Manuscript and Indian Culture

Manuscript and Indian Culture

Edited by

Projit Kumar Palit
Susmita Palit Saha

Kaveri Books
New Delhi-110002

First Published in 2017

ISBN: 978-81-7479-206-8

Published by
Kaveri Books
4832/24, Ansari Road
New Delhi-110002 (India)
Tel: 011-4707 2321
E-mail: kaveribooks@gmail.com
website: www.kaveribooks.com

Laser Typesetting by :
Tamalika Computers, Delhi

PRINTED IN INDIA

Dedication

To

Prof. Somnath Dasgupta

Former Vice Chancellor,
Assam University, Silchar

ोफेसर दिलीप चन्द्र नाथ
'rof. Dilip Chandra Nath

कुलपति
Vice-Chancellor

असम विश्वविद्यालय
(एक केन्द्रीय विश्वविद्यालय)
सिलचर 788011 असम, भारत
ASSAM UNIVERSITY
(A Central University)
Silchar 788011, Assam, India

Foreword

I am absolutely delighted to introduce the present volume entitled; 'The Manuscript and Indian Culture.' edited by two well-known scholars Dr. Projit Kumar Palit who is the Professor and Head of the Department of History, Assam University, (A Central University), Silchar while Mrs. Susmita Palit Saha, is working in Patha ṭBhavana, Visva Bharati University, Santiniketan, West Bengal. As many as twenty three distinguished scholars have articulated on various aspects of Manuscript and manuscript's Culture in India. The readers would be immensely benefited from the learned exposition of the Manuscript and how it has become a symbol of the Indian Culture.

From early times onwards, India has produced a large wealth of literature in the form of manuscripts. This tremendous knowledge was written on different kinds of material like birch bark, palm leaf, cloth, wood and stone and paper etc. India perhaps has the one of the oldest and largest collection of manuscripts in the world. The term manuscripts are used in various Indian languages - hastalekha, Pandulipi, matrka, pustaka, pustika, pusta, potha, pothi, pothaka, mulakosa, adarsa and so on. Manuscripts are available throughout India and those are in many languages and scripts, which cover religious, philosophical, historical, literary and scientific subjects. Various fields of human endeavour are stored on variety of medias viz. clay tablets, stones, metals, tree barks, palms leaves, animal skins, cloths, papers, etc. Manuscripts are primary sources of such heritage knowledge and it gives an opportunity for exploration of knowledge of Indian culture and exchanges it to next generation. The strength of this volume rests on the wide variety of the subjects as well as projects of the learned discourses.

I am confident that this volume will be well accepted by scholars and readers in the academic world. I congratulate the editors for his sincerity and successful efforts.

Date : 4th August, 2016

Prof. Dilip Chandra Nath,
Vice Chancellor

Phone : +91 3842 270801, 270273 (Office) Fax : 91 3842 270802 (Office), Cell +91 94350 73676

Acknowledgement

Manuscript means a manually written document but not printed from in any medium. The word manuscript has its origin in two latin words, namely 'manus' meaning hand and 'scribo' or scripture denoting the written character or script etc. Manuscripts have several forms i.e. book form, scrolls or in codex format. India has the largest collection of manuscripts in the world. Millions of manuscripts are lying in libraries, museums and private collections in all over India. All are the valuable sources of knowledge especially of ancient Indian history and culture. It is also exploring the knowledge of Indian cultures and exchanges the knowledge to next generation. Various type of scripts have been used for writing the manuscripts which are-, Devanagari, Tiglari, Sarada, Telugu, Kannada, Malayalam, Grantha, Tamil, Nandinagari, old Newari ,Persian and Arabic etc.

In the second half of the 18th century CE, a few British officers such as Sir William Jones (1746-1794CE), Sir Robert Chambers (1774-1779CE), Colin Mackenzie (1782 ṣ 1806CE) took a deep interest for studying the Indian culture. They started the collecting manuscripts, inscriptions and others antiquities for preserving, cataloguing and research. Sir William Jones established ṢThe Asiatic Society of Bengal¿ in Calcutta on 15th January, 1781CE for studying the manuscripts, inscriptions, scripts, languages and varieties of Indian cultures. Later on, in the last half of the 19th century CE, the Government of India deputed a few scholars such as G. Býhler, A.C. Burnell, R.G. Bhandarkar, R.L. Mitra, F. Kielhorn, G. Oppert, and G.B. Malleson for collecting the manuscripts in different parts of India. Since that time, the mission was started for collecting, preserving, cataloguing and editing the manuscripts on in and outside India.

In such context, the centre for Indological Studies, Assam University, Silchar, has planned to publish a monograph entitled "Manuscript and Indian Culture" edited by Projit Kumar Palit & Susmita Palit Saha. It is great pleasure to announce that the endeavour for the publication of a volume which has come out finally for the participation of twenty three distinguished scholars from various part of India and abroad.

I am expressing deep regards and gratitude to Prof. Dilip Chandra Nath, Vice Chancellor, Assam University, (A Central University), Silchar for his valuable Foreword.

I am also gratefulness to Dr. Amalendu Bhattacharjee, Former Head, Department of Bengali, G C College, Silchar, Assam for his unique Introduction of the Volume.

I would like to thank Swami Kamalasthananda Maharaj, Principal, Ramkrishna Mission Vivekananda Centenary College, Rahara, Kolkata, who has assisted me to complete the work. I am sincerely grateful and indebted to all authors who have contributed their research papers for this volume. I am thankful to Mr. Rakesh Goel and Abhisek Goel, Kaveri Books, New Delhi for publishing this volume within a very short time. I acknowledge my daughter Poulomi Palit for her encouragement and assistance for completing this work.

Projit Kumar Palit
Director and Professor,
Centre for Indological Studies,
Department of History,
Assam University,
(A Central University),
Silchar.

Contents

Diacritical Marks

Roman equivalents of Devanāgari Letters

a	अ	ka	क	da	द
ā	आ	kha	ख	dha	ध
i	इ	ga	ग	na	न
ī	ई	gha	घ	pa	प
u	उ	ṅ	ङ	pha	फ
ū	ऊ	ca/cha	च	ba	ब
ṛ	ऋ	cha/chha	छ	bha	भ
e	ए	ja	ज	ma	म
ai	ऐ	jha	झ	ya	य
o	ओ	ñ	ञ	ra	र
au	औ	ṭa	ट	la	ल
		ṭha	ठ	va	व
		ḍha	ड	śa	श
		ṇa	ढ	ṣa/sha	ष
		ta	ण	sa	स
		tha	त	ha	ह
			थ	ṁ	·
				ḥ	:

List of Contributers

Abira Basu Chakraborty, Assistant Professor, Department of History, Kandra R.K.K. Mahavidyalya, Burdawn, West Bengal.

Anil Kumar Acharya, Assistant Professor in Sanskrit, Ambedkar College, Fatikroy, Unakoti, Tripura 799290.

Anita Bagchi, Professor, Department of History, North Bengal University, West Bengal.

Asok Kumar. N.K, Assistant Professor, Department of Sanskrit Nyaya, Government of Sanskrit College, Tripuithura, Ernakulam, Kerala.

Bimalendra Kumar, Professor and Head, Department of Pali & Buddhist Studies, Faculty of Arts, Banaras Hindu University, Varanasi-221005 (U.P.)

Buddhadev Bhattachary, Assistant Professor, Department of Philosophy, Nava Nalanda University, Nalanda, Bihar.

Dhriti Roy, Assistant Professor, Department of Chinese, School of Languages and Literature, Sikkim University, Sikkim.

Jaydeep Chakrabarty, Assistant Professor, Department of English, Assam University, Silchar-788011, Assam.

Juthika Basu Bhowmik, Former Publication Officer, Department of Education, Government of Tripura, Tripura.

K. Maheswaran Nair, Former Professor, Department of Sanskrit, University of Kerala, Trivandrum, Kerala.

Krishnendu Ray, Associate Professor, Department of Ancient Indian History and Culture, University of Calcutta, West Bengal.

Nirmalya Karmakar, Research Scholar, Department of History, Tripura University, Tripura.

Paromita Das, Professor & Head, Department of History, Guwahati University, Assam.

Raj Kumar Mazinder, Assistant Professor, Department of Fine Arts, Assam University, Silchar-788011, Assam.

Rangan Kanti Jana, Curator, Museum and Art Gallery, The University of Burdwan, West Bengal.

Ravi Khangai, Assistant Professor, Department of History, Rashtrasant Tukdoji Maharaj Nagpur University, Nagpur, Maharashtra-440033.

Ruma Sarma, Professor, Department of Fine arts, Assam University, Silchar-788011, Assam.

S.K. Pathak, Former Professor, Indo-Tibetan Department, Visva Bharati, Santiniketan, West Bengal.

Satyadeo Poddar, Professor& Dean, The School of Arts, Department of History, Tripura University, Tripura.

Shanker Thapa, Professor, Department of History, Tribhuvan University, Kathmandu, Nepal.

Sudipa Ray Bandyopadhya, Professor, Department of Ancient Indian History and Culture, University of Calcutta, West Bengal.

Swadhinata Das, Research Scholar, Department of History, Assam University, Silchar-788011, Assam.

Swami Kamalasthananda, Principal, Ramkrishana Mission Vivekananda Centenary College, Rahara, West Bengal.

Swati Biswas, Assistant Professor, Department of Islamic History and Culture, University of Calcutta, West Bengal.

Introduction

It was around four thousand years ago the practice of putting things in record began in India. Different aspects of writing technology were mentioned in *Devipuran*. The media on which the exposition was given was termed as '*Pustak*'. But the word book or codex is not the appropriate synonym of *pustak* or *puthi*, which are essentially in manuscript form written on rustic materials like barks of tree, smooth wooden planks, dry and processed leaves or on hand made papers, with indigenous ink made from extracts of *pan*, *haritaki* and other matters. The following verse gives details of the process of *Pustak* production:

śrītādīpatrajenāñca suyantre svayamarccite |
vicitrapattikāpārśve carmmaṇām samkutikṛte | |
raktena atha kṛsṇeṇa múrddhanā rangikena ca |
dṛdasutrasuvaddhena evamvidhakṛtena ca | |
(91/37, 38)

The writing was done on Palmyra-leaf. The leaves were sized equally and kept compressed in a box made of animals' skin. Two pieces of wooden plank were used as the cover tied with black or red thread. Describing the writing style the verse records some words of appreciation for the scribe:

praṇastam smarate grantham śresthah pustakalekhakah |
nātisantatavicchinai rna ślaksai rna ca karkaśaih | |
nandināgarakairvarnai rlekhayecchivapustakam |
prārambhe pañcaślokāni punah śantintu kārayet | |
(91/52, 53)

It means, sacred books are to be written in *nāgar script*. The letters should neither be congested nor separated from each others in the group and must not be illegible. In the introductory part there should be five *vandanā śloka*, that is, invocation verses. The closing part must have *śānti śloka*, meaning benedictory incantation. The writing tools, as mentioned above were pen, ink pot, nib sharpener (*lekhanī ghatanam tiksṇam masīpātrantu Lekhanīm)*. Wrapped round with myriad coloured cloth the manuscripts were kept in a specially made wooden container. Manuscripts were written on diverse subject matters. The *Devipuran* mentions some such subjects:

siddhānta moksaśāstrāṇi vedān svargādisādhakān |
tadangānitihāsāni deyā dharmmavivṛddhaye | |
gārudam bālatantrañca bhutatantrāṇi bhairavam |
śāstrāṇi pathanāddānārmātarah phaladā nṛṇām | |
jyotisam vaidyaśāstrāṇi kalā kavyam śubhāgamān |
dānādārogyamāpnoti gāndharvvam labhate padam | |
(91/13-15)

The scholar who is committed to the cause of imparting knowledge has been referred to as a '*sarvalokapujya*', a man revered by all in all land. It has been said that learning is a never ending quest. The more one imparts it to others, the more it increases, and it is never exhausted. Therefore, teaching is regarded as the supreme act of benevolence to the society.

The spread of knowledge help develop the art of writing even in the remote places of the country. These huge writings are there in the monasteries, temples, academics and in the libraries or in private collections. It was the European scholars whose attention was drawn to this repository of traditional knowledge in modern times. At the behest of Sir William Jones the Asiatic Society was formed at Calcutta on January 15, 1784CE. There are about 47000 manuscripts in twenty-six varieties of scripts and languages under the possession of this centre for Indological studies. Notable other such institutions are Calcutta University (1857), Oriental Research Institute and Manuscript Library, (University of Kerala, Tiruvanantapuram), Oriental Research Institute, Mysore (1891CE), Khuda Bakhs Oriental Public Library, Patna (1891CE) etc. Numerous other institutions came in to existence thereafter.

To unearth the traditional knowledge stored in the manuscripts a massive hunt began in the 19th century CE. As a part of this venture the great discovery of 'caryāpada' from the royal archive of Nepal was made by Mahamohapadhyay Haraprasad Sastri in 1907CE. This primary source of several NIA languages in Eastern India, was brought out in book form in 1916CE by Bangiya Sahitya Parishad, Kolkata. Sri Sastri in its introduction had exhorted the future researchers to carry on similar hunt in Tibet, Nepal, Koch Bihar, Mayurbhanj, Manipur, Sylhet and other places where more such manuscripts might be available. Not very many scholars have responded to his biddings. Manuscriptology has not received due attention in the universities and in the similar institutions. At the initiative of central government NMM (National Mission for Manuscripts) was established in 2003CE.

In the present compilation, the seven out of twenty-three papers have dealt with the manuscripts of North East India. Assam has an ancient tradition of manuscripts. The '*Harshacharit*' by Banbhatta in its Book-VII, has it that Bhaskar Barman, the king of Kamrup, in 7th century CE had sent a gift of aromatic *pustak* wrapped up with the bark of the scented *Agaru* tree (*vetramayānāguruvalkalakalpitasañcayāni ca subhāsitabhāñji pustakāni*), along with brush for painting and a number of pots for the colorant (*avalamvamānatulikālāvukaMśca likhitānekalekhya-phalakasamputān*) through his emissary Hamsabeg.

The manuscript treasures of Manipur are rich in variety of their subject matter. The subject matters range from genealogy, mythology, rites and rituals, chronicles, descriptions of hills, dances, astrology, study of clouds, descriptions of nature, medicine and literature etc.

Question may arise, what is the relevance of manuscriptology in this techno-oriented 21st century CE. This is, in fact, necessary for the perpetuation of the civilization itself, the traditional knowledge stored in the manuscript needs be unearthed to enable us understand the glory of our past. This would show that, India has not only experienced advancement in philosophy and literature but also in science and worldly matters. There are innumerable manuscripts in different archives in the country on the study of science. Some examples of it are *Chikitsā sārasangraha* (Sanskrit/Ayurveda),*Kuruburarattamala* (Kannada/ Agriculture) , *Kitab-al-Hashaish* (Arabic/ Medicine), *Subika* (Manipuri/ Astronomy), *Chikitsa Manjari* ((Sanskrit/Ayurveda), *Ashvaphalaprakasha* (Sanskrit/veterinary science), *Hastividyarnava* (Assamese/ veterinary science) etc.

Aryan civilization had travelled from west to the east. The manuscripts in the land contain numerous sources to trace the process of this transmission.

The study of manuscripts opens new vista in the field of intellectual pursuits. During the pre-colonial period there existed two neighbouring kingdoms in the North East Indiaṭ Tripura and Hedemba or Cachar. When the practice of sacrifice (both human and animal) was forbidden by the royal court the Brihannāradiya Puran was translated into Bengali in both the kingdoms for the propagation of Vaishsnavite cult, a phenomenon very important in the context of cultural studies relating to this region.

Painted manuscripts are the wonderful specimen of manuscriptology. Assam occupies a place of pride in the production of this kind of manuscripts. Some of these are brought out in print form like, Chitrabhagbata (1949CE), Hastividyarnava (1976CE), Anandalahari (1993CE), Sachitra Ankavali (2013CE), Anadipatan (2013CE) etc. The manuscript painting is traditional art form of our country. These painting have an important place in the art history of India. The study of manuscriptology is closely connected with the study of art.

Manuscripts are the valuable source of study of the development of scripts and languages.

The manuscripts are the products of relentless effort of the scholars. The scribes used to preserve and perpetuate the *pustak* by making copies with great patience and expertise. They felt earnestly that these works should be preserved diligently. The Sanskrit *śloka* has it that—

bhagna pṛstha kati grīva stabdha dṛsti dhṛta vrata |
yatnena likhitām pusti putrabat pratipālayet | |

It should be our duty to honour the words of the scribe. It is hoped that the present book would create new awareness about manuscriptology.

Dr.Amalendu Bhattacharjee
Former Head,
Department of Bengali,
G C College, Silchar, Assam

1

Buddhist Sanskrit Manuscripts of Nepal: Continuity of Ancient Indian Textual Tradition in the Himalaya

– *Shanker Thapa*

Among all the ancient languages, Sanskrit excels in the sheer number of the works in the written form. Vast mass of Hindu and Buddhist Sanskrit literature has been preserved in different scripts on birch-bark, palm-leaf and paper in India and Nepal. These are the material of profound knowledge. To know about profoundness of knowledge, study of Buddhist Sanskrit manuscript is obvious. Not only in the orient, had the western world given priority to collect and study Sanskrit manuscripts. On oriental manuscript collection in the west, Klaus Ludwig Janert, a well known Sanskrit Buddhist scholar, opines that more than a million manuscripts in Indian languages (my addition: including that of Nepal's Sanskrit manuscripts) exist in libraries throughout the world. More than 600,000 of these have been listed or described with varying degrees of satisfaction since the inception of Indian studies in the West about a century and a half ago.[1]

A vast number of Sanskrit Mahayana texts were originated in North eastern India. Nepal's Buddhist Sanskrit manuscripts are precious heritage in the modern world but most of them are the continuity of Indian manuscripts. Although Nepalese manuscripts are extremely valuable, the problem with them is that, in some manuscripts, the editors need to modify readings towards more classical Sanskrit norms in order to compensate for various idiosyncrasies of spelling, *Sandhi* and punctuation found in them.[2]

After the decline of Buddhism in India due to Muslim invasion, almost entire body of Buddhist Sanskrit texts were lost, They survived intact in Nepal in manuscripts written in Kutila, Bhujimola and Pracalit Newari scripts. To some extent, Buddhist Sanskrit manuscripts were recovered from Gandhara, Kashmir, Central Asia and Tibet also. With an exception of Sanskrit Buddhist manuscripts availed in Tibet, manuscripts recovered in Gandhara and other parts of Central Asia are fragmentary and limed in types of texts. On contrary, manuscripts preserved in Nepal are extraordinary having greater religious as well as academic significance. Nepalese manuscripts are full text covering as many titles as possible. Newari manuscripts are special due to writing material. Different papers were used according to subject of manuscript. At the same time, varied Newari scripts were also used to write manuscript. To study Nepalese manuscripts is meant to learn about script, thematic aspects, narrative literature, writing material, art and so on. Nepalese scribes used thick papers in writing manuscripts. The significance of Sanskrit manuscripts of Nepal is well attested in the letter written by Pt. Radha Krishnan to the Vice Roy of India in 1868. In May 1868, Pt. Radha Krishnan, the Chief Pandit at Lahore Durbar wrote to Vice Roy Lord Lytton that the list of Sanskrit books and manuscripts will necessarily remain incomplete unless it contains the names of the books that are in the libraries of the Maharajas of Jaypur and Nepal. The oldest Sanskrit books are to be found there.[3] Buddhist Sanskrit texts have been found in fragments in the Central Asian region as well. In ancient times, each teacher had his personal collection of Hindu- Buddhist manuscripts kept in the houses, schools or temples. The educational establishments, monasteries and temples, and the royalties and nobilities also collected manuscripts and maintained manuscript repositories. Since the very beginning, the collection of Sanskrit manuscripts spread over distant parts in the Indian subcontinent and beyond. It reached as far as China and the Central Asian region in different times. Thus, Sanskrit Buddhist manuscripts proliferated to a large area from India to Nepal, Gandhara, Kashmir, Indonesia, Tibet, Central Asia, China, Korea and Japan. Important Sanskrit Buddhist manuscripts are also recovered in Gilgit, Swat and other adjoining areas. There are both happy and painful moments for Buddhist scholars in which valuable manuscripts were excavated or destroyed. Archeologists have uncovered, in Gilgit in 1931, a collection of invaluable manuscripts, written in Sanskrit, and stored in clay jars kept in an old Buddhist temple. Those manuscripts are Sarvastivada texts. This has been the most enjoyable event for the entire Buddhist world. On contrary, the Russian invasion of Afghanistan in the 1980's brought most regrettable casualty in Buddhism destructing rare Sanskrit manuscript collection of the Kabul Museum. During the rule of the Taibans, there was a movement to take out of Afghanistan every single Sanskrit manuscript retrievable. One of these collections is now deposited in the University of Oslo in Norway, which is popularly known as the 'Schoyen collection'. This collection has 1,400 titles of Sanskrit Buddhist manuscripts from Afghanistan. Foreign religious teachers, scholars and preachers took huge mass of manuscripts to various countries for study, transliteration, translation into the local languages or collection purposes. However, religious motives have been embedded in such efforts. The Indian expatriate monks and Buddhist scholars also took such manuscripts with them to the countries where they visited. As the result, a considerable mass of Sanskrit Buddhist manuscripts exists in Tibetan and Chinese translations.

Historical Context of Nepalese Manuscripts

Nepal's Buddhist Sanskrit literature has greater contribution in the development of Mahayana Buddhism in Northern countries. The mass migration of Indian Buddhists to Nepal ushered in an era of progress. The Muslim invasion in India made Nepal an abode for the fugitive Buddhists.[4] Before 13th century, India had vast collection of such manuscripts. But later the tradition was shifted to Nepal when a large number of Indian monks escaped Muslim invasion and reached Nepal.

Nepalese Buddhist monasteries could not accommodate all the Indian fugitive monks. Many of them had to support themselves by selling manuscripts, scriptures and antiquities which they carried at their arrival for personal use.

The famine in the 13th century during the reign of King Ari Malla Deva (1200-1216) caused death of many Indian expatriate monks. Their hosts claimed their belongings.[5] As a result, manuscript and antiquity holding of the deceased fell into the hands of the hosts. Another factor that caused an increase in the number of Buddhist manuscripts in Nepal was because of the popularity of copying tradition. Both copying or possession manuscripts was believed as the acts of merit making. Nepalese Buddhists were in the habit of procuring manuscripts in varied scripts.

All of these factors helped to accumulate an increase in the number of Buddhist Sanskrit manuscripts, Tibetan Buddhists also brought copies of Buddhist manuscripts to Nepal from Tibet. However, it has not been treated as important issue in Buddhist literary history. The accumulated Sanskrit manuscripts mostly consist of Sutra, Tantra and commentaries.

The accumulation of Buddhist Sanskrit manuscripts has turned Nepal into a warehouse of Buddhist manuscripts. Various original Buddhist manuscripts from India as well as Tibet written between 750- 1250 CE, were also copied later by Nepalese Buddhists from the 12th to 15th centuries. Buddhist manuscripts were regarded as very precious icon in the Newar society. Manuscripts are so important that they were even chosen as an object to exchange gifts to strengthen ties with neighbouring countries[6] In fact, Buddhist manuscripts became the gift of preference for foreign rulers. Their presentation always conveyed the most heartfelt feelings and cordiality.

Nature and Aims

Before 17th century, palm-leaves were used to write manuscripts. Thereafter, handmade Nepalese paper became popular material for manuscripts. This kind of paper was produced in the hill areas since the 16/17th centuries.[7] Thick paper was used to write manuscript which was prepared by pasting several layers together and cutting them into a rectangular shape. Texts were written on both sides. Individual manuscript sheets are tied with a string, which passes through two holes in the paper. This paper is coated with yellow coloured poisonous substance. Generally, Buddhist manuscripts were written on palm-leaf folios (*tad*), folding books (*thyasaphu*), bound books (*kitab*), and scrolls.

Buddhist manuscripts are written with black ink made from soot. Vegetable dyes were also used. Gold and silver were also used as ink. Bamboo pens were used to write manuscripts. The tip was cut obliquely, forming an oval shape. The tip was cut at a slant, which made it possible to write the thicker and thinner parts of letters with the same pen. The tip was halfway one to two centimeters long to hold ink. It is also said that iron pens were also made for writing purposes.

In most manuscripts, the aim of writing is clearly included in the ending remarks. The rulers of later medieval period sponsored copying texts to commemorate auspicious *puja* or rituals. Ritual books were written for the purpose of passing on tradition to the later generation.[8] On the other hand, the aim of each specific text varies. It is also said that books like *Dharmasastra* and rituals were intended to develop and increase piety and make the society systematic. Various other books were intended for later generations.

Newars and Brahmins were mostly involved in the copying of both Buddhist and Hindu manuscripts, Vajracaryas and Sakyas were concentrated in copying Buddhist texts. But not necessarily, they copied Buddhist texts only. References are found that the non-Buddhist scribes copied Buddhist texts as well. Names mentioned in colophons also created confusion in some cases as to whether they were authors or merely copiers. It is easy to distinguish in the case of *Sutra* and *tantra* manuscripts; however, this is not the case with the commentaries.

Subject of Manuscripts

Nepal has the largest repository of Buddhist Sanskrit literature dealing with different aspects of Mahayana. The monk scholars as well as Vajracarya Pandits have contributed in the production and preservation Buddhist manuscripts. One of the greatest services of Newars of Kathmandu valley is the preservation of Sanskrit manuscripts.[9] However, fragments of Sanskrit literature have also been recovered in Gilgit and other areas of Central Asia.[10] Those texts, however, are only in fragments. The work of Newar scholars is really praiseworthy, and is of immense significance in Mahayana Buddhism. It has great impact on Buddhist scholarship as well. The Muslim invasion had a direct impact on the movement of Buddhist Sanskrit texts from their places of origin to Nepal. Later on, those texts spread beyond Nepal. It had immense impact on religious life of the local people. The songs that were written on various Buddhist themes also reveal the mindset of the people in the contemporary society day.[11]

Nepal became the center of Buddhist learning after the Muslim invasion of India in the 13th century. The Vajrayana culmination of the Buddha's path also contributed to preservation activities. Similarly, the renowned monk scholars who escaped Muslims invasion and fled to Nepal continued the tradition of teaching and studying Buddhism in local Viharas in the Kathmandu valley. The spiritual sense of Nepalese Buddhists, devotion to the sacred scriptures and tradition of worshipping texts further contributed to its preservation. Nepal has a vast repository of Buddhist Manuscripts, which are kept in the National Archives of Nepal, Asa Saphu Kuthi, Keshar Library, TU Central Library, National Library, Vihara collections and in private collections in Nepal[12] and several repositories outside the country.

In Tibet, almost all the Buddhist texts have been preserved in translation as Kangyur and Tengyur. Most of the Mahayana texts have been translated into Tibetan. Kangyur contains the words of the Buddha which consists of Vinaya Prajnaparamita, Avatamsaka, Ratnakuta, Sutra-sutranta, Tantra, Pratantra, Kalacakra and Dharani. Similarly, Tengyur texts are the collection of texts written by Nepalese and Indian Pandits. It consists of Stotra, Prajnaparamita, Madhyamika, Lekha, Pramana, Savdavidya, Cikitsa, Silpa, Nitishastra, Viswashastra and Atisa texts.[13]

The preservation of Sanskrit manuscripts is attributed to the spirituality of Newar people. Also the practice of Vajrayana mantras has contributed to the preservation of Buddhist scriptures. In the Vajrayana tradition, the *Gurukul* style of Buddhist education is gradual. This tradition of studying Buddhism according to the *Gurukul* system was well preserved by the Vajracaryas of Nepal. The tradition of the Buddhist system of learning also contributed in the preservation of Buddhist Sanskrit literature in Nepal. Consequently, Nepal has the largest repository at present.

Many prominent Buddhist monk scholars from Nepal also lived in Nalanda and other monastic centers, and studied Buddhism. Some of them taught Buddhist philosophy and logic in those centers.[14]

Bharo (Shantibhadra), an eleventh century Vajracarya scholar from Cobhar near Kathmandu was the Guru of the Tibetan scholar Rwa Lotsaba (Vajrakirti).[15] The eminent Tibetan scholar Chag Lotsaba Chos rje dPal (13th Century), popularly known by his Sanskrit name Dharmasvamin lived in Nepal for some time and studied Tantras from two prominent Newar scholars Ratnaraksita and Ravindradeva. The Lotsaba had received a great deal of religious instructions from Ratnarakshita, who taught him the Guhyasamaja Tantra. He also studied Vajravalinamamandala Sadhana from Mahapandit Ravindradeva (Ni-ma'i ban-po'i-lha).[16] The individual Vajrayana Viharas of Nepal also gave rise to prominent Buddhist scholars. It is noteworthy that some of the Nepalese Buddhist scholars had tantric lineage in Tibet. The lineage of the Vajravarahi Tantra is a good example of this.

Many Tibetans have developed expertise in the fields of Sanskrit grammar, Kalacakra, Madhyamaka, Yogaratnamala, Hevajra, Guhyasamaja, Vajravarahi Tantra, Prajnaparamita, Vajravali, Buddhist logic, semantics and so on.[17] The destruction of Nalanda and other Mahaviharas in India in the 12th century paved the way for scholarly monks to come to Nepal.[18] The Buddhist scholars are of the pinion that the tradition of copying and writing manuscripts began as early as the tenth century in Nepal. However, there are references that refute this hypothesis. Thus, the true date merely remains the subject of speculation because the *Pancaraksa* dated N.S. 19 (899 CE), which is now in the Cambridge collection does not corroborate the idea. Similarly, a copy of the Prajnaparamita, which was written in 40 NS has also been found in Nepal which concludes that the tradition of writing existed even before tenth century.

At present, Nepal holds thousands of Buddhist Sanskrit manuscripts. After Brian Hodgson found out Nepal as the warehouse of Sanskrit manuscript, other scholars including Daniel Wright, Prof. Cecil Bendall, Prof. Junijiro Takakushu and Ven. Ekai Kawaguchi collected hundreds of Buddhist manuscripts.[19]

Since the ancient times, Nepalese rulers have patronized Buddhism. They made lavish donations to the *Viharas*, which provided favourable environment in which Buddhist scholarship could flourish.[20] King Våsa Deva, Siva Deva and Amsuvarma of the Licchavi dynasty patronized Buddhism. King Vrisha Deva was given the title of the 'Patron of Buddha's Rule' (*Sugata Sasana Paksyapati*).

Some of the texts which were started to write in Nalanda were completed in Nepal. The colophons of those texts mention this.[21] Nepal has a vast repository of Buddhist classics in the form of palm leaves, birch of bark folios, and *Thyasaphu*.

The tradition of copying Buddhist manuscripts is considered to be significant in the development of Buddhism. These texts were mainly compiled in Viharas. There was a tradition of copying both Buddhist and Hindu texts in Kathmandu, but Buddhist texts were copied in Patan because Patan itself has been always a predominantly Buddhist city. Usually, the Vajracaryas and Sakyas were involved in copying, which was done not only to further learning but also as an act of piety, which was considered to be a devotional act that accumulates merit.[22]

Manuscripts were originally copied on palm leaf folios. If not, the Buddhist manuscripts were written on birch bark folios, which had been prepared according to certain prescribed process. It is said that no manuscripts are written on birch bark in the book form. It was used to write charms and Mantras for amulets.

The Nepalese manuscripts are of different kinds. Beautiful pictures of Buddhist deities are depicted in manuscripts in the form of miniature paintings. It is interesting to note that wooden covers, which were lacquered and painted with related images of deities, are on every manuscript. In some cases, the cover is made up of carved brass metal, but normally manuscript covers are made from beautifully decorated wooden. These were added for protection. [23]

Nepalese manuscripts, both Buddhist and non-Buddhist, cover a wide variety of subjects, They are written in Newari and Sanskrit. Scripts used to write Buddhist manuscripts are *Ranjana*, *Bhujimol*, *Pracalit Newari* and *Devnagari*. Theses manuscripts cover areas such as - philosophy, commentaries, ritual, iconography, art and architecture, music, songs, eulogy, stories (Avadana Jataka), Dharani, Tantra, Sutra, Purana, Mahatmya, Pujavidhi and so on. The Buddhist manuscripts covered subject matters such as - philosophy, eulogy, commentary, art and architecture, painting, renovation, *Avadana*, *Jataka*, *Sutra*, *Tantra*, *Dharani*, *Caryagita*, *Stotra*, *Sastra*, *Pujavidhi*, *Mantra*, *Karmakanda*, *Vamsavali* and so on.[24]

The Buddhist Sanskrit manuscripts of Nepal which have been preserved in Nepal and abroad have several specific characteristics. As mentioned earlier, they are written in hybrid Sanskrit using *Newari* Scripts.

Although the manuscripts are written in Sanskrit, the colophons are in vernacular language. Most of those manuscripts were written or copied in Nepal. These documents also contain the date and name of kings. The importance of preserving manuscripts had always been stressed in Nepal. The climate too was favourable in the preservation of manuscripts. Later, the decline of Nepal's Buddhist scholastic tradition had direct impact on the study of Buddhist Sanskrit manuscripts. The decline in the scholarly importance of manuscripts among the Newars led them to remain untouched and unused. Devotion of people for religious texts and the tradition of manuscripts worship also helped in manuscript preservation. Chalk powder was also used to preserve manuscripts. Their excellent condition is due to the fact that manuscripts have not been used for centuries.

The time period in which manuscripts were written is very important for various reasons, because some of the dates on them may not be accurate. It is written in some of the manuscripts that they were written during the 8th and 9th centuries. But the scribes of some early Indian manuscripts carelessly wrote the date of the archetype on the copy. A.C. Burnell had doubts about the age of the Nepalese manuscripts for this reason, and did not believe that the manuscripts preserved at Cambridge were as old as they claimed to be.

Not only this, scripts also provide clue to determine the age of the documents. Some old Nepalese manuscripts are similar to traditional Bengali manuscripts. Some of such Bengali manuscripts are also recovered in Nepal. Certain manuscripts written in Nepal are identical to the Bengali manuscriprs. The *Astasahasrika Prajnaparamita* manuscript dated 285 N.S. (1165 CE) written in *Kutila* script during the reign of King Ananda Deva is identical to Bengali manuscript. Since the 12th century, certain changes have taken place in archaic letters. The style of manuscripts writing changed to the extent that even gold and silver ink was introduced.

Corpus of Indigenous Newar Buddhist Texts

The development of Buddhist scholarship, manuscript culture, emphasis on the study of Sanskrit language and literature, interactions with the expatriate Indian and Tibetan monks and other scholars, historical ties of Buddhist Newars with Nalanda and Vikramsila monasteries contributed in the development of Buddhist learning in Nepal. It facilitated Newar Buddhists to develop expertise in different branches of Buddhism especially tantric practices and ritual performances. Newar Buddhist society has produced eminent scholars of higher abilities. They became famous as learned Buddhist Masters and the practitioners in India and Tibet. As a matter of fact, Newar scholars and artisans were highly respected in Tibet. Entire situation led to accelerate scholarly and literary activities in the Newar Buddhist society. Their contribution made Nepal the largest repository of Buddhist manuscript. Manuscript culture was flourished in Nepal to great extent during the medieval times. Newar Buddhists have patronized the tradition primarily due to the religious reasons. Not only limited to reproducing Sanskrit manuscripts written in the India, Newar scholars also produced indigenous Newar Buddhist texts. They were the experts in producing and maintaining the intellectual products. Such texts fell under the categories of Purana, Stotra, Vidhi, Mahatmya, Katha, Vratavidhana, Jataka, Gatha, Caca, Karmakanda etc. It has created a corpus of indigenous Buddhist literature. Some of hose texts are also translated into Tibetan and Chinese. Svayambhu Purana, Nepalamandala-bhyantara-buddhaviharanamni, Jnanamala, Vasundharavrata Katha, redaction of 15, 16, 17 chapters of Buddhacarita, Vajradhatumukhakhyana Degurividhi, Degulipujavidhi, Adikarmapradipah, Mahamandala-devatanamavali Dharmasangraha-kosa, Nepaliyadevatakalyana, Vicitrakarnikavadana, Caca songs and various Puja Vidhi and ritual books, are important indigenous texts.

Proliferation of Manuscripts

Because of the significance of ancient and medieval Nepalese manuscripts, modern scholarship has given attention on their acquisition and study. The East India Company, realizing their historical value established a library in 1798 CE. Then the Company directed to its officers in the East to supply native literatures. The library was later named as the India Office Library. Finally, it received the bulk of the important manuscripts from India and other neighbouring countries including Nepal. Its elaborated collection of Sanskrit manuscripts is especially important. Later, Oxford University became the second rival with the foundation of Col. Joseph Boden's Sanskrit Professorship in 1827 CE and the appointment of Horace Hayman Wilson five years later.[25] Then after, attention was paid in the collection of ancient books and manuscripts. A large number of medieval Buddhist and Hindu manuscripts were collected from Nepal also. However, Nepal has no official record of written items that were taken out of the country. Later, many individual collectors also procured medieval manuscripts in Nepal and distributed them to different institutions in India, Tibet, China, Japan, UK, France, Germany, Russia, and the USA.

When Brian Hodgson, a British Residency official in Kathmandu, learned of Nepal's Hindu and Buddhist manuscripts, he found out massive repository of such manuscripts. He procured hundreds of texts, which he carried out of the country and distributed those texts to the academic institutions in India and Europe. The prominent British collectors Brian H. Hodgson, G.H.D. Gimlette, Daniel Wright collected manuscripts of Buddhist and Hindu texts in Nepal. On the other hand, Japanese collectors also showed up with keen interest on Nepalese manuscripts. Ven. Ekai Kawaguchi and Prof. Takakushu Junijiro of Tokyo University were the pioneers among the Japanese to procure Nepalese Buddhist manuscripts. The efforts of foreign Buddhist scholars, Sanskrit philologists and manuscript collectors finally made Nepalese Buddhist and Hindu manuscripts universal. As a matter of fact, Nepalese manuscripts are now deposited and preserved in various archives, libraries and institutions in different countries in original book form, hand written copies of original manuscripts and microfiche copies. Institutions where Nepalese manuscripts are abundant include the Asiatic society of Bengal, the CIHTS at Sarnath, the Oriental Institute at Baroda; Tokyo, Ryukoku, Bukkyo, Taisho, Tokai, Kyoto, Soka and other Japanese university libraries and the Toyo Bunko in Japan, the British Museum, British Library, Oxford and Cambridge Universities, SOAS library, Bodleian Library, the Royal Asiatic Society of London, Bibliotheque Nationale de France and Guimet Museum in France, German Oriental Society - Halle, University of Berlin, University of Hamberg in Germany and University of St. Petersberg and the Academy of Social Sciences - St. Peterberg in Russia and various monasteries in the distant lands of Tibet. Similarly, extensive microfilms of Nepalese manuscripts are kept at the Buddhist Library in Nagoya Japan. All those collections are very much valuable in the study of Sanskrit Buddhism. In addition, Nepalese manuscripts are abundant in many Tibetan monasteries procured from time to time during visits of eminent monks or other scholars. In the same way, Nepalese Buddhist manuscripts are also in the possession of various museums and libraries in China as well. The expatriate Indian *Pandits* in Tibet also carried with them Nepalese manuscripts for translation, academic or religious purposes. Those texts are now deposited in different monasteries. Tibet has historical relationship with Sanskrit Buddhist literature. Rahul Sankrityayan, the most eminent Buddhist scholar and a practitioner from India, has explored Sanskrit manuscripts in Tibetan monasteries such as Sa skya Zha lu Ri phug, Ngor etc. He also wrote about the Manuscripts he explored. He photographed Buddhist manuscripts which are now preserved in the K. P. Jayasawal Research Institute at Patna. One of the important texts he recovered is the Yogacarabhumi. At present, Buddhist scholars have switched to study those texts. Not only Sanskrit, Tibetan manuscripts available in Nepal are also very significant. Among others, the Oriental Institute Library of the Academy of Sciences in the Czech Republic also houses the collection of Tibetan manuscripts and block prints obtained from Tibet, China, India, Nepal, Mongolia and Buryatia. The majority of texts are represented by the canonical literature, Tantric and ritual works, philosophical treatises, literary texts particularly the story of prince Vishvantara, fairy tales and the love songs of the Sixth Dalai Lama.

Similarly, Giuseppe Tucci, an Italian Buddhist scholar, also collected, photographed or copied Sanskrit manuscripts during his quadruple visits to Tibet. The frequent interaction of Tibetans with the Newar Buddhists in the Kathmandu valley helped to accumulate Sanskrit manuscripts there. During the medieval times, Buddhist Sanskrit manuscripts were available for purchase in the Nepalese market. Tibetan Buddhists who visited Nepal either during that time for pilgrimage or study Buddhism procured Sanskrit manuscripts. As a matter of fact, Tibet has significant collection of Nepalese Buddhist manuscripts. However, further exploration in Tibet has not been allowed right since 1950 due to unspecified reasons.

Similarly, the Lhasa Newars also patronized copying Buddhist manuscripts. Many Newars took time and copied such texts by themselves while in Tibet. Not only this, Nepalese manuscripts are still preserved in China as well. We assume that visiting expatriate Chinese monks might have collected Nepalese manuscripts through their native counterparts. Among the repositories, the Cultural Palace of Nationalities in Beijing has Nepalese Buddhist manuscripts in its collection. Beside this, Sanskrit manuscripts are also kept in China Library of Nationalities - Beijing, Lushun Museum and Lin Yin Temple in Hangzhou, China. Very significant attempt is being made by the Chinese and Tibetan Buddhist and Sanskrit scholars to transcribe and study Sanskrit manuscripts. *Dasa Kriya* manuscript recovered in the Lin Yin temple, which has forty three palm leaves folios, has been transcribed by a Tibetan scholar named Serji very recently. Similar version of the manuscript is also found in the Nepalese collection. There are other places in China as well where Nepalese Sanskrit Buddhist manuscripts have been preserved.

The first Briton who deserves a due mention in relation to Nepalese manuscripts collection is Capt. William Kirkpatrick. He visited Nepal in 1793. During the visit, he has procured a copy of Astasahasrika Prajnaparamita Sutra and handed over to William Jones in November 1793.[26] It contains 303 folios of Nepali paper, which was copied in the 18th century. This one instance may be regarded as a significant moment as the beginning of movement of Nepalese manuscripts out of the country.

Brian H. Hodgson is a prominent name in connection with medieval Buddhist and Hindu manuscripts of Nepal. A Report of the Librarian of the India office Library stated that:[27]

> The Sanskrit and other oriental manuscripts sent by Mr. Hodgson are a priceless addition to our collection of most of these there are no other copies in Europe.

Hodgson discovered vast repository of Sanskrit Mss in Nepal.. He collected 381 bundles of manuscripts, which included 200 separate titles. He later donated his collection to various institutions in order to render them accessible to European scholars. He distributed the manuscripts to the Asiatic Society of Bengal Royal Asiatic Society of London, India Office Library, Bodleian Library, Oxford, Societe Asiatique and Prof. Eugene Burnouf.

Hodgson was a famous and exemplary collector of Nepalese manuscripts. Cecil Bendall has praised Hodgson's efforts of collecting manuscripts. European scholars are indebted to him for the development of oriental scholarship in Europe.

Prof. Eugene Burnouf writes[28]

> He (Hodgson) collected a larger body of original documents on Buddhism than had up to that time ever been gathered together either in Asia or Europe.

Until the later half of the 19th century, all the original works on Northern Buddhism in France, Gt. Britain and India were based upon material collected by B. H. Hodgson.[29] His collection contains as old as 700 years old manuscripts.

Daniel Wright, a Residency Surgeon later got involved in the collection of medieval Buddhist manuscripts of Nepal. Professor E. B. Cowel, a renowned Sanskrit scholar at Oxford, was familiar with Nepal's Sanskrit manuscripts. He studied and edited a catalogue of Hodgson collection at the Royal Asiatic Society of London.[30] Considering the importance of Nepalese Buddhist manuscripts, he requested Prof. William Wright, brother of Daniel Wright, to procure copies of Buddhist manuscripts from Nepal. Consequently, Daniel Wright procured manuscripts for the University library of Cambridge. He procured a series of original manuscripts. He even purchased them, and offered as much as 150 Pounds Sterling for a copy of *Mahavastu*.[31] He also donated Mss to the British Museum, the German oriental society at Halle, the University library of Berlin, the University library of St. Petersberg and the Library of the Imperial Academy of St. Petersberg.[32] Prof. E.B. Cowell studied Nepalese manuscripts at Cambridge in order to verify dates. He also collected Tibetan manuscripts, which were purchased from the son of a Nepalese merchant in Kathmandu. His collection at Cambridge consists of 330 books of Sanskrit manuscripts.[33] Prof. E. B. Cowell was very interested in Nepalese manuscripts. As soon as they were received, he commenced a descriptive work on a number of earliest and most interesting manuscripts.[34] Wright's collection contains the oldest Pancaraksa Sutra which was written in NS 19.[35] His collection of Nepalese manuscripts is listed in his book, *History of Nepal Translated from Parbatiya*. Cecil Bendall has thoroughly investigated Cambridge collection and prepared a detailed catalogue.[36] Bendall also rendered invaluable services in the study of Nepalese Sanskrit Buddhist manuscripts. He came to Nepal in November 1880 to pursue research on them. During that time, he also collected Nepalese manuscripts.[37] His collection has 212 Buddhist and

Hindu manuscripts.[38] He returned to Nepal during the winter of 1884-1885 to study old manuscripts. He again joined a joint expedition organized by the Asiatic Society of Bengal in the winter of 1889-90. The other members in the expedition were Pt. Hara Prasad Shastri and Binod Vihari Bhattacharya. They studied historical, archaeological and literary aspects of Nepalese manuscripts. Bendall has published a brief monograph of his first visit entitled *A Journey of Literary and Archaeological Research in Nepal and Northern India during the Winter of 1884-85.*[39] He has purchased *Candravyakarana* with the help of Resident A.C. Girdlestone.[40] Bendall was permitted to access manuscripts in various collections. He found premier's collection of manuscripts to be the finest in the entire Indian sub-continent.[41] It was impossible for such a marvelous collection to exist.

According to the catalogue of the Bodleian Library, A.F.R. Hoernle and H.H. Wilson donated Nepalese manuscripts to the library. Hoernle procured some important Buddhist manuscripts such as Astasahasrika Prajnaparamita (12th Century), Pitaputrasamagama Sutra (15thc), leaves of an unknown Sutra (15thc), Madhyamikavåtti (14thc), Niyamah (15thc), Margasataka Stuti (14thc), Tathagatajnana Stutigatha (12thc), Pancaraksa (11thc), Kriyapanjika (13thc), Mantr as texts(13thc) and Lalit Bhairava Mahatantra (11th&13thcc). Those manuscripts are now preserved at the Bodleian.[42] It is believed that he has purchased those manuscripts from the manuscript collectors in Nepal. Similarly, Wilson has collected Naipaliyadevatakalyana, Pancaviàsatika, Sapta Buddha Stotra and Astamivrata Vidhana. He handed over those manuscripts to W. H. Mills. In addition to prominent scholars from Britain and Japan, other manuscript enthusiasts also collected Buddhist and Hindu Sanskrit manuscripts in Nepal for academic purposes.

H. H. Wilson and S. H. Lewin were also the collectors of Nepalese manuscripts.[43] Trinity College and SOAS, London also has sixty four Nepalese manuscripts in its possession, out of which 56 are Buddhist, Srven are Tantric and the rest deal with Sanskrit and Nepali languages.[44]

In the same way, Japanese scholars were also keenly interested in the Buddhist Sanskrit manuscripts of Nepal, Thus, they also collected manuscripts in Nepal. There are large collections of Nepalese Sanskrit manuscripts at Tokyo University Library,[45] the faculty of letters at Kyoto

University,[46] Tokai University Library[47] and Taisho archives. However, the collection of Ekai Kawaguchi is first and foremost.[48] He has collected Sanskrit manuscripts in Nepal with the permission from the Premier Chandra Shumsher. The Premier also presented him several volumes of Buddhist Sanskrit manuscripts. Total collection of Prof. Takakushu contains 180 volumes, where as Ekai Kawaguchi collected 390 volumes of Buddhist Sanskrit Mss. Altogether they presented 570 volumes of Nepalese manuscripts to the Tokyo University Library in 1915 most of which are still in its possession. The Buddhist Library in Nagoya has a fine collection of microfilms of Nepalese manuscripts. It is an excellent collection of Buddhist Mss in Japan. Nepal's Buddhist manuscripts are also found in Tibet, the Royal Asiatic Society of London, the British Museum, the India Office Library, Library of the Central Institute of Higher Tibetan Studies at Sarnath, the Oriental Institute at Baroda, and in various libraries and archives in France, Germany, Italy, USA and Russia. Various archives and libraries in Nepal, India, Japan, U.K. and Germany have already published several volumes of catalogues of Nepalese Mss in Europe. The catalogues published in Nepal do not cover those Mss preserved outside Nepal. Nepalese Buddhist Sanskrit manuscripts are preserved elsewhere due to their historical, religious, literary and thematic significance. So, an authentic list of published and unpublished catalogues facilitates to study manuscripts.

Bir Library of Nepal has played a very significant role in the preservation of Sanskrit Buddhist manuscripts. It is also known as Durbar library which was established by Premier Bir Shumsher. It is likely that his exposure to western society in Calcutta during his college years created interest in Sanskrit Buddhist literature. He was inspired to preserve Buddhists manuscripts in the library. He is credited for the present government collection of Buddhist Sanskrit manuscripts in Nepal. Later the library handed over entire collection of manuscripts to the National Archives of Nepal. Some individuals also set up a private archive in Kathmandu. Mr. Dharma Ratna Vajracharya has donated 608 volumes of manuscripts from his collection to Asa Saphu Kuthi.[49]

The Nepal German Manuscripts Preservation Project (NGMPP) was supported by the German Oriental Society. It has microfilmed about 1,75,000 manuscripts preserved in the National Archives and also in the private collections.[50]

References

1. Klaus Ludwig Janert, An Annotated Bibliography of the Catalogues of Indian Manuscripts, Part 1, Verzeichnis der Orientalischen Handschriften in Deutschland, Supplementband 1, Wiesbaden: F. Steiner Verlag, 1965, p.347.
2. Douglas Osto, Power, Wealth and Women in Indian Mahāyāna Buddhism: the Gāavyūha Sūtra, Routledge Critical Study of Buddhism 51, London: Francis and Taylor, 2008, p. 6
3. Letter from Pandit Radhakrishna, Chief Pandit of the late Lahore Durbar, to His Excellency the Viceroy and Governor General of India, dated the 10th. May 1868, In: Archibald Edward Gough, Collection and Preservation of the Records Ancient Sanskrit Literature India Edited by Order of the Government of India, Calcutta: Office of Superintendent of Government Printing, 1878, p.1.
4. Rajendra Ram, History of Buddhism in Nepal 704-1396 A.D., Patna: Jana Bharati Prakashan, 1977, pp. 160-161; Also see: Rahul Sangkrityayan, Buddhacharya, Kashi: Sewa Upavan, 1931, p.14.
5. Luciano Petech, Medieval History of Nepal 75-1482, Rome: ISMEO, 1984, p.85.
6. King Madana Rama (1382- 1394 AD) sent an exchange delegation of Nepalese Buddhist scholars to Tai Tsu - the Chinese emperor. It was laden with gifts of Buddhist manuscripts, images, art objects and horses for the emperor. Rajendra Ram, f. op. cit., pp. 206-208; Giuseppe Tucci, Tibetan Painted Scrolls, Vol.2, Rome: Liberia Della Stato, 1949, p.692.
7. Hidenobu Takaoka (ed.), A Microfilm Catalogue of the Buddhist Manuscripts in Nepal, Nagoya: The Buddhist Library, 1981, p. V.
8. Janak Lal Vaidya, Rastriya Abhilekhalaya Sthit Nepal Bhasa Newari Abhilekh Grantha (A Research Report Submitted to T.U. Research Division), 2041 B.S., pp. 10-11.
9. Min Bahadur Shakya, 'Preservation of Sanskrit Buddhist Manuscripts in the Kathmandu Valley: Its Importance and Future', Paper presented at the seminar organized by Berkeley Buddhist Center, Berkeley: 1997, pp. 1-10.
10. Nalinaksha Dutta, Gilgit Manuscripts, Vol. 1, Delhi: Sri Satguru Publications. 1984.
11. Daniel Wright, History of Nepal-Translated from Parbatiya, Calcutta: Sushil Gupta, 1958, pp.192-197.
12. Jagannath Upadhyaya et. al., Suchipatra, Vol 1, Kathmandu: National Archives, 2054, pp.1-114; Purna Ratna Vajracharya (ed.),Brihat Suchipatram, Vol. VII, Pts. I, II, III, Kathmandu: Bir Library, 2021-23.
13. Tarthang Tulku, Guide to the Nyingma Edition of De-dge- bKagyur bsTan-'gyur, Berkeley: Dharma Publishing, 1980, pp. 1096-1097.

14. George N. Roerich (Eng. tr), The Blue Annals, New Delhi: Motilal Banarsi Dass, 1996, pp. 204-394 and 731-1053.
15. Hubert Decler, 'Vajracharya Transmission in 11th. Century Chobhar Bharo Maimed Hand's Main Disciple Vajrakirti, the Translator from Rwa', Buddhist Himalaya, Vol. VI, No. 1 & 2, Lalitpur, 1994-95, pp. 1-16.
16. George N. Roerich, Biography of Dharmaswamin, Patna: K. P. Jayasawal Research Institute, 1959, pp. 53-54; Shanker Thapa, 'Nepalese Buddhist Scholarship and Buddhist Sanskrit Literature of Nepal' research Report submitted to CNAS, Tribhuvan University, 2001.
17. Kamal Prakash Malla, 'Newar Bouddha Vidvata', Pasuka, Year: 9, No. 12, 2054 B.S, p.3; Kamal Prakash Malla, 'Newar Bouddha Vidvata-2', Pasuka year: 2, No.1, 2054, pp. 10-11.
18. See - Elizabeth Cook (ed.), Light of Liberation: A History of Buddhism in India Crystal Mirror Series , Vol. III, Berkeley: Dharma Publishing, 1992, pp. 302, 334-335, and 354-360.
19. For detail see: W W Hunter, Life of Brian Houghton Hodgson: British Resident at the Court of Nepal, London: Turner and Noble, 1896, pp. 261-282; Wright, op. cit., pp. 201-208; Cecil Bendall, Catalogue of Sanskrit Manuscripts in the University Library Cambridge, Cambridge: Cambridge University Press, 1902, pp. 1-2.
20. Dhanavajra Vajracharya, Licchavikalin Abhilekh, Kathmandu: Institute for Nepal and Asian Studies, 2030, pp. 320-335; Min Bahadur Shakya, Life and Contribution of Nepalese Princess Bhrikuti Devi to Tibetan History, Delh: Book Faith India, 1997, pp. 15-30.
21. Min Bahadur Shakya, A Short History of Buddhism in Nepal, Lalitpur: Young Buddhist Publication, 1986, p. 4; Hara Prasad Shastri, 'On a Manuscript of Aüöasahasrika Prajðaparamita Written in Nalanda and Discovered in Nepal', Journal of Asiatic Society of Bengal, 1899, Calcutta, pp. 39-40.
22. Sigfried Lierhard and Thakur Lal Manandhar (ed.), Nepalese Manuscripts Pt. 1, (Newari and Sanskrit), Stuttgart, Franz Steiner Verlag Wiesbaden GMBH, 1988, p. XVII.
23. Min Bahadur Shakya, Sacred Art of Nepal, Kathmandu: Handicraft Association of Nepal, 2000. p. 24; Aryamahapratisaradharani manuscript dated N. S. 898, It is now in the collection of the author. Also see: Shanker Thapa, Aryamahapratisara Sutra and Its Significance in the Buddhist Society of Nepal (Unpublished PGD Thesis submitted to the Department of Buddhist Studies, T.U. Kirtipur: 2001, pp. 70-71.
24. Raja Shakya, Asasaphu Kuthiya Saphudhala, Kathmandu: Asa Saphu Kuthi Guthi, 2000, pp. 1-84;

25. Arundel Esdaile, The British Museum Library: A Short History and Survey, London: George Allen and Unwin, 1948, pp.311-312; India office Library and Records: Report for the Year 1976, London: Foreign and Common Wealth Office, 1978, pp. 95-108.
26 Moriz Winternitz and Arthur Berriedale Keith (ed.), Catalogue of Sanskrit Manuscripts in the Bodleian Library, Vol. II, Oxford: The Clarendon Press, 1905, p. 249.
27. Rajendra Lal Mitra, Sanskrit Buddhist Literature of Nepal, Calcutta: Sanskrit Book Depot, 1971, p. XXXIV.
28. E. Burnouf, Introduction de' la Historie du Buddhisme Indien, Paris: 1876, p.1.
29. *Ibid.*
30. E.B. Cowell, along with Prof. J. Eggeling of Edinberg edited - 'Hodgson Manuscripts in the Royal Asiatic Society's Library', Journal of the Royal Asiatic Society, Vol. VII, 1876, pp. 1-52.
31. Hunter, op cit, p. 261-282.
32. Wright, op cit, p. 201.
33. *Ibid.*
34. Bendall, op cit, pp. VII-VIII.
35. Wright, op cit, p.207.
36. Bendall, f. op. cit., pp. VII-XII.
37. Binayak Lohani, Belayati Sangrahalayama Raheka Nepal Utpattika Puratatvik Samagriharu (Unpublished M.A. Thesis submitted to T.U. Dept of NEHCA), Kirtipur: 2049. B.S., p. 49.
38. Quoted from: Hara Prasad Shastri, A Catalogue of Palm-Leaf and Selected Paper manuscripts Belonging to the Durbar Library of Nepal, Vol. 1, Calcutta: 1905, pp. 2-3.
39. Cecil, Bendall, A Journey of Literary and Archaeological Research in Nepal and Northern India During the Winter of 1884-85, Cambridge: The University Press, 1886, pp. 16-20.
40. *Ibid.*, p. 4.
41. *Ibid.*, pp. 16-17.
42. *Ibid.*, pp. 250-267.
43. *Ibid.*, p. 249. Also see: Horace H. Wilson, Professor Wilson's Sanskrit manuscripts now Deposited in the Bodleian Library, Oxford, 1912, pp. 1-20.
44. Theodorr Aufrecht (ed), A Catalogue of Sanskrit Manuscripts in the Library of Trinity College, Cambridge: Deighton, Bell and Co., 1869, pp. 1-11.

The list of manuscripts of School of Oriental and African Studies, London is mentioned by Binayak Lohani - Quoted in Lohani, op cit, p. 50.

45. Matsunami Seiren (comp), Catalogue of the Sanskrit manuscripts in the Tokyo University Library, Tokyo: Suzuki Research Foundation, 1986, pp.1-386.
46. Kiyotaka Goshima and Keiyo Noguchi, (ed.), A Succinct Catalogue of the Sanskrit Manuscripts in the Possession of the Faculty of Letters- Kyoto University, Kyoto: 1983.
47. Yutaka Imamoto, 'Catalogue of Buddhist Sanskrit Manuscripts in the Library of Tokai University', Preceedings of the Faculty of Letters, Vol. 2, Tokyo: Tokai University, 1960.
48. Abhi Subedi, Ekai Kawaguchi: The Trespassing Insider, Kathmandu: Mandala Books, 1999, pp. 119-125.
49. *The Rising Nepal*, 2 June 1986, Part of those manuscripts (248 in total) are catalogued by Charles M. Novak on behalf of Asa Saphu Kuthi. See: Charles M. Novak, Catalogue of Selected Buddhist Manuscripts in Asa Saphukuthi, Kathmandu: Asa Saphu Kuthi, 1986, pp. 1-36.
50. Horst Brinkhaus, 'The NGMPP on the Threshold of its Five Year Phase', Abhilekh, year 3, No.3, Kathmandu, 2042 V. S. pp. 33-33.

2

Heritage of Tibetan Xylographs Related to Manuscripts of Indian Origin

– S.K. Pathak

According to the historical records available in Tibetan huge numbers of Indian manuscripts (henceforth mss) had once been carried over directly from India or via Nepal since the seventh century C.E. The earliest account of Manikabum *ma ni bka'bum* with its presumable authorship to Srongtsangampo *srong btsan sgam po* (d.650 C.E.) refers to advent of the Indian mss through Kashmirian routes in the land of snow. Oral traditions with the legendary account go as well.

Historically two avenues in movement of manuscripts from Bharatadesha *rga gar yul* to Bhotadesha *bod yul* are specifically determinable. Those were;

(i) Mss of Indian origin carried by the Indian Pandits in order to render in Tibetan.

(ii) Mss of Indian origin translated in the monasteries of their homeland like Vikramasila, Jagaddaloy Nalanda, monasteries with the assistance of either the author of particular text an expert on the particular subject concerned.

Thereby two kinds of mss have been available in Tibetan resources. Pandit Rahul Sankrityayana in course of his visit in Tibet during the thirties of the last century had an occasion to witness the Sanskrit mss of India. Those were then in the Nor Monastery of the Central West of Bhota desha.

Again, the brima (*bris ma*) mss in respect to the early Tibetan translation works had been preserved in the Royal Palace located near about Lhasa (*lha sa* in Sanskrit *deva bhumi*). Geza Bethtenfalvy has prepared a catalogue of the pa khan Tsal mss which may ge regarded as the early resource of Tibetan manuscripts of some Ka-Tan (*bka' 'gyur dang bstan 'gyur*),

Chronology of the Btsan Rulers

Srong tsan sgam po's father *Gnam ri srong Btsan* (c.600 C.E.) had been an energetic personality in the 6th century of the Land of Snow *gangs yul* around the Yere Gtsang river valley. He endeavoured to build up unity among various well-to-do families in order to consolidate unified cordiality.

His son, *Srong btsan sgam po* took its merits and could set up a powerful administration with several bands of warring groups. He established the *Btsan* Royal Dynasty in Central Tibet and its around. In due course he defeated the Chinese Western ruler and Nepal Thereafter, according to then practice, their daughters used to be the Victor's Spouse king Amshuvarman. Those royal spouses demanded to set up the teachings of the Buddha and king took advantage of those queens' merits. He invited Buddhist teachers from Kashmir, as the Tibetan records mention. He declared sixteen point Teachings for his subjects and that was credited to be a Moral Guidline how his subjects would be morally uplifted.

Two Buddhist temples were installed homely Jo bo khang and Ra mo che by the princess of A-zha in Western China; Wen Chen she invited Chinese Hva Shan Mahayana Masters from China. The Nepalies princess Bhrukuti Buddhist pandits from Kashmir had been invited. Thonim Sambhota was deputed to India to learn the writing the then Brahmi scripts as well as Sanskrit grammar in order to introduce writing in alphabetical format.

c. 650 C.E. Mang slon mang *btsan* succeeded as Srong bstan sgom po died in 659 circa. Strifes between the Chinese and Btsan rulers in capturing Turkistan continued.

c. (666-692) C.E. Khri 'dus srong *btsan* succeded and captured Turkestan to rule inclusive of 'Jam Nan chau in 680.

The Royal family has faced internal dispute between Chinese Hwashan priests and Bonpo practitioners in spirit of excellent Tibetan. Warring victory over several Chinese towns in 720, 727, 741 and Bru Zha (present day Gilgit in 737. Bon po established Kva in and managed to ban Buddhism 740.

c. 754 C.E. Khri Srong lde *btsang* ascended the Btsan ruling throne took measures to reinslitute Buddhism by inviting Shantaraksita from Nepal. Shantaraksita with his discriple Kamalashila succeeded to install *Bsam yas* (Acintya), the first Buddhist monastic installation a distant off from the Capital Lhasa under the Royal Declaration *bka' mchid* c.776. Pala rulers did not hesitate to pay tribute.

Prior to that the bilingual (Chinese-Tibetan) inscription *zhol rdo ring* was laid down territories like Kansu, Zuchuan, Yunan (757-61) prior to entry in the capital ch'ang in 762. later on Tibetan army occupied the Northen Gateway of China namely Dum-huang in 787 for silk route.

c.7 C.E. Ral-pa can took ovr the seat of *Btsan* ruling dynasty. He was so involved in spread of Buddhist faith as he was assassinated by the antagonists. Thereafter the *Btsan* Monarchy faced a set back.

Indo-Tibetan Cultural Negotiations

With the above polito-economical drastic drive in Central Asia and China in Central Asia, the Royal patronage to promote the Indian Buddhism opened cross-cultural negotiations an unpresidented avenue for exchange of wisdom between the Northern plateau of the Himalayas Bhota desa *toibot* (>Tibet, bod yul) and the Gangetic plateau of Bharatdesa in the following prerogatives.

1. *Bka 'tshigs* Royal Decree was issued for inaugaration of Buddhism in *bod* yul *Bhotadesha* as the Religion (c.779).
2. A centre for academic pursuits in rendering the Buddha's teachings from the original Indian resources was installed in the Bsam yas monastery. It was named *yig bsgyur bslabs sgra* Translation School.
3. Seven persons volunteered for learning Indian language *sad mi bdun* from the Indian learned pandits aroowed to render their lives for the cause.
4. Several Indian pandits volunteered to dedicate themselves for the cause of preparing Tibetan translated manuscripts after accurate rendering of the Buddha's sayings in collaboration with the Tibetan

expertise namely *lo tsa ba* (suggestively, those who hold *lo ca na* (faithful eyes how to render the *Buddhavacana*).

5. As the whole matter was conducted under the Royal Order since the holding of the public debating *shastartha*, the manuscripts having Tibetan rendering of the sayings Buddha *Buddhavacan* had been as the *Heritage Property* of the land after thorough revisions by the regarded veterans.

The above justifies the credibility of the Tibetan translations in manuscripts for stipulation of the Ruling authorities of the land of Snow. Those were subsequently xylographed wood lock printed editions.

In due course two separate Traditions of the Buddhavacana renderings developed, for the manuscrism in translation. Those are traceable in the Xylographs belonging to Groups.

(1) Narthang Manuscript Group (14th cent. C.E.)

(2) Tsal pa Manuscript Group (14th cent. C.E.)

Heritage

Lexiconically, *heritage* bolds reference to '*age*', a suffix in old French usage from Latin *Haticum*. In Modern Latin-*aginum*, as a post affix particle. Heritage is to toods and subjective ideas in quantum through generations in the course of 'age' or time. Heritage thus means what is or may be inherited. (OED) With Biblical reference 'the ancient Isralites, the Church' inherited lot' in the growth of Christianity in subsequent days. In the history of religions' in West Asia several instances of inheritance in conceptual growth from pluralistic deifications of the Nature around humans to the discovery of One God are traceable. That may be taken elsewhere. In this context some case studies are done how the Indian *manus* could inflect in compositions of Tibetan Buddhist literary heritage through literal renduring of the Buddha's sayings in *Bka' 'gyur* Buddhavacana collections.

Tibetan Translation Methods

Acarya Shanta Raksita with his Indian and Tibetan collaborators well versed if Indian languages and Tibetan could frame out a unique translating method:

i) Each person engaged in translation task must be master of either Tibetan or Sanskritic (Buddhist Sanskrit, Paninian, Sanskrit, Pali, Prakrit, Apabhramsha) along with their respective working knowledge as required. That means, a Tibetan translater lo-tsa-ba should have working knowledge in Sanskritic and an Indian Pandit should be conversent in Tibetan for proper performance.

ii) Acquaintance with derivative significance of a word for rendering from Sanskritic to Tibetan was essential in respect to an Indian pandit and that is equally required for a Tibetan *Lo tsa ba* translator.

iii) Themetically each Indian Buddhist text holds distinct conceptual deliberations. For instance, theme of the books on Buddhist Monastic Order is not similar to those of the Buddhist Sutras, nor those of Tantra in the *Tripitaka*. It is to note the Indian *Tipitaka* in Pali holds three sections, the Books of Monastic Discipline *Vinayapitaka*, the Buddhas usual discourses among the recluses and lay persons *Suttapitaka*. Those are distributed in five subdivisions according their size and numerical order in subject matter. The third one *Abhidhammapitaka* referring to psycho-spiritual guidance how to get rid of the suffering by measures for awakening in respect to each individual. Technically 'to be enlightened within' by the individual person in order in order to self-illumind *attadipo bhava*. Several Pali Tripitaka texts are available in Tibetan renderings of *Buddhavacana*.

iv) 'Unless and until' the equivalents be appropriately confirmed restrictions had been laid on to be entered in the translated text. In order to safe guard from arbitrary rendering by a translater as that has been in practice during the post-Srong btsan sgam po period (7th cent. C.E.) and post-Ralpacan period (9th cent. CE) a joint-effort had been undertaken by a wider number of Indian Pandits and Tibetan Lotsaba after their First Congregation in the 9th cent. C.E. in Central Tibet. Thereby a monumental compendium proper equivalent in renderings. That was known as *Mahavyutpalli* the first bi-lingual Sanskrit-Tibetan vocabulary deposit. It had been thus an achievement how to build up the Indo-Tibetan spiritual trend commonly among the inhabitants of the Roof of the World Bhota desha Bod yul with those of the Elevated country *'phags yul* arya desha.

v) Above these precautionary measures to avoid any sort lapse in transmitting the heritage of Indian erudition an Authority for Revision was set up to confirm those renderings as fit for preservation according to Royal Decree. *Bka' tshigs*.

Languages: Indian & Tibetan

In negoliating manuscript heritage cross-culturally, as that had been in case of Hebrew in the Old Testament, a few words on the geneses of two languages are necessary. In respect to ours, it is referred that Thon mi Sambhata had been deputed by the Second Btsan ruler of Tibet to India to formulate a morphological systematic language order in contrast to the mono syllabic Sino-Tibetan. Thereby the agglutinative Tibetan phonemes to generate a morphological base could form. In the span of about two centuries since the composition of Thon mi sabhota when the School of Translation *yig bsgyur bslab sgrwa* was established in the premises of *Bsam yas* monastery.

Despite that, some measures had been thoroughly laid down to appropriate renderings. Those may be jotted below.

i) Skt. *Buddha* (from the Sanskritic verb root *budh* to be aware of, to awake) suggests the Awakened one, the Enlightened one. In rendering Tib. *sangs rgyas* (constituted by two separate terms) agglutinate what is *Buddha* in Sanskritic means. Here *sangs* to be awaken from slumber and *rgyas* means thoroughly or widely with no lapse.

ii) Skt. *Deshayati* (Pali *desiti*; Budd. Prakrit *desayi*, Budh Apabramsa *disai*) means delivers teachings; (derived from the Skt. Verb root *dish*) holds a specific usuage in this case. Tib. *bka' gnang ba* (honorific is respect to Buddha by adding a specific word *gnang*; and, *ba* is a morphological particle generally added by agglutination.

iii) Skt. *Dharmam* (Sanskrtic from *dhammam* in all speeches) Tib. *chos* corresponds to *dhamma*. It is to note than no second ease-ending particle for the objective case in Tibetan is required; that requires in the Sanskritic speeches). Skt. *Bhudhah dharmam deshayati*. Tib. *Sangs rgyas chos bka' gnang ba* with no case ending signs in the Nominative and the accusative in Tibetan.

iv) Again for congation of the verbs in Sanskritic languages similar methods have been followed in course of translation.

v) As regards twenty pre-positional particles upasarga in Sanskrit (*upasagga* in Sanskirtic) twenty corresponding words are the agglulinatives particles used before the verbs. Tibetan particles floating occasionally for use.

Resultantly the Sanskrit structural model of has not been least disturbed and Tibetan Classical language *chos skod* is unique instance of language-reconstruction in the comparative Linguistics among the Asian languages.

Indian *Buddhavacana* mss. *bka' 'gyur*

An occasion of ruling the 'Freedom in Languages' to the Buddha's teachings had been granted by of the Founder of Buddhist Organisation *Sangha* during his lifetime. A request was submitted to the Buddha to use a particular language for use in the Sangha. He declined and allowed to use any language preferable to a nearer person. Resultantly, *Buddhavacana* Teachings of the Buddha had been preserved in multiple languages. Such as,

(i) Pali *Tipitaka* (three Baskets of Buddha's teaching in the Magadha-koshala Pali speech where Buddha had moved a major part as a recluse since he had left this Shakya royal palace in Kapilavastu. The Tipitaka collections were preserved by those hearers *savaka* (Skt. shravaka) of the Buddha directly. In Tibetan translations from Pali Tipitaka are available in the *Kanjur Bka' 'gyur*. Prajnaparamita section (Tohuku catalogue).

(ii) Gautama the Buddha had also moved to Mathura and around in Surashena mahajanapada. Those who had occasion to hear him directly preserved his sayings in their language, what is generally known as the Spoken Sanskrit. It was pre-Paninian 'unreformed', better to say Mixed Sanskrit for inclusion of the local peoples' speeches like *Prakrit* and *Apabhramsa* as required. Those hearers of the Buddha did not accept the Doctrine of Impermanence in the understanding what Magadhan hearers could follow. They daimed that all objects or phenomena were existent by a person's convensional knowing; but those were impermanent and liable to decay on account of being compounded or constituted. Those Buddhists were known as *Mulasarvastivadin*, the Primary group in holding the view of 'all existent' *sarvasti*.

Vinaya Pitaka: The Book of Monastic Discipline

The Buddhists in Tibet follow their Monastic Disciplinary rules of the above referred *Mulasarvastivada Vinayavastu*. Those texts were translated from the Indian Mulasarvastivada Mixed Sanskrit mss into Tibetan by the Kasmirian Pandits with the assistance of Tibetan devout Buddhist monks as early as the late Eight cent. C.E.

It is to note here that the Tipitaka in Pali and those in Sanskrit preserved by Mulasarvastivadin of Mathura and Sarvastivadins of Gandhara especially are in three folds; namely -

1) *Vinaya pitaka* in Pali; *Vinayavastu* in Sanskritic
2) *Sutta Pitaka* in Pali, *Agama* in Sanskrit i.e.
3) *Abhidhamma* in Pali; Abhidharma Shastra in Sanskritic

The Tibetans enumerate *Tripitaka* in Tibetan *sde snod gsonm* as,

1) *Dul ba* Disciplinary code for Buddhists recluses *Vinaya Vastu*
2) *Mdo rnams* the Buddha's teachings multiple occasions with aphoristic manuerism separately *sutrani* .
3) *rgyud sngags tantra mantra* in Sanskrit referring to the cryptic teachings of the Buddha in respect to these disciples who had been capable to follow with their sharp intellect tiksna-dhih. These deal with the extensive relationship between the part (individual person) and the whole (the Universe inclusive of cosmic space)

Vinaya Mulasarvastivada in Tibetan Translation

It is difficult to fix any historical data of sequence how the Indian mss had been carried to Tibet with reference to a text concerned. However the names of Indian Pandit leave a room to presume the period of translating the individual manuscript of the Indian Origin. Let us attempt for a case study in respect of seven *Vinaya vastu* works; namely -

1) *Vinaya vastu*: The version in Buddhist Sanskrit is found out and edited by Nalinaksa Dutt with its comparison with Tibetan renderings.
2) *Vinaya vibhanga:* No Indian manuscript is available the elucidation of the earlier text how to restrain a recluse oneself.
3) *Bhiksani Vinaya Vibhanga* : It would presumably be a unique text; as no such ms. Is available up till date.
4) *Bhiksuni Pratimaksa Sutra: -do-*
5) *(Bhiksu) Pratimoksa Sutra* : No Indian ms. Is traceable up till now. Pratimoksa-pada-bhismaranam by Danashila (visited Tibet in c. late 8th cent. C. E. and translated several Kashmirian treatises). It is investing that a Sautrantika household *kalyanamitra* a commentary of *Pratimoksa* entitled *Premotpadika*.
6) *Vinaya ksudraka vastu*: Minor rulings on monastic disciplinary rules in addition to the text no.1 above.
7) Vinaya uttara-sangraha: An Appendix of the monastic corde in respect to the *Mulasarvastivada* flourished in Kasmir. Afore said Sautrantika Kalyanamitra composed Vinayattaragama-Vishesagama-prashnavritti and that was rendered in Tibetan.

Some Instances of Collaborations

It may be added that several *Shastra(s)* composed by Several Kashmirian *Vinayadhara*(s) exponents of Monastic Discipline like Vinaya samgraha by Vishesamitra. The teams of Tibetan translation task from the Mulasarvastivada Vinayavastu mss were during the Early spread of Buddhism (9th and 10th centuries C.E.)

1. Indian Pandits

Sarvajnadeva of Kashmir, Vidyakaraprabha (rig gnas 'od) Tibetan Lotsaba; Dharmakara of Kashmir Dpal gyi lhun po Tibetan Lotsa ba

Kashmir Since Buddhist Council by Kaniska (c.1lst cent. B.C.E.) had been a strong hold centre of the Doctrine. If the Mulasarvadins the two numbered Teams for 'Revision' of the said translation in Tibetan was formed by Vidyakara prabha and Dpal brtsegs to confirm the merit of that rendering. Similar trenda continue.

It is to note that the Tibetan recluses followed the Mulasarvastivada and Sarvastivada Vinaya discipline coat is distinct from the Mahasmghika Vinaya disciplinary works. Therefore no Theravada (Magadhan Shavira Analytlatic bhajya method was followed. Among the Pali texts in buddhavacana no Vinaya text was rendered into Tibetan. *Vinaya vibhanga* analytes of Bhiksu *Vinaya* rules eludidations manus was entrusted to Indian Pandit Jinamitra Indian Pandit and Klui rgyal mtsan Lotsaba.

Whereas, more attention had ben given to case of the manuscript of Bhiksuni Vinaya Vibhanga of Mulasarvastivadin. Indian pandits like Sarvajnadeva of Kashmir, Dharmakara of Kashmir and Vidyakaraprabha of Tibet Dpal gyi lhun po of Tibet.

In respect to the Buddhist Monastic pureification rules by confession in the Uposatha Days in the Order *Sungha* the task for appropriate rendering was entrusted to Jinamitra of Kashmir and Klui rgyal mtsan of Tibet. They were also entrusted to deal with the Sanskrit manuscript of Bhiksuni Pratimoksa Sutra of the Mulasarvastivada.

Again, Vidyakaraprabha, Dharmakarabhadra and Tibetan Dpal 'khor in the 9th century took over the task of dealing the Indian manuscript of *Vinaya ksudraka vastu* for rendering into Tibetan. Those goes in hold a view that Kashmirians during the period seventh cent. C.E. downwards had been avowed to extend their Vinaya rules in order to claim their excellence among the Tibetan exponents with Sarvastivada order. As regards the procurement of the mss from Indian Buddhavacana texts like the Prajnaparamita Sutras, the colophons are found inadequate to examine their original. Presumably, Nepal had then advanced in Buddhamarga and manuscripts from Indian origin were with the practitioners. Let us take the case of Astasahasrika Prajna Paramita-sutra in Sanskrit manuscript is an important well read resource in doctrinal source of Prajna Paramita alias Shunyata. It is to admit that how and when the prime manuscript of the *Prajnaparamita Sutra* was formulated.

Its Tibetan version was prepared by Shakyasena, Indian Pandit. Jnanasiddhi Dharmata shila Chos nyid tshul khrims.

During the Later Spread of Buddhism in the 11th cent. C.E. Rinchen bzang po, a contemporaneous Tibetan erudite translator *Lo-chen* endeavoured to with the Indian Pandit Subhasita and Atisha Dipankara. Subsequently 'Brom rgyal ba'i 'byung gnas ventured to revise the said text Astasahashrika Prajnaparamita with Atisha Dipankara. After his demise, he attempted lonely to clarify some ambiguities in the Sanskrit mss, what had been then available in there. Finally Blo ldan shes rab revised some portions before it acceptance in the order of Narthang Xylograph with approval. Indian Sanskrit manuscripts from which the present edition is also been carefully edited as latest edition from Mithila Research Institute, Muzuffarpur Bihar with varient readings. This text demands an appropriate edition with its Tibetan and Chinese renderings.

Fourfold Tantra in the Kanjur

Among the Sanskrit manuscripts of vast Tantra Indian *Tripitaka*, the *Manjushri Namasangiti* is available in original. Mm. Vidhusekhara Bhattacarya prepared its bilingual (Sanskrit Tibetan edition and published by Calcutta University. Lokesh Chandra also published its another versionfrom Saraswativihara.

Similarly some Tantra mss in Sanskrit have been already published Such as,

Kriya Tantra

It is a wide section of Tantra mss which had been composed in India upto the eleventh and twelfth century C.E. More than one thousand mss on multiple aspects on how to start with Tantra rituals in respect to the Buddhist Tantric deities had been written by numerous Indian Tantric teachers of the Buddhist lineage. It is to add that Tantra ritualistic practices hold akin rites in many respect with the non-Buddhist Tantric orders.

Carya Tantra

Without strict mannerism in daily livelihood in determined mind Tantra practitioners fell to achieve their respective goals. In this respect the Siddhacaryas had composed *yogatantra* carya songs which had been to Tibet.

Literally *yoga* suggest 'unification' of the individual mundanences relatively confined in mind and in body. Thereby plurality prevails. A Tantric Unification how to practice is to be with the cosmic universe where individuality dissolves.

Anuttara yogatantra

It refers to the utmost state of experience in respect to a Tantra practitioner where duality percolates to ONENESS *advaya*.

In fine, our indebtedness goes to Alexandar Csoma de Koros, a Hungarian Tibetan researcher dedicated his life in the Asiatic Society Calcutta during the first half of the nineteenth century. He firstly brought to the notice of academicians the account of preservation of manuscript heritage in the cross cultural relevance between two neighbouring peoples, here the Indians and the Tibetan for about a millennium and a half.

The present attempt in this respect opens an angle how to be specific in locating multiple aspects of the Indian literary dimensions as those are historically evident while translated texts in Tibetan refer to their Indian Original manuscripts. Those had been written and copied number of times till they entered the Land of Snow for rendering each in Tibetan. Every text of the Kanjur *bka' 'gyur* holds its own history. In this respect the colophonrs in Tibetan editions are significal P. Cordier in the Catalogue do fonds Tibetain Repertoire du Kanjur of the Bibliotheca nationale have traced out in brief. A serious search is awaited to explore the 'heritage of manuscripts' numbering in the Dul ba (Vinaya vastu), in mdo (Sutra) and Rgyud sngags (Tantra mss.) according to Northang Xylographs. In the other versions like Derge, Peking, Zol edition vary those number vary. A list of catalogues of the Ka-Tan done so far is appended for future study.

About the distributions of Sutra and Tantra objectively no distinction in practice prevails. The Vaipulya Sutra texts occasionally include Dharani mantras in order to practice the spiritual extensions. In Tibetan those distributions are regarded as theory and applications of the Buddha's Silence *aruta-vaka*. According to the traditions, the instances of Dharma-cakra-pravartana had occurred. The Second instance was at Rajagriha (Rajgir) and the last one was at Dhanyakataka Srishaila peak in South India.

Appendix - I

Some Pali mss. in Tibetan Kanjur collection

A. *Vinayapitaka*

1. Dharma cakka pavattana sutra > Dharmacakra Pravartana Sutra (Derge edn. Tohoku Catalogue No.31 referring its Chinese renderings in Taisho Catalogue and Buniy Nanjio Catalogue Njo no. 379).

2. *Jataka Nidana* (Comparable to Khuddaka Nidana in Pali) Toh. Cat. No.32.

3. Atanutiya Sutta (Corresponding to Digha Nikaya in Pali No.33; *Dirghagama* vide Njo.974 with title Phl sha ma thian wan ching *vaishramana divyamnaya Sutra*. The textual content is similar.

4. *Mahasamaya* Sutta > *Mahasamaya sutra*, Toh. Cata. No. 34; deals with names of Deva(s) and Brahma(s) who are said to have appeared before Gautama the Buddha when he had been under deep meditation in Mahavana vihara of Kapilavastu Agrees with Dirghagama of Sarvastivadin Vide Chinese Catalogue Nanjio 545, 851.

5-6.*Maitri Sutra* (Toh. 35) and *maitri Bhavana Sutra* (Toh. 36) correspond to Metta Sutta in Khuddaka Nikaya referring to a *paritta manta* in Digha Nikaya. Its Chinese translation as referred by B. Nanjio in Catalogue agrees with Ekottara agama No. 544. It requires further probe with Taisho translation.

7-8.*Panca Shiksanu- samsha Sutra* (Toh. 37) and Giri-Ananda-Sutra (Toh.38). The latter text and appear to refer a paritta mantra in Pali Anguttara Nikaya, Similar may be *Nandopananda-naga-damana-sutra* (Toh.39).

9. *Nandopananda-nagaraja-damana Sutra*

   Buddhist mss on taming the Serpent King and other venomour reptiles are occasionally observed. Several Tibetan translated hand written mss rendered from the Indian mss are preserved in the Manuscripts Musuem, Asiatic Society Calcutta See Nanjio

Catalogue No.707 referring to the Mandgalayana for taming the Nagas for comparative note.

10. *Mahakashyapa Sutra*

11-12. Surya Sutra Suriya Sutta and Candrima Sutra/Canda Sutta refer to Samyutta Nikaya (Toh. Cata. 41 ī 42 respectively.

13. Mahamangala Sutra/Mahamangala Sutrta be referred to Mangala sutta in Pali Khuddaka Patha of the Fifth Nikaya.

14. Bandana Mukhapadhya in Gustar Roth Falicitation volume (pp.480ft) resource subject to verification. That opens a vista for manuscript studies. (Bihar Puravid Parisad, Patna 1998).

Appendix - II

Some Buddha Vacana mss. edited

1. *Astadasha sahasrika-Projnaparamita-Sutra*

   Ed. Edward Conze : *The Gilgit Manuscript* (fragmentary as available) *Chapters 55-70 Correspond the 5th Abhisamaya* Istituto Italino per li Medio ed. Estuemo Oriento, Roma (Is.M.E.O.) 1962.

2. *Astasahasrika Prajnaparamita Sutra* (ms located in *Bibliotheque Nationale de Paris*.

3. *Bhadracaripranidhana* ed. Suniti Kumar Pathak (mss with Tibetan rindering in Kanjur). Note. The Kholanese *Bhadracaripranidhanaraja* text with Buddhist Sanskrit original ed. Jes Peter Asmussen, Kobenhaven, Munkagaard 1961.

4. Bhadra-kalpika-sutra *ed. Sten konow* Saka Version of the Bradrakalpika Sutra Osto, 1929.

5. *Bhaisajya-guru-sutra,* vol. I ed. Nalinaksa Dutt. (Sanskrit edn.) Srinagar, Kashmir, 1939.

6. Buddha-baladhana-praliharya-vikurvana-nirdesha-Sutra. Ed. Nalinakasa Dutta : *Gilgit Manuscripts* vol. IV (Summary pp.XXV-XXVII) Calcutta Oriental Press, Calcutta. 1958.

7. Dashabhumika Sutra (pt. of Aratamshaka Sutra ed. by Edward Conze- London, Haripera Row, 1963 (Beyers Sanskrit text).

8. *Gandavyuha Sutra*
9. *Prajnaparamita-hrdaya Sutra* (in two separate versions) ed. Sumual Beal, Journal of Royal Asiatic Society, new Series 1865. pp. 25-29.
10. *K*arandavyuhasutra *ed. Samashrami (Bengali Script) Calcutta Prabhas Chandra Mazumdar. Its Metrical version, Indian Historical Quarterly 24, Calcutta 1948.*
11. *Karunapudarika* Isshi Yamado, Vol.I, School of Oriental and Africal Studies, London University.
12. *K*asyapapari *varta* Bhikkhu Pasadika in Link son Publication d'studies, bouddhologiques No I (Nov.1977) to (Nov.1979), German Scholars like Moritz Winternitz *Der* .
13. *Lalitavistara* ed. Rajendra Lal Mitra (Chap I-15), Asiatic Society, Calcutta 1881-86.
14. *Lankavatara Sutra* ed. Buniyo nanjio
15. *M*aparinirvana *sutra* ed. Kosho Yamamoto, 3 vols. The kerin Buddhalogical Series, Ubeshi, Karinnbanko, 1973-75.
16. Ratnaketu-dharani Sutra (It may be noted that the divisions like Sutra Tantra, Dharani among the Buddhists had been unknown on account of Buddha's deliberations to communication through 'deep mind') ed. Nalinaksa Dutt. Gilgit Manuscripts vol.IV (Summary pp iii-xiv) Calcutta. 1959.
17. Saddharma Pundarika Sutra ed. Nalinaksa Dutt, Asiatic Society, Calcutta.
18. Samadhiraja Sutra Summarized by nalinaksa Dutt in Gilgit Manuscripts Vol.II, pp. xiii-xxiii Srinagar Kashmir, 1941.
19. Sukhavalivyuha Sutra ed. F. Max Muller & Bunyiu Nanjio (Chap. 4, 9, 37, 44 in fragments) under the title *The Larger Sukhavuti vyuha,* Buddhist Mahayana Texts II p1-76, Oxford, Clarendon Press 1894) Indian edn. Matilal Banarasi Dass 1965.

19(a)The same text in (smaller manuscript) ed. by F. Max Muller. *Sanskrit Texts discovered in Japan* Journal of Royal Asiatic Society (new series) 12, 1880; *The Smaller Sukhavativyuha* Buddhist Mahayana Texts II pp.87-104) Oxford, 1894.

20. *Shurangama-samadhi-Sutra* ed. R. E. Emmerick *The Khotanese Shurangama Sutra*, Oxford University press. 1970. (Since the twenties of the last century academic ventures have been made to retranslate the lost Indian mss what are preserved in Tibetan translation. In this respect Mm. Vidhusekhara Shastri in Visva Bharati took leadership to retranslate Mahayana vimsaka from Tibetan and Chinese of the same text. Also N. Aiyaswami Shastri followed that method. Since the sixties those programs have continued).

    Thubtan Kalsang Rinpoche and Bhikkhu Pasadika retranslated into Sanskrit the text from Chapters I-5 under the title *Excerpts* from the *Shurangama-samadhi-Sutra* (Translation from Tibetan), Library of Tibetan Works & Archives, Dharamsala, 1975.
21. Suryagarbha Sutra (Manuscript Remains of Buddhist Literatures found in Eastern Turkistan ed. A. F. Rudolf harnale, Oxford 1918.
22. Suvarnaprabhasottama-Sutra ed. R. E. Emmerick Sanskrit text with English translation entitled 'The Sutra of Golden Light', London, Luzace 1970. (see Sacred Books of Buddhists, London)
23. *Upaliparipriccha* ed. Pierre Pythan *Vinaya-vinishcaya Upali Paripriccha* with French translation Paris, 1973 (vide Collection Jean Przyluski, Series No.5).
24. *Vajracchedika Prajnaparamita Sutra ed. Nalinaksa Dutt,* Gilgit Manuscripts *vol. IV, Calcutta, Calcutta Oriental Press.*
25. *Vimala Kirtinirdesha Sutra.*

Bibliography

Bethlenfavy, Geza, *The Catalogue of the Tsal pa palace Tibetan manuscripts*, Budapest, 1968.

Banerjee, Anukul, *Sarvastivada Literature*, Pub. D. Banerjee 1/5 Premchand Boral Street, Calcutta, 12, 1957.

Cordier, Pilliot, *Catalogue du Fonds Tibetan : Repertoire du Kanjur* par Marcelle Lolon avec une prefacede Paul Pelliot, paris 1933.

Dutt, Nalinaksa, *Gilgit Manuscripts,* Srinagar, Kashmir 1941.

Najjio, Buniyiu, *A Catalogue of the Chinese Translation of the Buddhist Tripitaka,* Oxford, 1882.

Hukuju Vi *et. al.*, *A Complete Catalogue of the Tibetan Canons*, Tohoku Imperial University, Japan 1934.

Mukhopadhyay, Bandana, Some Theravada Sutra Malarias in Tibetan Translations, *Facets of the Indian Culture*, Patna, 1998.

Sankrityaryan, Rahul, *Shabdavatara* (Tibetan) *Sgra la 'jug pa,* Mahabodhi Society, 1915.

Sinha, Cittaranjan Prasad (ed.), *Facets of the Indian Culture, Gustav Roth Felicitation Volume*. Bihar Puravid Parisad, Patna, 1998.

3

Pali Manuscripts in Asian Countries

– *Bimalendra Kumar*

Pali has always remained a language for scholars of Buddhist countries of Southeast Asia. It was influenced by commentators and grammarians and by the native languages of the countries in which Theravada Buddhism was established over many centuries. The oral transmission of the Pali canon continued for several centuries after the death of the Buddha, even after the texts were first preserved in writing. No one script was ever developed for the language of the canon; scribes used the scripts of their native languages to transcribe the texts. Although monasteries in South India are known to have been important centres of Buddhist learning in the early part of this millennium, no manuscripts from anywhere in India except Nepal have survived.

The bulk of the manuscripts surviving in Sri Lanka and Burma were copied in the 18th and 19th centuries. A considerable number of manuscripts in Northern Thailand, recently brought to wider notice by Prof. Oskar Von Hinuber, date from the 16th century. Only a handful of manuscripts known from elsewhere are older than that. The grammarians who systematized Pali grammar and prosody in Burma in the 12th century exercised considerable influence on how the language was written thereafter in Burma[1]. The oldest known Pali palm-leaf text is an anomaly: four folios from the *Culavagga* of The *Vinaya Pitaka*, written in a North Indian script and dating about the 9th century, preserved in Kathamandu, Nepal.[2] It seems to have been copied from a North Indian original some centuries later.[3] Somewhat older are the inscriptions on store or other durable materials from Burma and Siam, which give extracts from canonical texts.[4]

Oskar Von Hinuber has shown the pre-eminent importance of the Pali tradition of Northern Thailand. The ancient manuscripts from this region have preserved grammatical forms which in the traditions of Ceylon, Burma and Siam, have been lost due to later recensions by learned monks whose alterations have created puzzles and problems, unexplainable from the point of view of historical linguistics.[5] Some of these texts represent the oldest manuscripts that have survived, not only in the North, but in the whole of Thailand and South-east Asia. Other represents work of South-east Asian origin, including several that have been composed by scholars from Lan Na. Eighteen titles out of the total of 48 Pali texts have been identified and the remaining 30 Pali manuscripts are under research and investigation by the scholars through transliteration, phonematic transcription and translation systems.[6]

Otani University Library, Kyoto, Japan has also published a Catalogue of Palm leaf manscripts, kept in the Otani University Library. Sixty four of the manuscripts-59 in the Khmer script, 4 in Burmese and one in Mon-were presented in Koen Otani by King Rama V of Siam in 1900. The provenance of the Lânnâ manuscripts is not known. The oldest manuscript in the Otani Collection, the *Dâthâvansa,* dates to 1750; the youngest dated manuscript to 1887. The manuscripts include *Kammavâcâ*, non-cononical suttas, *Anisamsa*, *Jâtaka* and *Abhidhamma* texts. These manuscripts provide a valuable tool for future studies of Buddhist manuscript traditions of Pali and Lânnâ literature.[7]

The Library of the Siam Society has an important collection of ancient manuscripts, written in several languages and scripts, mainly on palm leaves with a small number of paper folding books. These manuscripts belong to the period from the 16th century to this century. Most of the texts belong to Buddhist literature, both canonical and non canonical. However, a number of historical records together with different kinds of manuals can also be found. A preliminary list of titles was made fifteen years ago by a team from The National Library of Thailand.[8] Later Dr. Oskar Von Hinuber made a catalogue of the 91 Pali titles, which was published in *The Journal of The Siam Society* in 1987.[9]

Unlike the other Buddhist peoples of South East Asia, the Burmese do not produce palm leave manuscripts; they transmit and preserve their literature in books made of handmade paper, either accordion books called *pâp-top* or *'pads'* sewn along the top called *pâp-ken*. On the average Shan books are much bigger than the accordion books of the Thai or the Burmese. The covers are often finely decorated in gilt lacquer, inlaid glass, or intricately carved wood. The letters are written in black ink on thick white paper. The Shans or Burmese have several different scripts of their own for writing Shan, but use the Burmese script for writing Pali. An abridged poetic version of the Tipitaka was composed in Shan by Sao Kaw-Lee of Muang Pan in the 18th century. This has been printed in three volumes namely *Vinaya, Suttanta* and *Abhidhamma*. Shan literature in European collection has not yet been properly catalogued. The Shan manuscripts in German collection are being catalogued by Chaichuen Khamdaengydtai. The University of Chiang Mai has catalogued the collection of one of the Shan temples in Chiang Mai, Wat Pa Pao. A perusal of the titles can give us at least a broad impression of the literature of the Shans.[10]

The preservation and restoration of the manuscripts in Cambodia has been started by the *Fonds pour l'edition des manuscripts due Cambodge (FEMC)*, Phnom Penh, which works under the auspices of the *Ecole francaise d'Extreme-Orient*, Hanoi. The goal of the project is to physically restore manuscripts-including those inscribed on palm-leave, both long and short in format and those written in folding accordion books made of hand-made paper, or on modern paper-and then to replicate the texts photographically. The texts are in several languages: largely in Khmer or Pali, but in a few cases in Northern or Lanna Thai, Thai or Burmese. From May 1991 to the present the FEMC team has visited more than 650 temples in Cambodia and has inventoried more than 7000 bundles. In addition, The *Bibliotheque Preah Vanarat Ken Vong* has collected ancient manuscripts of Phnom Penh, numbering 3400 the largest and most significant manuscript collection in Cambodia.

The manuscripts are also available in Mon language, which belongs to the Mon-Khmer family. With Pye, Cham, and Khmer, it is one of the earliest vernaculars in the region. The Mon adopted an Indic script, the so-called Pallava, and also used Sanskrit and Pali. The Pali inscriptions from Central Siam made during the 6th to 11th centuries-the time of the rich and cosmopolitan Dvâravatï culture which is believed to have had a Mon elite-are among the earliest surviving records of that language. The monasteries still keep large collections of manuscripts, both in Mon and Pali and these must be preserved for future generations.[11]

The Catalogue of Talaing manuscripts in the Bernard Free Library at Rangoon gives a list of 304 works. Of these manuscripts 190 deal directly with the Tripitaka and either give the Pali text or a Talaing Translations, usually a kind of word for word translation of the Pali. A number of Talaing manuscripts are preserved in The National Library at Bangkok, among them being a very complete version of the well-known *Milinda-Paüha.* The Ethnological Museum in Berlin, too, has a good collection, procured in Siam.[12]

On the evidence of manuscript and printed editions the *Äkâravattasutta* was a popular text in central South-East Asia. Padmanath S. Jaini has published a Romanized edition with English translation of one recension of the text from a single Khom-script manuscript belonging to Siam Society, Bangkok. The spelling and meaning of the title are uncertain. One Mon manuscript agrees with Jaini's title: two others give *Akkaravatta-sutta*. In three Tai Khun manuscripts it is *Äkâravatta-sutta*; the printed Mahamukuta version has *Äkâravatta-suttâ*. In the Mahamukuta version the *nidâna* is given only in Thai, not in Pali. Its substance is the same as that of the Pali edited by Jaini. The Mahamukuta version does not have the conclusion.[13]

It is interesting to note that Fragile Palm Leaves which is a non-profit project at Bangkok, dedicated to the preservation of Buddhist manuscripts and the literature, was able to provide copies of *The Apadâna* and its commentary to Sally Cutler, and of the *Samyuttanikâya* and its commentaries to Bhiksuni Vinita, both of whom are studying at Oxford. The originals include Khom script manuscripts from the library of Wat Bovoranives (Bangkok), a Mon-script manuscript from the library of Wat Paramayyikâvâsa and Burmese script manuscripts from the Fragile Palm Leaves collection. Oliver de Bernon and Peter Skilling are working on a Khom-script manuscript of a non-canonical Pali text entitled *Brah Mahâmûlakammatthânasutta*.

In Taipei, Chung-Hwa Institute of Buddhist Studies Manuscript Collection Summary Catalogue presents an assessment of the Burmese manuscript collection of The Chung-Hwa Institute of Buddhist Studies

(AD 1724-1930), which contains a total of 245 palm-leaf manuscripts: the *Vinaya* 127 titles, *Suttapitaka* 66 titles, *Abhidhamma* 67 titles, 49 grammars or lexical works.

The National Library of Laos together with The Lao-German Manuscript Preservation Program project works to survey, collect, microfilm and preserve palm leaf manuscripts. The most common texts found in Laos are *Nidânas, Anisamsa, Partitas, Chalongs, Kammavâcâs* etc. It should be emphasized that Pali canonical texts are often in the minority in these collections. There is a need of paying attention to the state of Pali and vernacular education in Laos.[14]

Under the auspices of *The Ecole francaise d'Extreme-Orient* (Paris), Jacqeline Filliozat has contributed her skills to the current survey of manuscripts in The Fragile Palm Leaves Collection. She has devoted her career to the cataloguing of Pali manuscripts in whatever script and wherever they may be.

The first edition of the *Dhamapada* in The West was prepared by V. Fausboll in 1855 and it was based upon three manuscripts. A new Pali Text Society (PTS) edition, edited by Osker Von Hinuber and K.R.Norman, was published in 1994. This edition makes use of Northern Thai (Lanna) Pali manuscripts, in addition to Burmese and Sinhalese script printed editions. The PTS has also published the computer generated *Indexes to The Dhammapada* by Moriichi Yamazaki, Yumi Ousaka and Masahiro Miyao (Oxford, 1995) which includes a Word Index, Reverse Word Index, Pada Index, and Reverse Pada Index. The manuscript of The Khotan Dharmapada or Gandhari Dharmapada is available in The Bibliotheque Nationale, Paris and Oriental Institute, St. Petersburg (Russia). It is probably dated of 1st or 2nd century AD and was discovered in 1893 near Khotan, Xinjiang. It was published by John Brough in 1962 by Oxford University Press, London (London Oriental Series 7).

The *Bhesajjamaüjusâ,* composed in Sri Lanka in The 13th Century is the only known medical treatise written in Pali. It was transmitted in South-East Asia. It was among the texts donated to a temple library at Pagan in Burma in 1442 and is found in Khom-script manuscripts in Siam. An inscription of A.D. 1442 in Burma also proves that this *Bhesajjamaüjusâ* was available in Burma. It mentions it in a list of books offered to the Sangha along with other things.[15] This is quite understandable in view of the religious contacts that existed between Sri Lanka and Burma from the 13th to the 18th centuries. A Burmese edition of the book is published in Rangoon in 1899. A copy of book written in Burmese script is available in the Cambridge University Library, bearing the Shelfmark Add MS 1252, (21). A large number of the manuscript of this book available in Sri Lanka indicates that it was widely used in the country. Bhesajjamanjusa chapter I-18 had been edited by Jinadasa Liyanaratne and published by Pali Text Society, London in 1996. It is based upon the five regional manuscripts of Sri Lanka and one manuscript of British Library.[16]

In 1994, a group of twenty-nine fragments of birch-bark scrolls containing various texts in Kharosthi script and Gandhari language was acquired by the British Library.[17] The birch-bark texts are probably the oldest Buddhist or even Indian manuscripts known to date. They were found, it seems, in an inscribed clay pot and are written in the so-called Gandhari language and Khrosthi script. They probably date from around the early decades of The Common Era. Ancient Gandhara, corresponding to modern northern Pakistan and eastern Afghanistan, was an important centre from which Buddhism was transmitted to China and other parts of Asia and was, as known from other sources, also a very important point of contact between India and The Western World even before the time of Alexander the Great.[18] These texts most probably belonged to a Dharmaguptaka monastery near Hadda in Afghanistan. The poetic compositions and compilations such as *The Dharmapada, The Anavataptagatha*, and the *Rhinoceros Horn Sutra*; texts in *Avadâna* and similar genres have been represented in these texts. Fragments from Abhidharma texts tend to confirm that Gandhara was an important early centre for Abhidharma studies.[19] R. Soloman, who is studying these manuscripts, says that there is no trace of Mahayana in these manuscripts. It is said that Mahayanists are known to have derived their canonical writings from The Sarvastivadins: The Sarvastivadins in Gandhara and Bacteria and their sub-school, The Dharmguptakas, used Gandhari and wrote Khrosthi in that early period.[20]

Subsequently, another collection of twenty-four Gandhari scrolls was acquired by a private collector, Robert Senior in the U.K. These texts are also currently being studied by the research team of British Library. Among the sutras for which parallels have been identified to date most correspond to sutras in Pali *Samyutta-nikâya* and/or the Chinese *Samyuktâgama*. The collection also includes Gandhari versions of at least one sutra of *Dïghanikâya* (*Samüüaphalasutta*) and one sutra of *Majjhimanikâya (Culagosingasutta)*

There are constant references in the colophans of the manuscript showing that those involved in making of 'Dhamma scriptures' ș as initiator, sponsor, or scribe-could expect certain benefits in terms of their own balance of merit and demerit. The wish most often mentioned in the Colophons is for the ȘThree Kinds of Happiness, The ultimate goal, of being Nibbana, which means that the scribe asks for happiness during his present and future lives in the World of Man, in the Heavenly Worlds as well as during his eventual stay in the World of Nibbana.[21]

Although it is possible to understand the main currents of Pali Buddhism through the study of the published texts, the picture they provide is not complete. Many non-canonical works, including sub-commentaries and sub-sub-commentaries are still not yet published and can only be consulted in manuscript form. There is no question that many aspects of Pali Buddhist culture still remain buried in their pagesṀ Since many scholars in the field of textual studies believe that it is important to consult extent manuscripts as well as published texts, interest in manuscripts has increased in recent years. Although an excellent critical edition may be at hand, it is still necessary to turn to the manuscripts and, using strict methods of textual criticism, reconstruct the original text. Only then can the original text be understood and interpreted. For this reason, manuscripts are of great value, even when a critical edition is available.[22]

Thus, the Pali manuscripts are invaluable and treasured. Not only were they difficult to produces, but they were also repositories of the Sacred Word, the Buddhavacana. They therefore had to be protected and cherished. They were wrapped in cloth and bound with specially woven ribbons. The cloths themselves were things of beauty: fine silks, brocades, and colourful weaves. In South-East Asia, the bamboo ribbed wrapper is used by the Mon, the Khmer, the Burmese, and the Thai. In South-East Asia, manuscripts that are not properly stored are threatened by damp. They need a clean environment, safe from insects and Era Manuscript Collections should be properly catalogued, and their contents protected against careless removal, theft, flooding or fire. Rare manuscripts should be replicated by micro-filming or scanning. There is a need of using modern technologies such as scanning and digital storage, to preserve the manuscript heritage of South-east Asia.

References

1. *A Pali Grammar* by Wilhelm Geiger, Revised and Edited by K.R. Norman, PTS, Oxford, 1994, p. xxv.
2. *Frgile Palm Leaves,* No.1, (Ed.) Peter Skilling, Nonthaburi, Thailand, 1997, p. 2.
3. Oskar Von Hinuber, 'The Oldest Manuscript', quoted in *A Pali Grammar* (Ed.) K.R. Norman, P.T.S., Oxford, 1994, p. xxv.
4. *Fragile Palm Leaves,* No. 1, op.cit.,p.2
5. 'The Colophons of 30 Pali Manuscripts from Northern Thailand' by H. Hundius in *The Journal of The Pali Text Society* Volume XIV (Ed.) by K.R. Norman, PTS Oxford, 1990, p. 19.
6. Ibid., pp. 20-22.
7. *Frgile Palm Leaves,* No.2 (Ed.) Peter Skilling, Nonthaburi, Thailand, 1997, p.4.
8. Ibid.p.6
9. Ibid.
10. *Fragile Palm Leaves,* No.5 (Ed.) eter Skilling, Thailand, 1999, pp.2-3.
11. *Fragile Palm Leaves*, No. 6(Ed.) Peter Skilling, Thailand, 2000, p. 1
12. *Fragile Palm Leaves*, No.6.(Ed.) Peter Skilling, Thailand, 2000, p.2.
13. Ibid.p.4.
14. *Fragile Palm Leaves,* No.7, (Ed.) Peter Skilling, Thailand, 2002, p.2.
15. Bode, M.H., *The Pali Literature of Burma*, Royal Asiatic Society,London, 1909, p. 108.
16. cf. *Bhesajjamaüjusâ* (Ed.) Jinadasa Liyanaratne, PTS, Oxford, 1996, pp. 15-21.
17. cf. 'The Senior Collection: A Second Group of Gandharan Buddhist Scrolls' in *The Abstracts of The XIIIth IABS Conference*, Bangkok, 2002, p. 195.
18. *Buddhist Studies Review*, (Ed.) Russel Web, Vol. 17, No. 1(2000), p. 110.
19. 'The Senior Collection:A Second Group of Gandharan Buddhist Scrolls in *The Abstracts of The XIIIth IABS Conference*, Bangkok, 2002, p 196.
20. cf. 'Sarvastivada Developments in Northwestern India and in China' by Charles Willemen in *The Indian International Journal of Buddhist Studies* No.2, 2001, BJK Institute of Buddhist and Asian Studies, Sarnath, Varanasi, pp. 164-165

21. cf. The colophons of 30 Pali manuscripts from Northern Thailand' by H. Hundius, in *The Journal of Pali Text Society*, Vol. XIV, PTS, Oxford, 1990, pp. 29-30.
22. cf. Hojun Nagasaki, 'Catalogue of Palm Leaf Manuscripts Kept in The Otani University Library, Kyoto, 1995, quoted in *The Fragile Palm Leaves*, No.2, 1997, p.5.

4

A Brief Note on Manuscriptology

– *K.Maheswaran Nair*

Mastery of man over nature began with the development of hand. Hand is the organ as well as the product of labour. Labour caused members of the primeval society to come closer which in due course created the point when they had something to say to each other. Necessity created the organ; the larynx of the ape was transformed by modulations and the organs of the mouth gradually learned to pronounce articulate sounds. This process which began about five hundred thousand years ago has been elaborated by Charles Darwin.

The great Sanskrit poet, Dandin has proclaimed-

> The progress of the world has been maintained by the grace of words which have been endorsed by the authoritative scholars. All the three worlds would have been in complete dark, had there been not the light of speech.

Language began in oral tradition and was grown into written form about six thousand years ago. Both the oral and written traditions of language have been subjected to serious studies in modern times. The former has given birth to the branch of knowledge called morality studies while the latter has formulated manuscriptology. Orality studies concentrate on the oral lore of mankind whereas manuscriptology is concerned with manuscripts.

What is a Manuscript?

A hand-written document is called manuscript (mss.). The term ms. is derived from Latin manus meaning 'hand' and scriptum (v. scribere) meaning 'to scratch' that meant later to write. Hence, a mss. is 'some thing that is written with the hand.'

In the latest context of Personal Computers giving way to Electronic Note-books, Thinkpad etc. and also key-boards giving way to touch screen technology, one has to rethink about the old concept of stylus and palm leaf. Since one can write with one's fingertip on the screen and get the same saved in hard disk, the definition of manuscript need not be altered.

Towards a Definition of Manuscriptology

Manuscriptology can be shortly defined as the science of manuscripts. Deciphering mss. is its primary concern and some people call it as the science of deciphering manuscripts. Manuscriptology has to be distinguished from paleography which is the science of writing. In fact Manuscriptology is not merely the science of deciphering manuscripts. It also specializes in the procurement, preservation, documentation, reading, transcribing, editing and publishing of various kinds of manuscripts. And in these matters, the boundaries of Manuscriptology border with other specialised branches like Textoloy, Conservation Science etc.

Nature and Scope of Manuscriptology

Manuscript will be in a language and it will certainly be pertaining to a subject. As such, manuscriptology by its nature demands the student to have expertise in, the language in which it is written and also the subject dealt with in it. An expert manuscriptologist should have knowledge of both the language and the subject of the manuscript.

The scope of Manuscriptology does not confine to mere reading, writing, transcribing or editing of manuscrrpts. It extends to literature, conservation science, cultural criticism etc. Emergence of New Manuscriptology, in recent times, as a trend of literary criticism, especially criticism related to the genesis of the literary piece, has further enlarged the scope of Manuscriptology. Possibilities of utilising Manuscriptology in such areas of studies such as criminology, psychology and certain paramedical sciences have to be explored too.

Manuscriptology and Textual Criticism

Textual criticism is a branch of literary criticism that is concerned with the identification and rectification of transcription errors in the texts of manuscripts. It is also called lower criticism in contrast with 'higher' criticism, which is the endeavor to establish the authorship, date and place of composition of the original text. To err is human and scribes make errors or alterations when they copy manuscripts by hand. Based on one or many copies of a manuscript, but not the original document, the textual critic seeks to reconstruct the original text, the archetype or autograph, as closely as possible. The same process can be applied to reconstruct intermediate editions or recessions, of a document's transcription history. The ultimate objective of the textual critic is the production of a 'critical edition' containing a text most closely approximating the original.

Manuscriptology and Paleography

Paleography is the art of analysing and reading handwriting. Some would like to call it a science, in fact, it is an art, with some scientific props. Paleography functions at different levels. At its most basic level, it is a decoding process which allows a student or researcher to read what someone at an earlier time has written, even though the communication code has changed over the centuries.

Paleography is history in itself. Changes to styles and form of writing over the centuries reflect historical and social change. The content and style of manuscripts mirror the changing concerns of society. The history of writing is a major component of our cultural heritage. Writing as a craft and writing as a communication skill are inseparable in our cultural development.

Paleography as a science can be used for intricate historical tracing. Analyses of the precise mode of delineation of letters, the identification of local script styles or individual scribal hands and the intricacies of punctuation and abbreviation can be used to trace influences across time and space, and even to trace the movements of individuals.

Manuscriptology in the Indian Context

Millions of manuscripts are lying in libraries, museums and private collections all over India. India has a collection of nearly five million manuscripts, of which some are very rare. They are the valuable sources of knowledge especially of our ancient history and culture.

The materials used to write manuscript are paper, palm-leaf, bark, cloth, metal etc. Various scripts have been used in mss. Some of the scripts are—Grantha, Tamil, Nandinagari, Devanagari, Tiglari, Sarada, Telugu, Kannada, Malayalam, old Newari etc. Many manuscripts are available in foreign scripts such as Persian, Arabic etc.

Ancient Indian texts, many of which have a history of more than a millennium, are based on manuscripts whose lifespan is normally not more than a few centuries. From early times onwards, efforts have been made to collect, store and preserve the manuscripts in libraries inside and outside India. In the second half of the 18th century, a few British officers such as Sir William Jones (1746-1794), Sir Robert Chambers (1774-1779) and Colin Mackenzie (1782-1806) took a deep interest in Indian culture. They tried to get acquainted with the Sanskrit language and literature, and started collecting inscriptions, epigraphs, and manuscripts privately. An institution named "The Asiatic Society of Bengal" was established in 1781. One of its aims was the collection and preservation of valuable manuscripts, a huge number of which was lying in the houses of scholars, in schools and pathasalas, in religious mutts, monasteries, chaityas, temples, palaces and village libraries in Bengal and different parts of India. Later on, in the latter half of the 19th century, the then Government of India took an active part and allocated funds for the collection of manuscripts. Scholars such as G. Buhler, A.C. Burnell, R.G. Bhandarkar, R.L. Mitra, F. Kielhorn, G. Oppert, G.B. Malleson and a few others were deputed to tour in different provinces of India in search of manuscripts, to make a list of the available ones and to purchase the more important of them. Since then, the mission of the collection, preservation, and cataloguing of manuscripts, and the preparation of critical editions of important texts conserved in them, is going on in and outside India by scholars with an interest to protect and study this rich cultural heritage.

Apart from the Asiatic Society in Kolkata there are reputable repositories of mss. in different parts of the country– Sarasvati Mahal Library, Tanjavur, The Adyar Library and the Government Oriental Manuscripts Library in Chennai, Oriental Research Institute, Baroda, Oriental Research Institute and Manuscript Library, University of Kerala, S.V. Oriental Research Institute, Tirupati, Bhandarkar Oriental Research Institute, Pune and so on. Collections outside India, for instance, the Van Manen collection of palm leaf manuscripts of the Kern Institute, Leiden, are also valuable.

Why Should Manuscripts be Preserved?

Manuscripts preserve our heritage. The constitution of India states, under Fundamental Duties in Article 51A :

> It shall be the duty of every citizen to value and preserve the rich heritage of their composite culture.

Hence, there is an urgent need to collect, conserve, preserve, collate and provide access to these precious documents through the standards established by the Ministry of Culture & Tourism, Govt. of India. In the year 2003, the Govt. of India has started a project called 'National Mission for Manuscripts (NMM)' for the mss. collection, preservation, trainings and seminars. The NMM has worked tirelessly to realize the goal by collecting five lakh manuscript, through their partner Manuscript Resource Centers (MRCs) and Manuscript Conservation Centers (MCCs). The University of Madras has adopted a prestigious project called 'New Catalogus Catalogurum (NCC) in the year 1935 which is in succession to Theoder Aufrecht's Catalogus Catalogorum.

It may be noted in this connection that most of the manuscript, are inaccessible for various reasons. Many manuscripts are almost destroyed by insects or by hostile weather conditions. The best way to preserve them in the modern context is digitisation.

Critical Edition

Critical edition of texts, is one of the major outputs of manuscriptology. All the old books, especially of Sanskrit, which we access today are transcribed from the preserved manuscript BORI, Pune has brought out the first critical edition of the great epic Mahabharata. Out of the one lakh verses in it, only 73 thousand verses are found to be original. This was decided based on the style, grammar etc. of the verses. Twenty-seven thousand verses seem to differ in style, grammar etc from those of 73 thousand written by Sage Veda Vyasa. Students/researchers should be encouraged to take up critical editions to decide the accuracy of the textual content. Anyone who attempts for a critical edition of any text must compulsorily go through the Prolegomena of the Adiparvan of Mahabharata by V.S. Sukthamkar who was the first editor of the critical edition of Mahabharata.

Manuscripts and Kerala

The manuscript heritage of Kerala is very rich. The Trivandrum Sanskrit Series is one of the oldest Oriental Series comprising a series of Sanskrit books edited from Sanskrit palm-leaf manuscripts dating back to 1400 A.D. available in the Trivandrum Oriental Manuscripts Library. The palm leaves available in the Library have been famous for their contents and great Sanskrit scholars like Dr. T. Ganapathi Sastri, K. Sambasiva Sastri etc. have been the editors of the library. The content of these Sanskrit works and their authenticity have been well known in the field of Indology and Sanskrit. These Sanskrit series comprises books from various disciplines of Sanskrit like Jyotisha, Silpa, Ayurveda, Kavya, Nataka, Kosa, Tantra to name a few.

Kerala and ORI and Mss Library, Trivandrum can always be proud of the famous Bhasa Natakas brought out under the Trivandrum Sanskrit Series. Ganapathi Sastri, while touring in search of Sanskrit mss in south Trvancore found out from the collection of mss of the brahmin family of Manalikkara near Nagercvil, a codex about four centuries old written on palm-leaves in Malayalam characters and containing ten Sanskrit plays hitherto unknown. Later three more plays were found out.

Three plays namely Svapnavasavadatta, Pratijnayaugandharayana and Pncaratra were published as volumes 15, 16 and 17 of the Trivandrum Sanskrit Series in 1912 and it created history. These plays were written by Bhasa who was famous but whose works were supposed to be lost. There is difference of opinion among scholars as regards Bhasa's authorship of all the thirteen plays. No doubt, some plays are certainly from the pen of Bhasa, all scholars agree with this.

The plays became classics in the area of Sanskrit drama. The practice of these dramas have made one understand the stage practice of Indian Sanskrit theatre prevailing in ancient times. The plays found out and published by Ganapati Sastri came to be known as Trivandrum plays or Bhasa plays. Ganapati Sastri was awarded with doctorate degree by Tubingen University of Germany.

5

Ecological Perception in Ancient India Through Manuscript Study

– *Swami Kamalasthananda*

Manuscript is generally called a manually written document but not printed from in any medium. Before the arrival of printing device i.e. press or printer, all documents and books were called manuscripts as all these were produced manually. Manuscripts are not defined or rather classified by the nature of contents present in the same, which may include arts, literature, facts, fictions, esthetic creation, history, geography, mathematical calculations, maps, explanatory figures or illustrations or any type of human endeavour which has leaded man onward and forward. Manuscripts have several forms i.e. book form, scrolls or in codex format. The word 'manuscript' is derived from the medieval Latin term 'manuscriptum' that indicates hand written documents. Manuscript is a hand written composition on bark, cloth, metal, palm-leaf, paper or any other material that has significant scientific, historical or aesthetic value. Manuscripts are found in hundreds of different languages and scripts (www.indianetzone.com). The manuscripts have a long history of its existence. According to the Chambers Dictionary, 'Manuscript is a book or document written by hand before the invention of printing' (Allied Chambers (India) Limited, 2000). Modern time manuscripts refer to autographs, correspondence, and any personal type-written text required for the publication of book or monograph.

The Antiquities and Art Treasures Act, 1972 gives the legal framework for custody of manuscripts. Antiquities, defined under the Act include 'any manuscript, record or other document which is of scientific, historical, literary or aesthetic value and which has been in existence for not less than seventy-five years'.

Preservation of Manuscript

The preservation of manuscript is a serious concern for the people of library science, information science, literary person, social study, historical study, etc. from very ancient time people have a great concern for this subject. Many ancient civilizations also deeply thought over this issue. Babylonia, Assyria, Sumeria, China or India; the scribes were always worried to preserve their writings for posterity with whatever means they had. Scholars like Aristotle, Ovid and Horace were also worried about the safety of the manuscripts from the insects[1]. With the technological breakthrough new scientific techniques are evolved for the preservation of the manuscripts. But the importance of the indigenous methods is still present for the preservation process. The all indigenous processes are time tested practice and are evolved in specific regions and climate condition. It has the following advantages:

- These are not hazardous for human health.
- These do not have any adverse effect on the materials.
- The methods do not require much expertise, equipment and money[2].

So the idea to preserve the manuscript is not the new concept in the present day. People knew that the environment factors like light, dust, moisture and the different warms are highly detrimental for all these manuscript. So people solve this problem in their own way of preventive measure. Some of these preventive measure are given below which ancient people used to conversant:

(a) Safe upkeep of manuscripts is ensured even before writing on the leaf. Seasoning of the leaf by burying them under the mud or boiling them in water are considered to have some antiseptic effect against the damage caused by the insects.

(b) Usually to fasten the manuscripts, holes are punched on the leaves and cords are passed through them. These are then placed in between two stiff flat wooden boards having the same type of holes for passing the cords. The wooden boards press the leaves from both the sides, prevent curling at the edges and chipping by abrasion.

(c) Wrapping the manuscripts in clothes, protect them from dust, worms and also to a great extent from variation in atmospheric humidity and absorption of acidic fumes.

(d) Palm leaves are usually wrapped in red or yellow colour clothes. It is believed that red is a repelling colour for the insects and yellow colour if, produced by turmeric possess some germicidal power that repel the insects from getting in contact with the manuscripts.

(e) Manuscripts are also wrapped in silk clothes as silk is remarkably free from bookworms for which its extensive use has been seen.

(f) The bundles of manuscripts are also kept in heavy wooden chests to reduce the rigorous changing of climate.

(g) Exposing palm leaves in the kitchen have the scientific fact that smoke particles have the capacity to repel the insects. Though the smoke deposits bring out undesired changes on the leaves yet this system is effective for prevention of insect attack over the palm leaf manuscripts.

(h) Exposure of the leaves to the tender rays of the rising or setting Sun destroys the traces of growth of insects and micro-organisms.

(i) The palm leaves are usually arranged and strung together with the help of a needle made of bamboo and a string of cotton or silk which keep the leaves intact.

(j) At some places underground cells are prepared for preservation of manuscripts.

(k) Manuscripts are generally exposed to the Sun in the Lunar month of Bhadraba i.e. in August as the rays of the Sun in that particular month are very favorable. By this the worms are killed under the Sun.

(l) The indigenous method is to take out palm leaves on Vijaya Dashami day then they are cleaned and kept back[3].

Many herbal and natural products are used as the pesticides or insect repellents or processing materials for giving the long life of the organic matters which are used as writing materials. Some herbal products are given below for their use in manuscript preservation purpose:

1. Dried and powdered leaves of Aswagandha in small packets are kept with the manuscripts covered in clothes to repel insect attack..
2. Along with bundles of manuscripts pieces of Vasambu or dried ginger are kept to save these from insect attack..
3. Coatings of lemon-grass oil are given to strengthen the leaves of manuscripts and destroy the growths of micro-organisms.
4. In some repositories people use vermillion or kumkum fruit powder (which is red in colour) that act as a very good insect repellant.
5. Powdered roots of dried sweet flag known as Bacha, filled in small bags are kept in cup-boards of manuscripts which has got very good medicinal value and insecticidal power.
6. Oil extracts of some natural products like black pepper, sandal wood or clove facilitate in the restoration of flexibility to the palm leaf manuscripts.
7. The use of fresh palm leaf extract has also the possibilities of imparting flexibility to the old and brittle leaves.
8. Powdered Ajwain also acts as an insect killer and fungicide.
9. Custard-apple seeds powder is used to kill the insects that thrive on manuscripts.
10. The mixture of neem laves, karanja, nirgundi and citronella are known to have insecticidal properties for which it could be used in the manuscript libraries.
11. Dried Tamakhu leaves also protect the manuscripts against attack of insects. The leaves are generally packed in small cloth bags or spread on the shelves where manuscripts are kept. The nicotinic acid of the leaves keeps the insects at bay.
12. Leaves of the Five-leaved-chaste tree (Vitex Incisa) are dried in Sunrays and kept along with the bundles of the manuscripts. As

these trees are grown in abundance in Orissa, its use is very common here.

13. Naga-damani known as Indian worm wood bears an essential oil whose sweet aroma and insect repellant action helps to eradicate insects from the manuscripts.
14. Mint leaves also repel ants and cockroaches.
15. Black-Cumin (Kala Jeera) which gives a strong aromatic smell also used as an insect repellant. Scattering of the seeds at the manuscript storage keeps away insects.
16. Sandal wood dust is commonly used by many libraries to ward off insects.
17. Neem oil contains limonoids, a class of compounds that acts as anti-feedants or growth regulators in insects; they don't kill instantly but wipe out a whole generation of insects by preventing the young ones from maturing and adults from reproducing. Dried Neem leaves and seeds are also useful in keeping away insects. So its use has been widely recognized since ancient times.
18. As the wooden planks attached to the bundles of manuscripts are prone to insect attack, in some libraries the planks are made of neem wood which can ward off termite.
19. The annual ritual is to apply coconut leaf juice (Coccinia Indica), wood charcoal and turmeric paste with a clean cloth and after wards it is wiped away to make the leaf proof against insect and fungal attack.
20. Another natural product ş Camphor (Karpura) is commonly used in India to protect valuable documents. Filled in small cloth bags it is kept inside the storage of manuscripts. Besides, synthetic Camphor Oil is also used to protect palm leaf manuscripts against insect attack.
21. Small bags of a sort grass ş Panadi by name (which is grown in Jaisalmir and used in making perfumes) are placed among the bundles of manuscripts to save them from white ants.
22. Application of turmeric paste to the seasoned palm leaves is well known for its dis-infecting effect.

The tradition of the manuscript preparation, copying and preservation continues till the end of the 19th century and the downfall started on the beginning of the 20th century for the popularity of the printed books and printed media. After that handwritten practice for the document is completely shifted to the printed books and document.

Manuscript: India and Abroad

In one of the surveys made by Dr. S. C. Biswas and Mr. M. K. Prajapati on behalf of INTACH during 1988- 90 and on the basis of scrutiny of about 1100 printed catalogues and hand lists belonging to 70 libraries, institutions and individuals, the following estimates were made:

1.	Total number of manuscripts in India	5,000,000
2.	Indian manuscripts available in European Countries	60,000
3.	Indian manuscripts in South Asia and Asian Countries	150,000
4.	Number of manuscripts recorded in catalogues	1,000,000
5.	Percentage of manuscripts languages wise Sanskrit	67%
6.	Other Indian Languages	25%
7.	Arabic/Persian/Tibetan	8%

(Source: Project Document, NMM, 2003)

The classification and indexing the collection of the manuscript is first evident in Jain period. As far as the data found, in 1383 a Jain monk whose name was not known wrote Brihattipanika. The Brihattipanik, covers some manuscripts in the collections in several places, such as Patan, Cambey and Bharauch. It furnishes data of authors' names, time and grantha-parimana (extent of texts). The manuscript of this catalogue is still preserved in the Shaninatha Bhandara. Next the celebrated name of the monastic Kavindracharya of Varanasi (Kashi) comes Kavindracharya built up a good library of manuscripts. He compiled his subject wise classified catalogue of 2192 manuscripts between the year 1628 and 1688[5]. Collection of different manuscripts from different regions in a particular topic is used practice in ancient times for writing any commentary or illustration on a particular subject. In medieval period among the independent rulers, Tippu Sultan of Mysore (18th cent. C.E.) built up a library of oriental manuscripts in Arabic, Persian and Hindustani languages.

After his defeat and death, while fighting with the British forces, his library was taken over by the Britishers. The manuscripts from Tippu's library were studied and catalogued by General Charles Stewart; the Catalogue was published from Cambridge (A Descriptive Catalogue of the Oriental Library of the Late Tippu Sultan of MysoreṀṀCambridge: University Press, 1809). Native rulers in the British period took initiative for collection and preservation of manuscripts. The rulers of Travancore, Cochin and Mysore are important names in this field. The Travancore Palace Library collection was started by Maharaja Vishakham Tirunal (1880-1885). The manuscripts collected and preserved in this Library were subsequently catalogued by eminent traditional Sanskrit scholars, such as K. Sambasiva Sastri and K. Mahadeva Sastri, and a catalogue in 8 volumes was published (A Descriptive Catalogue of the Sanskrit Manuscripts in H.H. the Maharajah's Palace Library, Trivandrum. Trivandrum: V.V. Press Branch, 1937-38)[6].

Outside India the manuscript written Pali, prakrit and Sanskrit are found in the important libraries in neibhbouring countries like Japan, Nepal Sri Lanka, Japan, etc. This is because in ancient times a good communication was established with neighbouring countries through trade, education and preaching mission of the Indian sublime thought. So all connections with the neighbouring countries demand some communication medium and the old languages like Sanskrit, Pali, etc spread these countries through the manuscripts and other collections. Outside India, Sanskrit, Pali and Prakrit manuscripts are available in almost all the famous libraries in Europe, Japan, Srilanka, Pakistan, Bangladesh, Thailand, Myanmar, et al. At Bibliotheque Nationale, France cataloguing of manuscripts started in eighteenth century and the first catalogue, Catalogus Codicum Manuscriptorum Bibliothecae regiae, was published under the supervision of Stephen Fourmont in 1739. This series continued for a long time and Department des Manuscripts Catalogue Somaire des Manuscrits Sanskrits et Palis published catalogues in 1806, 1844, 1854, 1880, 1882 and 1907-08.

Tuebingen University (Germany), St. Petersbourg Academy and Bodleian Library were in forefront in publishing catalogues of Indian manuscripts. A large number of Indian manuscripts are there in the custody of various institutes and libraries in Germany, England and France[7].

Ecological Idea in Vedic Manuscript

Vedic people believed that man has certain relation with the gross elements which are responsible for the formation of body and after death these elements go to the respective sources. ".... It may be observed that the Vedic Risis did believe in some kind of union with different elements (bhutas) after death, and that the different components of the gross (earthly) body united with the corresponding subtle elements, the tanmatras of the Upanisads. Further, it may be pointed out that the fine constituents members of the bhutas occurs in the Rigveda in the form of of five defined natural objects. The words prthivi, ap, agni, vayu and akasa (or dyaus) have been deified in the Rigveda. These divinities may be regarded as prototypal gross elements (bhutas). A number of myths and legends have been woven around them to bring out their essential nature and characteristic features, that might have led the post-vedic thinkers to conceive and transform them into the five bhutas constituting the physical universe."[8]

In nature every time there is a constant interaction between living world and non-living world with inflow and outflow of matter in equilibrium condition. In different vedic texts we find the cyclic order of these interactions present in the environment. This cycle is called Rita, the term coined by Vedic people. Rita is an universal law which control and monitor the everything in the whole universe. S.R.N. Murthy considers it as a law of gravitation i.e. common attractive force present between all beings, in simple form. According to H.W. Wallis 'The principle of the order of the world, of the regularity of cosmic phenomena, was conceived by the Rishis to have existed as a principle before the manifestation of any phenomena. The phenomena of the world are shifting and changeable, but the principle regulating the periodical recurrence of phenomena is constant; fresh phenomena are continually reproduced, but the principle of order remains the same; the principle, therefore, existed already when the earliest phenomena appeared' [9].

In the early vedic time people used to live in the high mountain. So the mountain valley is the chosen area for settlement of the people. Mountains with firm rock and high altitude indicate the nearness to the God. Even Agni or Fire who eats everything but leaves aside the rock stone. Fire sometimes burns all trees plants on the mountain and appears like shaved head ṣ Who in his wrath shaves a hill as a barber shaves a head (Rigveda, X.142, 144). Vedic people are settled on the banks of rivers. River is by nature is flowing continuously with an untiring zeal. Vedic people understand the importance of the flowing river.

Trees have an important role on this earth which is understood by the vedic people. In vedic texts several indications are mentioned about the praise of the plant and its utilities. In Rigvedic period trees are treated as different embodiments of God. Generally Vriksas and Virudh are used in Rigveda and Samhitas to indicate the term tree or plant. The most celebrated plant Soma is mentioned in Rigveda. Other trees are mentioned in Rigveda are salmali or silk cotton tree, khadira, sinsapa and vibhidaka. In Atharvaveda the two trees sami and plaksa are mentioned. Iksu or sugarcane was also cultivated in the vedic period. In vedic texts several types of the fruits bearing trees and flower bearing trees are mentioned. In Rigveda Soma, a name of plant is praised as creater: These herbs, these milch-kine and these running waters, all these, O Soma, thou hast generated. The spacious firmament has thou expanded and with light thou hast dispelled the darkness. Rigveda, 1.91.22)

Atharvaveda claims the ability of herbs and plants in controlling the age of human beings: Ye arise: it is thundering and crashing, Ye plant, since Parjanya (the God of rain) is favouring you, O children of Prisni (the spotted cloud) with his seed (water). In Atharvaveda says that certain plant can remove the sinful or evil effect (Atharvaveda, 7.65.2). This Goddess is addressed as Aranyani, in Rig Vedic text as the goddess. She is the part of the whole cosmic order. In this cosmic order everything is sacred. All these are the part and parcel of one rhythm.

'Aranyani is sacred as part of [ta, the Cosmic Law and order and because all Nature is sacred not because it was created, but because it is intrinsically sacred. She is sacred as a mother who gives all she has and in turn requests only respect and love; she is sacred because she must be well taken care of to enable her to carry on the work of her own generous self. She is a deity in the sense that she is an abstract-form, the summation and integration of a concept that cannot be seen physically as a separate self-contained body, she can only be sensed through her parts and works; she is a deity with her own attributes, forms and functions; she is elusive and beyond grasp; she is perhaps better represented mentally as the spirit of the jungle. As appropriate of the feminine nature and of all mothers, although selfless and generous, she may cause death if ill-treated, misused or insulted by the wayfarer, the villager or 'another' (verse 5) who does not know her manners and restrictions'[10].

Huge trees are usually called Vanaspati or lord of the Forest. Vanaspati is the Lord of the forest is due its big appearance, usefulness and helpfulness to humankind. Vanaspati is also the Lord of all the plants and animals which live in the domain that he oversees from his roots in the soil up to the lofty, majestic height of the canopy. Alive and standing, the tree overrules the living forest and when recumbent over his mother's bosom (Rigveda. III; 8, 1) after being felled by age or man, he becomes the material for the worship of all gods by nourishing Agni who sublimates the material into spirit and is the intermediate between man and the Supreme'[11].

Man in vedic period has established the friendly relationship with the animals. Gradually, with passage of time people try to overpower other species also:

During perhaps more than 99 percent of man's history so far, man's religion has been neither the worship of himself nor the quest of the rational-spiritual reality behind the phenomenon of the Universe. It has, as we have noted, been the worship of the forces of non-human nature: animals, trees, stones, earth, water, winds, rain, storm, sun, moon and stars. Throughout the food gathering stage of human history, which has been the first stage of it and by far the longest stage so far, mankind was at the mercy of non-human nature; and we worship things in whose power we feel ourselves to be. Conversely, we cannot worship things that we have mastered; and since man has mastered nature the primeval religion of nature-worship has receded[12].

So man are very much like to interact with surrounding animals. It is represented in the Atharvaveda:

> Born on Thee, on Thee move mortal creatures;
> Thou bearest them - the biped and the quadruped;
> Thine, O Earth, are the five traces of men, to whom,
> Mortals, Surya (sun) as he rises spreads,
> With his rays the light that is immortal. (Atharvaveda, 12.1.15)

Vedic people are very much cautious about the importance of the cow and the utility of cow in the daily human life. They have praised in many names to indicate the utility of cow. Several legends are depicted to describe the power and divinity of the cow.

For thee were forest beasts and sylvan creatures placed in the wood, and small birds, swans and eagles. Food, lord of beasts! Contain thy living beings: to smell thy strength flow the celestial water (Atharvaveda, 10.2.24).

Ecological Idea in Upanishadic Manuscript

Upanishads deals with different gods in the mantra and samhita portion of the literature. The idea of Gods like Agni, Vayu, Earth, Indra, Varuna, etc. are evolved to highlight their role and importance. So the ecology which is nothing but the interrelatedness of different elements present in the nature is one of the important aspects in Upanishads.

In different Upanishads the embodied deities are described to represent the various ecological phenomenon present in the earth. The following are portions of different Upanishads which vividly describe the five great elements or *panchamahabhutas*, plant, animals and other biotic-abiotic world.

In the beginning all this verily was Atman only, one and without a second. There was nothing else that winked. He bethought Himself: 'Let Me now create the worlds.' He created these worlds: Ambhah, the world of water-bearing clouds, Marichi, the world of the solar rays, Mara, the world of mortals and Ap, the world of waters. Yon is Ambhah, above heaven; heaven is its support. The Marichis are the interspace. Mara is the earth. What is underneath is Apa (Aitareya Upanishad, 1.1.2).

How the gross elements and prana are related is clearly explained in this Upanishads through the example of chariot wheel.

These ten objects (what is spoken, smelled, seen, & c.) have reference to pragna (self-consciousness), the ten subjects (speech, the senses, mind) have reference to objects. If there were no objects, there would be no subjects; and if there were no subjects, there would be no objects. For on either side alone nothing could be achieved. But that (the self of pragna, consciousness, and prana, life) is not many, (but one.) (Kaushitaki Upanashad 2.6.).

The essence of all these beings is the earth; the essence of the earth is water; the essence of water is plants; the essence of plants is a person; essence of a person is speech; the essence of speech is the Rig-Veda; essence of the Rig-Veda is the Sama-Veda; the essence of the Sama-Veda is the Udgitha which is Om (Chandogya Upanishad,1.1.2).

Water is, verily, greater than food. Therefore if there is not sufficient rain, then living creatures are afflicted with the thought that there will be less food. But if there is sufficient rain, then living creatures rejoice in the thought that there will be much food. It is water that assumes the form of this earth, this midṭregion, this heaven, these mountains, these gods and men, cattle and birds, herbs and trees and animals, together with worms, flies and ants. Water indeed is all these forms. Meditate on water (Chandogya Upanishad, 7.10.1).

M. Winternitz has told - When ripe old approaches however, he may leave his house and as forest dweller (Vanaparparastha) he may now perform sacrificial service only in a limited manner, but to that extent meditate on the mystic and symbolic significance of sacrifice. But only when he feels his end approach shall be give up even his sacrifice and meditations, renounce al action-based piety and as a recluse ascetic (sanyasin) meditate only on Brahman, the highest World principle and strive for union with the same.

With this doctrine of the Brahminic ideal in life are also connected the chapters of the Brahmanas which as Aranyakas or 'forest book' i.e. texts to be studied by hermits (Vanaprasthas) in the forest...[13].

Aswamedha Yajna or sacrifice is mentioned in Brihadarnyaka Upanishad. Aswamedha Yajna is the great sacrifice where horse is an essential item. In this description two things are found ṣ firstly the meticulous description of the different organs of the horse and secondly the comparison of different natural phenomena with the different organs of the horse. The whole life is nothing but the sacrifice to nature. The manifested world is not a static affair, it is full of dynamic nature, ever changing, ever modifying. So the natural phenomenon which constitute the world are represented by the horse, well known as the symbol of motion.

Om, verily, the head of the sacrificial horse is the dawn, its eye the sun, its vital breath the wind, its open mouth the Vaisvanara fire and the trunk of the sacrificial horse is the year. The back is heaven, the belly the intermediate region, the hoof the earth, the sides the four quarters, the ribs the intermediate quarters, the limbs the seasons, the joints the months and half-months, the feet the days and nights, the bones the stars, the flesh the clouds. Its half-digested food is the sand, the blood-vessels the rivers, the liver and lungs the mountains, the hair the herbs and trees. The fore part of the horse is the rising sun and the hinder part the setting sun. Its yawn is lightning, its shaking of the body is thunder, its water is rain and its neighing is indeed voice (Brihadarnyaka Upanishad, 1.1.1.).

The following verse describe the relationship between the different beings. Right from the gross elements to the human beings all are integrated closely. So any break in the close chain like relation leads to the utter destruction in the living world.

The earth is verily the essence of all these beings, water is the essence of the earth, herbs of water, flowers of herbs, fruits of flowers, man of fruits and semen is the essence of man (Brihadarnyaka Upanishad, 6.4.1.).

The prana is, verily, food; the body is the eater of food. The body rests on the prana; the prana rest on the body. Thus food (the body and vital force are both foods) rests on food (Taittiriya Upanishad 3.7.1).

Water is, verily, food; fire is the eater. Fire rests on water and water rests on fire. Thus food (the fire and water are both foods) rests on food (Taittiriya Upanishad 3.8.1).

The air is important element which is essential for life. This air enters into the body and does different functions.

He it is who sends prana upward and who leads apana downward. All the devas worship that adorable One seated in the middle (Katha Upanishada 2.2.3)

The primordial energy enters into the food grains, food items and all plant worlds. The expression of the energy in the plant is in different forms. All human beings, animals, insects etc. are dependent upon the plant world.

The sun is, indeed, prana, life; the moon is rayi, food. Food is, indeed, all thisṭwhat has form and what is formless. Therefore everything having form is, indeed, food (Prasna Upanishad 1.5.).

Cosmogony deals with the beginning of the universe and the theory related to the subject. Whereas Cosmology deals with the study of the total universe and its different aspects. The universe is broadly made up Earth, Stars, Planets, sun etc. The relation and interrelation between different all these elements give the correct picture of the whole universe. In Upanishadic time people are aware of the world made up seven land masses together with nearby ocean and seas.

The worlds in the ascending and descending orders belong to him who, knowing this, meditates on the fivefold Saman as the worlds. (Chandyogya Upanishad 2.2.3)

It is mentioned in Upanishads that universe is comprised of space, sun, moon, stars with their clusters and earth with its atmospheric envelop. In the Hume's translation of Upanishads one notices the world-form consisting of the Earth, atmosphere and the sky[14].

Commonly the space surrounding the Earth has been described as Sky. There are references to Solar-Lunar realms, Surya-Chandra Mandala or Ravindra Mandala as the integral and indivisible part of the empty space. The sky has been described into the categories i.e. supreme or divine sky (paramakasa), infinite sky (mahakasa) and solar sky (suryakasa) illumined by millions of suns (Hamsopanishad,7). The sky has been call the essence of all creatures (Brihadarnyakopanishad, 2.5.9). The Earth has its support in the Sky (Chandyogya Upanishad 1.9.1). It is tantamount to indicate that the atmosphere lies in the sky or the space (Chandyogya Upanishad 1.9.6).

In Modern atmospheric science the atmosphere above the Earth surface is grossly divided into five parts.

a) Troposphere: It is the immediate range of the atmosphere and it is extended upto 12 km. and it is denser layer.

b) Stratosphere: It is extended upto 50 km. The temperature increases with the increase of the altitude.

c) Mesosphere: It is extended upto 80 km. The temperature decreases in this layer and the minimum temperature is -90^0 C.

d) Thermosphere : It is extended upto 500 km. Here the temperature increases with rise in altitude due to the absorption of X-ray or other high energetic wave.

e) Exosphere: Beyond 500 km the gas molecules are so feeble that gas molecules can easily escape from this layer to the space.

In Mandalabrahmana Upanishad, 2.1 it is defined that three types of atmosphere are present on the earth. First one is Fire Sphere, middle one is Lunar sphere and the last one is Solar sphere[15].

1. Fire Sphere: It is known as *Agni Mandala* and it is the immediate nearby layer on the Earth. Its name indicates that it is hot. So this layer may indicate the Troposphere and Stratosphere.
2. Lunar Sphere: It is known as *Chandra Mandala* and it is the middle layer between upper and lower layers. As moon light is cool in nature, the temperature in this layer is low. So this layer may indicate the Mesosphere.
3. Solar Sphere: This layer is also called *Surya Mandala* and it is the upper layer. The name indicates that the sunlight directly enters into this layer and some portion is also absorbed. Due to the absorption of sunlight it remains hot. So this layer may indicate Thermosphere or Ionosphere.

Ecological Idea in the Manuscript of Ramayana

But the basic problem for finding out the actual time period is the existence of three types of Ramayana version i.e. the Valmiki Ramayana; the Ramopakhyana of the Mahabharata and the Dasaratha Jataka (DJ), (the Buddhist version). Each has considerable difference from other.

The whole epic has ample reference where the rain, mountain, cloud and vegetation are enumerated in different forms.

In his Ramayana, Valmiki also portrays the forest as a place of shelter and refuge. When Sita takes her twin sons to Valmiki's ashram and raises them there, that gives a whole new sense to our understanding of the forest. The city has banished her but the forest welcomes her.

Yet another aspect of the forest is revealed in the story of Shambuka, a Shudra ascetic who does so much penance that an anthill grows around him while he sits and focuses his mind in utter stillness. When Rama finds Shambuka in the forest, he asks him, "Are you a Shudra?"[16]

The Ramayana brings before us a picture of great biodiversity. For example, consider Hanuman trying to locate the life-giving Sanjivini herb.

But there are so many herbs on that hill that Hanuman simply cannot remember the name of the herb that he was supposed to bring back. To me that is an example of the great diversity of herbs that existed during the time when forests covered nearly all the South Asian subcontinent [17].

Ramayana describes the term 'Physiography' of earth which indicates the earth's natural resources in its three major divisions i.e. Lithosphere, Atmosphere and Hydrosphere. The broad feature of the earth is mainly continent and ocean described as *Relief features of the first order* by R.D. Salisbury. In Ramayana , the earth is regarded as lying hidden in the heart of vast ocean and land mass is surrounded on all sides by vast water bodies[18]. In Ramayana all mentioned about the continental mass and water bodies are mythical but have no scientific proof. Ramayana describes the genesis, types and geomorphological features of the mountains. The mountains are considerd unstable due to tectonic movement since the past[19]. Besides, the phenomenon of tectonic movement and submergence[20] of rising of a mountain in an ocean deep[21] of horizontal and vertical movement of a mountain or earth's crust[22], of submergence due to earthquake amidst the ocean[23], of submergence of a very high mountain and genesis of level plain[24] are also referred to the Ramayana.

The Sanskrit term refers to the plain are *samaḅhumitala* or *samabhumih* and *sthali*. The Ramayana clearly reveals the plains of northern and peninsular India composed of fine alluvial sediments which were agriculturally very rich and significant besides coastal plains are referred to the Ramayana[25].

The Ramayana mentions the descent of rivers from the mountains and flowing towards sea. Here the vivid description of the flow path of Ganga from its origin in the Himalaya and its confluence in the ocean. The Ramayana refers to vertical as wella s lateral erosion by the rivers in the rainy season and on non-resistant steep banks[26]. The upper course of the Yamuna was termed *Silavaha* which signifies the presence of boulders and pebbles in the bed. From the study of the Ramayana it is clear that topography, relief building agents and their resultant topography are known to the people of Ramayanic age and which is vividly represented by the poet Valmiki.

The climatic variation from time to time is minutely observed by the people in the Ramayana period, they divided the whole year into six seasons which are formed as a result of sun's position in the northern and southern hemisphere. The name of the seasons are Vasanta ritu, Grisma ritu, Varsa ritu, Sarad ritu, Hamanta ritu and Sisira ritu.

Of all the elements on the earth wind is prominently described in the Ramayana. It appears that the people of the Ramayanic age had marked and named winds according to their strength and climatic phenomena associated with them. The Vayu appears to be used in the sense of delightful breeze free from dust. The term Vata or Mahavata is used in the sense of violent wind or storm. The name Marutas is used to describe the monsoon winds. This wind blows strongly and vehemently with huge noise causing rains by carrying the clouds to higher altitudes.

The Ramayana mentions the formation of clouds and rainfall caused by the sun [27]. It is the sun during nine months through its heats attracts the water into upward direction and which is subsequently in three months goes down to the earth as rain. The process of cloud formation includes isolation, moisture evaporation and causing increase of humidity[28]. The classification what we know in modern time, same is found in Ramayana as different synonyms of the cloud.

- Abhra: These cloud do not bring any rainfall. They may correspond to Cirrus Clouds
- Megha: These sprinkle water are called Megha. They are likely correspons to Nimbus, Nibostratus.
- Varidhara or Toyadhara or Balahaka: As the name suggests that they all are rain bearing cloud in the rainy season. They have lightning and assumes various forms. They are full of profuse water and bring excessive rains which is destructive. They probably Altostratus and cumulonimbus cloud[29].

In Ramayana we could not get any direct evidence regarding weather-forecasting, but the clear description and classifications of seasons indicates that they have some indigenous method of forecasting system. This forecasting is useful in agriculture, trade and other important aspects of human life. The following methods are used in practice during Ramayana age:

1. Methods of weather-forecast based on the observations of speed and direction of the wind.

2. Methods of weather-forecast based on the observations of the changes in trees and creepers etc.
3. Methods of weather-forecast based on the observations of the activities of some mammals, birds, reptiles, amphibians, fish and insects.
4. Methods of weather-forecast based on the observations of some physical changes in the atmosphere appearing to be around the sun and moon viz. halo etc.
5. Methods of weather-forecast based on the study of location, movements, conjuction etc. of the planets and stars.
6. Methods of weather-forecast based on the study of the cloud forms and other sky features such as lightning, hurricane, thunder, rainbow, etc[30].

In Ramayana age, there are dense forests are mentioned in the texts which are abounded in wild life. The eventful life of Rama is mostly spent in the different forests. According to the description found in Ramayana the natural vegetation is classified mainly in two groups i.e. Forests and Grasses. The different types of forests follows physical and chemical properties of soils and meteorological conditions and elevation of the land. Major forests of Ramayana are Caitraratha Vana, Sala Vana, Kurujangala, Bharunda Vana and Varutha Vana, Naimisaranya, Saravana, Tatakavana, Citrakuta Vana, Alaksitavana, Dandakaranya, etc. The different forests of Dandakaranya are known by different names ṣ Pippalivana, Madhuka and Nyagrodha vana, Pancavati vana, Krauncaranya, Matangaranya, Velavana, etc.

Grassland is present extensively all over the country. These lands are the main supply source for the food item of domestic animals. Moreover in religious and social activities grass plays an integral role in the Ramayanic period. The main grasses are in the text are Durbha, Kusa, Munja, Kasa, Sadbala , Sara, etc.

The importance of forest is found in all ancient ages. In Ramayana these forest is the source of economic and social prosperity. Ramayana has attached great importance of afforestation[31]. The following are the major advantages from forests are enumerated in the Ramayana:

a) The forests were used as pasture lands.

b) They were a great source of fuel and the forests dwellers used to cut them.

c) Houses, carts, chariots, cots, wooden seat, wooden sandals, combs, umbrellas, palanquins, boats, ships and various musical instruments such as Vina, Vipanci, Vallaki, Mridanga, Muraja, Pataha, Panava, Dundubhi, Dindima, etc were made of wood.

d) The trees like bilva, khadira, palasa, sleamataka, deodara, plaksa etc. were very important from the religious point of view because their wood was used in the sacrifices.

e) Various powders, scents, cosmetics and unguents were prepared from forest resources.

f) Medicinal herbs obtained from the forests were very common for besmearing the body.

g) Honey formed the principal item of food and people were in the habit of drinking it during the Ramayanic age. It was easily available in the forests.

h) The hermitage and forest dwellers collect their food, dress from the different plant items available in the forests[32].

The animals in The Ramayana are classified under two heads:

1. Domestic animals ;

2. Wild animals.

The position of cow among all domestic animals has an important place in the epic. It is used in all sphere of life ranging from religious to social aspects. Horses, camels, asses and mules are used for pulling chariots, carts and carrying burden. The use of elephant is known in Ramayan ages, there are different names mentioned in the Ramayana. The goats and sheeps are given freely as gifts in epic ages. In Ramayana the wild animals are mentioned like– lion, tiger, elephants, bear, pig, deer, jackal, hare, leopard, wild buffalo, antelope, yak, gayel and porcupine. Among birds different bird species are mentioned – crow, swan, peacock, wild duck, water-fowl, crane, vulture, parrot, heron, howl, pigeon, eagle, owl, etc[33].

Ecological Idea in the Manuscript of Mahabharata

In Mahabharata ample description of the five great elements are present. Trees and other plants mentioned in different parts of the Mahabharata vividly indicate the perpetual practice of Environmental Consciousness. According to Maharsi Vyasa the immovable are called Udbhijas and these are of five types – trees, shrubs, creepers, plants and bamboos. All these types of trees and plants were found at different places of Mahabharata. Description of Meru mountain is beautifully depicted in the Adi Parva, where it is said: the mountain was covered with many medicinal plants are of great use in human beings in their daily life. Many fearful beasts were roaming here and there on its weight. This mountain was also covered with different types of trees such as Ashoka, Champaka, Cutas, Atimuktakas, Punnagas, Karanikaras, Bakulas, Divya-Patala, Patala, Narikelas, Chandanas, Arjunas and various other beautiful and sacred trees full of fragrant flowers and sweet fruits. Richness of forest with varieties of flora and fauna, has been a distinct feature of Mahabharata age. Cutting down of trees was supposed to be heinous action even at that time and those who cut down the trees, also be killed. A great importance has been attached to the trees and leaves in the Adi parva. Lakes having cool water, tanks, ponds were integral part of human life and the different types of trees are present in the bank of the water body. Fragrant and pure air blowing though the forest carried perfumes of celestial flowers. Furthermore, the presence of herbs and plants having medicinal value are known in Mahabharata age. People in the great epic used to worship forest, mountains and rivers[34].

Different types of animals are mentioned in Mahabharata. It is mentioned that the killing of animal is sin in general. The Yudhisthir, eldest Pandava was not in favour of war with the Kauravas, because of the innumerable human beings as well as animals would be killed in this war. A man who commits crime of killing some animal, he should declare his sin in publicly and should also go on fast for three nights.

In Mahabharata the planning of villages and town are ecologically sound. All villages and towns were situated near the developed gardens full of plants, trees and creepers. People are highly dependent upon the different plant items as their life sustenance. Khandavaprastha, kingdom of Pandava was covered with so many charming gardens and trees with full blossom in their season and used to lean towards earth with the weight of their fruits.

People know the use and utility about the water in Mahabharata. The storage of water for domestic and agriculture purpose is known in Mahabharata. Moreover water is used in religious rites for its pure and sacred nature. People used to make their habitation on the vicinity of river like water bodies.

People at the time of Mahabharata, saved water in big tanks, that's why the problem of water-storage was rarely noticed. After suffering to get water in the country king Yavakri c constructed so many ponds and tanks for the well availability of water. The wells were constructed in the palaces and the houses for daily use and the water was stored in the earthen pots, of which there were two benefits; (i) the water remained cold at every time, and (ii) it was pure and hygienic in the earthen pots. The king also ordered to dig wells on the road sides of the big Rajamargas for the comfort of the travelers. Description of so many rivers, lakes, tanks. etc. is found in the different places of Mahasharata depicted the beneficial and sacredness of waters. The river Malini used to flow through the maintain valley which attracted so many ascetics on its banks for its pure, transparent and sacred water. The river was flowing through many islands and cleaned shores. About the sacredness of the river Ganges water, it is said by Maharshi Vyasa 'this auspicious and celestial river is accessible to all times. The Ganges water has external value so one should certainly take a dip into it. Like the river Ganges, the river like Sukumari, Kumari, Sitasi, Venika, Mahanadi, Manijala, Caksusa and Vardhanika were also considered as sacred. In the Kingdom of Chedi, the lakes in the forests were full of sacred and clean waters. The Gandhamardana mountain the lakes were neat and clean banks and it is water is having a good healing power because of the cane tree[35]'.

In Mahabharata people know the different form of Tejas or fire. The fire in form of house-holders fire helps man to do the yajna which is helpful for environment purpose. It is present on the stomach of animal as well as man. Fire in form of sun is essential item for the growth and expression of life on the earth without sun there is no question of life on the earth at all. So people on the Mahabharata revere the sun. Its existence generates different seasons, day and night. It is the cause of water cycle on the earth.

'Sun is the most powerful planet of the universe. If the sun would have no existence in the sky, there would have been no light and no heat, to which life on the earth would have been impossible. The sun shine in the great lightning and inspiration it dispels the darkness everywhere. Due to its brightness all the stand in the sky seem to disappeared because some of the stars have their shine only due to the sunlight. Keeping fore towards east and west one should offer prayers to the sun god in both the joining times and in the morning and evening. Due to the continuous motion of the sun different seasons are created. For six months he travels towards north ward course and then for the six months n southward course. This traveling course of the sun creates winter and summer seasons for the creatures. The sun beams are very helpful for the healthy growth of plants, creepers etc. The sun has been one of the main cause of rain on the earth because the sun soaks up waters and justices from the earth. Then he again, at proper time and proper season gives back the water in the form of rain[36]'.

Similarly *Vayu* or air is described in Mahabharata in different forms. The name of pancha prana i.e. *prana, apana, udana, vyana* and *samana* are found in texts of Mahabharata.

Manuscript is an important tool for the formation and preservation of any knowledge in time. People in ancient time try their level best to explore the developmental process of writing skill and preservation skill. Ultimate result of all efforts give the different form of manuscript in ancient period. The manuscript of Vedic, Upanishadic, epic like Ramayana and Mahabharata give vivid reference for the ecological perception of Ancient People in India. The awareness for environment compels man to decipher the secret behind all natural phenomenon existing in the environment. So we see from Vedic to epic period the awareness level of human being towards environment is evident from the manuscript study. So the manuscript study and introspection give the idea of development of knowledge process about environment or ecology from ancient to modern time.

References

1. Sahoo J. and Mohanty B. "Giving Life to Palm Leaf Manuscripts: Technological Aspects", *The Orissa Historical Research Journal,* Vol. XLVII, No. 3, p. 28.

2 Ibid. p-29
3. Ibid. pp. 29-30
4. Ibid. pp. 30-31
5. http://crl.du.ac.in/ical09/papers/index_files/ical-14_227_489_2_RV.pdf
6. http://crl.du.ac.in/ical09/papers/index_files/ical-14_227_489_2_RV.pdf
7. Gaur, Ramesh C. & Chakraborty, M. (2009). Preservation and access to Indian manuscripts: A knowledge base of Indian cultural heritage resources for academic libraries. (S M DhawanṀ et al.).(Ed.) (pp. 90-98), *Proceedings of the International Conference on Academic Libraries* (ICAL-2009), Delhi. Retrieved March 14, 2011, from http://crl.du.ac.in/ical09/papers/index_files/ical-14_227_489_2_RV.pdf
8. Kapila Vatsyayan, (ed.), *Prakriti: The integral Vision.* Vol.2, Indira Gandhi National Centre for the Arts, New Delhi. 1995, p. 7.
9. H.W.Wallis, *The Cosmology of the Rigveda*, Cosmo Publications, 1999, pp.94-95.
10. M. Vannucci, '*Human Ecology in the Vedas*', D.K. Printworld (P) Ltd., New Delhi, 1999, p.262.
11. Ibid., p.267
12. Arnold J. Toynbee, '*Change and Habit*', London, Oxford University Press, 1966,p.171.
13. M. Winternitz, *A History of Indian Literature, Vol. I*, Reprinted 1996, MLBD, New Delhi., pp.215-216.
14. Robert Earnest Hume, *The Thirteen principal Upanishads*, Oxford University Press, 1921, p.35.
15. B.G. Tamaskar, *Geographical Knowledge in Upanishads*, Indus Publishing Company, New Delhi, 1989, p. 25.
16. Rangarajan, Swarnalatha, *Ecological Dimensions of the Ramayana*, Volume 25, Number 1 (2009), p.25
17. Ibid. p.27
18. Ramayana, I.5.2, II.110, 24-25, VII.23.21.
19. Ramayana, V.1.94
20. Ramayana, I.45.27
21. Ramayana, III.33.6, V.1.101, VI.50.32
22. Ramayana, V.1.94
23. Ramayana, V.1.125-126
24. Ramayana, V.56. 49-50
25. Ramayana, II.35.26
26. Ramayana, II.63.46, II.64.74, III.46.21, V.25.15

27. Ramayana, VI.105,13, 22

28. Ramayana, II.63.15-16, IV.28.3-5

29. Shukla, R.K., *Ramayana: A Study in Ancient Indian Geography*, Ph.D Thesis, Bundelkhand University, Jhansi, 1984, Ch.II, pp 65-66.

30. Ibid. p.68.

31. Ramayana, V.14, 43, V.15.1-15, V.61.8.

32. Shukla, R.K., *Ramayana: A Study in Ancient Indian Geography*, Ph.D Thesis, Bundelkhand University, Jhansi, 1984, Ch-III, pp 83-91.

33. Ibid. pp. 93-95.

34. Biswal, Amarendra: 'Research Analysis and Evaluation'. *Relevance of Mahabharata with Regard to Environmental Consciousness,* Vol. I, Issue-9, 2009, Kurukshetra University, Kurukshetra, Haryana.

35. Ibid.p.28.

36. Ibid. p.29.

6

Architectural Motifs in Pāla Manuscript Paintings of Early Medieval Bengal

– *Sudipa Ray Bandyopadhyay*

An 'architectural motif' signifies the delineation of an architectonic form either in part or in whole in any work of art, and is used mainly for enhancing the decorative value of the concerned work. Being related to a structural monument an architectural motif exists in time and taste and hence the sculptural or pictorial works which betray preferences for some of these motifs can be reasonably dated or at least the period of their creation can be reasonably guessed.

There are almost no extant religious edifices of the Pāla-Sena period either in Bihar or in Bengal, the two major territories over which the Pāla-Sena empire extended. The absence of extant religious edifices forms a major constraint in the proper appreciation of the religious architecture of the period. A study of the architectural motifs of religious edifices depicted in the art objects of the period provides us with a fair knowledge of the temple architecture of the period. These motifs can be seen in works of art of different media— stone sculptures, manuscript paintings, wood carvings and terracottas. Among the various religious architectural motifs that appear in Pāla-Sena art, *stūpas* and *deuls* are the most widely depicted ones. This paper concentrates on these two motifs depicted in the manuscript paintings of the Pāla period in eastern India in the early medieval period.

All the manuscript paintings of the Buddhists, such as the *Ashmasāhasmikā Prajñāpāramitā* (ASPP), the *Pañchavi śatisāhashikâ Prajñāpāramitā* (PVSPP) the *Pancharakshā* (PR), the *Kāraṇḍavyūhasūtra* (KVS), *Dhāram-grantha*, etc. are of incalculable help for studying architectural motifs in Pāla-Sena art. Chronologically they belong to the time-bracket of eleventh-twelfth century under different Pāla rulers like Mahīpāladeva I, Nayapāladeva, Mahīpāladeva II, Rāmapāladeva, Gopāla IV and Madanapāladeva; Varman ruler Harivarmanadeva; and Sena King Lakshmanasena.

The paintings which include such motifs are drawn in outline. The inner space created by such outlines is filled up with distinguishing pigment. Though most of these manuscripts have been discovered outside the territorial limits of the Pāla-Sena empire, they bear distinctive traits of the Pāla art idiom. Some of them are hazy and indistinct; others, which are still clean and bright in colour, are full and square. In almost all cases the motifs represent full architectonic forms of some temple or *stūpa* in their frontal delineation, recalling similar items of the lithic and metal repertoire.

The labels accompanying the relevant paintings in each case identify the respective shrines, their locations, and deities installed. The artists of the period under review painted at least thirty two important shrines of different parts of the Buddhist world. Of these about two-thirds are from Eastern India.[1]

Among these illustrated manuscripts displaying architectural motifs of different designations and allowing some inferences in regard to their elevation, the most important is the ASPP preserved in the Cambridge University Library and copied in Newar Samvat 135, corresponding to 1015 CE.[2] Among other similar types of illustrated manuscripts mention may be made of the following pictorial representations:

- Maitreya Buddha with a *stūpa* dated 14th regnal year of the Pāla king Nayapāladeva preserved in the Cambridge University Library manuscript of *Paṇcharakshā*, No. Add. 1688; [3]
- *Prajñāpāramitā* Uddhāra or Rescue of *Prajñāpāramitā* with the depiction of a *mahāstūpa*, dated 8th regnal year of Harivarmadeva (marginal years of eleventh-twelfth centuries CE) preserved in the Baroda Museum of Art[4;]

- A tantric goddess seated within a shrine, dated 18th regnal year of the Pāla monarch Govindapāladeva of twelfth century preserved in the Asiatic Society, Kolkata manuscript of ASPP No. G. 9989A[5];
- Portrait of Maitreya Buddha with a miniature *stūpa* placed in front of the matted hair of the deity of about eleventh-twelfth century CE preserved in the Tokyo University Library[6];
- A heavily illustrated manuscript of the *Kāraṇḍavyūhasūtra* dated around 1100-1125 CE, depicting a large number of architectonic forms of various types preserved in the British Library[7]; and etc.

The shrine motifs depicted in all these paintings may conveniently be classified under *bhadra*, *stūpa-śīrsha-bhadra* and *śikhara-śīrsha-bhadra deuls*. A number of manuscript illustrations of the period provide us with a glimpse of the architectonic varieties of contemporary Buddhist *bhadra deuls*. In many instances, they carry the depiction of the shrine along with the labels describing the divinity installed and the location of the shrine (e.g. Chandradvīpe Bhagavatī Tārā, PuGravardane TriśraGa-Buddha-Bhammârakah, etc). The painting titled PuGravardane TriśraGa-Buddha-Bhammārakah shows the architectural type of this order existing at that time in Eastern India. This has led some scholars to suggest that such representations of shrines are not products of the painter's imagination only.[8] Of late, a scholar has argued that these miniatures are helpful in forming an idea of the temple architecture of the time, but it is unsafe to accept them as actual replicas of the shrines concerned.[9]

The manuscript painters are more meticulous in representing the frontal view, sometimes with linear dimensions. The manuscript paintings carry in each case the front view of the edifice in question, but on occasions they give us an idea of its ground plan too. The notable features of these *bhadra deuls* of different descriptions are:

(i) In certain instances the tiered stages of the *gaGī* of the temple look like a sloping roof similar to that of a hut in the Bengal region with a single or duplication of such roofs,

(ii) In many cases the decorated *stūpa* replicas being accommodated at the corners of the tiered stages introduce diversity in the skyline beside the *mastaka* in the central plane of elevation like some Brahmanical temples with miniature *śikharas* surmounting the main one,

(iii) In some cases sectarian affiliation of the shrines is represented by such elements as *makara*-like *āmalaka* surmounted by a miniature *stūpa* finial, while in some others the *stûpa* or the *śikhara* forms the principal part of the structure in its plane of elevation leading to a composite form of architectural design which cannot be classified simply as *bhadra deul.* In the latter cases the *śikhara* or *stūpa* or both surmounts the *pitha* molding of different numbers including even a single one.

This varied set of compositional elements, has led some scholars to classify these *bhadra deul* motifs as follows:

(i) Tiered type surmounted by an *āmalaka* and/or finial-*bhadra*,

(ii) Tiered type surmounted by *stūpa— stūpa-śīrsha bhadra* and,

(iii) Tired type surmounted by *śikhara— śikhara-śīrsha bhadra.*

Bhadra deuls

Manuscript illustrations of the period reproducing *bhadra deul* motifs of pure formation are fairly large in number. Of these, the paintings depicting the temples of Mahattarī Tārā in Varendra[10] and Lokanātha of Chandragomin at Nalendra[11] in the Cambridge University manuscript of *Ashmasāhasmikā Prajñāpāramitā* copied in Newar Samvat 135 (corresponding to 1015 CE) deserve attention. The pictorial representation of the former shows a three-tiered roof gradually diminishing at every stage surmounted by an *āmalaka* and two distinctly visible *khaṇḍi* between the tired roof. At the projected corners of the uppermost tier, figures of two sitting antelopes or bulls facing opposite directions are seen. In the latter, like the former one, the shrine is composed of a three-tiered roof headed by *āmalaka* and *stūpa* finial. In both the cases the shrines are fronted by a three-lobed arch. But in the latter further transformation has been sought by providing replica *stūpa* cresting on either side of the corners of the third stage of the tiered elevation by ensuring a diversification of the skyline. Further, the employment of floral design to decorate the tiered stages in both the shrines shows that the shrine architecture of the Pāla-Sena period was not devoid of artistic embellishments. Illustrations in pigment depicting similar type of *bhadra deul* are also available in another manuscript of the period. An illustrated manuscript of a late Mahāyāna text *Kāraṇḍavyūhasūtra*, assignable to Eastern India and to a date around 1100-1125 CE contains a fair number of illustrations depicting shrines of a similar order.[12] The paintings illustrating the shrines of twelve-armed standing Lokeśvara[13], Lokeśvara with Tārā and Hayagrīva[14]; and Tārā with Jāṅgulī and Ekajamâ[15] are some of the remarkable specimens of this type of shrine motif from the aforesaid text, now in the British Library.

Rekha or Nagara deuls

Representations of *rekha* or *nāgara deul* motif including pure *śikhara* variety in the art of the period are fewer than their counterparts of *bhadra* and composite type shrines. A handful of examples of *rekha deuls* are available as a motif. The temple replicas show almost all the elements of the *gaṇḍī* and *mastaka* of a *rekha deul*, which includes *bhūmi*, *bhūmi-āmalakas*, *bicama*, *beki*, *āmalaka* and *kalasa*. The vertical curvatures of the *gaṇḍī* indicate that the *deuls* had *rathaka* projections. In one of the manuscript paintings, a two-armed Avalokiteśvara with the right hand in *varadamudrā* is shown seated in *lalitāsana* inside a *rekha deul* with all its salient features[16].

Composite type of shrines

The *śikhara* of a shrine surmounted by *āmalaka* and/or finial is known as *bhadra deul*. Other two types of *deuls* — *stūpa-śīrca bhadra deul* and *śikhara-śīrsha bhadra deul* — are two representative examples of the composite type of temples.[17] A good number of composite forms of shrine are found in the Pāla manuscript paintings of Bengal, Bihar and Nepal region. According to Sarasi Kumar Saraswati, the composite form of temples led to the diversification of the design, breaking up the usual monotony of the tiered courses.[18]

The basic form of these types of architecture being *bhadra*, they are designated as *stūpa-śīrsha bhadra* and *śikhara-śīrsha bhadra*. In the former, the *stūpa* forms a distinctive part of the elevation of the structure over some tiered courses, while in the latter the role of the *stūpa* is noticeably played by a *śikhara*. Unlike a *bhadra deul* with *stūpa* finial, here the *stūpa* or the *śikhara* is a part of the elevation. As in some of the *bhadra deuls*, here also in both cases, the composite form led to the diversification of the design, breaking up the visual monotony of the tiered courses.[19]

In every instance of the eastern Indian (including Nepal) pictorial illuminations of *stūpa-śīrsha bhadra deul* and *śikhara-śīrsha bhadra deul*, the *stūpa* or the *śikhara* is found to be complete with all its elements. Sometimes in a *śikhara-śīrsha bhadra deul* a finial of *stūpa* replica over the *āmalaka* is also seen. That the *śikhara* portion of this type of composite form received equal treatment *vis-a-vis* to the basic part of the form of elevation is proved by the delineation of vertical planes on the face of the *śikhara*, which further suggests a cruciform ground plan of a *nāgara* type of temple.

Motifs exhibiting *śikhara-śīrsha bhadra deul* are found in art objects of different media like stone, terracotta, and pigment but so far as composite form of *stūpa-śīrsha bhadra* is concerned, it is to be found only in pigment. Some dated manuscript illustrations of the Pâla period provide us with a good number of *deul* motifs of this group. Both the Cambridge University manuscript of ASPP and the *Kāraṇḍavyūhasūtra* of 12th century CE bear a large number of miniatures depicting *śikhara-śīrsha bhadra deul*. In the manuscript illustrations, the upper part of the elevation of the *śikhara-śīrsha bhadra deul* is marked by two important features:

(a) only the skyline is affected in *deuls* in which *śikhara* surmounts the tiered courses; and

(b) *stūpas* fill the empty background in *deuls* in which in addition to the *śikhara* a number of *stūpas* occurs on either side.

A miniature of the Cambridge University Library manuscript of *Aṣṭasāhasrikā Prajñāpāramitā* shows a shrine fronted by a three-lobed arch on supporting pillars and with a superstructure of three-tiered courses surmounted by a *śikhara* which in its turn is crowned with an *āmalaka* and a *stūpa*-finial; it delineates a deity standing within a shrine which has been described as Lokanātha of Tulākshetra of Varendra. Here the *śikhara* and the flat tiered courses are decorated with some floral and geometric designs.[20] A slight variation is found in the formation of the tiered courses of another miniature *śikhara-śīrṣa bhadra deul* in the same manuscript representing Puṇḍravardhane Triśaraṇa-Buddha-Bhaṭṭārakaḥ. In this *deul* motif the lowest part of the four-tiered course of a *śikhara-śīrṣa bhadra deul* is slanting in construction, not flat. A careful observation reveals that the slanting course is not an inseparable part of the actual tiered stages over the *garbhagṛiha* of the shrine. Sign of an enclosure around the open portico of the shrine indicates that this slanting course of tiered roof probably served as a shade over the portico meant for using as a circumambulatory path. For all practical purposes, the *bhadra* formation of the *deul* motif of this illustration consists of three-tiered courses.[21] Several miniatures representing *śikhara-śīrṣa bhadra deul* also appears in the manuscripts of *KVS*. In a painting depicting Avalokiteśara on folio 12b of the manuscript, the deity is seen standing within a shrine of three-lobed arch surmounted by three-tiered courses and a *śikhara*.[22] Another miniature from *PVS PPM*, dated 8th year of Harivarmadeva (1192 CE) preserved in the Baroda Museum Art Gallery, Gujarat, shows Tārā with Aúokakāntā Mārichī and Ekjamā sitting within a *śikhara-śīrṣa bhadra deul* with a three-lobed arch. The tiered courses and the *śikhara* of the *deul* have been vividly depicted by the manuscript painter.[23]

The second type of composite form of shrine motif discernible in the art of the period is that of a shrine with a superstructure of a number of tiered stages of the *gaṇḍï* surmounted by a complete *stūpa* which in its turn is crowned by an *āmalaka* and a finial. Unlike a *bhadra deul* surmounted by a decorated *stūpa* finial, the present motif shows the *stūpa* as a principal element of the elevation of the structure, which does not serve the purpose of an ornamental finial like the previous one.[24] This type of shrine motif, categorized as *stūpa-śīrsha bhadra* shrine, is only noticeable in manuscript paintings and not in any other art media of the period. The Cambridge University Library manuscript of *Aṣṭasāhasrikā Prajñāpāramitā* represents as many as eight miniatures delineating such a *deul* motif. The miniature accompanied by a label describing the god as Maṅgakoshmha Vajrapāṇi at Oddiyana, portrays the deity seated within a shrine fronted by a three-lobed arch resting on pillars and with a superstructure rising up in three well-built decorated receding tiered stages above which is a *stūpa* of a fairly large size crowned by an *āmalaka* and a finial. Obviously, the *stūpa* here is a principal element in the elevation of the superstructure.[25] Another elegant example of this type of *stūpa-śīrsha bhadra* in the same manuscript is the miniature showing Jamā Lokanātha in Rādhyārāmā. In this miniature, the lavishly decorated three-tiered stage is not only surmounted by a *stūpa* of a smaller size than that of the previous miniature, but also crowned by an *āmalaka* and finial.[26]

In both the cases the void of the backdrop is filled up by miniature *stūpas* in the upper stages of the frontal view of the shrine, labelled as Mahāchīne Buddharūpaka Lokanātha; it has on its front a trefoil arch and a superstructure of four-tiered stages surmounted by a *stūpa*. Here also two miniature *stūpas* are found placed on the corners of the central tier.[27]

The second type of *stūpa-śīrsha bhadra deul* is composed of a superstructure of single or two-tiered sloping roof surmounted by a *stūpa* with a finial. In a superstructure of a single tiered sloping roof, the roof from four different sides of the edifice converges at the top in an ascending order. But in the case of a superstructure of a two-tiered sloping roof, in addition to a set of the above type of roof, there is a duplication of a sloping roof, particularly where the sanctum cella is surrounded by a running corridor. The lower tier of the roof obviously does not converge at the top, but merge on the four sides of the outer surface of the walls of the sanctum cella. Shrines of this type with one and two-tiered sloping roof call to mind Bengal's *chārchālā* and *āmchālā* huts respectively.[28] From the front, the superstructure with such receding tiered courses appears like a *bhadra*, and when a full-fledged *stūpa* and a finial surmount it, it is nothing but a *stūpa-śīrsha bhadra deul* shrine. Representations of such *stūpa-śīrsha bhadra deul* are found in some of the manuscript paintings of the period. A miniature of the Cambridge University Library manuscript *ASPP* depicts a multi-armed Lokanātha (described as *sahasrabhuja*) and describes him as the deity of Sivapura of Konkana (apparently the well-known region of the same name in Maharashtra). Here the deity is seen standing in *samapada* inside a shrine with a roof of two sets of sloping tiers, the edges of the lower one are found resting on pillars. The upper part of the wall of the sanctum cella with a *chaitya*-window is visible between the two-tiered stages of the sloping roof. The upper tiered stage is surmounted by a *stūpa* and a finial.[29] Representations of this type of *stūpa-śīrsha bhadra* shrine are seen in some other manuscript paintings of the period. In a miniature in the *PVSS PP*, the goddess Mahattarī Tārā is seen in a sitting posture within a temple of this type. But here the artist, in order to represent a bigger appearance of the deity within the small available space, refrains from drawing the front portion of the lower sloping roof and indicates its presence by showing only two side-wings of the same resting on pillars on either side. The temple is as usually surmounted by a *stūpa* and a finial.[30] Representation of a two-tiered sloping *stūpa-śīrsha bhadra shrine* with such visual ingenuity is also noticed in a miniature of *Kāraṇḍavyūhasūtra*, where Khaṣarpaṇa Lokeśvara is seen standing within such a temple. Here the figure of the deity has been so enlarged as to encroach on the wall-space of the sanctum cella between the two tiers. Like the previous one, the artist has drawn only the side-wings of the lower tier to indicate its presence. The temple is surmounted by a well-shaped *stūpa* forming a part of the elevation and finally by a finial.[31]

Chaityagarbha deul

Deul motifs of an altogether different type also appear in some art works in stone and pigment of the period. They are essentially Buddhist in inspiration. Barring a few, the deity installed in such a shrine is usually Mārīchi, a dominant goddess in the Mahayana pantheon. Mārīchi is often depicted in sculptural art and manuscript painting within an architectural structure following a description in the *Sādhanamālā* where the deity is mentioned as *chaityagarbhasthitā* i.e. residing within the womb of a *chaitya*.[32]

In the manuscript of the *ASPP*, preserved in the Cambridge University Library, an illustration of Aśokakāntā Mārīchi bears the descriptive label *Dvibhujā-Mārīchi-chaityah*.[33] Ushṇīshavijayā, another deity of the Mahayana pantheon also appears in a painting. Ushṇīshavijayā is described as *chaityaguhāgarbhasthita*[34] in the *Sādhanamālā* [35]. It appears from the description of the residing places, i.e. *Chaityagarbha* and *Chaityaguhāgarbha* of Mārīchi and Ushṇīshavijayā respectively, that *chaitya* in these contexts probably means a shrine.[36] Nothing is known so far about the principal elements of such a religious edifice from any text, but from the use of the above two terms in *Sādhanamālā* and from a close scrutiny of the representations of such edifices in the sculptural and pictorial works of the period it appears that the shrine looked like a barrel-vaulted niche with superstructure.

Representations of the *chaityagarbha* motif are mostly found in images of Mārīchi, both in stone and in pigment. The motif is meticulously carved in deep relief in stone sculptures of the early medieval period. Here, however, only examples of the motif occurring in manuscript paintings will be cited. Compared to their sculptural counterpart, painted representations of the *chaityagarbha* motif are less numerous. A few of the miniatures appearing in the manuscript of *Kāraṇḍavyūhasūtra* show depictions of this motif. A miniature representing an eight-handed Mārīchi in folio 43a of the manuscript of the *Kāraṇḍavyūhasūtra* shows the superstructure of a *chaityagarbha* shrine up to the vaulted roof. Unfortunately, the upper margin of the folio is missing, and as such the portion delineating the *chaitya* above the vaulted roof is not visible. The pilasters supporting the vaulted-arch of the shrine have some faint marks of colourful decoration and show the *tulāpīmha* at the top ends merging with the declining ends of the arch of the vaulted-roof.[37] But in a miniature in folio 41b of the same text depicting Parṇaśabarī there appears a fuller representation of the superstructure of a *chaityagarbha* shrine. In this motif, a well-shaped *āmalaka* and a sun and crescent are seen atop the vaulted-roof.[38] In the same text a twelve-handed Nāmasaṁgīti seated in *vajraparyāṅkāsana* is also seen installed within a *chaityagarbha deul*, the *mastaka* of which is missing.[39]

Stūpas

Among the architectural motifs depicted in Pāla-Sena art, the *stūpa* is the most widely depicted one. Sometimes multiple representations of this motif are found in the pictorial art of the period. The stylistic evolution of the *stūpa* architectural form can be discerned through the transformation of the different components of the *stūpa* under different stylistic idioms.[40] The *stūpa* motif in Pāla-Sena art registers almost all these transformations.

Stūpa forms in pigment are of different designations. Among depictions of architectonic forms that appear in their fullness in the art of the period, the *stūpa* motif is the most widely visible motif. The main components of a fully developed *stūpa* from ground level upwards are:

(a) ***Vedī*** or ground balustrade separating the sacred precinct

(b) ***Medhi*** or drum

(c) ***Aṇḍa*** or dome

(d) ***Harmikā*** or a pavilion for setting a shaft

(e) ***Chhatras*** or umbrellas surrounding a *yashmi* or shaft and

(f) ***Dhvaja*** or finial.

The basement of a *stūpa* i.e. ***vedī*** demarcates the sacred precincts from the outside and much of the elevation of the superstructure of a *stūpa* and its formation depends on it. The *stūpa* motifs in the art of the period reveal two types of *vedī's* — circular and four-sided. A circular *vedī* can be seen in the painted representation of Lokanātha in the illustrated manuscript of *ASPP*, housed in the Cambridge University library.[41] A four-sided *vedī* can be seen in a painted representation of *Prajñāpāramitā* Uddhāra in the illustrated manuscript of *PVSPP* of the 8th regnal year of Harivarmadeva (an eleventh-twelfth century ruler of the Varman dynasty of Bengal), now housed in the Baroda Museum and Picture Gallery.[42]

Medhi or drum is the terrace surrounding the *aṇḍa* or the dome. The *medhi* is of varied shapes: circular, four-sided, hexagonal, and lotus-shaped. Among the four different types of *medhi*[43], an illustrated manuscript of *ASPP* preserved in the Asiatic Society, Kolkata, shows a pair of *stūpa* motifs with lotus-shaped *medhi* on either side of a palm tree on the right of the painted representation of Dīpaṅkara Buddha.[44]

Among the various components of a *stūpa*, *aṇḍa* is the most important. Generally three types of, *aṇḍa* are discernible in Pāla-Sena art – hemispherical *aṇḍa*, bulbous *aṇḍa* and lotus-shaped *aṇḍa*. The first variety can be seen in an eleventh century miniature in the ASPP, preserved in the Cambridge University Library with the accompanying label 'Tulākshetre Vardhamāna Stūpa'. A perfect hemispherical *aṇḍa* is seen in the *stūpa*s depicted.[45] Another representation of a *stūpa* with hemispherical, *aṇḍa* can be seen in the same manuscript bearing the label 'Dharmarājika Chaitya in Rāha'.[46] To this may be added the depiction found in a manuscript of the ASPP in the Asiatic Society collection, Kolkata, dated 1071 CE. bearing the label 'Siṁhaladvīpe Dīpaṅkara Abhayahasta'.[47] Another variety of hemispherical *aṇḍa* (flattened at the top) can be seen in a painted representation of *Prajñāpāramitā* Uddhāra in the illustrated manuscript of PVSPP preserved in the Baroda Museum and Picture Gallery. Bulbous *aṇḍa* and lotus-shaped *aṇḍa* are rarely seen in the manuscript paintings of the period.

Harmikā or little pavilion in an arc or cube is built above the *aṇḍa* and is either circular or square in shape. It is usually fenced in by a *vedīka* or railing. A circular *harmikā* appears in the painted manuscript of the ASPP preserved in the Cambridge University Library with the accompanying label 'Varendra Tulākshetra-Lokanātha'.[48] Another instance can be traced in a painting of *Prajñāpāramitā* Uddhāra in PVSPP, preserved in the Baroda Museum and Picture Gallery. In the painting a *stūpa* motif has been endowed with knob-like projections on either side of the circular *harmikā*.

The final stage of elevation of the *stūpa* is ***chhatravali*** and ***dhvaja***. A manuscript painting of Dīpaṅkara in the ASPP of the Asiatic Society collection, Kolkata, carries a *stūpa* motif of seven *chhatras*.[49] But in art works of other media of the Pâla-Sena period the *chhatras* are not restricted to seven; there are one, three, five, seven, nine, eleven, and thirteen *chahatras* as well, forming a conical shape around the *yashṭi* or shaft.

Finial or ***dhvaja*** is the final point of the uppermost phase of a *stūpa* elevation. Finials of different forms appear as motifs in the art of the period: flamboyant finial, vase-shaped finial and finial with crescent and sun, occasionally with a rain-water disc or *varshāsthala* placed below the crescent and sun. Among these, crescent and sun finial with *varshāsthala* can be found in the manuscript paintings of the period. In an illustrated manuscript painting of Dīpaṅkara Buddha in the ASPP of Asiatic Society, Kolkata, a palm tree is seen flanked by two *stūpa* motifs showing a decorated canopy with two suspending festoons and *varshāsthala*.[50] Finial with crescent and sun is also distinctly visible on the right side of the central figure of Avalokiteśvara in the manuscript painting of the KVS.[51] Finial surmounted by *varshāsthala* is also found in a manuscript painting of Lokanātha in the ASPP, housed in the Cambridge University Library, where two rows of *stūpa* replicas are painted on either side of a temple on the ground level.[52]

On the basis of the pictorial representations of the *stūpa* motifs in Pāla-Sena art it can be said that unlike stone, metal or wooden sculptures, the specimens of the pictorial art are all drawn in outline; the inner space created by such outlines is filled up with distinguishing pigment. Most of these manuscripts have been discovered outside the territorial limits of the Pāla-Sena empire, but they bear distinct marks of the Pāla art idiom. Some of them are hazy and indistinct; others, which are still clean and bright in colour, are full and square. Colour compositions of these paintings are sometimes remarkably contrasting. In almost all cases the motifs represent full architectonic forms of some temple or *stūpa* in their frontal delineation, recalling similar items of the lithic and metal repertoire. The labels accompanying the relevant paintings in each case identify the respective shrines, their locations and deities installed. The artists painted at least thirty-two important shrines of different parts of the Buddhist world of the period, of which about two-thirds are from eastern India. The advent and spread of the Mahayana sect led to the importation of various deities into the fold of Buddhist iconography. The Buddhist art of the Pāla-Sena period thus became more and more idol-centred. This also explains the appearance of *stūpa* motifs in large numbers in the various art forms of the period.

Concluding Observations

A large number of *stūpas* and *deul* motifs can be found in manuscript paintings as well as in art objects of other media. Quantitatively *deul* motifs are fewer than *stūpa* motifs. But this comparative paucity of *deul* motifs does not necessarily indicate their relative insignificance as an architectural form. During the tenth-eleventh centuries, at least two types of composite *deul* forms were devised by the builders. Miniature paintings demonstrate that their basic form was *bhadra*, but as they were surmounted by a *stūpa* or a *śikhara*, they were designated as *stūpa-śīrsha bhadra* and *śikhara-śīrsha bhadra deuls* respectively. Some of the manuscript paintings of the period bearing a composite type of *deul* motif— classified as *stūpa-śrsha bhadra deul* — show a superstructure of a single or double-tiered sloping roof, four-faceted or eight-faceted, as the case may be, surmounted by a *stūpa* as a finial. This type of single and double-tiered sloping roofs is very common in building constructions in rural Bengal; they are designated as *chārchālā* and *āṭchāla*. Besides different types of *rekha*, *drāviḍa* and composite shrines, there are also *chaityagarbha* and *chaityaguhāgarbha deul* motifs that are unique in formulation. Data obtained from sculptural art and pictorial repertoire and corroborative evidence from *Tantrayāna* iconographic texts like the *Sādhanamālā* and the *Kāraṇḍavyūhasūtra* show that some sort of cave or monolithic architecture developed during the period; the structural configuration of such a *deul* appears from the front like a barrel-vaulted niche which is surmounted by a *chaitya*, sometimes tiered in formation. The impressive number of specimens executed in different media exhibiting such a unique form of *deul* architecture proves its existence and popularity.

Notes and References

1. Saraswati, S. K. (1975) 'Rare Architectural Types in Manuscript Illustrations' in *Bangladesh Lalitkalā*, I.1,Bangladesh, pp.2-3.
2. Ibid., pp.1.
3. Saraswati, S.K. (1977) with introduction and notes, *Tantrayāna Art: An Album*, Calcutta: The Asiatic society, Pl. 259.
4. Bautze-Picron, Claudine (1999), 'Buddhist Painting During the Reign of Harivarmadeva (end of the 11th C.) in South East Bangladesh' in *Journal of Bengal Art*, Vol.4 (ed.) Enamul Haque, ICSBA, Dhaka, Bangladesh, pp.159-197, including 43 colour Plates.
5. Sarasi Kumar Saraswati (1978), *Pāl Yuger Chitrakalā* (in Bengali), Kolkata: Ananda Publishers, Fig. in p. 101.
6. Ibid., p. 131.
7. Losty, Jeremiah P. (1989) 'An Early Indian Manuscript of the *Kāraṇḍavyūhasūtra* in Debala Mitra and Gauriswar Bhattacharya, (ed.) *Studies in Art and Archaeology of Bihar-Bengal: Nalinikanta Satavarsiki* [Dr. N.K. Bhattasali Centenary Volume (1888- 1988)], Delhi: Indian Books Centre, 1989, pp.1-21, Figs. 1-77.
8. Sarasi Kumar Saraswati (1975), p.1.
9. Losty, Jeremiah P. (1989), p.4.
10. Saraswati, S. K. (1976) *Architecture of Bengal*, Book I (Ancient Period), Calcutta: G. Bharadwaj & Co., Pl. XV, Fig. 29.
11. Ibid. Pl. XV, Fig. 28.
12. Losty, Jeremiah P. (1989), *op. cit.*, p.1.
13. Ibid., Fig. 5, see also Enamul Haque (2007) *The Art Heritage of Bangladesh*, Dhaka, Bangladesh: International Centre for Studies in Bengal Art (ICSBA), Pl. 391, p. 323.
14. Ibid., Fig.6 , see also Enamul Haque (2007), Pl 387, p. 323.
15. Ibid., Fig.13, see also Enamul Haque (2007), Pl 396, p. 323.
16. Enamul Haque (2007), Pl. 401, p. 323.
17. Bandyopadhyay Sudipa (2002), *Architectural Motifs in Early Mediaeval Art of Eastern India (Pāla-Sena Period)*, Kolkata: R.N. Bhattacharya, pp. 80-81.
18. Saraswati, S. K., (1975), pp. 2-3.
19. Ibid, p.7.
20. Bandyopadhyay Sudipa (2002), Fig. 31, p. 86.
21. Ibid., Fig. 55, p. 86.
22. Ibid., Fig. 57, p. 87.

23. Goetz, H. (1987), *Hand Book of the Collections: Baroda Museum and Picture Gallery*, Baroda, 1952; Reprinted, Ahmedabad, Pl. XXXI (middle of the lowermost row).
24. Saraswati, S. K. (1975), p.7.
25. Bandyopadhyay Sudipa (2002), Fig. 58, p.87.
26. Saraswati, S. K. (1975), Pl. I, p.4.
27. Bandyopadhyay Sudipa (2002), Fig. 59, p. 87.
28. Saraswati, S. K. (1975), Pl. I, p.4.
29. Bandyopadhyay Sudipa (2002), Fig. 60, p. 88.
30. Bhattacharya, Benoytosh (1958),*The Indian Buddhist Iconography mainly based on the Sādhanamālā and Other Cognate Tantric Text of Rituals*, Second Edition, Calcutta, Fig. 10; E.G. 128.
31. Bandyopadhyay Sudipa (2002), Fig. 62, p. 88.
32. Sādhana No. 134 of *Sādhanamālā*.
33. Saraswati, S. K. (1977), p. XLI.
34. Bhattacharya, Benoytosh (1958), p.214.
35. Sadhana Nos.191, 211, 212 of *Sādhanamālā*.
36. Saraswati, S. K. (1977), p. XLII.
37. Bandyopadhyay Sudipa (2002), Fig. 67, p. 90.
38. Ibid., Fig. 42, p. 90.
39. Losty, Jeremiah P. (1989), Fig. 76. See also Sudipa Ray (Bandyopadhyay) (1999), 'Chaityagarbha Deul Motif in Pāla-Sena Art' in *Kalyan Bharati*, Vol. III, Calcutta, pp. 96-99 and Pl. II.
40. Pereira Jose (1987), 'The Evolution of the *Stūpa*: A Summary of Stylistic History' in B. M. Pande and B.D.Chattopadhyay (ed.) *Archaeology and History* (Essays in Memory of Shri A. Ghosh), II, Delhi, pp. 451-65.
41. No. Add 1643: folio 174 verso right panel; N.S. 135/CE 1015, Nepal.
42. Sarasi Kumar Saraswati (1975), p.7.
43. Circular medhi; Four-sided medhi; Hexagonal medhi; and Lotus-shaped medhi.
44. No. G. 9989 A; year 18 of the reign of Govindapāla — c. CE 1179-80, Eastern India.
45. Foucher Alfred (1900), *Etude sur l'Iconographie Bouddhique de l' Inde d'apres des documents nouveaux*, Paris: Ernest Leroux, Editeur.Pt. 1, Cat. I. 13, Pl. I.3.
46. Ibid., Pt. 1, Cat. II. 34, Pl. I.5.
47. Bandyopadhyay Sudipa (2007), 'Stūpa Motifs in Pāla Manuscript Paintings' in *Journal of Ancient Indian History* (ed.) Subid Chattopadhyay, Vol. XXII, Kolkata: University of Calcutta, pp. 11-14 & Plate I.

48. Bandyopadhyay Sudipa (2002), Fig. 31.
49. Ibid., Fig.45.
50. Bandyopadhyay Sudipa (2007), pp. 11-14 & Plate I.
51. Preserved in the British Library, London. For details, see Losty, Jeremiah P. (1989), pp.1-21.
52. Saraswati S.K. (1977), Pl. 241.

7

Two Indigenous Manuscripts of Assam:
A New Paradigm in the History of Traditional Knowledge in India

– *Anita Bagchi*

The modern breeds of the domestic horse are all descended from the wild horse that roamed in large herds in the steppes of central Asia and Europe.[1] Among the causes of destruction of *Harappan* culture, the theory of Aryan invasion or foreign invasion cannot be rejected. The general literature still reiterates the theory as we may refer to Basham. Among the scanty remains of the invaders there is clear evidence of the presence of the horse. The Indus cities fell to barbarians who triumphed not only through greater military powers, but also because they were equipped with better weapons and had learnt to make full use of the swift and terror-striking beast of the steppes[2] (i. e. the horse). The issue of the existence of horse in the *Harappan* sites is not beyond controversy. Different views have been offered by the scholars with regard to identification of the bone remains of horses and their stratigraphic existence.[3] But reference to horse in the Vedic literature is sufficient to make us believe that with the advent of the Aryans, a new phase began in Indian history though the continuity of earlier cultural tradition did not wither totally. In the hymns of the Rgveda, the horse is praised as the best strength givers, with wide jaws (R.V. 1.28.7. p. 17) and having the power to unbar the doors to wealth (RV, IX.64.3. p. 492-493).

It is already pointed out that the remains of horses are not sufficient to justify the use of horses by the *Harappan* people. Horse bones appeared only in the upper levels and hence cannot be assigned to the mature Indus phase.[4] Naturally, the study on horse may be started from the days of the *Rgveda* as their earliest literary composition is replete with different information not only of the horse but also of other living world around. Thus in an ancient country like India, her people had to make incessant effort for developing a knowledge system on different aspects of plant and animal life in order to meet up their needs in everyday life. The knowledge obtained through observation generally does not contradict experiments because experience is gathered through observation and through a process of trial and error. Empirical science, so to say traditional knowledge system thus flourished gradually and we may find its existence in the encyclopedic works like the *Arthasastra*, the *Agnipurana*, the *Brihat Samhita*, *Sukraniti* and others. Specific texts on horses and elephants are also available like the *Samhita* of *Salihotra*, the *Asvasastra* of Nakula or the *Hastyayurveda* of Palakapya and *Matanga Lila* of Nilakantha. Practically the texts mentioned above may be treated as the source book of all the later works on these animals. This is logical to hold that knowledge database remained stored in manuscripts for long and later these were published for the readers in edited books and mostly in translated form. In this context, it should be taken into consideration that the works of the authors bear their own individual entity though they deal with the same content. Variable information and pattern of composition attract reader's attention. The authors generally did remain concerned to their time and space. Naturally they could leave for their posterity the works of variant nature. The writer of the present article shall make an attempt here to deal with two such works on ethology ṣ one on horse and another on elephant which are the native products of Assam. The manuscripts were edited and published under the initiative of the Government of Assam.

Horse and elephant both the animals constituted the essential components of *Chaturanga Sena*. A text on horse lore known by the name *'Ghora Nidan'* deserves our attention as an instance of original text produced in Assam.[5] The author as well as the date of its composition is not definitely known. The original manuscript was handed over to T. C. Bhattacharjee by the *Kamrupa Anusandhan Samiti* through Pandit Hemchandra Goswamy. The original *Puthi* contains 40 leaves and written in old Assamese scripts. It was discovered from Mangaldai subdivision in the Western part of Assam. It was the main centre of horse trade in the past. A Guha has shown that unlike the trade with Bengal, Ahom trade with Tibet and Bhutan was favourable. The bulk of this Caravan trade was between the Ahom kingdom and Lhasa and was negotiated at a place in the foothill.[6] Thus the Western part of Assam particularly Mangaldai and Kamrup became the main centre of horse trade. According to Dr. Baishya, a traditional veterinary knowledge system developed at that particular area for treating the horses on the way when required.[7] A number of manuscripts containing the essential knowledge of native medical treatment of the horse have been traced in the locality. Bhattacharjee refers to two more *Puthi* on horse lore dissimilar in style and composition, namely *Ghorar Lokshana* and *Ghotoka Ratna*. There was only one manuscript in the custody of Srijuta Padmakanta Goswami of the Kulbil Satra in Kamrup which resembled exactly the text of the Ghora Nidan though with minor variations. He also makes mention of a number of copies of *Ghora Nidan* which differs a lot in style of composition. The traditional horse lores extant in that part of Assam may not be called purely scientific as such but it can easily be accepted as clear proof of development of an empirical knowledge system flourished through a process of exchange of ideas, concepts and over and above with the help of indigenous practice of herbal medicine. This science or better to designate as proto-science obviously grew out of its utility to the people who in some way or other were connected with the activities as mentioned above.

Bhattacharjee observes, 'the method, style and treatment of the subject are so peculiar that it can be recognized at a glance that it is not a translation from other Sanskrit treatises'.[8] Bhattacharjee takes this lore as Assam's native production as there is no mention of any spices or herbs which are rare in Assam. The *Puthi* is distinctly divided into two parts: the first part deals with classes, colour and character of the ponies and the other with diseases, its symptoms and curative medicines. It may be safely held that this handbook on horse lore reflects an individual and distinctive local character and is free from the influence of ancient Sanskrit treatises on equestrian science. The text as is evident from the contents deals with *Tatuk* (Bhutan pony) and the *Turki* i. e. *Turki* pony and typical indigenous terms and words have been profusely used in the text. Bhattacharjee also points out that nearly 50 technical words used in the 'Ghora Nidan' could not be deciphered; even Rai Sahib G. C. Barua, the well known the Ahom translator could hardly extend any help to the writers in deciphering the archaic terms which had been in use long before.

The first and the foremost task of a scholar interested in the study and rediscovery of traditional Indian knowledge system of early India is to get at the proper meaning and connotation of technical terms in such indigenous texts especially written in regional languages. This edited and translated version of the 'Ghora Nidan' with a glossary at the end facilitates the clear understanding of the content to the reader. Infact such a difficult task by a scholar opens a new chapter in the history of early scientific knowledge and its practice in a frontier kingdom like Assam. The first part of the text has delineated the characteristics of the horses belonging to two types namely the Bhutan pony and the Turki pony. These two are mentioned in the text as *Tatuk* and *Turuki* respectively, the males being known as *Tangon* and a female as *Taji*. There are instructions for testing the physical and mental fitness of the horse. For this the author (unknown) makes allusion to colour, shape of different parts of the body, skin, hair, whorl, natural marks along with few instructions about riding. The second part deals with the diseases, their symptoms and remedies. In this section as much as 109 names of diseases and their antidotes are prescribed.

In the second edition of the book, an additional glossary of diseases and of plant medicine has been furnished by D. Baishya who is an expert in zoological science. In this context, a few words about the *Asvasastram* of Nakula will not be out of context. It is a rare illustrated Sanskrit manuscript and was edited first in 1952 by S. Gopalan in three versions – Sanskrit, Tamil and English. The manuscript was in the possession of Sarasvati Mahal library of Tanjavur. It is generally held that Nakula, the fourth *Pandava* compiled the work on horse on the basis of Salihotra's original text. Gopalan states, 'this work on horses illustrates how ancient is our knowledge of horses and how, from time immemorial, it has been systematized and reduced to easy practical rules to be applied in harnessing them for the use of man'.[9]

The book is a compendium on the subject and contains coloured pictures of horses. On the other, the *Ghora Nidan* of Assam has a section on horse diseases and their herbal remedies. A list of disease and the names of the roots and herbs with their scientific names is given in the appendix by D. Baishya. This part practically makes the text unique in nature.

Now the writer of this article wants to draw the attention of the reader to another manuscript dealing with elephantology. The word *Hastisastra* may be translated into English as 'Elephantology'. The science deals with topics like genealogical, physical, mental and intellectual characteristics of elephants, techniques of tracing and capturing elephant from forests, nourishment for healthy growth and general upkeep, taming and training them for war and work and diagnosis and treatment of their diseases. It was seriously studied in India since very ancient times in great details and has a continuous written and oral tradition.[10]

There are two species of elephant, viz., African and Asian, their scientific names are *Loxodonta Africana* and *Elephas maximus* respectively.[11] It is obvious that the elephantologists of India in the ancient past must have studied and recorded their observations on the details of the Asian type. Among the animal remains excavated from the Indus site, the most popular animal reproduced on seals are various types of bulls and the next popular one on the seal is elephant figure. We get several references to elephant in ancient literature. The powerful and huge animal has got nice expression in the hymns of the *Rgveda*. One of such hymns is as follows:

'Mighty, with wondrous power and marvelously bright, self strong like mountains, ye assume your strength among the bright red flames' (RV., 1.64.7).[12]

The ancient Indian kings maintained huge armies in which foot soldiers and warriors riding on chariots, on horse backs and on elephants formed the four divisions, constituting the *Caturanga Sena*. Breeding, maintaining and training of elephants, studying their behaviour and treatments in ailments, therefore, automatically occupied a place of vital importance in military department for defense of any empire or kingdom. In the state building process elephants and horses constituted indispensable element and we find the mention of *danda*, i. e. coercive power among the seven elements of the state in Kautilya's Saptanga theory of state. Kautilya further adds that the victory of kings in battles depends mainly upon elephants, because elephants being of large physical frame are capable not only of destroying the arrayed army of an enemy, his fortifications and encampments, but also of undertaking works that are dangerous to life.

The qualitative classification of elephants done by Kautilya is fascinating. According to Kautilya, 'Elephants bred in countries, such as Kalinga, Anga, Karusa, and the East are the best; those of the *Dasharna* and western countries are of middle quality and those of *Saurastra* and *Panchajana* countries are of low quality. The might and energy of all can, however, be improved by suitable training'.[13] The forests in Eastern country probably is identical with the *Prachyavana* mentioned in the *Manasollasa* of Someshvara III. The extent of *Prachyavana* has been described in the following stanza:

> *Gangasagara-Himadri-Prayaganam chamadhyatah /*
> *Vanam prachyam=iti Proktam Lohita-bdhischa=paschime //*[14]

It means that the *Prachyavana* extended from *Gangasagara* in the south to the *Himadri* in the North and from *Prayaga* in the West to the *Lohitya* (lower course of the Brahmaputra) in the East which understandably indicates the Assam region.[15] So it is clear from the above evidences that the forest in Assam infested with elephants falls under the category of *Hastivana*. Shihabuddin Talis who accompanied Mir Jumla in his invasion of Assam during the middle of 17th century CE makes mention of the large number of elephants abounding in the hills and forests of Assam.[16] Elephant catching was a very old practice in Assam and the Assamese people bear traditional knowledge of high order in elephantology which deals with different aspects of the behaviour, characteristic features, health and diseases and also the medicines to combat with the ailments of the elephants. A very interesting treasure house of knowledge on elephants entitled *Hastividyarnava Sarasamgraha* may be mentioned here in this context. *Hastividyarnava Sarasamgraha* written in Tai-Ahom language is a comprehensive manual based on elephant ethology. It is exclusively an indigenous production of Assam. The illustrated manuscript copy of the *Hastividyarnava* was in the custody of Late Mahidhar Buragohain, the grandson of Purnananda Buragohain, the legendary Prime Minister of Assam (1783-1817). The late pundit H. C. Goswami recovered this manuscript as early as 1912 and the copy of the manuscript was handed over to the Department of Historical and Antiquarian Studies, Assam.[17] The original manuscript had 193 folios out of which 135 still remain. The folios are of the measurement of 58 ṅ 16 cm. the folios till 162 deal with the types of elephants and from 164 to the end with their ailment and treatment. From the colophon we come to know that it was composed in Saka 1656 i. e. 1734 CE under the order and instruction of the Ahom king Siva and his queen Ambika Devi[18] Sukumar Barkath composed the *Hastividyarnava.*[19] Dilbar and Dosai the two painters painted the pictures therein under the order of the King and Queen.[20] The total number of paintings is 170. Dr. S. K. Chatterjee comments, 'the coloured miniatures... show a very vigorous school of Hindu painting which flourished in the 18th century Assam ... the style is distinctive, and this pictorial art of Assam deserves a worthy place besides Rajasthani, Rajput, Kangra and Mogul Schools... Apart from their topical and historical value, these miniatures have an aesthetic charm which makes them a possession for ever, which lovers of art cannot ignore'.[21]

In *Hastividyarnava*, there are chapters like:

1. Different Types of Elephants,
2. The Tuskers: the mode of training,
3. Female Elephants: mode of the training,
4. Description of Elephant stable, measurement of ropes for elephants etc.,
5. Functions of Elephants delineated in the *Nitisara* of Kamandaka,
6. Varieties of elephants as described by Vyas,
7. Characteristics of different varieties,
8. Bad types,
9. Variant characteristics of elephants of different regions,
10. Technique of training of the newly caught elephants and the infants,
11. Measurement of body of the elephants according to age,
12. Treatment suggested for the elephants captured in aged stage,
13. Treatment of the newly caught elephant,
14. Medicine for ailing elephant,
15. Medicine for rutted elephant.

The text describes nearly about 500 herbal and faunal antidotes and most of the ingredients for preparing medicines are available in Assam. The illustrated *Gajasastrabhasaprabandha* of Maratha king Sarfoji Bhonsle was composed in 1820 CE. But the *Hastividyarnava* was composed in 1734 CE. So there is no doubt that the Assamese composition is a pioneering work in this discipline. With the illustration of the types, categories, colours, physics, mood, taming, training and application of medicines etc. the *Hastividyarnava* stands ahead than the illustrated manuscript of the *Gajasastrabhasaprabandha*. This is an outcome of the original thinking of king and the queen of the Ahom kingdom. The huge store house of knowledge in herbal medicine for the elephant as preserved in the *Hastividyarnava* reveals that Kamrup or Assam constitute the natural habitat of elephants and the study on elephant had become a principal area of investigation and in this task the royal as well as the common people were equally interested. Without the initiative as well as direct involvement of the people, the production of such an encyclopedic work was not possible. It required the total involvement of the kings, the pundits, the plant scientists, the physicians and over and above the sincere observation and efforts of the common folk and the riders who were well acquainted with the nature and the natural habitat of the elephants.[22]

Notes and References:

1. Chakravarty, R. S., ṢRigvedic India, A Centre of Domestication of the Horse in Y. N. Nene (ed.) *Glimpses of the Agricultural Heritage of India*, Asian Agri-History Foundation Secunderebad, 2007, pp. 178-184. The article was originally published in the Annals of the Bhandarkar Oriental Research Institute, Pune, Vol. LVI, pp. 129-139.
2. Basham, A. L., *The Wonder That Was India*, 3rd Revised Edition, Rupa & Co., New Delhhi, 1999, p. 27.
3. Singh, U., *A History of Ancient and Early Medieval India*, Pearson Education, New Delhi, 2009, p. 157.
4. Sahu, B. P., *From Hunters to Breeders* (Faunal Background of Early India) Anamika Prakashan, Delhi, 1988, p. 159.
5. Bhattacharjee, T. C., (ed.) *Ghora Nidan*, This is a Handbook on the disease of the horse and their remedies. It was first edited by late T. C. Bhattacharjee of Tezpur in 1932. It was published under the order of the Government of Assam. The latest edition of the Ghora Nidan has been published by society

for appropriate Technology, Guwahati with a preface containing the scientific analysis of diseases and medicinal plants by Dr. D. Baishya in 2006.

6. Guha, A., ŞThe Medieval Economy of Assam¿ in T. Ray Chaudhuri and I. Habib (ed.) *The Cambridge Economic History of India*, Vol. I (c. 1200-1750), Orient Longman, Delhi, 1984, p. 492.
7. *Op. cit.* Bhattacharjee, T. C., Preface to the Second Edition by D. Baishya.
8. *Ibid.*
9. Gopalan, S., Asvasastram, Sarasvati Mahal Library, Thanjavur, 2001 (2nd ed.), p. vi.
10. Sadhale, N. and Nene, Y. L., ŞOn Elephants in Manasollasa ş 1: Characteristics, Habitat, Methods of Capturing and Training¿ in Y. L. Nene (ed.) *Glimpses of the Agricultural Heritage of India*, Asian Agri History Foundation, Secunderabad, 2007, p. 215.
11. *The Asian Elephant*, 2001, Himalayan Nature and Adventure Foundation, Siliguri and Jalpaiguri Science and Nature Club, p. 4.
12. Griffith, R. T. H., *The Hymns of the Rgveda*, Motilal Banarsidass Publishers Pvt. Ltd., Delhi, 1991, p. 43.
13. Shamastry, R., *Kautilya's Arthasastra*, Mysore Printing and Publishing House, Mysore, 1961, p. 49.
14. Sircar, D. C., The Elephant forests of Ancient India in D. C. Sircar, (ed.) *The Bhakti Cult and Ancient Indian Geography*, University of Calcutta, 1970, pp. 160-172.
15. Bagchi, A., Paintings as source of Science in the Past: Understanding Indian Elephants in *Karatoya: NBU Journal of History*, Vol. II, 2008, pp. 24-35.
16. Choudhury, P. C. (ed.) *Hastividyarnava Sarasamgraha*, Publication Board Assam, Gauhati, 1975, p. v.
17. *Ibid*, p. iv.
18. *Ibid*, pp. 198-202.
19. *Ibid*, p. 202.
20. *Ibid.*
21. *Ibid*, p. vii.
22. *Op. cit.*, Bagchi, A., pp. 29-30.

8

Assam Buranji Manuscript No. 43 and Fortifications of Guwahati under Ahom Rule

– *Paromita Das*

The state of Assam possesses a rich store of historical literature of the Ahom period in the form of chronicles known as *Buranji*. A number of them have been edited and published by different scholars like S.K. Bhuyan, G.C. Barua and others, but the majority of them are yet to be published. This paper proposes to examine the importance of one such *Assam Buranji* preserved in the Department of Historical and Antiquarian Studies, Panbazar, Guwahati. In his introduction to the *Tungkhungia Buranji* S.K.Bhuyan writes:

> The Buranjis were to the Assamese what the *Bakhars* were to the Mahrattas, the *Tawarikhis* to the Moghuls and the Persians, the *Yazawins* or *Rajawins* to the Burmese and the *P'ongsawadans* to the Siamese. The term *Buranji,* originally a word of Ahom or Shan origin has been naturalized in assamese, being applied to all chronicles or histories. The Ahoms maintained regular chronicles of their ruleṀcompiled by duly appointed officers who were grantyed free access to the deliberations of the court and the archives of the state. They were also compiled by private scholars with the help of other existing chronicles and materials collected by them. The Buranjis are a direct product of the universal custom in vogue among the Tai race, the Shans, the Burmans, the Siamese and the Chinese of reducing all important things to writing, and they are profuse and varied. Assamese

> historical literature is the legacy which the people of the Brahmaputra Valley have received from their contact with the Ahom invaders and settlers. The Buranjis were first compiled in the Ahom language and later on in Assamese as well; The Buranjis are valuable studies in as much as they have conserved the customs, the taits, the hopes and aspirations of the people. (Bhuyan: 1990:xv).

Manuscript No. 43 was recovered from the house of Upendra Chandra Lekharu of North Guwahati. It is an Assamese manuscript composed on the bark of the aloe tree that is locally known as *sanchipat puthi*. A major part of the manuscript is difficult to decipher due to weathering and fading of the ink used. A few leaves are also in danger of falling apart. Although the manuscript bears no title as such, keeping in view its contents, it is recorded as *Asamar Rajnoitik Bhugol* in the manuscript register. The Department also has a transcription of a few pages of the manuscript (no. 311), which contains a description of the fortifications of Guwahati during the time of the Ahom-Mughal conflict in the 17th century. As the manuscript records the name of Mansur Khan, erstwhile *Thanedar* of Rangamati who occupied Guwahti in 1679 C.E. it is reasonable to assume that it was composed in the last two decades of the seventeenth century C.E. The importance of the manuscript lies in the fact that it gives a detailed account of the fortifications of Guwahati erected prior to the Battle of Saraighat in 1671.

The evidence of epigraphs and the existence of moats and ramparts scattered around the modern city testify to the fact that the city of Guwahati was a theatre of war from the early 13th century C.E. till the end of the 17th century C.E. During this period it witnessed a series of invasions. Guwahati witnessed a long drawn conflict for its occupation by the Muslim rulers from the west, and local and regional ruling houses. First the Turko-Afghan Sultans of Bengal, and later the Mughals attempted to occupy the city. During the interlude it was a part of the Koch Hajo kingdom of Raghudeva.

The Ahom *Buranjis* do not mention any Muslim invasion of Assam prior to 1527. (Barua: 1988: 175) .The division of the powerful Koch kingdom in 1581 following the rebellion of Raghudev, son of Chilarai paved the way for its subsequent annexation by the Ahoms and the

Mughals. The annexation of Koch Hajo by the Mughals in the reign of Siu-Seng-Pha (1603-1641C.E.) led to a series of conflicts between the Ahom and the Mughals during which time the modern city of Guwahati occupied a position of importance. After the death of Naranarayana, in 1584 C.E., problems arose between the two Koch states of Koch Hajo and Koch Behar. Raghudev refused to acknowledge the suzerainty of Lakshmi Narayana, (the son of Naranarayana) and struck coins in his own name (Gait: 1963: 64). Lakshmi Narayana was not strong enough to reduce Raghudev to submission. So he encouraged the latter's son Parikshit, to rebel against his father. The rebellion failed. Parikshit was imprisoned, but succeeded in escaping to the court of Koch Behar where he was cordially received. When his father died in 1603 C.E. he returned to his own kingdom. Parikshit established his capital in North Guwahati and built a palace near the Asvakranta hill (Gait: 1963: 65). Like his father, Parikshit now refused to acknowledge the supremacy of Lakshmi Narayana, and worsted him in battle. Both kings now sought Ahom help, and in 1605 C.E. Parikshit gave his daughter Mangal Dahi to the Ahom monarch Siu-Seng-Pha. Earlier in 1596 C.E. Lakshmi Narayana had declared himself a vassal of the Mughal Empire. The next year, i.e. in 1597C.E. he gave a daughter in marriage to Raja Man Singh, the Mughal Governor of Bengal. Man Singh sent troops to Koch Behar to protect his father-in-law. As the conflict between the two Koch states continued, Lakshmi Narayana went in person to Dacca and begged the Nawab for help. When the latter's troops invaded Koch Hajo Parikshit requested Ahom aid. The Koch ruler however could not agree to the conditions laid down by the Ahoms. He battled on alone, ultimately surrendered and was taken to Dacca. The Mughal Emperor Jehangir, according to local accounts agreed to restore him to his throne in return for four lakhs of rupees. On the way back home, he fell ill and died. In 1613C.E. his lands as far as the Barnadi were annexed to the Mughal Empire. Parikshit's brother Bali Narayana was given asylum in the Ahom kingdom. (Gait: 1963: 66ff) This resulted in the invasion of the Ahom kingdom by the Mughals.

The Ahom chronicles or *Buranjis*, while describing this conflict, incidentally makes numerous references to the city of Guwahati. This city and its surrounding area became the central arena in the prolonged war between the Ahoms and the Mughals. We learn from the *Buranjis* that in the period between 1615C.E. and 1682C.E. the city was alternately occupied by the Ahoms and the Mughals several times, in keeping with their changing fortunes in war. The conflict commenced with the invasion of Assam in 1615C.E. Saiad Abu Bakr led the Mughal troops. The Ahoms were successful in repelling the invaders. They installed Bali Narayana (renamed as Dharma Narayana) as the tributary Raja of Darrang in 1616C.E. (Gait: 1963: 68). The following year the Ahom king Siu-Seng-Pha attacked and occupied Pandu (in Guwahati) and fortified it. He however failed to occupy Kamrup (a district, as opposed to the old state of Kamarupa) proper. Although the Ahoms suffered a setback their general Langi Panisiya had distinguished himself in battle. So he was rewarded with the newly created post of *Bar Phukan* or 'governor' of the conquered provinces west of Kaliabor. His headquarters were established at Guwahati. The Rajas of Darrang were also required to take his counsel before taking action on important matters.

In May 1619 C.E. the hill chiefs of South Kamrup rebelled against the Mughals. The Ahoms and the Raja of Darrang aided them. In September, the Ahoms took the fort of Ranihat (Gait: 1963: 69). The war continued with varying fortunes. By 1637 C.E. the Mughals had consolidated their rule in Kamrup. A financial settlement was effected and Mir Nurullah was appointed *Thanedar,* with headquarters at Guwahati. In 1638 October, the Mughals invaded Upper Assam, were repulsed, and retreated to Guwahati. In February 1639 C.E., a treaty was concluded between the Ahoms and the Mughals. It bought peace for nearly thirty years. According to the terms of this Treaty of Asurar Ali, signed in February, the Barnadi on the North Bank (of the Brahmaputra River) and the Asurar Ali on the South Bank were recognized as the boundaries of the territories of the Mughals and those of the Ahoms in Assam (Barpujari: 1992: 164). Thus Guwahati continued to be under Mughal occupation. Trade and commercial intercourse was established between the Ahoms and the Mughals. Allah Yar Khan was the Mughal *Faujdar* (military governor) of Kamrup. The Mughals shifted their headquarters to Guwahati, then an important town on the north bank of the Brahmaputra (Barpujari: 1992: 165).

The conflict was renewed during the reign of Siu-Tam-La (1648-1663C.E.) and Guwahati once again occupied center stage in this political upheaval. In 1657C.E. the Mughal Emperor Shah Jehan fell ill and a war of succession broke out among his four sons. In the resulting turmoil when the Mughal *Thanedar* of Guwahati fled, Pran Narayana, the Raja of Koch Behar seized Goalpara, northern Kamrup as well as Hajo. Meanwhile, the Ahoms who had advanced with a huge army arrived at Guwahati. As the Mughals had already abandoned the town they occupied it along with Pandu and Srighat. They also defeated Pran Narayana and occupied the Koch territories. The Ahoms became masters of the entire Brahmaputra valley (Barpujari:1992:169).

When Aurangzeb became the Mughal Emperor of Delhi, he dispatched Mir Jumla, the *Subedar* of Bengal, to recover the Mughal possessions in Assam. In 1661C.E. he recovered Koch Behar and in the following year invaded Assam proper. On 4th February, 1662 C.E. Srighat fell, and the Mughals once again occupied Guwahati. Here, a number of chiefs, including the Raja of Darrang, submitted to Mir Jumla. After a few days halt at Guwahati, Mir Jumla started on his march to Garhgaon, the capital of the Ahoms. It was occupied on 17th March 1662 C.E. following the flight of the Ahom king and his army. In January 1663 C.E. peace was concluded. Rashid Khan was installed as the *Faujdar* of Guwahati. The Mughals established a form of military rule in Assam by appointing *faujdars* and *thanedars*. (Barpujari: 1992:169-178).

During the time of Siu-Pung-Mung (1663-1670C.E.) the conflict was renewed as the Ahoms refused to comply with the terms of the peace treaty. From Guwahati, Firuz Khan (who had succeeded Rashid Khan as *faujdar*) sent a strongly worded letter to the Ahom king demanding payment of outstanding dues. The Ahoms, who were preparing for an offensive against the Mughals, made this (i.e. the letter) a *casus belli*. In 1667C.E. an army was dispatched under Lachit Bar Phukan to recover Guwahati. He succeeded in taking the Mughal outposts at Kajali and Bansbari. Next to fall was the fort of Itakhuli, on the night of 4th November, 1667 C.E. Shortly afterwards the Mughal defenders of Guwahati fled. In the middle of November the Ahoms occupied the city. After the arrival of reinforcements the Mughals renewed the offensive. However, the naval supremacy of the Ahoms resulted in their ultimately winning the war. This event is recorded in three Sanskrit inscriptions, one, on a stone pillar at Fatasil in Guwahati, and two in North Guwahati. An old canon recovered from Silghat bears an inscription in Sanskrit that also records the defeat of the Muhammedans in battle in 1558 Saka (1667 C.E.) by

Chakradhvaj Singha, as Siu-Pung-Mung was also known. Another old canon at Dikom bears a similar inscription referring to a victory in the following year. This canon also bears an inscription in Persian stating Ṣit was placed in charge of Saiad Ahmed Al Hussain for the purpose of conquering Assam in 1074 *Hijri* (1663 C.E.). (Gait: 1963: 158). Thus the account of the Ahom *Buranjis* is borne out by epigraphic evidence.

Due to its topography Guwahati was found eminently suited for defensive warfare. Montgomery Martin in his description of the city in the 19th century C.E. writes, "Goahawtee occupies an extent of hilly country on both banks of the great stream; the hills on each side form a specious amphitheatre which have been equally well fortified by nature and art." (Martin: 1976: 630) The Ahoms, who occupied Guwahati, made it the headquarters of their Governor styled Bar Phukan. As it functioned as the seat of the Ahom Viceroy it also enjoyed political importance, for this officer conducted and maintained the relations with Bengal in the west as well as with the neighbouring chieftains in the area under his jurisdiction. Thus, Guwahati, due to its strategic location, was both a military base and an administrative headquarters. The river Brahmaputra that divided the ancient settlement into two parts viz. north and south was the lifeline of the city. It facilitated transportation of men and material during times of peace and war.

The *Buranjis* give us many details about Guwahati during this period of conflict, as well as the defensive measures taken after the war. Thus we learn that the fort of Itakhuli was near Sukreśvar Temple while one of the gateways to Itakhuli fort was at Latasil. The eastern gateway was at Jaiduar, near modern Chandmari. Guwahati was thereafter made the headquarters of the Bar Phukan in the inevitable struggle ahead, with the Mughals. During the period of Ahom -Mughal conflict in the 17th century C.E. the Ahom general Lachit Bar Phukan aptly remarked: "We could fight as if we were sitting in our own homes." (Bhuyan: 1960: 93) Guwahati was chosen as the war base due to its strategic location.

To avenge the defeat of Firuz Khan, Aurangzeb sent Raja Ram Singha at the head of an imperial army to Assam. It reached Rangamati on February 1669 C.E., and shortly afterwards, Hajo. The Mughals failed to take Saraighat and proceeded towards Darrang. The war continued with changing fortunes until a truce was declared just before the death of the Ahom king. The war was renewed during the reign of his successor

Siun-Yet-Pha (1670-1673C.E.). The defeat of the Mughals in the Battle of Saraighat in 1671C.E. sealed their fate.

The Ahoms had occupied Guwahati in 1667 C.E. Two inscriptions on the Kanai Barasi Bowa Rock state that the Ahoms after killing Syed Sana and Syed Piroz in 1667 C.E. had erected ramparts (*Garh*). (Neog: 1974: 6). The *Kamrupar Buranji* also records that ramparts were erected on both banks of the Brahmaputra (Bhuyan: 1987: 91) prior to the invasion of the Mughals under Ram Singh. However, details of these ramparts are found only in the manuscript under discussion. Thus it describes how *garhs* or defensive ramparts protected the gaps between the passes. As for instance it states that a rampart was constructed from the end of Asuror Ali which measured 2215 *beuns*, a *beun* being the distance between two outstretched arms of an adult male, i.e. about seven and a half feet. At a distance of every two *beuns* three soldiers were posted, numbering a total of 3322. Another *garh* was constructed from Itakhuli where the Bar Phukan had his headquarters. The manuscript states that from Bar Phukan's *ghat* (landing stage) up to Udmarir Barsil was the Simali Garh which measured 900 *beuns*, and a soldier was posted one *beun* apart, numbering a total of 900 soldiers. The next line is undecipherable, but from there up to the middle of an unspecified place there was a rampart measuring 400 *beuns*, and two soldiers were posted every *beun* numbering a total of 800 soldiers in all. From there up to Juria, the rampart measured 500 *beuns* and thence to Sarai (ghat) 400 *beuns*. Apparently there was a second line of defense on the riverside, for the next line records the construction of another rampart from Juria to Sarai that was 530 *beuns*. From Sarai, up to the (*kekuri*) bend in the river (Brahmaputra) the rampart measured 180 *beuns* and 3 soldiers were stationed at every *beun* numbering 420 in total. Elsewhere in the text it is recorded that there was a sand rampart measuring 600 *beuns* from Udmari and another up to Juria measuring 700 *beuns*. The record gives further details of the earthen rampart on the north bank of the river from the point opposite Sarai up to Lathiya Parbat, which measured 220 beuns, and upon which a total of 550 men were stationed, the Lathiya Parbat itself measured 333 *beun* and 450 men were posted there. From thence to Lorhagarh it was 920, from thence to Ghorabandhaloi 386, to Sat Paghor 1420, thence to Satalua, 680, to Barkhana 320 and from there to Saloni 240. All measurements are given in *beuns*.

The 17th century thus witnessed the construction of defensive ramparts on an extensive scale, which encircled the city on both banks as stated in verse 161 of the *Kamrupar Buranji* and also in the *Assam Buranji*. (Bhuyan:1987:92;Bhuyan:1960: 92-94) Some of these ramparts survive to this day. Inscriptions on stone and rock discovered in the city mark the entry points called *duars,* during this period. They were five such *duars* or *chowkis* on either side of the Brahmaputra as corroborated by contemporary literature of the time. The western entrance on the South Bank, called *Duar Garila*, was at the southern foot of the Nilachala Hill. The eastern entrance called *Jai Duar* was located near Chandmari. The northern entrance was through the *Pani Duar* at Latasil. It was accessible by the river. Another entry point near the river was at Pandu, to the west of the Nilachala Hill. The southern entrance to the city called *Dharam Duar* was at Fatasil Ambari. On the North Bank of the river the town "occupies the space within the following passes through the fortified hill, viz. - *Kanaibarasibowa, Sillar Chowki, Sindurighopa, Pat Duar* and *Pani Chowki* or *Korai Chowki.*" (Martin: 1976: 631) Thus, Guwahati was a fortified city in the medieval period.

Besides the construction of earthen ramparts which closed the gaps between the hills surrounding Guwahati, barrages and sand ramparts were also constructed along the river bank, as for instance the Shahburuz and the Rangaliburuz (barrages were called *buruz*) on the north and south bank of the river respectively, near the area of the modern Saraighat bridge, right up to Lankeswar and Sat Mile. A list of what appears to be supplies needed for the construction of a sand rampart are also recorded, like *choti-khuta, sarua choti* measuring around 12 feet (*baro hat*) in length and 12 fingers ((*baro anguli*) in breadth and around 13 feet of *berhe* (?) and 6 fistful (*soi muthiya*) in circumference *choti* and numbering 1000 and 2000 poles were also necessary. Moreover, 1320 *Sampator Sur* (?), (probably the leaves of the Surot plant which caused whoever touched it to itch and scratch) It is also recorded that when Mansur Khan had come (to reoccupy Guwahati in 1769 C.E.) to construct a barrage (*paniguj garh*) the requirement had been 1280 *ora soukha*. Leaf/page number 17 of the manuscript states that ramparts should be constructed between two hills to close the gap and at the corner of each there should be a *thana* or chowki: '*Tar kakhate kariba thana*'

The next two pages deal with locations of other fortifications and places: 'To the north is the river (Brahmaputra?). Upstream of Manaha is Rouroua, at a distance of two days journey (presumably on foot or by boat?). Upstream from Rouroua, is Borholiya (6 days), further upstream is Sesa, reached in one afternoon, Dhorajan is reached in one and a half days *(der poror bat)*, Barnadi in *chari daror bat,* Mangaldoi in *derdinor bat,* Dhansiriya in a day and Rota in two days'. Similarly, distances are given in similar terms, to Kalahi, Bitta, Gorhal, Tandaruwa, Dibru, Mitani, Kapili, Hanrhiya, Diju, Boko, Dilinga, Jaipur, Khaliha, etc. We find interesting names of villages like Baukakota, Nagaon, Ratanpur, Bamunigaon, Saruratanpur, Barratanpur, Chaigaon, Dhaniyagaon, Khaseriya, etc.

The text also refers to different people, presumably *paiks* or servitors like *Kapur-dhowa,* (washermen) *Baman doloi,* (Brahman priest) *Nangata Raja,* (Naked king?) etc. Names of localities on the north and south banks of the Kalang river, references to Mirigaon, Kacharigaon, locations of different *duars* or passes are also recorded.

The foregoing discussion adequately reveals that the said manuscript contains a wealth of information on a variety of subjects and is a valuable source of historical geography of Assam in the last quarter of the eighteenth century. At present the manuscript contains 20 leaves, i.e. 40 sides. The last leaf has the number 28 B written on it in ink of a different colour. So probably the manuscript may have originally been of 56 sides. Microfilming and preservation of the manuscript is the need of the hour to stop its further disintegration.

Notes and References:

1. Bhuyan, S.K., trans & ed., *Tungkhungia Buranji,* 1990, 3rd Edition, (1933) published by Department of Historical and Antiquarinan Studies in Assam, Guwahati.
2. Barua, K.L., *Early History of Kamarupa,* 1988, 3rd Edition, (1933) published by Lawyer's Book Stall, Guwahati, Assam.
3. Gait, E.A., *A History of Assam,* 1963, 3rd Revised Edition (1905) published by Thacker Spink & Co. P. Ltd, Calcutta.
4. Barpujari, H.K., ed., *The Comprehensive History of Assam, Volume II,* 1992, Publication Board Assam, Guwahati.

5. Bhuyan, S.K. ed., *Assam Buranji*, Guwahati, 1960, 2nd Edition, published by Department of Historical and Antiquarinan Studies in Assam, Guwahati.
6. Martin, M. *The History Antiquities Topography and Statistics of Eastern India, Vol. V*, 1976 1st Indian Reprint, New Delhi.
7. Neog, M. ed, *Praschya Sasanavali,* (Texts) 1974, Publication Board of Assam Guwahati.
8. Bhuyan, S.K. ed, *Kamrupar Buranji,* 1987, 3rd edition, (1958), Department of Historical and Antiquarian Studies, Guwahati.

9

Manuscript Painting Tradition in Assam: A Concise Overview

– *Raj Kumar Mazinder*

In Assam, the art of painting has been developed around the culture of illustrating manuscript in line and colour. In other words painting as an art form is unique, valuable treasure of cultural heritage of Assam. Manuscript is simply hand written collection of both text and image for number of readers or viewers. Till late part of nineteenth century in Assam and before launching printing technology and printed book by Missionary people from western origin, manuscript book had great role as spreading, flourishing and also preserving wisdom and knowledge.

In the preface note on Assamese manuscripts S.K. Bhuyan wrote radically as, 'From time immemorial the ancient kingdom of *Kamrupa* or Assam has been swept by a wave of Hindu civilization which has maintained its cultural homogeneity with the rest of India. Monarchs have resigned here whose exploits and achievements have been recorded in the Hindu epics and *Puranas*. Physically isolated, Assam was not outside the cultural hegemony of Aryyavarta. One vast means of conservation and transmitting Hindu civilization and culture was through *puthis* or manuscripts, elucidated by the verbal comments and explanations of the learned.'[1]

It had no evidence of writing book on art in particular till twentieth century, though some important rhetorical word has been found in numerous old books of Assamese epic, poetry, '*Charit puthi*'/biography to signify various skill and aesthetics of art or eminent personality. In the context, the book entitled 'Descriptive Catalogue of Assamese Manuscripts, by Pandit Hemchandra Goswami would be mentioned as earliest, which was published by Calcutta University in 1930. 'According to Dr. Naren Kalita, the effort of Pandit Goswami fructified in the formation of a repository with a few illustrated transcripts in the library of Kamrup Anusandhana Samiti.'[2]

That period few number of people as Jyotiprasad Agarwalla, Sarbeswar Kataki, Rajmohan Nath was a few art loving connoisseurs in Assamese society. Sarbeswar Kataki, a renowned scholar and archaeologist, wrote an article, in the Assamese monthly, *'Awahana'*, in its second year of publication (Vol. IV, p. 385-388) accompanied by 6 monochrome and 4 multi-coloured paintings from the manuscript titled *'Anadipatan'*, (Pl.9.1 & Pl.9.2) in order to draw the attention of the people and the scholars to

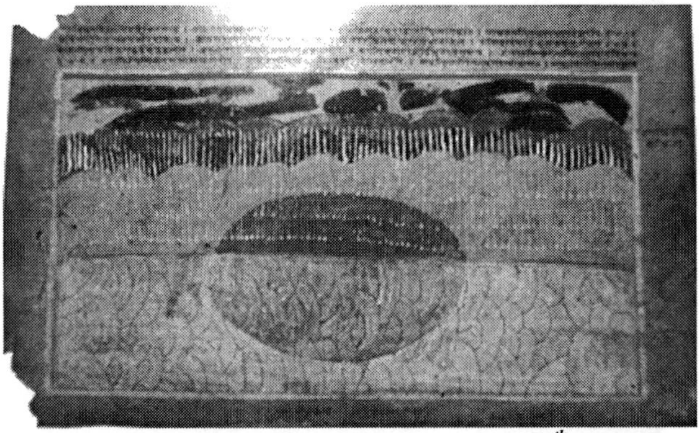

Pl.9.1: Anadi-patana *manuscript, mid-18th century*

Pl.9.2: Anadi-patana, *Kuji Xara, Nagaon, mid-18th century*

the rich heritage with a long tradition of about three hundred years of artistic activity.[3]

'The publication of the *Chitra Bhagavata* (Pl.9.3) with paintings from the *Bhagavata-purana*, Book X (*Adya* portion) in 1949 was an epoch-making event. It was for the painstaking effort of Sahityarartna Harinarayan Dutta Baruah, a celebrated devotee of Srimanta Sankardeva's neo-Vaishnavism, that the original illustrated treatise in the name of *Adi Dasham*' of *Bali Xatra* in Nagaon got published.'[4] And for the first time the people of Assam came to know about a rich tradition of artistic activities around the culture of painting. The *Chitra Bhagavata* is also significant for the scholarly introduction ever written in Assamese language on the growth and development of painting tradition in India. It was, in fact, a single man's effort, a challenging task to publish an illustrated book with large number of monochrome and 117 multi-coloured paintings despite the limitation of print media and constraint of fund.

Pl.9.3: Bhagavata-purana (Adi-dasama) *popularly known as* Chitr Bhagavata, *Late 17th century*

Afterwards great scholars as Maheswar Neog, Kapila Vatsayan, Rajata Nanda Dasgupta, Nilmani Phookan, Satyendra Nath Sarmah, Jugal Das, Birendranath Datta, Naren Kalita, Narayan Das, Rabin Deb Choudhury, Samiran Baruah, Kakoli Barkakoti immense input, detail and analytical study on the topic has enriched further in particular. Worth to mention that, the book entitled 'Descriptive Catalogue of Assamese Manuscript', based on the collection of Krishnakanta Handiqui Library of old manuscript books of Assam has been published by Gauhati University in 1999 which was edited by Dr. Satyendra Nath Sarmah.

In the present time, a rare scholar of Assamese language, literature, enduring devotee of neo-vaishnavite culture and former professor of

Anundoram Dhekial Phukan College, Nagaon Dr. Naren Kalita, with his deeper study, scholastic thinking and analysis on old manuscript painting and art tradition, raise into academic vibes as well as in a higher perspective of glorious heritage of India. Associated with Srimanta Sankaradeva Kalakshetra in Guwahati since its inception this great personage has been not only collected lots of old books and but also working in various ways as research, conservation and also preservation and write several books in the context. As huge attainment of his life, two books are '*Axomor Puthchitra*' in Assamese language (Publication Board, Assam, 1996) and another 'An Alphabetical Index of Illustrated Manuscript of Assam' (Published by Indira Gandhi National Centre for Arts, New Delhi, 2009). In various perspectives of erudite study and research on old manuscript books of Assam and related art discourses, these two books has certainly regarded as a milestone in course of time and textual resource.

In the next of title page of Dr. Kalita's book '*Axomor Puthichitra*' has been remembered and inevitably dedicate to those unknown, anonymous artists- 'who was he, what's his name, that *Khanikar*/creator of '*Chitra-Bhagavata*' manuscript and similar unidentified artists- *Khanikar* clan and namely as *Khankari* fragrance has been known to all: some of their name as Dilbor- Dosai, Bishnuram- Purnakam, Sashadhar Ata, Durga Panchanan and Ghanashyam Khargaria Phukan, in remembrance to those artists'.[5] He not only inscribes identity of those unknown, anonymous artists and their creation of manuscript, but also discussing comprehensively inner aesthetical juice and values along with study of text and feeling of those artists. To discuss about art in Assamese language, required art terminology or meaningful simile words are rather inadequate in numbers. In this aspect Dr. Kalita engages himself quite sincerely to look into authentic word from original Sanskrit text, English glossary and also various oral languages; and use those words in both powerful command and perfection.

The contribution of Assam in various art practices since ancient period has been known from old Sanskrit text and copper plates of local kings. Story of political goodwill and cultural co-operation between Gupta empire of *Pataliputra* and old royal king of *Kamrup*a had mentioned in various texts of history in India. '*Dau Parvatia*' ruins of Tezpur and the impression or influence of Gupta period would be certainly narrating in detail that coloristic history of cultural connectivity.

In the circumstances, three main artist-clans have been mentioned in '*Nagnajit*', an oldest text of art discourses. Among them, one is *Prahalad* and other two namely *Biswakorma* and *Nagnajit* respectively. According to old stories, *Banasur* was from that *Prahalad* clan. As looking into stories of *Sonitpur* and *Banasur*, Usha and *Chitalekha*, that *Prahalad* clan can be well connected with ancient Eastern India. *Chitralekha,* an expert of virtuosity in painting-dance-music, had done portrait-drawing in India for the first time. It must be an enduring tradition of various art practices for developing such a talent at the reign of *Banasur.*

In the text of *Harshacharit* several gift items had been mentioned as sending to Kaunoj's Emperor *Harshavardhana* by *Bhaskarvarman* royal king of *Kamrupa* during seventh century. Some of items were manuscript books, art brushes, colour vessels, picture and blank art board. Evidence of decorated royal palaces during later kings of *Bhaskarvarman* has been mentioned in the excavated land endowment plates of that time.

During sixteenth and seventieth century Assam, *Srimanta Sankaradeva* launched a vigorous movement against numerous idol worship and awful belief/custom with his vernacular literature based on *Vaisnavite* text and preaching. He was alone responsible for the great bulk of literary output of his time. He translated many chapters of the *Bhagavata-purana* into old Assamese verses, wrote several Kavyas, composed six dramas and inaugurated new style of dramatic art, composed many devotional songs and the most celebrated work, the *Kirtana*, besides *a kanda* of the *Ramayana* and Sanskrit compendium, the *Bhakti-Ratnakara*, on *bhakti*. The culture of vernacular literature and Neo-Vaisnavite preaching was not only creating enthusiasm among common folk and learned people but also bring the entire people under one umbrella.

The art of painting got a new life in the hands of the extremely skilled artist of this era, Srimanta Sankardeva. "He drew the *pat* (pictures) of seven *Baikunthas*/ heavens for the performance of *Chinha Yatra Bhaona* (a folk theatrical performance) himself. Apart from these, the exquisitely painted '*Brindavani Bastra*' (a kind of cloth) gifted by Srimanta Sankardeva to the king of Koch Bihar, Naranarayana, stands as a clear testimony to the excellence attained by this form during Sankardeva era."[6]

The foundation and proliferation of the religious organisation called *Xatra* as a central institution for dissemination of religious morals among the people was a great boost for the promotion of literary activities and art. The 17th and 18th centuries were most active not only for the proliferation of different *xatras* in the entire warp and the weft of the Brahmaputra valley but also for the development of art and culture in the society. The emergence of a regional art form of painting can be attributed to the culture of manuscript copying in the *xatra* circles. Different *Xatras* patronized and supported the penmanship of craftsmen, called the *Khanikaras* under their wings. These craftsmen were involved various activities of *Xatra* as traditional carving as primarily associated with woodcrafts, viz, the carving of the lion-seat called *Simhasana* for enshrining the holy book, associating them with traditional theatre referred as *Bhaona* in mask-making, make-up men related imperative job. Their familiarities with colour and form of traditional theatre inspired them to create parallel pictorial forms in line and colour on the surface of the picture space left vacant by the scribe in the folios of manuscripts.

In the context, the *Sachiitra Puthis* (books having pictorial illustrations) which have been in various parts of Assam also proves the artistic talent of this land. Those pictorial illustrations were mainly found on *Sanchi* pat (i.e., the bark of *Sanchi* tree specially prepared for writing purpose) *tulapat* or *tula*-leaf and muga clothes. But due to frequent calamities occurring in Assam and inadequate techniques of preservation, a large number of manuscripts with valuable have become extinct. The Putichtras or painted manuscripts that have been rescued till now are- *Chira Bhagavata, (Dakham Skandha), Mahabharata, Ramayana, Kirtanghokha, Adi Dakham, Bhakti Ratnawali, Kumar Haran, Lava-Kusha Yudha, Darrang- Rajbonshawali, Hangkhasur Badh, Geet- Govinda, Kalki Purana, Ananda Lahari, Hasti Vidyanava, Dharma Puran, Ajamil Upakhyan, Ahom-Jyotish, Banamalidevar Charita, Matsya Charita* and *Shamudra Manthan*. Among these, *Namghosa* and *Ahom Jyotish* are inscribed on *muga* clothes and the others are inscribed on *Sanchi* leaves. Although majority of the pictorial manuscripts are related to religion, yet few of them are secular too.

Thus illustrated manuscripts of Assam has been originated from the *Xatras,* the pictorial style inaugurated by the *Khanikars* of the *Xatras* may be designated as *Xatria.* As the within periphery of Xatra the *Xatria* style of manuscript painting evolved and develop in own formal ideal and motifs, but later period the *Xatria* style became more mature, enrich by exotic pictorial elements in connecting each other with Royal *Ahom* court manuscript painting style of 18th century which was influenced by the *Mughal* principles of pictorial art. Among the collected manuscripts with illustration till now, *'Adi Dasham'* of *Bali Xatra*, Nagaon has been described by the scholars as earliest dated manuscripts of the end of 17th century possibly. Printed version of this manuscript is known as *'Chitra-Bhagavata'*.

Stylistic Variety of Painted Manuscripts in Assam

In the medieval times, basically in royal families and in the Xatras, the art of painting was widely practiced. In due course of time, the pictorial manuscripts in the two respective places acquired two different styles. Dr. Suniti Kumar Chattopadhyaya has divided the two styles into;

- Secular Royal style
- Religious *Xatria* Style

On the other hand, Dr. Rajatananda Dasgupta, who has done extensive research on Eastern India's *Chitraputhis* or *Puthichitras* (books with pictorial illustrations), has divided them into seven styles. Various other research scholars have categorized the *Puthichitras* of Assam in their ways. After analyzing the results of the various researches, we can divide the medieval painted manuscripts in to following styles:

- Tai Ahom style, based on the religious books written in Tai-Ahom language.
- Imperial or court style developed through the patronage of Ahom monarch.
- Religious Xatriya style.
- Darangi style developed on the basis of folk art.

Tai-Ahom Style, Based on the Religious Books Written in Tai-Ahom Language

The Ahoms were great patrons of book illustration like their Thai cousins. 'The Ahoms brought manuscripts dealing both with religious and with secular matters.'[5] All the Thai tribes between Upper Assam and

Upper Burma were designated as the Naras by the people of Assam. Painting was popular among these tribes. They were linked by marriages as well as religious ceremony; paintings often were prized as dowry among these tribes and also sacred offering to monastery. Thus even after settling down in Assam, the Shan style of painting was continued due to constant contracts with the native land and kinfolk across the border of the Patkai. The style in Assam has been designated as the Tai-Ahom style.

Few books with pictorial illustrations belonging to this style group could be found. 'The earliest extant examples of manuscript illustration in Assam are from the *Phung Chin* manuscript (Pl.9.4), dated 1473 CE, belongs to Phake community and in the Tai-Ahom language/ script, which has been preserved in Namphake monastery near Dibrugarh town, Assam. It is a treatise on the Phake conception of heavens and hells as modified by animism as well Hinayana Buddhism.'[7] There are a number of Tai manuscripts, mostly belonging to Buddhist Tai groups, in which are found

Pl.9.4: Phung Chin Manuscript, 1473 CE

various kinds of illustrations-from rough sketches and symbolic drawings to elaborate paintings. 'While some of the paintings depict the other worlds and the plight of the souls in each of them according to the belief of the particular Burmese Buddhist sect with which these groups have religious links, some others illustrate Jataka stories. A good numbers of other *Ahom* manuscripts on indigenous oral chants has to be seen some monochrome illustrations of chicken-leg or chicken-bone in various positions from which predictions are to be made.'[8]

Another earliest evidence of painted manuscript, *Suk-tanta kampong* has several painted illustration of Buddha. These are written on folios of 'tulapat' or locally made paper, folded and stitched together. "Painted manuscript '*Gileswar Bailung Nemi Mang*' of 17th century and 18th century Assam on *Sanchi* tree bark (Aquillaria Agallocha), is a unique discovery of Tai-Ahom treatise, digitisation recently by British Library, London. Mainly with line and less colour, lone *Sachi* tree bark leave has shown picture of a king like personality, smoking along with a deer, looking at the monkey in offering posture."[9]

Significantly during 2006, with the publication of Catalogue of Ahom and Tai Manuscripts edited by Dr. Jogendra Nath Phukan and published by Department of Historical and Antiquarian Studies (DHAS), Assam have created land-mark in the field of Manuscript-studies as well as historical research in North-East India in general and Assam in particular. Since its establishment in 1928, DHAS has been collected a good number of manuscripts written in Tai language, original language of the Ahom of Buddhist origin, who were the ruling people for six centuries in the Brahmaputra valley before it came under the occupation of the British in 1826. Later on manuscripts written in other Tai languages like the Khamti, Aiton and Phake have been added to its collection.

Imperial or Court Style Developed Through the Patronage of Ahom Monarch

Historically, it is a fact that Assam in the early 18th century witnessed the exodus of several families of craftsmen from Mughal India which was on the verge of disintegration and decay. 'The families, of course, immigrated to Assam at the behest of the Ahom king Swargadeo Rudra Simha (1695-1713 CE), showing his keen interest in search for skilled artisans in the Mughal territories of India. Thus the Mughal School of painting as well as its principles immigrated to Assam through these persons.'

The prominent painted manuscripts with pictorial illustrations of this style include- *Hastividyarnava,* (Pl.9.5) *Ananda Lahari, Hangkhasur*

Pl.9.5: Hastividyarnava *manuscript, Saka 1636 (CE 1734)*

Badh, Gita-Govinda, Dharma Puran, Kalki Puran, etc. '*Hastividyarnava* (Pl.9.6) was composed in Saka 1636 (CE 1734) as known from the colophon, under the patronage of Ahom king Swargadeo Shiva Simha and his queen Rani Ambika. It appears perhaps that, originally compiled in Tai-Ahom language, may be without pictures of elephants, the text of the treatise Hastividyarnava was recomposed by author Sukumara Barkath (Kayastha), with materials drawn from *Gajendra-cintamani*. The paintings in the painted manuscripts were done by two eminent Muslim artists Dilbar and Doshai. They were undoubtedly expert in the line and used their brush with adroitness.There are 171 colourful pictures in *Hastividyarnava*. The colours used in the paintings are black ink, prepared from *Silikha* (terminalia citina) and bull's urine, indigo, yellow ochre (*Gerumati*), vermillion (*hengul*), green and lamb black, taken from natural products in the main.'[10] The background is portrayed with green and blue colours. The faces of the animals and men in the painting are set facing aside. All classes of elephants are illustrated with great precision, and their ailments and their appropriate remedies detailed in full.

Pl.9.6: Hastividyarnava *manuscript, Auniati Xatra, Majuli, late 18th century*

During the time of the Ahoms there was a famous book belonging to the *Shakta Dharma* (the religious faction that worships Goddess Sakti) named *Ananda Lahari*. The paintings found in this book done by the most skilful artists of the time under the careful supervision of *Borraja Phuleswari Konwari*. As per the direction of king Swargadeo Shiva Simha and queen Phuleswari Konwari, the two books '*Geet Govinda*' and '*Hangsur Badh*' were translated by Kabiraj Chakraborty into the ancient Assamese language. The main themes of these two books were beautifully represented through paintings by the most eminent artists of the time under the direction of the royal authorities. The book '*Dharma Purana*' was translated into Assamese language by the poet Kabichandra Dvij as per the orders of King Swargadeo Shiva Simha and queen Konwari Ambika Devi and, later on, the book was given a pictorial form by a ligira (a personal attendant). The epic 'Kalki Puran' was composed by poet Rusinath Kandali under the orders of king Rudra Simha and the paintings in it were ordered to be done by the most skilled artists of the time. Besides these, Bhagawatar Sastha Skandha' (AD), Kirtan Gokha', 'Darrang Rajbangkhawali', the eminent arist Durgaram's pictorial version of the 'Brahma Khanda' of 'Brahma Baivarta Purana' (Pl.9.7) kept in the

Pl.9.7: Brhma-Vivarta-purana *(Brahmananda-khanda), British Museum, London, 1836 CE*

British Museum, 'Kumar Haran' that lies preserved in Budhbariya Xatra of Nazira are noteworthy.

Religious Xatriya Style

The pictures of Xatriya style and those carved out by the sculptor/ painter of *Xatra* on main worshipping book-keeping throne (*Simhasan*), cover of books, boxes for keeping books, on the walls of Xatra, etc. using *hengul-haital* (red and yellow pigments). We find that majority of the *Chitraputhis* or *puthichitras* (books with pictorial illustrations) belong to the Xatriya style.

Amidst these the '*Adya Dakham Skanda Bhagawat'*, by Srimanta Sankardeva found in Bali Xatra of Nagaon, is one of the oldest. It is recorded in the literature (*Shastras*) that the poems and paintings in this book were composed during the time period of 1539 A.D. to 16th Century. There are paintings and poems showing and describing the childhood and adolescent period of Lord Krishna's life, Raslila (a festival of dance, music and games enjoyed by Lord Krishna with Gopinis/female attendants), *Vastraharan* (Lord Krishna stealing the clothes of Gopinis), *Gubardhan dharan* (Lord Krishna carrying the Govardhan Parvat), *Hangkhasur badh* (killing of *Hangkhasur*), *Naradar agaman* (coming of Narad Muni), *Kangkhabadh* (killing of Kangkha) are most informative and fascinating ones. Some other valuable painted manuscripts of Xatriya style include— 'Dasam' illustrated by Rusi Bapu in 1765 A.D.; '*Samundra Manthan'* found in Sivsagar; 'Adya Dasam' preserved in Dakshinapat Xatra; two volumes of '*Bhagawat Puran'* prerseved in the British Museum of London; '*Sachitra Ramayana*'that lay preserved at Ahataguri Satra, Nagaon; '*Langka kanda'* preserved by Upendranath Lekharu; '*Sribhagawat Matsya Charitra'* and '*Kumar Haran'* found in Mayaram Dinajay Xatra; '*Bhakti Ratnavali'* found in Karatipar Xatra of Nagaon; '*Bhakti Pradeep'* found in Samaguri Xatra of Nagaon, 'Chitra Kirtan' of Karanga, Jorhat; 'Sachtra Parijat' '*Parijat-haran*' (Pl.9.8) of Aibheti Na-Xatra, '*Rangali Kirtan*' of Pub-thoria Madhav Ata Xatra, *Anadi-patana*, Samaguri Xatra, majuli (Pl.9.9) etc.

Darangi Style on the Basis of Folk Style

Another school of manuscript painting saw its birth in the court of the Koch principality known as the Darang Raj of Mangoldoi in the district

Pl.9.8: Parijata-harana *manuscript, 1836 CE*

Pl.9.9: Anadi-patana, *Samaguri Xatra, Majuli*

of Darang. Closely similar to the *Xatria* School of neo-Vaishnavism, from which originated, it soon developed its own characteristics which was later patronised by the Ahom Monarchs and Koch chiefs of the 17th and 18th centuries. The highly sophisticated Ahom courtly school of miniature painting also influenced that of Darrang. 'The most important example of the later Darrang manuscript miniatures is the Darrang Rajvasvali (1791 A.D.), but it is proper to deal under Imperial style of Ahom monarch though its province is different.'[11] Among the works belonging to Darangi style, *Tritiya Skandha Bhagavat*, Dvijram's *Sahapari Upakhyan, Astam Skandha Bhagavat* and *Tirtha Kamudi* are the most prominent. It is worth mentioning that this style evolved and developed in the Darrang region because of which it came to be known as the *Darrangi* style.

Conclusion

With the rise of the Neo-*Vaisnavism* under *Shrimanta Sankardeva*, from 16th century onwards, we get a host of concrete examples that can be called painting in its real sense that flourished until the last part of the 19th century. These polychrome paintings, popularly known as manuscript painting, done on *sanchi* pat or *tulapat*, were the illustrations of the stories of the *Bhagavata*, the *Puranas,* the Ramayana, the Mahabharata, etc., which contained written descriptions along with these paintings. At least one hundred manuscripts, each containing on an average forty such paintings, have been discovered so far. From these paintings, it is apparent that both their form and spirit are traditionally integrated with the basic aesthetic concept of the Indian painting tradition. For example in almost all these paintings the Hindu spirit of religious fervour is clearly visible.

During reign of *Ahom* rulers of Mongoloid/South-east Asia origin in the Medieval Assam the *Mughal* influence became evident, yet it had been able like the *Rajasthani* and *Pahari* School to synthesize that influence to its own advantage, and thus had been able to maintain its distinct regional entity. That is why we find the similarity of manuscript paintings of Assam to be more striking with the *Kangra* School than with the *Mughal* School because of the thematic connotation and stylistic similarities. In the paintings of the manuscript of the first book of *Brahmaavaivarta Purana* which is now prescribed in the British Library, London, the *Shankhachuda Vadha,* the *Hastividyarnava* (of *Auniati Satra*), *Kumara Harana* (of both *Budhbari* and *Dichial Satras*), we experience the highest manifestation of this assimilation.

On the other hand, in the paintings of the *Chitra Bhagavata* we experience something very original in its vigorous lines, contrast of colors and uniqueness of composition, which very well establishes its distinct identity. However, in all the above mentioned paintings we feel the same confident and effortless control of the painter over his job that reflected in the vigorous lines, arrangement of space and choice of colors. In his expert hands even the otherwise irrational and awkward arrangement of space become normal, perfect and pleasing. There is also a separate genre of paintings where, instead of trained, expert and confident hand we encounter the lines of confusion and simplicity of a child, where colors and composition also become arbitrary and irrational. But this irrationality often opens up a vista for a kind of innocent pleasure of fantasy which the rational thinking always fails.

It is worth to be mentioned that the paintings were traditionally done using vermillion red, yellow, blue, black, the colour produced from grey *hilika* (a kind of bitter fruit) and dhol or kharimati. A kind of simplicity is reflected in the use of colours in *Xatria* art. On the other hand, one can find indigenous influence on the style of various objects like *Simhasan, harai*, etc. There is a picture of camel found on the *Sanchi-puthi* (book on bark leaves) '*Samudra Manthan*' that has been kept in Sivasagar. Apart from the above mentioned *chitraputhis* or painted manuscript, there are numerous other painted manuscripts found to be preserved in the *xatras* located in the nook and corner of Assam. All these painted manuscripts done on *Sanchi* bark found widely in the nook and corners of Assam especially in Brahmaputra valley, beautifully illustrate the rich artistic tradition of Assam.

It may be mentioned here that all illuminated manuscripts do not contain paintings proper. Some of the folios of a manuscript are decorated with geometric and floral designs along with their borders and also at the centre. 'Generally such designs are not frequently, sometimes each folio is treated with a specific design. Significantly, floral and geometric designs of similar nature are almost consistently found in the carvings and paintings on wood panels of and other articles associated with the neo-*Vaishnavism* order. A specific term- *Lata-kata*- has been traditionally used to designate such designs.'[12]

Taking into account what has been said earlier about apparent popular or folk style associated *patuas* and *natas,* coupled with the fact that paintings of some of the known illustrated manuscripts have obvious folk link, we can venture the conclude that at least some of different schools of manuscript painting has grown out of, or in mingling with, some indigenous folk styles; in some cases this had come about through a process of natural and independant evolution, and in some others as off-shoots of earlier refined styles, or as new development s through contact with more advanced styles developed elsewhere. 'In paintings of the *Hastividyaarnava* it is to be seen to what extent the style of Hindu and Mughal (i.e. Indo-Persian with European influence) paintings were transformed by Mongoloid Boro or Ahom influence.'[13]

In early nineteenth century came the Burmese invasion in Assam with not only disastrous impact on socio-economic life, but also it almost ruined hundred years' long art and cultural traditions of Assam. In 1826, after the *Yandaboo Treaty*, the British took over power from the Burmese. The Christian missionaries introduced printing technology at this time.

British imperial reign had not only exploited that deplete situation of Assam as collecting some of treasured manuscripts to their own country, but also never encouraged nourishment of that manuscript painting tradition of Assam. In this juncture government, non-governmental agency, corporate bodies and above all viewers/public has to be really responsive to take special care, attention and nourishment, also proper initiative towards those painted manuscripts tradition in this troubled torn part of our country.

References & Bibliography:

1. Goswami, H, *Descriptive Catalogue of Assamese Manuscripts*, Historical and Antiquarian Studies, Assam, 2nd Edition, 2009, pp. xv-xxx.
2. Kalita, N, *An Alphabetical of Illustrated Manuscripts of Assam*, Indira Gandhi National Centre for Arts, New Delhi, p. 2.
3. Phookan, N, *'Rup Borna Bak'*, Students' Stores, Guwahati, 1998, pp. 30-31.
4. Dutta Baruah, H. N, ed., *'Chitra Bhagavata',* Nalbari, 1949.
5. Kalita, N, *'Axomor Puthchitra'*, Publication Board, Assam, 1996.
6. Bhuyan, S. K., *The Administrative System of the Ahoms*; p. 94.
7. Hamilton, F, *An Account of Assam*, pp. 78-79.
8. Datta, B, *Folk Paintings of Assam,* Tezpur University, Tezpur, 1998, p. 8.
9. www. britishlibrary.typepad.co.uk/ 15.07.2013.
10. Chouddhury, P. C. Ed., *Hastividyarnava,* Publication Board of Assam, Guwahati, 1976, pp. iv-xi.
11. Das Gupta, R, *Art of Mediaeval Assam*, Cosmo Publications, New Delhi, 1982, p. 120.
12. Datta, B, Ibid., p. 9.
13. Chatterjee, S. K., *The Place of Assam in the History and Civilization of India,* Gauhati University, Guwahati, 1970, p. 56 Datta, B, Ibid., p. 9.

10

Writing the Environment of Early Medieval Bengal: Gleaning from Manuscripts (CE 600-1300)

– *Krishnendu Ray*

Innumerable varieties of artefacts like axes, daggers, bowls, *hāndis*, pots and other useful objects from archaeological sites such as Dholavira, Kausambi, Ter, Rajagriha,[1] Nagarjunikonda,[2] and many other sites in the Indian subcontinent confirm human engagement with occupying a particular space for their settlement on the earth. The objects found from the excavated sites in India drive home the fact that humans transformed their settlement spaces into places by performing different activities social, economic as well as cultural. Thus we find them to have related their activities to different parts of the earth such as the mountainous regions, riverine areas, forests, plain lands, agrarian land, or coastal area.[3] Gradually they have made[4], as we learn from early Indian history up to 1300 CE, many historically important places like Magadha (south Bihar), Kāñchi (Kanchipuram), Pāmmānām, Avanti (Ujjain and Mandhata, western Madhya Pradesh) and Malwa etc.[5] In doing so they have interacted with rocks/stones, lands, water bodies, trees and plants on the one hand; on the other; they have adapted themselves to climatic/weather changes through ages. Thus they have interacted with the environment. Naturally at this point we may pause for a while to understand what the environment is. We are told that the environment is 'the aggregate of surrounding things, conditions or influences especially as affecting the existence or development of someone or something'.[6] Nature is represented by trees and plants, animals, rocks, water and air minus humans; culture is 'socially constructed.'[7] Now, we are told that human activities constitute what is called culture[8]. By performing cultural activities human beings have constructed and changed societies through times. Thus the environment includes Nature and culture. Historically it appears that humans have changed the patterns of their interactions with the environment through ages. These may be understood from the attempts by the people to settle in the Gangetic plains during the days of the Vedas (c. 1500-600 BCE) or human efforts towards agrarian production in early India up to c. 1300 CE.[9] In doing so as they have influenced the environment, so they have also been affected by the environment. In passing their lives they have acquired experiences which they have preserved not only in archaeological materials or monuments, but also in manuscripts.[10] In early India we find humans to have preserved their cultural, artistic, scientific and philosophical ideas and thoughts/perceptions in different languages like Sanskrit, Prākrit, Pâli, Tamil etc. in shells, stones, copper, bronze, clay seals, bricks, palm leaves (*tālapatra*), birch leaves (*bhurjapatra*), cloth, paper, wood etc.[11] Thus manuscripts are important historical documents containing the treasures of the knowledge of the early Indians about their interaction with their surroundings. Therefore efforts have been made to preserve these historical resources in different academic libraries/ institutions in India.[12] At this point we wish to propose a few literary texts such as the *Kṛṣṁparāśara*[13], *Saduktikarnāmṛta,*[14] *Āryāsaptaśatī*[15] etc prepared on the basis of manuscripts from the Asiatic Society, Kolkata, Sanskrit College Library, Kolkata, and the Bhandarkar Oriental Research Institute, Pune etc. Similarly we have also other texts; for example mention may be made to the *Subhāsitaratnakoca* of Vidyākara based on manuscripts.[16] From scholarly studies[17] relating to these texts we learn how the people of ancient Bengal passed their lives, how they interacted with others, how they earned their livelihood, how they thought, how they worshipped the gods and goddesses of their choice, how they developed their beliefs and rituals, how they used the environmental resources like land, water, trees and plants etc. Thus we have some insights about the different aspects of the social life of the people of early medieval Bengal.

But in regard to the interactions with their surroundings also we may have gleanings from these texts of early medieval Bengal. Therefore the aim of the present essay is set to an understanding of their use of the environmental resources in early medieval Bengal.

We may start our discussion with water one of the most essential environmental resources for humans. Bengal is well known to have been watered by a large number of rivers, viz, the Bhagirathi, Ganga, Padma and Meghna, to mention a few. Early medieval Bengal also witnessed no exception to this.[18] Several *caryas* referring to the boat as *nāvī, nāve, nâva, nāvahi, nāhi* in the *Caryāpadas* provide indications towards the fact that the people interacted with rivers by using a boat.[19] It appears from a *caryā* that the boat was plied by the man called *Nauvāhī*.[20] The word *Nauvāhī* might have signified a sailor (*Nāvika*); for the word *Nāvika* was used in the sense of a sailor as known from an epigraphic text of the eleventh century.[21] He might have been an ordinary sailor. Possibly there was another one who played the more vital role than the ordinary sailor in plying a boat across the river. This helmsman might have been represented by the word *karnahāra* in the *Caryāpadas*.[22] It may be noted that one became *karnahāra* out of his experiences that he had gathered by plying a boat across the river. The point may be supported by the *Amarakoca* (c. fifth/sixth century CE) in which we read the *karnadhāra* as holding (*dhārayati*) the steering oar (*karna*).[23] In connection with interactions with rivers a big-sized boat might have been used as indicated by the word *vāja Gāva*[24] occurring in the *Caryāpadas*. It is not difficult to understand that the rivers and boats were used for the purpose of communication 'between the littorals and the interior'[25] of Bengal. Besides, the rivers with silt deposits on their banks have also ensured agricultural prosperity for the people of Bengal. In Khanā's *Vacanas* (c. 9th -13th centuries) we read different types of soil fit for the production of different types of agricultural crops such as clayey soil for the production of jute, lime-rich soil for sugarcane, saline soil for the growth of coconut trees etc.[26] In another contemporary text *Rāmacaritam* (11th-12th century) by the Bengali poet Sandhyakaranandi prepared by M M Haraprasad Shastri on the basis of a palm-leaf manuscript from Nepal we read the agricultural prosperity of Varendri (north Bengal including the Rajshahi, Bogra and Dinajpur districts of Bangladesh) expressed through various kinds of paddy plants (*bahudhānya*), good quality bamboo clumps (*sadvaṁśā*) and flourishing plants of sugarcane (*prasphura-dikcvāku*) in the soil of the region.[27] The production of cardamom plants, creepers (*lavaśga*), arecanut trees etc in the land of Varendra is also known from the text of the *Râmacaritam.*[28] In the text we also find some spaces dotted with wooden apple trees (*śrīphala*), edible *kāṇḍa* roots etc.[29] The soil of the Varendra region is also known to have been congenial to the growth of various flowers like *kanaka, ketaka* etc.[30] In the text we read that Rāmapala caused to be constructed large lakes for the use of the people in general. On both the sides of the lakes palm trees were planted.[31] These works were certainly in favour of keeping the environment healthy for the public. In other words, the soil of the Varendra region was congenial to the cultivation of various kinds of agricultural crops. The excellent production of rice and sugarcane in early medieval Bengal is reported from the *Saduktikarṇāmṛta* of Śrīdharadāsa.[32] In the *Āryāsaptaśatī* we find a variety of autumnal paddy called *jātiśālini* being compared to the character of a clever elite class woman of the society.[33] The acquaintance with this variety of paddy may lead one to assume that the paddy was cultivated in early medieval Bengal. This may be corroborated by a literary reference to the farmer's hut rich with the *Śāli* variety of paddy in the *Saduktikarṇāmṛta*.[34] The text also brings out the fact that another variety of paddy called *kalama* was cultivated in early medieval Bengal.[35] In the contemporary text *Āryāsaptaśatī* also we find this *kalama* variety of *Śāli* rice to have been cultivated in early medieval Bengal.[36] In this connection it may be noted that this variety of *Śāli* rice had come much earlier into cultivation in Bengal.[37] These textual references to the production of crops indicate the inclination of the people towards agriculture. At this point we propose a good number of epigraphic references of the earlier period in Bengal during the period from the fifth to the seventh centuries.[38] These references point to the prayer for *khilakcetra* (uncultivated land) and the land measurements in *droṇavāpa* (the land sown with one *droṇa* of seeds), *kulyavāpa* (the land sown with one *kulya* of seeds)[39] etc The evidences drive home the fact that the people of Bengal made the fallow land resource of Nature fertile for agricultural production and consumed its products. In order to fulfil their agricultural needs they might have utilized the river water for irrigation. At this point we like to propose Niharranjan Ray. Ray draws our attention to the fact that large ponds were dug by the Pāla authority and these were used to facilitate the task of agriculture. Probably for the same purpose, as we learn from Ray, the Sena king Vallâlasena (c. CE 1159-79) caused to be constructed an embankment at the confluence of the Gaṅgā-Jamuna-Sarasvati in Sumha (a large part of the Hooghly district, south of Burdwan and Howrah districts).[40] Before leaving the point of using water for irrigation, we can take note of the fact that the fisherman spread his thick net in the river and caught fish therefrom.[41] In other words the poet did not forget to note the use of the river as a resource. Side by side our attention is also drawn to the weather conditions in early medieval Bengal. In summer the surface level of the water of the pond remained hot (*agre taptajalā*), but very cool beneath (*nitāntaśiśirâ mūle*). But the wells of the wayside dried up.[42] It is not difficult to understand that the travellers suffered due to this condition of the wells. But the scorching heat went when the rains came. After the rains a gentle wind used to blow and the scent of the *kadamba* flower wet in the rains also blew[43] around. In the autumn the peasants were happy when they saw the ripening sugarcane and the high rice. Some leading peasant families (*ādikula*) invited and fed Brāhmaṇas.[44] Thus the peasants expressed their happiness with the crops. The farmers were also happy with their 'first harvest of the winter rice'. They also stored grains in the jars. This might have some impact on the mind of the villager. We learn from the *Kṛṣiparāśara* that the villagers had probably the mind to entertain respected humans, gods and guests with food.[45] In the *Saduktikarṇāmṛta* we are introduced to the hospitality the villagers showed to the wayfarers. In the text we find that the villagers accommodated travellers in their village temple.[46] Some of the villagers might have earned their livelihood by serving as agricultural labourers in the field. They were called Pâmaras. They were very poor probably so much that they did not have sufficient clothes to cover their body in cold.[47] At this point we are told that the young tribal girls used leaves to cover their breasts,[48] In the *Āryāsaptaśatī* we are told that the Pulindas and Śabaras lived by hunting animals.[49] The villagers also used to earn their livelihood by making earthen pots because these pots were used by the people.[50] They are also known to have lived by making wood work as wooden objects like mortar and pestle (*mucala*),[51] bullock-cart *śakama*),[52] oil-pressing instrument (*cakra*) etc[53] are noted in the manuscripts of the *Saduktikarṇāmṛta* and *Āryāsaptaśatī*. The villagers are also known to have taken to cotton carding for sustenance. In the *Caryāpadas* we find that cotton was very pleasant thing to the people. This is supported by the *śabarapāda*[54] of the *Caryāgīti*. People used to live on carding cotton. It appears that cotton was carded and the fibre was produced out of it.[55] We also learn from the text that there might have been one or more than one in early medieval Bengal who was/were well versed in the art of weaving.[56] Even in the poor Brahmin families women were involved in the act of cotton carding. The contemporary poet has noted this in his literary creation *Saduktikarṇāmṛta*.[57] Beside their efforts to survive humans have also made attempts to get over tensions they have faced. Thus they have prayed for refuge from the god of their choice. In this direction also human endeavours are known from manuscripts. In the *Subhāsitaratnakoca* it has been noted that the villagers worshipped a forest goddess.[58] Possibly they worshipped the goddess in order to preserve the forest wealth. They also worshipped the god of the field (Kcetrapāla) under the tree.[59] Probably the god maintained/protected (*pāla*) the agricultural wealth of the field. In the *Āryāsaptaśatī* we find that the banyan tree was considered as the abode of the god/ goddess and therefore people sought its protection from the stroke of the axe. That the tree is valuable in human life has also been noted in the relevant verses of the *Āryāsaptaśatī*.[60] We learn from the *Kṛṣiparāśara* that the people practised a ritual called *muṣṭigrahaṇa* in the field. The ceremony included sandal-paste, incense, flowers, two and a half handfuls of crops and with these ritual objects the farmer worshipped the paddy plants (*dhānyvṛksakān*) on an auspicious day (*śubhavāsare*) in the month of *Agrahāyaṇa* (November-December). After the completion of the ritual the farmer took the paddy to his home and placed it in the main room (*mukhyāniketane*) in the east (*pūrvabhāge*).[61] The villagers are also known to have practised certain popular beliefs centring round the crow in daily life. For the crow (*karata*) was believed to be the judge (*pramāṇapuruṣa*) of what was good and what was bad for the people. Therefore the crow was thought to be worthy of receiving worship (*karamapūjya*) from the villagers.[62] From the *Āryāsaptaśatī* we learn that some creepers (*vallī*) were used in order to remove the suffering due to poison (*garalotāpahāriṇya*).[63] It was also a vital part of the popular beliefs which the villagers had developed and practised in their daily life. Besides their popular beliefs they might have also been devoted to the Brahmanical gods like Śiva, Viśṇu and Pārvatī.[64]

The people seem to have enjoyed Indian classical music. That the sweetness of a song depends not on its words, but upon one of the modes of Indian classical music was also known to the people of early medieval Bengal. This is supported by a verse of the *Āryāsaptaśatī*.[65] Their songs were accompanied by musical instruments like *kambu* (musical conch), *baṁśī* (clarion), *vipañcī* (*vīṇā*) etc.[66] People are also known to have practised performing arts like dance, dance-drama as gleaned from the relevant verses of the *Āryāsaptaśatī*. The same text provides indication toward acting on the open stage.[67]

Conclusion

It appears from the above discussion that in interaction with Nature human beings have utilized their surrounding environmental conditions in early medieval Bengal. Thus in order to fulfil the needs, aspirations, dreams of their lives they have built up society, developed their ideas and thoughts, manners and customs and left behind the impressions of their life experiences through their cultural achievements/creations through ages.[68] The individual author has coded these human achievements into words. Therefore the manuscripts of early medieval Bengal contain significant information about the environmental conditions in which the people used to live their lives.

References and Footnotes

1. Chakrabarti Dilip K, *India: An Archaeological History Palaeolithic Beginnings to Early Historic Foundations*, Second Impression, New Delhi, 2003.
2. Soundararajan K.V., *Nagarjunakonda (1954-60)*, Memoirs of the Archaeological Survey of India No.75, Archaeological Survey of India, New Delhi, 2006.
3. Chattopadhyaya B. D, *Studying Early India Archaeology, Texts and Historical Issues*, Permanent Black, New Delhi, 2003, p.50.
4. Anderson Jon, *Understanding Cultural Geography Places and Traces* (hereafter *Understanding Cultural Geography*), Routledge, London and New York, 2010, pp. 1-3, 132ff.
5. Chakravarti Ranabir, *Exploring Early India up to C. AD 1300* (henceforth *Exploring Early India*), Second Edition, Macmillan Publishers India Ltd, New Delhi, 2013.
6. *Webster's Encyclopedic Unabridged Dictionary of the English Language*, Newly Revised Edition, Grammercy, New York, 1989, p.477.

7. Massey, Geraldine, *Reading the Environment: Narrative Construction of Ecological Subjectivities in Australian Children's Literature*, Ph.D. Thesis, 2009, p. 23 (Collected from the Internet).
8. Anderson, Jon, *Understanding Cultural Geography*, p. 3.
9. Chakravarti, Ranabir, *Exploring Early India*.
10. Chattopadhyaya, B. D, 'Space, History and Cultural Process: Some Ideas on the Ingredients of Subregional 'Identity' in Hermann Kulke and George Berkemer (eds.), *Centres Out There? Facets of Subregional Identities in Orissa*, Manohar Books, New Delhi, 2011, p. 22, fn. 5.
11. Sircar, D. C., *Indian Epigraphy*, Motilal Banarsidass, Delhi, 1965, pp. 70-79, 61-69.
12. Gaur, Ramesh C and Chakraborty Mrinmoy, 'Preservation and Access to Indian Manuscripts: A Knowledge Base of Indian Cultural Heritage Resources for Academic Libraries' in *International Conference on Academic Libraries (ICAL), 2009 Vision and Roles of the Future Academic Libraries*, New Delhi, 2009, pp. 90-98; Sahoo Jyotshna et al, 'Indian Manuscript Heritage and the Role of National Mission for Manuscripts', *Library Philosophy and Practice* (e-Journal), 2013, Paper 984.
13. Majumdar, G.P and Banerji S.C. (ed & tr), *K[ciparāśara*, Reprinted, The Asiatic Society, Kolkata, 2001.
14. Banerji, S. C. (ed.), *SaduktikarGām[ta of Śrīdharadāsa* (hereafter *SaduktikarGām[ta*), Firma K.L.Mukhopadhyay, Calcutta, 1965.
15. Chakraborty, Janhabi Kumar (tr.), *Āryāsaptaśatī O GauvaEga* (hereafter *Āryāsaptaśatī*), (in Bengali), Sanyal & Co, Calcutta, 1971.
16. Kosambi, D.D. and Gokhale V.V. (eds.), *The Subhāsitaratnakoca Compiled by Vidyākara*, (hereafter *Subhāsitaratnakoca*), Harvard University Press, Harvard, 1957, p. XVIff
17. Sarkar, Soumyendra Nath, *Caryāgītikoca*, Modern Book Agency Pvt. Ltd, Calcutta (Kolkata), 1978, pp. 183-205; Banerjee, Asit Kumar, *BāEglā Sāhityer Itiv[tta* (*History of Bengali Literature*), Vol. I, Third Edition, Modern Book Agency Pvt. Ltd, Calcutta (Kolkata), 1970, pp. 196-204; Ray Niharranjan, *BāEgālīr Itihās Ādi Parva* (hereafter *BāEgālīr Itihās*) (*A History of the Bengali People: Early Period*), Dey's Publishing, Calcutta, 1993, relevant pages; Gopal Lallongi and Srivastava V. C (eds.), *History of Agriculture in India (up to c.1200 AD)* (hereafter *History of Agriculture in India*) in *D. P. Chatopadhyaya* (Gen. ed.), *History of Science, Philosophy and Culture in Indian Civilization*, Vol. V, Part I, Concept Publishing Company, New Delhi, 2008, p. 489ff; Husain Shahanara, 'Poet Yogesvara and Some of his verses depicting Village Life in Early Medieval Bengal', *Journal of Varendra Research Society*, Vol. 8, 1994, pp. 20-28.

18. Bhattacharyya, Amitabha, *Historical Geography of Ancient and Early Mediaeval Bengal*, Calcutta, 1977, pp. 11-35; Ray Niharranjan, *BāEgālīr Itihās*, p. 70ff.
19. Sen, Nilratan, *Caryāgītikoca*, Dey Book Store, Calcutta, 1978,
20. - -, *ibid,* p. 146, *caryā* 38.
21. Gupta, K. M, 'The Bhatera Copper-Plate Inscription of Govinda-Kesavadeva (c.1049 AD)', *Epigraphia Indica*, Vol. XIX, No. 49, 1927-28/1983, pp. 277-286.
22. Sen, Nilratan (ed.), *Caryāgītikoca*, Calcutta, 1978, *caryā* 13, text-line 9; the word *kaGGahāra* stands for *karGadhāra*.
23. Ramanathan, A.A. (ed.), *Amarakośa*, Vol. I, Reprint, Madras (Chennai), 1989, pp. 162-163, verse. 11; cf. Chakravarti, Ranabir, *Trade and Traders in Early Indian Society* (hereafter *Trade and Traders*), Manohar Books, New Delhi, 2002, pp. 127, 139, fn. 65.
24. Ramanathan, A.A. (ed.), *Amarakośa*, *Ibid*, pp. 123, 151, 164 *caryā* 49; *Vāja Gāva* might have been a *Vajra-naukā*.
25. Chakravarti, Ranabir, *Trade and Traders*, p. 169.
26. Chaudhuri, Rita, 'Agriculture as known from Khana's Vacanas' in Gopal Lallongi and Srivastava, V.C. (eds.), *History of Agriculture in India*, p. 529.
27. Sastri, Haraprasad M M (ed.) and Basak Radhagovinda (rev. & tr.), *Rāmacaritam* of Sandhyakaranandin, Reprint, Memoir Series Vol. III, No. I, The Asiatic Society, Calcutta, 1969, p. 66.
28. --, *Ibid*, pp. 67-68, vv. 18-20.
29. --, *Ibid*, p. 64, v.3/12.
30. --, *Ibid*, p. 67, v.3/22.
31. --, *Ibid*, p. 75, v.3/42.
32. Banerji, S.C. (ed.), *SaduktikarGām[ta*, p. 238, 2/84/3ṭ*brīhi% stambakāri% prabhutaṭ prtyujjībitam-ikcuGāṭ*.
33. Chakraborty, Janhabi Kumar (tr.), *Āryāsaptaśatī*, p. 199, *āryā* 237bṭ-*ayi śaradanurupaA tava śīlamidaA jātiśālinya%*
34. Banerji, S.C. (ed.), *SaduktikarGām[ta*, p. 363, v. 1353 (*śāliccheda-sam[ddha-hālikag[hā%*)
35. --, *Ibid*, p. 358, verse 2. 173. 2.
36. Chakraborty, Janhabi Kumar (tr.), *Āryāsaptaśatī*, p. 168, v. 101, p.174, v.130, p.189, v.192, p.225, v.346.
37. Bhattacharyaya, G.N., *Amarakosa*, Sanskrit Pustak Bhandar, Calcutta, 1988, p.261, verse 70.

38. Mukherji, Ramaranjan and Maity, Sachindra Kumar (ed.), *Corpus of Bengal Inscriptions Bearing on History and Civilization of Bengal*, Firma K.L. Mukhopadhyay, Calcutta, 1967, pp. 41, 45, 50, 59, 71,
39. Sircar, D.C., *Indian Epigraphical Glossary*, Motilal Banarsidass, Delhi, 1966, pp. 101, 165.
40. Ray, Niharranjan, *BāEgālīr Itihās*, pp. 202, 117.
41. Chakraborty, Janhabi Kumar (tr.), *Āryāsaptaśatī*, p. 203, v. 252 (*ghanajālruddhamīnā nadī*).
42. Ingalls, H. H. Daniel (tr.), *An Anthology of Sanskrit Court Poetry* (hereafter *Anthology of Sanskrit Court Poetry*), Oxford University Press, London, p. 123, v. 206; Kosambi, D.D. and Gokhale, V.V. (eds.), *The Subhāsitaratnakośa*, p. 39, v. 206, text-line 1.
43. --, *Ibid,* p.42, v.220, text-lines 1, 3 (*āsarāntam-[dupravṛttamaruto*), (*dhārāklinnakadambasaAbh[tasurā-mododbahā*).
44. Ingalls, H. H. Daniel (tr.), *Anthology of Sanskrit Court Poetry*, p. 141, v. 291 (*t[Garājapākasaurabhasugandhaya% pariGatāśavo*); Kosambi D.D. and Gokhale, V.V. (eds.), *The Subhāsitaratnakośa*, p. 54, v. 291, text-line 1.
45. Majumdar, G.P. and Banerji, S.C. (ed & tr), *K[ciparāśara*, pp. 26, 73, v. 98, text-line 2 (*pitrdevatithīnāA ca nānnadāne bhavet kcama%*); cf. Choudhary, Abhay Kant, *Early Medieval Village in North-Eastern India (A.D.600-1200)* (hereafter *Early Medieval Village*), Punthi Pustak, Calcutta, 1971, p. 250.
46. Banerji S.C. (ed.), *SaduktikarGām[ta*, pp.360-361, 2/174/4-5; Choudhary, Abhay Kant, *Early Medieval Village*, p.250.
47. Banerji S.C. (ed.), *SaduktikarGām[ta*, pp.358-359, v. 4; Do, *Ibid*, p.98.
48. Banerji S.C. (ed.), *SaduktikarGām[ta*, p.226, v.1; Choudhary Abhay Kant, *Early Medieval Village*, p.104.
49. Chakraborty, Janhabi Kumar (tr.), *Āryāsaptaśatī*, pp. 206, 210, vv. 264, 283; Choudhary, Abhay Kant, *Early Medieval Village*, p.104.
50. Banerji, S.C. (ed.), *SaduktikarGām[ta*, p.237, v.1.
51. --, *Ibid,* p. 237, v.1.
52. --, *Ibid,* p.238, v.2.
53. Chakraborty, Janhabi Kumar (tr.), *Āryāsaptaśatī*, p.277, v.592; Choudhary, Abhay Kant, *Early Medieval Village*, p.196.
54. Sen, Sukumar, *Caryāgīti Padābalī*, Ananda Publishers Pvt Ltd, Calcutta, 1995, p. 77, verse 50, text-line *Heri ye meri tailā bāī kha%same samatulā/ Yukaa ese re kapāsu phumilā//*; Ray, Niharranjan, *BāEgālīr Itihās*, p.149.

55. Sen, Sukumar, *Caryāgīti Padābalī*, p. 65, verse 26, text-line *tulā dhuGi dhuGi añsure aüsu/añsu dhuGi dhuGiṭ-*; Ray, Niharranjan, *BāEgālīr Itihās*, p.149.
56. --, *Ibid*, p. 149; Ray, Krishnendu, 'Understanding Glimpses from the *Caryapadas* on Cotton-Carding and their Probable bearing on Seaborne Trade and Commerce of Early Medieval Bengal (c. 9th-10th Century to 13th)', *Journal of Bengal Art*, Vol. 17, 2012, p.63.
57. Banerji, S.C. (ed.), *SaduktikarGām[ta*, p.392, 3. 17. 2; Ray, Niharranjan, *BāEgālīr Itihās*, p.150.
58. Kosambi, D.D. and Gokhale, V.V. (eds.), *Subhāsitaratnakośa*, p.213, v.1191; Choudhary, Abhay Kant, *Early Medieval Village*, p.234.
59. Ray, Niharranjan, *BāEgālīr Itihās*, p.482.
60. Chakraborty, Janhabi Kumar (tr.), *Āryāsaptaśatī*, p. 205, v.262, p.295, v.674.
61. Majumdar, G. P. and Banerji, S.C. (ed & tr), *K[ciparāśara*, pp. 51-52, vv. 206-209; Choudhary, Abhay Kant, *Early Medieval Village*, pp.241-242.
62. Chakraborty, Janhabi Kumar (tr.), *Āryāsaptaśatī*, *Ibid,* pp. 275-276, v.584.
63. --, *Ibid,* p.164, v.84.
64. --, *Ibid*, pp136 (vv. 6, 8), 186 (v. 178), 217 (v. 311).
65. --, *Ibid,* pp. 94, 272, v. 566 (*Śruta eva śrutihāriGi rāgotkarceGa kaGthamadhivasati I Gīta eva tvayi madhure karoti nārthagrahaGaA sutanu% II*
66. --, *Ibid,* pp. 95, 278, (v. 597), 193, 244 (vv. 211, 437), 193-194 (v. 211).
67. --, Ibid, pp. 181 (v. 155), 266 (v. 538), 185 (v. 174).
68. Ray, Niharranjan, *Bhāratetihās Jijñāsā*, Bengali, Dey's Publishing, Calcutta, 2003, p. 17.

11

History of Tripura:

A Study on Manuscripts and Tradition in Tripura

– *Juthika Basu Bhowmik*

Tripura is a land of multi-ethnic diversity as a result; various languages have been and are in vogue for long. However, Bangla had emerged as the medium of literature, culture and social exchange under the patronage of the erstwhile princely rulers of the land. The tutelage to 'Bangla' from the Royal court is evident in the numerous copper plates, rock inscriptions, stamps and coins of the period. However, the most prominent of these have been the several manuscripts (Manuscripts) whose historical importance has been growing over the years. It should be noted that the National Manuscript Mission states that 'Manuscript is a handwritten composition on paper, bark, cloth, metal, palm leaf or any other material dating back at least seventy-five years that has significant scientific, historical or aesthetic value'. Interesting to note here that in Tripura, though primarily written in Bangla, these Manuscripts often included sections written in Sanskrit and had substantial usage prior to the advent of printing in a mass form. As a result, the hand written Manuscripts remained the foremost medium of literary and cultural pursuits in the state.

It has been observed that the Puranic traditions and the epics were the mainstay of these Manuscripts but these handwritten treatises had a different dimension owing to the incorporation of the contemporary events, particularly royal, in the process. However, it was not always that the Manuscripts were written only at the instructions of the royal families, rather these were often written at the initiative of many private individuals or families. The absence of the knowledge of printing had made the Manuscripts as the most important means of documentation during the time. Even though, the publication of Halhed's 'Bengali Grammar' marks the beginning of the printed Bengali books, the use of Manuscripts continued even later not only to suffice the orders or desires of the rulers but also as a means of expression and creation. Thus, today Manuscripts remain as the source of social, political, religious and literary history.

The exact number of Manuscripts found in Tripura is yet to be determined but whatever has been found appears to be originated between the 17th and the 19th century. Tripura here obviously refers to the present state as well as the Tripura district of the British period. Generally, the manuscripts writers began or ended their narrative with a eulogy to the king, ruler or the sponsor, but in course of the narrative also details out their individual profile in terms of names, genealogy, habitations, occupations, hobbies, religion and social preferences which certainly are important ingredients for the reconstruction of history of the time. Thus, hand written Manuscripts like 'Rajmala', 'Krishnamala', 'Champakvijay', 'Gazinama', etc have emerged as the reference books of history in later periods. It should be noted here that the earliest historical text of Tripura, 'Rajabali' has also been accepted as one of the earliest texts of the Bengali prose, but unfortunately, the book is no longer traceable.

The chronicle of Tripura's royal history, 'Rajmala' was edited by Kaliprasanna Vidya Bhusan on the basis of the hand written Manuscripts of Durgamani Ujir which is preserved at the Government Museum, Agartala. The Manuscript belongs to 1238 T.E. (1838 CE) and comprises of 149 pages made of cotton pulp measuring 41.5 cm by 13.5 cm. The author identifies himself as the son of Maharaja Ram Ganga Manikya and narrates the history for the period beginning with Maharaja Daitya to that of his uncle, Maharaja Kasichandra Manikya, who was at the throne during that time.

'Champaka Vijaya' written during the reign of Maharaja Ratna Manikya II (1682-1711 CE) narrates the events of the king's recapture of the throne after being removed from power by his uncle Narendra Manikya. Sheikh Mohuddin authored this narrative on the directives of the Mir Khan Gazi, the general of the king.

"Sri Mir Khan Gazi Bhuban Durjoy I
Tahan Aadeshe Dhori Mohuddiye Koy II"

....

'Champak Bijoy Kotha Madhu Ros Bani
Sheikh Mohuddiye kohe Yuddher Kahani' II

(GoT, 1977; pg 61)

This Manuscript has a lot of Arabic and Persian words possibly because the author is a Muslim, but it also incorporates events related to Hindu Gods and Goddesses attesting the secular relation of the time and place. A copy of the same has been made by Ramnarayan Deb resident of Vidyakut village in the Nurnagar Pargana. The referred village, presently in the Brahmanbariya district of Bangladesh is credited to be the residence of several learned men and scholars. Interestingly, the same person comes to the fore as the copyist of the Rajmala ManuscriptS which is preserved at the Bangiya Sahitya Parishad and later published in a printed book format by the Education Department of the Government of Tripura in 1967. In this context one may infer that Manuscript copying and compiling might have been a prevalent vocation during the time.

It should be noted that Nurnagar was one of the most distinguished parganas of Chakla Roshanabad. Chakla Roshanabad as the plains of Tripura were commonly referred had 24 sub-divisions. It is said that a Mughal Feudal lord, Nurbulla Khan annexed the three provinces of Heuing, Beuing and Kailargarh and combined them as a unit naming the new region in his name. It is further observed that a custom had emerged whereby many of the royal officials and servants used to rename certain portions of the subdivision in their name. A similar reference can be made about Champaknagar as referred in the Chaitanyamangal. The origin of Champaknagar is credited to Yuvaraj Champak Manikya, who was at the helm of Nurnagar during the reign of Ratna Manikya II (Singha, 1984; pp, 199).

We may recall here that presently, there is a place called Champaknagar at a distance of 28-29 kms from Agartala on the National Highway 44, which has a very interesting historical fact attached though of a different dimension. During a visit to the state in 1948, the Chief Minister of West Bengal, Dr. Prafulla Ghosh offered Rs. 10000 for the construction of a school for the Tribes of the state of Tripura. Accordingly, Tripura Lok

Shikshalaya, a school exclusively for the tribals of Tripura, was set up at Champaknagar on 7th May, 1949 with the internationally famed painter Dhiren Krishna Debbarman as the Director. The faculties included Gopal Chandra Bhattacharya, Tarit Mohan Dasgupta and Ajit Bandhu Debbarma while Phanibhusan Debbarma and Durga Mohan Debbarma joined as Mechanical Instructor and Teacher in Smithy class (learnt from the eminent painter of Bengal School Dhiren Krishna Debbarman in 1977).

On the other hand, we find that the date and time mentioned in the Manuscripts generally provided links to the reign of the kings as is seen for the Kriya-jog-sar Manuscripts. Maharaj Jagat Manikya directed the Brahmins to copy and transcribe the Padmapurana to facilitate noble thoughts among his subjects. The author Mukunda Brahmin also says that the king offered Five Coins as honorarium for each chapter which is a proof of the benevolent nature of the ruler as well as gives an impression that there were a sizeable number of Manuscripts writers in the kingdom. We quote-

> *"Basu veda rasa Arka saka Pariman,*
> *Baishakh masher dasadin abasan,*
> *shombar amabassya punya tithi jani*
> *karila dharmer chinta bipragana ani"*

The period can be identified as 1648 saka era (1826 CE), because basu = 8; veda= 4, rasa= 6; arka= 1; which corresponds to the reign of Maharaja Jagat Manikya on the throne of Tripura. In the latter day Manuscript of 'Ramayana (Uttarakanda)' reference to Rajdhar Manikya is made in the post colophone statements along with the mention of 'Rajdhani Hastinapur', 'Sarkar Udaipur' and 'Chakla Roshanabad' similar to that of the copper plate inscriptions. Interestingly, the kings of Tripura claimed to be descendent the mythological King Yayati of Hastinapur, thus naturally, their capital was also referred as Hastinapur. Udaipur had been the traditional capital of the kings of Tripura for long, however, during the Mughal period much of the plains of Tripura were annexed by them. The lost land was initially called as Sarkar Udaipur and later renamed as Chakla Roshanabad and it was during the rule of Nawab Shujauddin (1727-37 CE) that Maharaj Dharma Manikya obtained the zamindari rights for the place.

Interestingly, the period quoted in the Manuscript Ramayana are 1203 BE, 1206 TE and 1718 CE. Moreover, Rajdhar Manikya is at times refered as the Zamindar King definitely suggesting that the King of Tripura was the Zamindar of Chakla Roshanabad and that area was also known as Sarkar Udaipur. Rajdhar Manikya II who reigned from 1785 to 1804 CE was the nephew and inheritor of Maharaj Krishna Manikya and it was on his directives that the book 'Krishnamala' was written. The book written by Ram Ganga Bisharad in a prose format depicts the life and times of Maharaj Krishna Manikya and accounts rare and unknown facets of the time.

Another important historical Manuscript from Tripura is the Gazinama written by the poet Manohar Ali from Dakshin Shik. The Manuscript tales the war between Samsher Gazi and Tripura represented by the King Indra Manikya and prince Krishna Manikya. Moreover, we also have reference of another historical chronicle of the royal family in 'Srenimala' written by Durgamani Ujir.

During the time of Rajdhar II, copies of Sanjoy's Mahabharata and Bharat Sabitri were also made. We find that these two Manuscripts along with that of Ramayana were copied by Gangagovinda Bardhan, a resident of Maniyanda. This corroborates our proposition of the existence of the vocation of copyists. On the other hand, Maniyanda is a village in the Kamalasagar region of the present day Bangladesh. The Bardhans of the region were an illustrious family. An inscription of Maharaja Ram Manikya, the son of Maharaja Gobinda Manikya dated 1093 TE (1683 CE) refers to the event that 'Sri Sangram Choudhuri has been granted a tax free grant of 51 Dronas in the Muni Yando village' (Singha, 1984). Over time, Muni Yando transformed as Muniyando (narrated by Dwijendra Chandra Dutta in 1976).

After the demise of Rajdhar II, Prince Durgamani inherited the Chakla Roshanabad region in 1809 AD. The script of 'Sri Ramayan Lankakanda' copied by Haragobinda Das Baishnab in 1812 CE refers to Roshanabad, 'Rajdhani Hastinapur' and 'Sarkar Udaipur'. It also mentions about Gopinathpur, a place between Kasba and Mogra in the present-day Bangladesh. The culture of Manuscript writing and copying continued also during the reign of Maharaja Krishna Kishore Manikya, also. The focus of the period however was Baishnav literature as many such pieces have been compiled during that time. The 'Geetkalpataru' written in 1835 CE is pictorial in nature with illustrations from the famous Muslim artist Alam Karigar. The said Manuscript attests to the cultural insight of the rulers of Tripura making it a unique creation. Maharaja Ishan Chandra Manikya ascended the throne after Maharaj Krishna Kishore Manikya in 1850 which is evident in the eulogies of the King.

Tripura's history characterises well documented evidences of proficiency of Bengali language particularly among the women of the royal families. Moreover, we also find reference of Subhadra Baishnabi as the compiler of the 'Prembhakti Chandrika' Manuscript. A resident of Agartala, her Manuscript dates to 1244 TE (1834 CE), a time when the ruler of the state Maharaja Krishnakishore Manikya had shifted the capital to Agartala. It is true that education and learning did spread through Tolls, Chatuspatis, etc but the number of females in such institutions was very limited. No doubts, that Manuscript copying had emerged as a vocation by then but such employment opportunities for females were certainly very limited. It is not certain whether Subhadra Baishnabi was a professional or not, but her case certainly deserves special mention. However, during the same time, we have references of Sanskrit proficient women like Hati Vidyalankar, Priyambada Devi, Anandamayi Devi, etc at various other places. The queen, princess and other royal females of Bishnupur used to read and write Manuscripts, as is evident in their own hand written books. However, the fact that Subhadra Baishnabi took up the task around 177 years ago in Agartala is a big event for the state and its history.

Nevertheless, it can be said that Manuscripts, particularly, the Bengali Manuscripts do tell us a lot of events and provides us significant narratives of the period. However, on the basis of the above discussion it should be reiterated that the Manuscripts of Tripura allows us to make two major observations which deserves special merit and acknowledgement. These two are -

- Prevalence of Manuscript copying and compiling as a profession &
- Existence of lady manuscript copyist in Agartala, Tripura.

However, it should be noted that the present paper is just a snapshot view of some of the historical facts and would call for greater investigation by other scholars of the present time to decipher the several untold stories of the bygone era.

References

Govt. of Tripura (1977), 'A Descriptive Catalogue of Manuscripts in the Library of the Government Museum, Agartala.'

Chakraborti, Bhupendra Chandra (1941), 'Rajmala', Indian Photo Engraving Co., Kolkata.

Singha, Kailash Chandra (1984), '*Rajmala or Tripurar Itibrityo*' Ed (Chakraborty, et al); Barnamala Prakashani, Agartala.

Govt. of Tripura (1967), 'Rajmala'; Education Department, Agartala.

Bhowmik, Juthika Basu (1999), 'Bangla Puthir Pushpika', Subarnarekha, Kolkata

12

Manuscripts of Tripura:
A Cultural Heritage

– *Satyadeo Poddar & Nirmalya Karmakar*

Introduction

Manuscripts have always remained a major resource of knowledge of any society. India was exceedingly advanced in intellectual activity during the ancient and medieval times. This country has the distinction of multiplicity of thoughts, languages, scientific, artistic, cultural, philosophical perceptions and knowledge system. These composite knowledge is perceived as the key resource for developmental activities. For centuries, the Indian knowledge Systems have passed down from generation to generation through oral and written traditions. A variety of writing materials such as stones, copperplates, birch bark, palm leaves, parchments and paper had been in use to preserve the intellectual heritage. This treasure of wisdom containing the ancient knowledge systems has come down to us in the form of manuscripts. Indian manuscripts are the richest collection of written documents that provide information on the existence of different civilizations and the cultural affluence of the nation. Written in different Indian languages; these manuscripts are spread all over the country in different monasteries, temples, libraries, museums, with individuals and in several private institutions. In fact, India has possibly the oldest and the largest collection of manuscripts in the world.

In the development of intellectual tradition of India we observe a big leap forward from scripts to manuscripts, handwritten materials. A manuscript seeks of the past, reveals history, unfolds perspectives and reflects the socio-cultural, even socio political scenario of time . Its contents are significant literally, scientifically. As it forms fascinating palaeographically, calligraphically, and technically. Thus manuscripts are concrete examples of the humanistic and artistic activities of the past. Record of Indian wisdom is lying in the books written by host of authors in the form of manuscripts for millennium against all odds. Manuscripts are useful sources for building history of the respective people , place and period. Material preserved in manuscript form is the primary source databank of written material from the earliest period. Manuscripts provide not only the most authentic witnesses to life, but also a record of what aspects of life were considered to be of sufficient importance to immortalize in the medium. Every manuscript written in the medieval era is an authentic artifact of that era. However, every manuscript was not penned by its author, and every author was not a living witness to the events he or she penned. Scribes existed in every era, chronicling events of many generations past. After all, they were writing for their times, not for curious readers hundreds of years in the future. Written records can be used in a diversity of ways to make inferences about historical questions which could not have been further from the minds of the scribes who penned the words. The granting of privileges or the dispensing of justice reveals much about social conditions, relations and expectations. The importance of manuscripts, especially chronicles in the reconstruction of early history cannot be denied; however, manuscripts also tend to reflect opinionated versions of actual facts.

The North East India is the meeting ground of various cultures since pre historic period. Before independence, it consisted of independent Kingdom of Assam, Manipur, Tripura and some hills region. The area is notable for its rich cultural heritage in the form of temples, monasteries, stupas, traditional arts and crafts, dances, festivals, rituals and so on. During medieval period the state of Manipur and Tripura were ruled by Hindu Kings. The same was the case in Assam; with the coming of the Ahoms in Assam (13th-14th Century), a number of Buronjies were written. Simultaneously with the growth of Neo Vishanavism propounded by great, saint Shrimant Shankar Dev. The cultural heritage of Assam was given a new flip one of the finest contributions of the Ahom Kings as well as Shankar Dev was to popularised the writings of manuscripts. The Buddhist monasteries in Tawang area as well as Theravada Buddhist manuscripts in eastern part of Arunachal Pradesh and some parts of Assam also patronized, writing of manuscripts as well as manuscript painting. In Tripura also the Manikya King and in Manipur after the introduction of Vishanavism in 17th century writings of manuscripts were patronised by the rulers.

Tripura kingdom (Sanskrit: Tripura; Anglicized: Tripera) was one of the largest ancient kingdoms of the Tipra people of the Bodo Kachari ethnicity in the North Eastern region of Indian subcontinent. It is believed that after 1st century BC. the Tipra - Kingdom was established around the confluence of the river Brahmaputra (Twima) with the Meghna and the Surma rivers in todays' Central Bangladesh area. The capital was called 'Khorongma' and was in the Syllet district of the present Bangladesh. Triura, small but culturally developed hilly picturesque state having total area measuring 10,486 Sq.km with a population of 3.1 million only. This state with its capital at Agartala is bounded by Sylhet district of Bangladesh in the North, Cachar district of Assam in the North East, Mizoram state in the East, the districs of Noakhali and Chittagong East, the districts of Noakhali and Chittagong of Bangladesh in the West. No less than 19 tribal communities belonging to different ethnic and linguistic groups are to be found in different parts of the state. The plain people from indeterminable times have been hiring side by side with tribal communities resulting in cultural exchanges. This state is famous as an abode of fourteen deities of our age long tradition; recognized as one of the 51 shakti peethas of India hearing the sacred shrine of the Mother Tripureswari, in the southern pond a Saiva tirtha named as Unokoti, an extraordinary sculptural erection of heavy and quity images of Hindu gods and goddesses on the body of hillocks situated in the north district of Kailasahar. This land is also affluent with so many archeological sites specially that of Buddha cult at Pilak in the south.

There is a common belief that the name of Tripura has originated from 'Tripura Sundari' - the presiding deity of the land which is famous as one of the 51 Pithas of Hindu Pilgrims. Apart from this traditional view it is believed that originally the land was known as 'Tuipra' meaning a land adjoining the water. It is fact that in days of yore the boundaries of Tripura was extended up to the Bay of Bengal when its rulers held sway from Garo hills to Arakan. According to the 'Rajmala', the rulers were known by the surname 'Fa' which means 'father'. The rulers of Bengal helped the Tripura King in the 14th century, the king of Tripura had to face frequent Mughal invasion. They defeated the Mohammedan Sultans Bengal in Several battles. Another meaning of the Tripura has been coined from two Tripuri word 'Tui' which is meaning water and 'Pra' means near.

There are about nineteen different tribes living in Tripura, the Tripuri, Jamatia, Noatia, Reang, Halam, Chakma, Mog, Garo, Munda, Lushai, Oraon, Santhal, Uchoi, Khasi, Bhil, Lepcha, Bhutia, Chaimal and Kuki. They have their own cultural heritage. It is to be noted that 15 tribes out of 19 scheduled tribe in the state viz, Tripuri, Jamatia, Reang, Noatia, Halam and Uchoi share same linguistic chords and rich cultural identity. Tripura is the traditional home to the indigenous tribals over the past decades. Tripura had beckoned and welcomed the settlement of non-tribals down the annals of history. As attested by the enumeration of the first imperial census conducted in 1872, Tripura had a non-tribal population of 30% which grew substantially in the succeeding decadal censuses. In accordance with the returns of 2001 census indigenous tribals comprising altogether 19 communities constitute 31.05% of the state's population while 69.95% are non-tribals including a fair sprinkling of Manipuris. Tripuri is big tribe in terms of population Bhutia tribe being the least in the state.

Amongst the tribals, Tripuri or 'Debbarman' community form the vast majority of around fifty percent while the non-tribal population comprising by and large the Bengalis and a minuscule number of Meithei and Vishnupriya Manipuris belong to various castes and sub-castes. Tripura is largely dominated by Bengali Community, in spite of the 19 Schedule Tribes, that form a major chunk of the population. Fringe tribal communities-in the context of Tripura, to be precise-like the Bhils, Santhals, Mundas and Oraons who had settled in the state from the early decades of twentieth century as tea-garden labourers grace Tripura's ethnic mosaic. While 'Kokborok' has emerged as Tripura's lingua franca among the tribals, fringe communities continue to speak their own languages. Being dominated by the Bengalis, the state's prevalent dominating culture is Bengali. In fact, Tripura is also home to thousands of migrants from West Bengal and Bangladesh. Bengali is spoken and understood by more than 50% of the state's population. However, Kok-Borak as well as Bengali are the official languages of Tripura. Hinduism is the most practiced religion in Tripura. Both Bengalis and Tripuris follow Hinduism with ardent fervor. Islam, Buddhism and Christianity are also followed by people in minority.

Tripura - a hilly state proverbially known as 'Paandava Barjita Desha' a land despised by the Pandavas. It was our grave misfortune that the Mughals plundered the land time and again, the British stigmatized it by putting our fellow brethren behind the forbidden iron curtain of 'Excluded Area', it has been a great tragedy that colonial hangover still haunts us even after 65 years of Independence. Alexzander Mackenzie in his book- 'History of the Relationship of Government with Hill Tribes of North East Frontier of Bengal' (1884) described Tripura in the following words- 'Covered with jungles and inhabited by tribes of whom nothing was known, save they were uncouth and not particular as to clothing, the hills were looked upon as something apart. The Rajash claimed to exercise authority with them, but did not as it seemed derive much profit from them.'[3]

The Tripura ruling house was traditionally believed to be the oldest Princely dynasty in the country and claim their descent from Yajati, the sixth descendent of the Lunar Dynasty. According to traditional belief Prince Druhya being exiled by his father embarked upon a career of conquest and political adventurism and in the process defeated and overthrew the king of Kiratas and had set up a new dynasty in North - Eastern India. The same sources further go on to suggest that king Trilochana of the dynasty attended the 'Rajsua Sacrifice' performed by king Yudhisthira and was greatly honoured by him. Dr. H.L. Chatterjee a very distinguished historian who spent long years in Tripura and closely studied its history, had a different opinion. He said. ȘSober history is however, inclined to treat accounts such as these as legendary and dismisses as fictitious the claims of the Kings of Tripura as being scions of the Lunar race. Undoubtedly, they are a Hinduised Indo-Mongoloin people significantly termed 'Kiratas' by the great linguist Dr. Suniti Kumar Chattopadhay (JASB, Vol. VI, No.2, 1950, p.216) having close affinity and Kinship with races of outlying tribal areas widely scattered over the entire North-Eastern frontier of our country.[5]

There is no doubt that the earl history of Tripura is shrouded in the mist of legends and there is paucity of the historical source materials. It is really a difficult job to discuss the social history of Tripura because of the great scarcity of data in this regard. Besides, some accounts given by few colonial writers on North East India and some administrative reports of the British Political Agents stationed in Tripura almost no reliable in formations.Only two authentic sources the two Manuscripts Sri Rajamala in Bengali and Rajatatnakara in Sanskrit can help reconstruct the ancient and medieval history of Tripura. The history of Tripura is primarily recorded in the Rajamala, the state chronicle and the Rajaratnakar a Mahakavya, written in Sanskrit. Like other sources of history Sri Rajmala contains the description and legends of the kings of Tripura, origin of the royal family and their reigns etc. Rajmala was first composed during the reign of 143rd. King of Tripura Dharma Manikya (1431 AD-1461 CE). The royal priest Durlabhendra Chantai recited the Rajmala in Tripuri language. After hearing to that recital, two eminent Sanskrit poets of the royal court, viz. Durja Baneswar and Durja Sukreswar translated these stories or wrote afresh in Bengali language. The 1st Lahar on 1st part of Rajmala written in Bengali verse is considered as one of the ancient books of Bengali language and literature. This 1st part of Rajmala compiled in the beginning of the 15th. century CE the subsequent parts were compiled at later periods.

The Rajmala has four parts, written in different times & by different authors. 'Rajmala' the royal chronicle of Tripura's ruling dynasty created more problems and confusions in determining the authentic history of Tripura. The Royalist school as ardent followers of Rajmala and other mythological evidences, strongly believe that 'Druhya' as the first formal Ruler of Tripura Kingdom claiming his descent from Yajati had established his independent empire at a Tribeg near the river Kapili flowing down the Kamakshya hills of Assam. Thus the claim of descent from Lunar race, according to them, is justified. Further in all royal proclamations of Princely Tripura, till the time of the last independent ruler the state capital had always been mentioned as 'Rajdhani Hastinapura'- which in fact was the capital of Kauravas and Pandavas.

E.F. Sandys, a British official in the Tripura royal court in his book entitled. 'History of Tripura' claimed that Tripura finds a mention in the 153rd. chapter of 'Vanaparva' of Mahabharata and according to him Tripura kingdom existed far before the beginning of Christian era. In the absence of any concrete historical evidence, numismatic, epigraphical or archaeological such claim can hardly be entertained. But the mention of 'Tripura Kingdom' in the Ashokan Piller dating back to 400 BC and Allahabad Stone Inscription of Samudra Gupta (c. 350 CE) again make the claim of the royalist school about their ancient heritage rather stronger for the Allahabad inscription clearly mentions -'Rulers of neighbouring states which include Kamarupa, Nepalaka and Tripura'. This Tripura is certainly not the Mahabharatan 'Tripura' which was located near Jabbalpur of Madhyapradesh adjacent to ancient 'Koshaldesha'. The very geographical proximity of Tripura to the Kingdoms of Kamrupa, Nepalaka etc. obviously refers to Tripura of Manikya Dynasty.

It is again curious that Rajmala is quite silent about the presence of Buddhist Rulers in some parts of Tripura. Whereas the 7th-8th century archaeological findings of Mainamati (now in Bangladesh) Complex near Comilla a few kilometers away from Tripura's State Capital Agartala, bear striking similarity with the findings of Pilak and Deotamura in South Tripura. Samatata was once ruled by very powerful Buddhist Rulers and held in their sway a vast area extending from Arakan to Kamrupa. It, therefore looks most improbable that Tripura could survive that powerful onslaught. Even T.H. Lewin in his book 'The Hill tracts of Chittagong and Dwellers therein' (1869) mentioned about 'Buddhist King of Amarpur in South Tripura - once capital of the Kingdom of Tripura. A German scholar visited Tripura around 1967-68 and he was of the firm opinion that Tripura's southern portion was under the sovereign authority of Buddhist rulers at least from 7th century. It is explicitly mentioned in the Rajaratnakara, the famous historical manuscript of Tripura that king Farusena of Tripura went to Ayodhya to attend the sacrifice performed by king Dasaratha. He was accompanied by Rsis and Yogis and was guarded properly by his soldiers. In that sacrifice the Tripura king was honoured duly by King Dasaratha. (Sri Rajaratnakara - 1st Part, 9th Sanga 86-87). The above mentioned two historical documents - Rajaratnakara and Rajmala are not self sufficient to come to any final conclusion.

The Library of British Museum preserves a manuscript since January 8, 1842 written on Sanchi-Pat made of the bark of aloes wood. It was written in Assamese language by two emissaries of Ahomraj Maharaja Rudra Singha (1696-1714 CE) namely Ratna Kandali Sarma Kataki and Arjun Das Bairagi Kataki who were sent to the court of Maharaj Ratna Manikya (1698-1772 CE) of Tripura. They visited Tripura on three occasions between 1709 and 1715. King Rudra Singha was extremely annoyed with the Governor of Benal, Nawab Mushid Kuli Khan who used to send 'Khelats' to Sargadeo Rudra Singh 'insinuating' thereby that the Ahom Monarch was subordinate to the government of Moghuls. Rudra Singh was 'therefore' keen on organizing a formidable confederacy against the Moghuls whom he described as 'enemies of Hinduism'. He dispatched his envoys to the Rajas of Morang, Bana-Vishnupur, Nadiya, Cooch Behar, Burdwan, Barahanagar and Tripura seeking their support and cooperation in the fight against the invaders. The account of the visits to Tripura by the two emissaries was recorded by them in 146 folios incorporated at the end of the manuscript there was a table of contents. The name of the manuscript was 'Tripura Deshor Kathar Lekha'. It was completed in 1724. Dr. Surjya Kumar Bhuyan an eminent historian of Assam closely studied this manuscript at the British Museum London in the year 1937 and edited the Chronicle and publish it in the year 1938. This 300 years old manuscript is an unique document that provides not only the account of three diplomatic missions but also incorporates the contemporary social, economic, cultural and political tradition prevailing in the region in the first and second decades of 18th century. Dr. Surjya Kumar Bhuyan described the book in the following words "on the whole 'Tripura Burnji' constitutes a distinct landmark in the history of Assamese prose and Assamese historical literature with regard both to its contents and expression, occupying a position far above the average Buranji". It also reveals significantly about the contemporary socio-political history of Tripura as well.

The eternal flow of Sanskrit has drenched all the parts of Indian soil. But it is surprising that the deep forests and Chester of hills surrounding the North East, did not stand on the way of Sanskrit, and the Sanskritic culture was eagerly embraced by this princely state of Tripura even in the mysterious past. The cultural history of Tripura would have been written in a different manner had there been no favourable attitude of the tribal kings towards Sanskrit. So far the earlier history of Tripura is concerned, it can be learnt from available manuscripts, different inscriptions, coins, deeds, oral traditions and other records. The history of Tripura is primarily recorded in the Rajmala, the state chronicle and the Rajaratnakar a Mahakavya, written in Sanskrit. The brahmanical culture apparently stepped in the state of Tripura for the first time during the middle of seventh century CE while Adi Dharmapa was reigning the state. History, however, tells us that the brahmanical culture and religion had already spread in Bengal and Assam in the 6th and 7th Century, CE. It is therefore, reasonable to believe that Tripura could not steer clear of the influence of that culture. At the request of Adi Dharmapa, the then Mithila king Balabhadra sent five erudite Vedic Brahmana Scholars to the capital of Tripura state. Te five brahmins were Sri Nanda, Ananda, Govinda, Sripati and Purusottama belonging to vatsa, vatsya, Bharadwaja, ksnatreys and Parasara gotras respectively. They performed a great Vedic sacrifice at the behest of the king in the district of Sylhet. The name Adi Dharmapa was conferred on the king for his religious bent of mind. A copper plate inscription, written in Sanskrit states that those five brahmanas were favoured with grant of land for their stay in the kingdom.

The date of the inscription appears as 51 Tripurabda. Those Vedic brahmanas had drawn subsequently five other brahmanas from Mithila belonging to the Katyayana, Kasyapa, Moudgalya, Swarnakausika and Goutama gotra together with their brahmana attendents and barbers. In flux of brahmanas from other parts of India also continued. One copper plate inscription reveals that during the Gupta period brahmana priests, expert in sacrificial rites, came from North West India to being by way of establishing many Sanskrit tols in Bengal. Sanskrit learning became firm footed in the state due to arrival of many brahmana pundits, and also with the composition of many valuable books by them on philosophy literature, Smrti, astrology and ayurveda. Since then the flow of Sanskritisation continued in the royal culture of Tripura. At a much later date, during the regime of king Dharmadhara, the son of King Megha, a great Vedic sacrifice was performed in kailashahar (in 1195 CE). This is stated by Sri Dinesh Chandra Sen in his book 'Brhat Banga' (Part II, P. 1086). A copper plate relating to donation of lad as an offering, 'daksina' to the sacrificial chief. It is interesting to note that during the last part of 14th century CE when Sylhet came under the Muslim rule, then too Sanskrit tradition in Tripura did not cease to continue. Some landed deeds, written in Sanskrit during that time, as mentioned in the 'Srihatter Itivrtta', bear the truth of this statement. We are aware that Maharaja Dharma Manikya took resort to the Sanskrit Pundits Banesvara and Sukrisvara to record the history of his ancestors. Kailash Chandra Singha's Rajamala records the fact of the arrival of many brahmana pundits at the time of king Ratna Manikya built the temple and installed the idol of goddess Tripura Sundari kali and orderly placed a stone slab in the temple bearing a sloka inscribed on it. After Dhanya Manikya inscriptions, inscribed in Sanskrit Slokas, were installed in different temples and buildings at different times by Maharaja kalyana Manikya, Vijaya Manikya, Rama Manikya, Govinda Manikya and Tadha Kishore Manikya. In 1901 Maharaja Radhakishore Manikya installed a stone inscription while laying the foundation stone of other magnificent Uajjayanta Palace at Agartala.

Mog Manuscripts

There is a controversy over the origin of the word 'MOG' or 'MOGH'. According to a periodical magazine of the Burmese Research Society, this 'word' has been desired to originate from Bengali. But in the Bengali Dictionary of Bangiya Sahitya Parishad, the origin of this word is 'unknown'. In another Dictionary this word is claimed to have originated from a Burmese word 'Mogh' which is generally used as an epithet before the name of a gentleman. Some others of course referred to the ancient Mogadha (Magadha) Empire for its origination. But it is sad that when the domination of Hindu religion began to thrive in this ancient center of Buddha religion, a branch of Mogadha dynasty left for Chitagong and subsequently settled down in Hill Chittagong. Probably the Word 'Mogh' came from 'Mogadhi'(one who hails from Mogadhaor one who is a resident of Mogadha). In English dictionary the words Mog, Mogen, Mouge have been shown as surnames to the inhabitants of Arakan in 15th and 16th centuries. Bengalees, of course refer to the inhabitants of Arakan as 'Mog'. Mogs are also known as Marma in Bangladesh.

According to 'Rajmala' the historical record of the royal lineage of Tripura, the Mog (Burmese origin) were the powerful Buddhist kings of Tripura. The people of 'Mog' community claimed to have come from Arakan and settled down in Tripura in 957 CE. Buddhism flourished in Tripura from 2nd to 9th century CE. Both Theravada and Mahayana forms of Buddhism were practiced, though Theravada Buddhism have stronghold in many parts of Tripura for many centuries. The Buddhists of Tripura also had to meet the same fate. The Buddhist king of Tripura was defeated by the Hindu king and Muslim invaders. The defeated Buddhist king along with his subjects had to flee and settle in different parts of Myanmar and Bangladesh. By the 11th century CE, Buddhism totally disappeared from Tripura. It is in the 17th century CE that the Mog (of Burmese origin) re-entered Tripura. With the re-entry of Mog there was revival of Buddhism in the state.

The Mogs are Buddhist by religion and almost all the people are the followers of Buddhism. The three major Buddhist communities of Tripura, viz. Mog, Chakma and Barua, have close relation with each other and observe vassa, Buddha Purima, Kathin Chīvara Dāna etc. in uniformity. Mog (Burmese origin), Chakma, Barua and Uchai are the followers of Buddhism in Tripura. Their cultural background and customs resemble with that of Burmese and Thai Buddhist tradition. The Mog Buddhists have close affinity with Burmese Buddhism in all socio-cultural and religious aspects. Though they live in Tripura, almost all Dhamma books such as Tripītaka, Aīhakatha, Burmese (Myanmar) Translationss etc are brought from Myanmar and Dharma teaching is done in Burmese (Myanmar) script. The dialect that the Mog people speak is similar to that of Burmese (Myanmar) and Arakanese (Rakhine) language with little variation in pronunciation, but the script is the same (Burmese Myanmar) script.

The Mogs are indigenous community of Tripura. They constitute sixth largest indigenous people of the state. Mog comprises 3.06 per cent population in total tribes of Tripura. By religion they are Buddhist. Their major concentrations are at Sabroom and Belonia in South Tripura. Their language is grouped under Tibeto-Chinese family. Mogs are dependent on Jhum cultivation. Mogs social culture and belief are centralized with Burmese culture. Mog community by tradition is famous for their folk medicine. The Mogs had a dynasty in Arakan, situated in present Myanmar. There were instances and records of wars between the Arakan king and Tripura kings. They were fierce fighter, and the Mogs was inducted in the Tripura royal forces, there were many soldiers belonging to Mogs community in the past. It is presumed that the Mogs started settling in Tripura since then, almost 5-6th. centuries. The Mogs are basically agriculturist, but now a day they are found to take profession of every modern discipline. As a community the Mogs are very disciplined, self reliant, and peace loving and meek. Maintenances of internal discipline are the distinct responsibility of the head man who in the past used to lend helping to the king of Tripura by maintaining peace within the community.

The Mogs have a large number of manuscripts with them specially the palm leaf and manuscripts made from bark of a tree. Though many of them have already destroyed and some are about to. According to these manuscripts we have come to know few occasions, festivals and also the Mog months. Tripura is one of the states of North East which remains the least well-known part of India, linguistically and anthropologically. At a time of great social change and also increasing interest in the region, new research is constantly being produced. However, there are many older sources which are not easy to access, either because they are out of print or because they are only available from limited outlets. This paper aims to help those who are interested in the region. Effort has been made to focus on socio-cultural as well as historical facts about the Mog people in the light of manuscripts and not all of them have any great value. Some indeed seem to be actually untrustworthy, forwarding ethnic agendas rather than any objective description. It needs more time to discover the several unwritten history of the Mog tribe. Further, a deep & serious study of the these Mog manuscripts may open a new chapter or historical research on Tripura and adjoining regions.

Manipuri Manuscripts

Tripura State was known by the name 'Takhen' in a number of manuscripts written in Meetei Script like 'Takhen Ngamba', 'Cheitharol Kumpaba', 'Sanggai Phammang', 'Langthaballon', 'Pamol Khunthoklon', 'Nongchup Haram' and others. Meetei (in larger connotation, Manipuri) settlement in Tripura was mostly the outcome of the matrimonial relations between the royal families of the two kingdoms. Another one is historical reason. Inter-state migration between Takhen (Tripura) and Kangleipak (modern Manipur). It is written in the old manuscript 'Khamlangba Khunkumion' that Khamlangba, a well known adventurer, in the first quarter of the first century CE, left Kangleipak for Takhen (modern Tripura). It is mentioned in the manuscript that the Takhens (people of Takhen, Tripura) had known him as 'Kalika'. In Khamlangbals return journey to Kangleipak, he was accompanied by a group of emigrants and they had settled at Uripok near Imphal City and Kakching in the south-east region of Kangleipak. It is the first recorded inter-state or inter-community migration episode between Takhen (Tripura) and Kangleipak (modern Manipur). Khamlangba had a wife during his outside journey.

Eminent scholars are of the opinion that his wife was a Takhen woman. It is also opined that some of the Meeteis (major community of Kangleipak) who were associated with in the adventure journey of Khamlangba had setteled in Takhen having Takhen wives.

On the other hand, matrimonial relations are the important causes of Meetei settlement in Tripura. Some selected examples may support the fact. During the regime of Meetei King Khagemba (1597-1652 CE), Akoijam Chanu Yangnu was married to Takhen king and she became 'Takhen Leima', Takhen queen as recorded in manuscript 'Cheitharol Kumpaba'. Meetei attendants of Takhen Leima and retinues had permanently settled in Tripura. Harisheshori, a daughter of King Chingthangkhomba (1759-1798 CE) was married to king Rajadhan of Tripura (1785-1804 CE). Meetei princess Kutilakshi had been married to Tripura King Kashichandra Manikya (1826-1829 CE) and Krishna Kishore Manikya and Birchandra Manikya the following kings of Tripura had Meetei ranis. All the attendants and retinues of the Meetei ranis had settled in Tripura. Here, the reigned periods and some names of Tripura Kings are not mentioned in the Meetei manuscripts. There are added from other sources for convenience.

The manuscripts 'Ningthourol Lampuba', 'Cheitharol Kumpaba' and 'Kangleirol' had mentioned a number of battles fought between Tripura and Manipur which showed the Inter-State Military Conflict between these two states. Mention may be made of a few of them. In Maliya Kum 2926 (Kangleipak era used since the regime of King Maliya Phambalch coroneted in 1397 BCE), that is, 1529 CE, Langai (an area of Langai river, a tributory of barak river) was a region of Tripura. Kangleipak King Kabomba (1524-1542 CE, that is, Maliya Kum 2921-2939) had sent a military force to invade Langai region of Tripura. Langai region was attacked and occupied by the Meetei troop in 1929 CE. To take a revenge, Tripura force attacked kangleipak (Manipur) in 1533 under the command of Pancham. The Tripuri troop advanced up to Leimatak area of Kangleipak. The Meetei troop had defeated the invaders and some important persons were captured. To commemorate the victory, Takhen Khong (Tripura Canal) was dug jointly with Takhen personalities and they became bonafide citizens of Kangleipak. There were also military conflicts between the two kingdoms during the regimes of King Chalamba

(1545-1562), Mungyamba (1562-1597), Charairongba (1698-1709), Pamheiba (1709-1748) and others.

In Tripura also, the Manipuri emigrants had brought Sanamahism with them along with recently adopted Hinduism. But before the second quarter of the eighteenth century CE, they had settled in Tripura professing only Sanamahi religion. Under the patronage of Tripuri Kings, four deities of Sanamahi religion were formally worshipped in Takhen. A temple of goddess 'Panthoibi' was constructed at Likman Khuman in Taltola and another temple of goddess 'Lamden Lairembi' at Bajal Ghat. A temple of the same goddess 'Lamden Lairembi' had also been constructed at Bamutia in Tripura. Two temples of the two male gods 'Pakhangba' and 'Puthiba' were constructed at Banamalipur and Abhoynagar in Tripura. The Tripuri emigrants had also professed two religions Sanamahism and Hinduism as they had been native Meeteis. Both Tripuri and Meetei Manipuris are mongoloids. Their appearance, facial cuts and skull forms are the same. Therefore, assimilation and adaptation process is quick and speedy and that is why indigenous Tripuris are all bonafide Meeteis in Manipur. They are never mentioned as Tripuris in the manuscripts of Manipur which are written in Meetei script.

Kokborok Manuscripts

According to the views of Santimoy Chakraborty this Kokborok manuscript is the oldest one and was composed far most back in 590 CE. It is comprehended that the manuscript was transcribed, may a time in the successive reigns of the kings of Tripura. As revealed in the verse No. 5 of the Mantras (incantations) the manuscript was last transcribed by some Krishna Ballav Deb Sarmano during the reign of king Mahendra Manikya in 1699 CE. It was further stated in the verse that Shri Durgaprasad Narayan Tripuṛ was the custodian of the Manuscript. The original composer of the Mantras (verses)was not indicated anywhere. Thorough research is also required regarding the oldness of the manuscript.

However, there are some hints and references of old literature written in the Kokborok language under the Royal patronage. First, there is a mention that the 'Rajmala' the chronicle of the Tripura dynasty, was written in the Kokborok by Durlabendra Chantai. King Dharma Manikya during his reign (1431-1462 CE) engaged two brahmin-brothers Sukreswar and Baneswar for translation of the 'Rajmala' from Kokborok Language to Bengali. But, the manuscript of the Kokborok 'Rajmala' is still missing. The second reference of the Kokborok manuscript is 'Surchya Pujar Khonaimani' (worship of the Sun-God) as published by Santimoy Chakraborty in his book 'Kok-boroker Utsa Sandane' in 2000. The manuscript is being preserved in the Agartala Museum. The manuscript is of the Mantras (incantations) for worship of the Sun-God and other Gods and Goddesses being worshiped by the tribal people of the State. There are forty Slukas (verses) containing eight lines in each of the Slukas (verses).

Again we find a mention of the Kokborok cultivation by prince Radhakishore Manikya in the Official Reports. I.E. Cox, head, Esq. C.S. Officiating Political Agent, Hill Tipperah in his Annual Report of 1876 stated - 'The Joobraj has, moreover, at my suggestion, set about the compilation of a Tipperah vocabulary. He is perfectly acquainted with the vernacular of the hill people, and I am in hopes that the result of his undertaking will have some scientific interest.' (No. 134, date Agurtollah, the 26th June, 1876). In the next year, C.W. Bolton, Esq. Officiating Political Agent, Hill Tipperah, in his Annual Report of 1877 stated - 'The Jubraj is still engaged in the compilation of Tipperah - Bengal Dictionary.' (No. 196, dated. Agartala, the 17th July, 1877). But the aforesaid work of the Jubraj was not published and the manuscript thereof was not found elsewhere. Doulat Ahammad was the pioneer in the venture of composing the Kokborok Grammar. He wrote a book of Kokborok Grammar 'Kokborma aung Tripura-Byakaran' published in 1897 A.D. (Poush 1307 Tring). After publication of this book he wrote another Kokborok Grammar 'Kokma Kalai' (Easy Grammar), but it was not published. At the instance of Nehar Uddin Ahmmad, the youngest son of Doulat Ahammad, the manuscript was found out from their homestead Kulubari, Sonamura, in 1970.

Conclusion

Tripura state has very less numbers of manuscripts, where Tripura University has taken an initiative to preserve the available manuscripts. Manuscripts of Tripura belongs to the Chakma Culture dealing with subjects like the history of ethnic tribes, their culture, herbal medicine practices, music and Hinayana Buddhism. In Tripura University, National Mission for Manuscripts has sanctioned a Manuscript Resource Centre and Manuscript Conservation Centre (MRC & MCC) in the Department of History on 20th December, 2010. The scenario of manuscript preservation is not so satisfactory in our country and there are many important manuscripts vanishing gradually in absence of proper care and emphasis of such documents. Northeast India is a treasure house of various cultural heritages and it is very important to preserve those heritages for future generations. The present study shows that except a few states of North East India, manuscript preservation process is still in dark. National Mission for Manuscripts is working on few projects to recollect those cultural heritages for preservation. There is a lack of manuscript preservation policy in the Northeast states. Only a few studies on manuscript have been conducted in this region. Launching of manuscript repository will definitely touch a mile stone in the area of manuscript preservation digitally along with its availability for use. Thus, the manuscripts, which are of at most importance to know the history and culture of the people of the area, are lost forever. The importance of manuscripts cannot be over estimated from the simple fact that these manuscripts contain ideas regarding cultural interaction of North East India with Tibet and parts of South East Asia. Thus, the manuscripts of Tripura form the soicio-cultural heritage of the region and it is needed to streamlined with National Heritage of India.

References

1. Barua, Golan Chandra, *Ahom Buranji: From the Earliest Time to the End of the Ahom Rule* (Guwahati: Spectrum Publications, 1985, Reprint).
2. Bernier, Francois, *Travels in the Mughal Empire*.
3. Bhattacharya, Banikantha, *Tripura Administration: The Era of Modernisation*, 1870-1972.
4. Bijan, Mohanta, *Tripura in the light of Socio-Political movements since 1945*, Progressive Publishers, Kolkata, 2004.
5. Brook, Douglas Renfrew, *The Secret of the Three Cities: An Introduction to Hindu Sakta Tantrism*.
6. *Census of India 1961 XXVI*, Tripura, Part V-A.
7. Chatterji, Suniti Kumar, *Kirata-Jana-Krti* (Calcutta: Asiatic Society, 1974, 2nd ed).

8. Chaudhari, D.K., *The Political Agents and the Native Raj*, New Delhi 1999,
9. Das Gupta, Rajatananda, *Eastern Indian Manuscript Painting*.
10. Das, Utpal, *Importance of Preserving Historical Materials of Assam*. New Spectrum, 2006.
11. Debbarma, Chandramani, *Glory of Tripura Civilization: History of Tripura with Kok Borok names of the kings*.
12. Doulat, Ahmed, *Kokborma Aung Tripura-Byakaran*, 1897.
13. Dutta, Jyotish Chandra, *An Introduction to the History of Tripura: From Monarchy to Democracy*.
14. Gait, Edward, *A History of Assam,* Calcutta: Thacker Spink & Co. (1933).
15. Gaur, R.C. and Chakraborty, M. (2009), 'Preservation and Access to Indian Manuscripts: A Knowledge Base of Indian Cultural Heritage Resources for Academic Libraries', in ICAL 2009 *Vision and Roles of the Future Academic Libraries*, University of Delhi, New Delhi.
16. Ghosh, Rituparna (2012), 'Palm-leaf Manuscripts Conservation: A Study, *Global Research Methodology Journal*, Vol.4, Feb-Mar 2012.
17. Guha, Upendrachandra, *Kacharer Itibritta,* Guwahati: Asom Prakashan Parishad, 1971.
18. *India, (2002)* 'Department of Culture: National Mission for Manuscript', 'Project Document' (2004).
19. Kharbade, B.V. (2010), *'Research and Innovation in Conservation of Manuscripts: An Interim Report'*, Research Project of National Mission of Manuscripts (NMM).
20. Kumar, Udaya D, 2009, 'Traditional writing system in Southern Indiaș Palm-leaf Manuscript', *Design Thoughts* (IDC, IIT Bombay),Vol. 2,
21. Maharaja Kumar Sahadev Bikram Kishore and Dr. Jagadis Ganchoudhury, *Tripura Historical Documents*, Calcutta, 1994.
22. Nandi, Subodh Gopal, Projit Kumar Palit, *Manuscript and Manuscriptology in India*, Kaveri Books, New Delhi.
23. Naresh Debbarma, *Kokma Kalai,* Hachukni Khorang Publishers, Agartala, in 2007
24. Ng. Kangiia Mangang Takhen (Tripura) As Reflected in The Manuscripts of Manipur (Former Kangleipak).
25. Parratt, Saroj Nalini Arambam, *The Court Chronicle of the Kings of Manipur: the Cheitharon Kumpapa* (London & New York: Routledge, 2006).
26. Rama Prasad Dutta, T*ripurar Prachin Punthi*, Agartala, Tripura.1998,
27. Ramana, Y. V. (2005), 'Digital Preservation of Indian Manuscripts: An Over View', in 3rd International CALIBER 2005, Cochin University, Cochin, 8-10 February 2007.

28. Ray. S. K: *India's North-East and the Travails of Tripura*, Minerva Associates, 2003.
29. Rev. James Long, *Analysis of the Rajmala or Chronicles of Tripura*. Tribal Research institute and Museum, Government of Tripura, (Reprint), 2008,
30. Roychoudhury, Nalini Ranjan, *Tripura through the Ages: A short history of Tripura from the earliest times to 1947 A.D.*, Sterling, 1983.
31. S.N. Guha Thakurta: *Tripura*, Publish by the Director, National Book Trust, India, New Delhi.
32. Sahoo, J. and Mohanty B. (2004), Early Writing Materials: A Historical Perspective; *The Orissa Historical Research Journal (OHRJ)*, Vol. XLVII, No. 4, 2004
33. Santimoy Chakraborty, *Kok-Boroker Utsa Sandane,* 2000.
34. Sen, Kaliprasanna, *Sri Rajmala,* Agartala: Tribal Cultural Research Institute, 2003, Reprint.
35. Singh, G.P., *Researches into the History and Civilization of the Kirātas.*
36. Sinha, Kailas Chandra, *Rajmala or Annals and Chronicles of Tripura* (Comilla, 1896).
37. Sircar, Dineschandra, *Some Epigraphical Records of the Medieval Period from Eastern India*, Abhinav Publications.
38. *Tripura District Gazetteers*, Volume 1, Educational Publications, Dept. of Education, Govt. of Tripura.
39. Bhaumik, D.L., *Tribal Religion of Tripura*, Tribal Research Institute, Govt. of Tripura, Agartala.
40. Bhattacharya, N.N., *Religious Culture of North-Eastern India*, Manohar Publishers, New Delhi.

13

Mrigavati Kavya of Abdul Alim:
A Bengali Manuscript of Medieval Bardhaman

– *Rangan Kanti Jana*

To reconstruct the history of land and people ancient literature can be considered as one of the major sources of information. In case of Indian sub continent the story in same. In ancient India there were a number of examples; with the help of these writings anybody can glimpse the past upto a certain limit of a particular period. Six main categories that help to the elucidation of the problems of history namely manuscript, epigraph, coin, sculpture, painting and architecture. In this present study basic attempt is to show how the literature illumines the historical events, more precisely history in literature. The discovery of rare manuscript do help to understand the past's time and space or to supplement other sources. In this regard, the vernacular literature of medieval Bengal may be considered as the immense sources of information of the political-social- economic-cultural aspects. It is to be remembered that authors of these vernacular literatures were not historians at all of their respective periods, but they incorporated various types of contemporary information in their works to give more authentic outlook of their works. These volume of information are corroborated by the other types of sources namely inscriptions, archaeological specimens, as well as foreigners' descriptions.

A manuscript (Kalmi puthi) written in Bengali languages has been found from a majar at Suyata village in Ausgram in the district of Bardhaman in the State of West Bengal. The name of the Kavya as mentioned in the manuscript is 'Mrigavati (Jana, 2010-11). So far as known, the main story is a folk tale which was circulated in the Radha region during that time. One Abdul Alim has been depicted as the poet of this very work. Thepoet stated that he was a resident of Suyata (now in Ausgram, district Bardhaman). This Kavya bears eight hundred and eightly six stanzas in two forms namely-'Payar' and 'tripadi', (Jana, 2010-11). Apart from this text atleast eight Mrigavati texts are known to have been discovered from undivided Bengal which were compored between the CE 7th century and the CE. Nineteenth century in Bengali Language, and the poets are – Dvia Pasupati, Muhammad Mukim, Muhammed Khater, Ebadatullaha and Safatullaha-Sarkar, Divjaram, Khalil, and Krimullah. The coposition inder study is earlier thus the other works. But it is interesting to note that before Abdul Alim's composition in Bengali Language, One Mrigavati was compered by Sk. Kutuvant in Oud language, who was the court poet of Sultan Hoain Shah Sarki of Jaunpur. This Hosain Shah Sarki took shelter under Sultan Hosain Shah of Gaur after his defeat to the Sultan of Delhi Sikander Lodi. Abdul Alim had incorporated the name of Sk. Kutuvant in his composition (Jana, 2010-11). On the basis of that it can be inferred that Sk Kutuvant's composition is earlier than the composition under study. Another point is to be noted here that Sk. Kutuvant's and Abdul Alim's composition & bear the same name of the Kavya, but in Kutuvants's story live the poet describes the Prince died and his wives followed the prince's way, where as in Abdul Alim's Kavya the prince of Kamkoti marred to the princess of Indrani. It reflects a happy ending tale.

According to the composer that he heard this tale from his paternal grandmother. The paternal grandmother had been described as a store of the stories (Jana, 2010-11) which indicates that this very folk tale was existed in the Radha region of Bengal prior to the date of composition. Abdul Alim's Kavya apart from the Mrigavati's folk tale, it consists of a number of sections (Jana, 2010-11) namely (Vandanas ii invocations)-Nabi Vandana, Pir Vandana, Raj Vandana, Pir Shah Mahamud Vandana, and a section deals with the birth of human being (stated as Nara-Nari Janma Katha). Fallowing poets's statement, it is known that he took one year to compose the Kavya. The date of composition has been incorporated twice in different ways such as (Jana, 2010-11)- 'Ritu Netra Veda Sasi Parimita Saka, Alauddin Hosain Shah Nripati Tilaka'. It indicates 1436 Saka i.e. CE 1514. In another way it is described as "Vachhar Dharia

Rachi Mrigavati/Alima Sunite Mon/Hijri Saner Nsokudi Holo/Mrigavati Samapon'' means 920 Hijri or CE 1514. In the 'Rajvandana' section (Jana, 2010-11) the poet described the perspective of the composition. Accordng to him during the visit of Sultan Hosain Shah at Suyata in Pir Bhahamani's majar to pay homage to the Pir, he (the poet) got the rare opportunity to sing the folk tale composition in front of the sultan, After hearing the composition the Sultan highly appreciated the poet for his unique composition. Further the Sultan advised the poet to write the composition. In this way ultimately Abdul Alim composed the Mrigavati Kavya.

The Kavya illumines the historical fact that Sultan Allauddin Hosain Shah visited the village Suyata to pay his homage to Pir Bahamani and from Suyata he moved towards Valki to inaugurate a masjid and a gateway. Besides this Kavya, three inscriptions of Sultan Hosain Shah have been found now which are fixed on the wall of Pir Bahamani's majar. Inscription No.1, bears the name of Sultan and the scribe-Kaji Minaji, ayat no 25 and 26 of the 3rd Sura and the date i.e., 902 Hijri or Ad 1496-97 (Karim, 1992). Inscription No.2 states the name of Sultan, his epithet (the conqueror of Kamrupa and Kamta), scribes name ie Kaji Minaji, the date ie 902 Hijri or CE 1496-97 (Karim, 1992) Inscription No.3, mentions the name of Sultan, his epithet, Scribe's name (iei Nasar-al-din), reason behind the inscription (ie the construction of one masjid and one gateway), ayat no 25 of the 3rd Sura and the date (i.e. 909 Hijri or 1502-03) (Karim, 1992). With the help of these aforesaid inscriptions, it can atleast be said that Sultan Hosain Shah had some connection with the village Suyata and adjacent Valki in the district of Bardhaman or Burdwan. Inscription No 3 indicates that Sultan came here in the year CE 1502-1503 or near before after the conquest of Kamrupa-Kamta. This is the first inscription which mentions Sultan's conquest. About this masjid and its gateway, there is no definite information particularly about masjid's location. Though till today an area between Suyata and Valki in known as the Masid danga or Masjid danga. But this area now does not bear any archaeological relics in connection with the mosque (Dasgupta 2011).

The poet Abdul Alim said that he took one year to complete Mrigavati in the year CE 1514 i.e. Hijri 920 ie Saka 1436 (Jana, 2010-11). It means poet Alim composed his Kavya twelve yeas after the visit of Sultan Allauddin Hosain Shah at Suyata and Valki. But the question is, why the poet Abdul Alim composed the Kavya twelve years after Sultan Hosain Shah's visit. There is no information where Abdul Alim Claimed himself as a court poet of Sultan Hosain Shah. He described himself as a petty village poet of Suyata son of a 'naquib' of Pir Bahaman's Majar (Jana, 2010-11). His meeting with the Sultan was a rare event. In his composition apart from the main folk tale to felicitate the meeting with Sultan perhaps he composed the 'Rajvandana' along with other invocations. It is interesting to note that the 'Rajvandana' section certainly reflects the impression of the common people towards the supreme power to Bengal. During that time ie early CE sixteenth century in the perspective of local history the visit of Sultan Hosain Shah at Suyata and Valki reflects a rare as well as a important event. This is the only literary source which bears the rare historic event supported by these inscriptions. It also indicates the common man's attitude towards the supreme power of the then Bengal.

The main story line of the Abdul Alim's composition ṣ Mrigavati is a folk tale. The geographical space as shown in the composition is the Indrani pargana. Which is located in the Katwa sub-division in the present district of Bardhaman or Burdwan on the westernside of the river Bhagirathi (Jana, 2010-11). Abdul Alim's composition is named after Mrigavati (Jana, 2010-11) the princess of Indrani. She was the main character of the folk tale. Mrigavati was the only daughter of King Rup and queen Rupa. In her childhood days she used to play with fawns. Mrigavati thought that in her earlier birth she was a female deer. She and her male partner with their two fawns lived in a forest. One day due to forest fire her male partner left her and two fawns to save his own life. Mother deer with her two sons were burnt to death by the forest fire. Afterwards in her human life she could not forget her male partner's selfish behaviour what he had done in the deer's life. So in her human life she did not believe any male except her father. Kamal Kumar the prince of Kamkoti was very much attracted by Mrigavati's beauty, but he failed to proceed due to her rigid nature towards male. To cope with the problem Kamal Kumar made one plan to counter the princess and he formulated one story same as Mrigavati's story. The only difference in Kamal Kumar's story is, he and his two little fawns were killed by the forest fire, the female deer had fled the forest to save her own life. The gardener and his wife helped the prince to spread the constructed story to the country of Gopbhum. When the princess heard this new story, she complained against Kamal Kumar to her father the King of Gopbhum. The parents of both Kamal Kumar and Mrigavati came forward to solved the problem. During the time of debate Mrigavati became very angry to hear baseless aligetion against her and suddenly came out behind the curtain. She became spell bound to see the prince Kamal Kumar, ultimately the problem was solved and Mrigavati agreed to marry Kamal Kumar the prince of Kamkoti. At last they happly united.

Mrigavati's main tale bears the idea of re-birth, which is a Buddhist idea as revealed by the Jataka stories. It can atleast be said that the folktale, which the poet heard from his maternal grandmother was certainly influenced by the Buddhist Jataka stories. There is no such source in hand, apart from the discovered archaeological materials, which can help to formulate a concrete idea about the Buddhist religio-cultural activities in the Bardhaman district before the Muslim invasion in Bengal (in the first decade of the CE thirteenth century). Not only that about early Buddhist activities till roughly CE seventh century within this geographical space no information such as archaeological as well as literary have yet been come into light. With the help of archaeological data an overall picture about the Buddhist activities in the early medieval period may be glimpsed (jana 2011). The geographical area concerned (ie the district of Bardhaman or Burdwan) is now situated between the Lati. 22°48'-23°53'N and Longi. 86°48'- 88°25' E. The district is situated in the middle of the Radha region. Some of the major autiquities in connection with the Buddhism are as follows ṣ a brick built Pancaratha base stupa at Bharatpur (PS Budbud), which was built in the CE 7th.- 9th. century (Ghosh 1989); a finely executed sand stone image of Vaisravan the god of wealth (chattopadhyay and Jana 2011) found from Kanchannagar (P.S. Bardhaman); a seated Buddha, which was discovered from Bacharhat (P.S. Bardhaman) of the CE eleventh century (Jana 2003); An inscribed small image of Jambhala (the god of wealth) discovered from Natunhat (P.S. Mangalkot) of the CE eleventh century (Jana 2008-09); a fragmented stone part of a Buddhist shrine from Birhata (P.S. Bardhaman), (Chattopadhyay and Jana 2001); a painted Hariti in the village Susna (P.S. Manteswar), (Jana 2011); apart from these, there are a number of stone images, which are reported to have been discovered. On the basis of excavated and explored materials, it can atleast be assumed that the Buddhist religio cultural activities within the said geographical space were in full swing. It also indicates that the very religion had received partronage from the local individuals like samanta, trader, cultivator etc to propagate the same religion in the very land. The political, economic and social condition of this geographical space as well as other parts of Bengal did not obstruct the propagation of different religions (such as Buddhism, Pouranic Hinduism, Jainism etc.) in the early medieval period. Probably the surplus from the agricultural expansion and local trade had given a big impetus to the growth of different religio-cultural communities (Jana 2011). The core story of Mrigavati Kavya reminds the rich Buddhist cultural heritage of the geographical space of the early medieval period.

Lastly it can at least be said that the Kavya under study had been composed in the medieval age, but the main story line, which is a folk tale (Kamal Kumar-Mrigavati love story), had its origin quite earlier before CE thirteenth century. It is true that the original manuscript of the Kavya is still missing, what we have, is theKalmi puthi of 1181 Bangabda. A question may now arise about the Language, which is quite modern than the exact date of the composition, 'Mahid Chandhury's manuscript copy of Abdul Alim's 'Mrgavati' is composed in pure Bengali and the Language appears to be near modern. This is not surprising as Chaudhury himself stated the date to be in the late eighteenth century; the manuscript may well be a modernized copy of the early sixteenth century original. But there is an every chance that the Bengali original may actually be a much later version of Kutuban's Awadhi Mrgavati. Kutuban wrote his 'Mrgavati' in 1512 as against Alim's stated date of 1514-15 for his own Bengali version. That puts the two versions very close together, if we are to believe in the autiquity of the Bengali version. However in terms of the language of composition and in content, the Bengali version seems to be later than Kutuban's writing (Dasgupta-2011).

References

1. Jana, Rangan Kanti (2010-11), (ed) Mrigavati Kavya of Abdul Alim, Sanskrita Pustak Bhandar-Kolkata, PP 1 ff.
2. Jana (2010-11), p.3
3. Jana (2010-11), p.5.
4. Jana (2010-11), p.3.
5. Jana (2010-11), p.3.
6. Jana (2010-11), p.3.

7. Jana (2010-11), p.3.
8. Karim, Abdul (1992), *Corpus of the Arabic and Persian Inscriptions of Bengal*, Dhaka, pp 240-42.
9. Karim (1992-11), pp.241-42.
10. Karim (1992), pp.256-57.
11. Dasgupta, Nupur, (2011), The Evidence of Words: In Search of the Popular in Medieval Bengali literature, in *Aspects of History* (ed) Haider, N and Hussain, E, New Delhi, p 83.
12. Jana (2010-11), p.3.
13. Jana (2010-11), p.54.
14. Jana (2010-11), p.11.
15. Jana (2010-11), p.23ff.
16. Jana, Rangan Kanti, (2011), Tracing the Archaeology of Buddhism in the Early Medieval Bardhaman, West Bengal, in *Pratna Samiksha. Vol. 2, New Series*, Kolkata, pp 115-118.
17. Ghosh, A (ed) (1989), *An Encyclopaedia of Indian Archaeology, Vol.2*, Munshiram Manoharlal, New Delhi, pp 66-67.
18. Chattapadhyay, Bhaskar and Jana, Rangan Kanti, (2001), *Descriptive Catalogue of Sculptures Museum and Art Gallery,* The University of Burdwan, Burdwan, pp 28-29, Pl. 9 No 73.
19. Jana, Rangan Kanti, (2003), A Note on an Insribed Image of Dhayani Buddha, in *Journal of the Asiatic Society,* 45(1), Kolkata, pp. 46-47, Pl. 156.
20. Jana, Rangan Kanti, (2008-09), An Inscribed Jambhala Image from Mangolkot, Burdwans, *Journal of History*, Department of History, Jadavpur University, 26, Kolkata, pp 146-148, Pl.16.
21. Chattopadhyay and Jana, (2001), p 27.
22. Jana (2011), p. 117.
23. Jana (2011), p. 117.
24. Dasgupta (2011), p. 82.

14

The Sacred Books of the East:
A Colonial Representation

– *Abira Basu Chakraborty*

From the year 1600 CE, when Elizabeth-I granted permission to the East India Company for having trade relations with India, it was a fairly normal trading company with huge profits from major trading ports of India. Even over India, the Anglo-French hostile relationship in Europe had cast its shadow and both fought for the hegemony over the undivided Indian sub-continent. A strong position and supremacy over India was necessary for the British to offset the power of France on one hand, and on the other, to dominate Asia. The Indian empire was vital for Britain because a major part of its economy was dependent on India. This dependence eventually compelled the British to think about this country from a different angle. East India Company decided to expand the empire and therefore, heavily recruited Indian soldiers to strengthen their position as well as to increase the size of the British army. According to Lawrence James, the British had a general feeling that they were not only ideally qualified to rule India because of their racial superiority, additionally they also had to fulfill its historic destiny concerning the lesser breeds[1]. Though it is surprising that a country with deep convictions about personal liberty could even imagine of an authoritarian empire, the answer was ready: the lesser breeds need a benevolent despotism.

When Bengal and Bihar fell under the rule of East India Company in A.D. 1765, they found it difficult to administer the Hindu law of inheritance. Through the Regulation Act of 1773, Warren Hastings had been appointed as Governor General in India and simultaneously Calcutta was declared to be the capital of British India. Warren Hastings was the embodiment of British Policies regarding India. He had a firm belief that to rule a country better, it was important to know the country better. Though there were various avenues available to achieve the required knowledge, one of the key techniques was to attain it through intellectual exercise. According to the wish of Governor General, the Hindu and Islamic laws of the country were translated into English and in contrast, the company regulations were translated in different vernacular languages. It was also under consideration that to make a bridge with the natives, to know them better, to know the country better it was essential to identify the base of their intellectual achievement. Therefore, the authoritarian *Manusmriti* was translated into English in CE 1776. *Pandits* were associated with British judges to administer Hindu civil law and for that of the Muslims, *maulavis* administered the same. It is interesting that in 1783, Mr. Jonathan Duncan received Rs.15,000 for translating the Company regulations in Bengali language. However, the initial efforts to understand ancient Indian laws and customs continued largely until the eighteenth century; the process gradually culminated in the establishment of Asiatic Society of Bengal (Calcutta) in 1784, The Bombay Asiatic Society in 1804 and The Asiatic Society of Great Britain (London) in 1823[2]. The foundation of Asiatic Society of Bengal in 1784 was the result of an idea that this organization would meet up the intellectual requirements of the British administrators. This could be achieved safely through the translation of both secular and religious literary works of India into English language.

Prof. Gyan Prakash has rightly observed,

> No sooner had the East India Company acquired territorial power in India than its conduct was subjected to a blistering attack. I refer here, of course, to Edmund Burke's impassioned denunciation of Warren Hastings, the Governor-General of the Company in the late eighteenth century. Hastings believed firmly that the Company ought to respect India's oriental laws and customs, but this belief did not prevent him from imprisoning and displacing Indian Chieftains, and annexing their territories[3].

Burke and Hastings both shared 'the guilt of colonial rule' and both agreed that the indigenous customs and laws should guide Company rule in India[4]. But they never thought of leaving the Indian people free from the power of the foreign intervention. In fact, the English authority over the Indian population was not put into question in any way. But Burke was of the opinion that in course of time, the Company could lose its control over the Empire, which has actually happened. The fear of Burke was soon became reality: 'Parliament gradually enlarged its control over the affairs of the Company, and colonialism entered the fiber of British life'[5]. According to Prof. Prakash, this was the reason, for which Disraeli could mastermind the coronation of Queen Victoria as the Empress of India in 1877 as a 'domestic political maneuver because the empire was already domesticated as something out there, outside Britain and to be shared by all Britons'[6]. Therefore, the early policy of the East India Company of not to intervene in the Indian social life gradually changed its course and understanding about the subject population, their social customs, manners and ethical codes were regarded as a necessary prerequisite for developing permanent institutions of rule, as it has been observed by Prof. Sekhar Bandyopadhyay. No doubt, Hasting's tenure was a gradual move towards cautious intervention in the matter of Indian Social institutions[7].

In this backdrop, the of eighteenth century European scholars looked to the East in context of British India. Sanskrit, as a language, was begun to be studied by Western scholars since the late eighteenth century. On the other hand, the serious study of India and its past began in the late eighteenth century beginning with the works of scholars known since as Orientalists or Indologists. This theory was further intensified by Sir William Jones, a civil servant of East India Company and a scholar of repute, who set up the Asiatic Society of Bengal. He was the first man to suggest that Sanskrit, Latin and Greek belonged to the same family of languages and emphasized that originally the European languages were very similar to Sanskrit and that of the Iranian language. This theory motivated European countries like Germany, France and Russia to embark upon Indological studies. During the first half of the nineteenth century, Chairs in Sanskrit were established in the UK and several other European countries[8]. During this century, the study of Sanskrit also played a crucial role in the development of comparative linguistics of the Indo-European languages. The ultimate goal, at the back of their mind, was to establish a relationship between Sanskrit and certain European languages and cementing a base for 'common Indo-European heritage'[9]. On the other hand, this study of comparative linguistics helped the Orientalists to establish the past of Indian sub-continent almost as a 'lost-wing' of early European culture.

All over the late eighteenth and early nineteenth centuries, the British Parliament began to assume an increasingly larger role in the affairs of the East India Company. Regulating Act of 1773, Pitt's India Act of 1784, Charter Act of 1813, a series of Acts of Parliament were passed to establish the sovereignty of the Crown over the territories it had acquired. But the eventual end of the Company was precipitated by the Rebellion of 1857[10]. The British government dissolved the Company and assumed direct control over India through the Government of India Act 1858. On the contrary, the Revolt of 1857 made Britain realize that it badly needed a deeper knowledge of the manners and social systems of the unfamiliar people whom they are ruling. British Raj was established with an appointed Governor-General to administer India. Queen Victoria was crowned as the Empress of India. India became the empire's most valuable possession, turned out to be the most important source of British strength and came to be known, as expected, as 'the Jewel in the Crown'[11].

In one hand, British supremacy incessantly tried to subsume India into their custody; on the other due to their various policies, socio-economic and political turmoil of the country was going to be irreversible. In fact, the late eighteenth and nineteenth centuries witnessed a very unstable period. Series of Acts of Parliament annoyed the Indian mass a great deal; the merciless persecution of Indian people in the struggle of Rebellion of 1857 caused anarchy all around; also a series of crop failures in the late nineteenth century led to widespread famines in which over fifteen million Indian people had nothing to do but decease. As a result, it could be predicted clearly that the nature of the forthcoming British government in India was definitely going to be different, particularly when in every aspect (political, social and economic rule) the policies of East India Company failed miserably.

The point of fact is, the British Raj encompassed only the three-fifths of the sub-continent. The other two-fifths continued to be independently governed by over five hundred and sixty large and small principalities with mutual co-operation. Accordingly, the British Raj adopted a set of new policies. Government of India combined the spirit of co-operation and conciliation with a policy of coercion and force. Though the ultimate goal of the empire was nothing but its own financial growth, yet experience had educated them that to govern efficiently they need the assistance of indigenous 'collaborators'[12], which was indispensable. They understood very clearly that only 1,200 Indian Civil Servants could not rule 300 to 350 million Indians properly, particularly when the question of authority and supremacy was concerned. But in true British tradition, they also preferred sophisticated and intellectual arguments to justify and explain their rule. Most iconically this notion was expressed by T. B. Macaulay in 1833:

> 'that... by good government we may educate our subjects into a capacity for better government, that, having become instructed in European knowledge, they may, in some future age, demand European institutions. Whether such a day will ever come I know not. ... Whenever it comes, it will be the proudest day in English history.'[13]

At once the observation of Prof. Hobsbawm along with V.G. Kiernan and D.R. Headrick comes to our mind, 'The colonial conquests of European forces had been achieved not by miraculous weaponry, but by greater aggressiveness, ruthlessness and, above all, disciplined organization'[14]. Therefore, under disciplined and organized machinery, historical writings as well as translations of Indian literary works received a great fillip in the hands of the British Civil Servants and administrators which was intensified from the second half of the nineteenth century. In contrast, to win over the converts and strengthen the British Empire the Christian missionaries tried whole-heartedly to find out the vulnerabilities in the Hindu religion. But at the same time the writings about Indian history not only helped the British to strengthen its power, but also gradually engulfed the thought process of Indian colonized people very successfully. For example, the works of foremost British historian James Mill (as an employee in the offices of East India Company had access to every paper from India), practically dominated the intellectual paradigm of entire nineteenth century. On the basis of the papers, he tried to interpret Indian History and 'carefully' divided the historical periods under the captions of Hindu period, Muslim period and British (surprisingly not 'Christian') period! To support the British rule he energetically put forward that as Hindu and Muslim forms of government had failed miserably to perform their duties, it was the responsibility of more enlightened British Rule to bestow its utmost effort to the improvement of conditions of Indian people. Strangely enough, Mill had never been to India once! But that never deterred him to formulate a theory on Indian history and that too based on the division of religion! It was sheer misfortune on the part of the Indians that this theory had practically dominated the intellectual domain of this country for an entire century. Even today it is almost a common practice to describe medieval period in Indian history as 'Muslim period'!

According to Hobsbawm, the late nineteenth century was marked by the characteristics of –

> 'two sectors combined together into one global system: the developed and the lagging, the dominant and the dependant, the rich and the poor. Even this description is misleading. While the (smaller) first world, in spite of its considerable internal disparities, was united by history and as the common bearer of capitalist development, the (much larger) second world was united by nothing except its relations with, that is to say its potential or actual dependency on, the first.'[15].

In general, almost over a century the Western scholars had few firm believe about the Indians that they 'lacked' sense of history, they were accustomed to despotic rule and had never experienced any form of self-governance or nationhood. Though in reality, it is not that the Indians 'lacked' the historical sense, but the problem is, their sense of history perhaps do not match the European logic of history; and as far as despotic rule is concerned, probably all countries having monarchy as ruling system had faced such a phase in their history as well. Prof. R.S Sharma has aptly put it, 'British interpretations of Indian history served to denigrate the Indian character and achievements, and justify colonial rule'[16]. The British administrators in India as well as the elite class in England strongly believed that India had no glory to talk about at par the European one ţ not in science, nor literature. Gradually they started to endorse the concept of responsibility on the part of the British Government to 'educate' the 'natives' appropriately. It can further be proved by the Minute of Honourable Macaulay (1835). From the opinions of the Committee of Public Instruction prescribed by the British Parliament in 1813, it is known that a sum (of Rupees One lakh) is set apart 'for the revival and promotion of literature, and the encouragement of the learned natives of India, and for the introduction and promotion of a knowledge of the sciences among the inhabitants of the British territories.'[17] Further, Hon'ble Macaulay said in the same Minute of 1835, that:[18]

> 'I have never found one among them who could deny that a single shelf of a good European library was worth the whole native literature of India and Arabia. The intrinsic superiority of the Western literature is indeed fully admitted by those members of the committee who support the oriental plan of education'.

Again he opined,

> 'In one point I fully agree with the gentlemen to whose general views I am opposed. I feel with them that it is impossible for us, with our limited means, to attempt to educate the body of the people. We must at present do our best to form a class who may be interpreters between us and the millions whom we govern, a class of persons Indian in blood and colour, but English in tastes, in opinions, in morals and in intellect. To that class we may leave it to refine the vernacular dialects of the country, to enrich those dialects with terms of science borrowed from the Western nomenclature, and to render them by degrees fit vehicles for conveying knowledge to the great mass of the population'[19].

Therefore, to know the root of the country better and to meet the need of the hour, ancient scriptures had begun to be translated on a massive scale. The European scholars began to edit many Sanskrit texts that was survived in manuscript forms and it was them who first gave the manuscripts the shape of published format. The study of Sanskrit grammar and philology remained important both in the fields of Indology and Indo-European studies. Translations of major Hindu texts were published, e.g, *Shakuntala* by William Jones (in 1791), Max Mueller's edition of the *Rigveda* appeared in series (published from 1849 to 1875 by The East India Company), a series known as The Sacred Books of the East (from 1879 to 1910) under the editorship of Max Mueller, *Panini*'s Grammar edited by Otto von Bohtlingk (in 1887) and a systematic editing of key Sanskrit texts *Bibliotheca Buddhica* by a Russian Orientalist, Sergey Oldenberg (in 1897). There are many more translated works that could have been cited here, but only few that have been considered as landmarks are mentioned here.

Not only the translation works, but Indological studies in an all-encompassing manner, got the greatest impetus at the hands of the German-born scholar Friedrich Max Mueller, who was largely based in England and like Mill 'had never even visited India'. As far as India is concerned, Max Mueller as well as other European scholars had contributed many important literary works. But due to space constraint, it will not be possible to review all the literary works, and so for this article, the line of argument would be confined only to the monumental work of the period, The Sacred Books of the East (SBE), edited by great intellectual and Orientalist Friedrich Max Mueller (1823-1900).

The monumental effort of Max Mueller is comprised of a total fifty volumes. Max Mueller himself translated three of the volumes in the series and collaborated on three others. The series was his dream project. For this project he worked not less than ten hours a dayṭ not counting the time spent in correspondence with the translators, well-wishers, publisher and others. This was the chief occupation of Max Mueller to which the last twenty five years of his life were devoted! The entire series took thirty one years of hard work ṣfrom 1879 to 1910 and was proudly published by Oxford University Press. The series was comprised of the translations of key sacred texts of Hinduism, Buddhism, Taoism, Confucianism, Zoroastrianism, Jainism, and Islam. All the religious texts published in the series were by and large kept as manuscripts in different countries. The credit goes to Max Mueller who not only collected but also organised the collection efficiently. In fact, the patience and hard work on the part of Max Mueller is really amazing!

In the Preface of the first volume of the series Max Mueller has acknowledged,

> 'To watch in the Sacred Books of the East the dawn of the religious consciousness of man, must always remain one of the most inspiring and hallowing sights in the whole history of the world; and he whose heart cannot quiver with the first quivering rays of human thought and human faith, as revealed in those ancient documents, is, in his own way, as unfit for these studies as, from another side, the man who shrinks from copying and collating

> ancient MSS., or toiling through volumes of tedious commentary.'[20]

Max Mueller was one of the persons who competently introduced the study of Indology in the West. But quite the reverse, while translations were going on, Max Mueller felt that being a foreigner, it seemed difficult to understand perfectly the cultural nuances of a completely unfamiliar country as disparity in habits and ideas were apart from the Europe. He was rather confused and put it straightforwardly –

> 'In using, what may seem to some of my fellow-workers, this very strong and almost irreverent language with regard to the ancient Sacred Books of the East, I have not neglected to make full allowance for that very important intellectual parallax which, no doubt, renders it most difficult for a Western observer to see things and thoughts under exactly the same angle and in the same light as they would appear to an Eastern eye'[21].

He further put it unpretentiously that the difference was such wide that an Indian *Saṅgīta* seems to the Europeans without melody, harmony, or rhythm, while a symphony of Beethoven's would be 'mere noise to an Indian ear'. The sharp cultural contrast and disparity in thought process was a real dilemma. The traditions so natural to India, was somewhat surprising to them. For example, his observation on meditation on the syllable *Om* could be taken into consideration –

> '... a long continued repetition of that syllable with a view of drawing the thoughts away from all other subjects, and thus concentrating them on some higher object of thought of which that syllable was made to be the symbol. This concentration of thought, ekâgratâ or one-pointedness, as the Hindus called it, is something to us almost unknown. Our minds are like kaleidoscopes of thoughts in constant motion; and to shut our mental eyes to everything else, while dwelling on one thought only, has become to most of us almost as impossible as to apprehend one musical note without harmonics. With the life we are leading now, with telegrams, letters, newspapers, reviews, pamphlets, and books ever breaking in upon us, it has become impossible, or almost impossible, ever to arrive at that intensity of thought which the Hindus meant by ekâgratâ, and the attainment of which was to

> them the indispensable condition of all philosophical and religious speculation.'[22]

Difference between two countries, India and England or so to say Europe, was well-defined and certain. It was known to all. Geographically, culturally, historically and sociologicallyṭ both the countries are apart in various aspects. Then why the English people wanted to know the religions of 'East' so intensely? Is it pure inquisitiveness? Why the British administration suddenly felt so curious about the religions of East that are thousands of years old, particularly when it had already been proved that they came and stayed here for monetary gains only! Did they anyway feel attracted towards the ancient religions of the East like Hinduism, Buddhism, Taoism, Confucianism, Zoroastrianism, Jainism, and Islam? Why Max Mueller gave his utmost endeavour to go for most of the renowned scholars from Europe who could contribute in his project? Perhaps one of the motivations at the rear can be traced in the words of Max Mueller in the Preface of the first volume of the series—

> 'We want to know the ancient religions such as they really were, not such as we wish they should have been. We want to know, not their wisdom only, but their folly also; and while we must learn to look up to their highest points where they seem to rise nearer to heaven than anything we were acquainted with before, we must not shrink from looking down into their stony tracts, their dark abysses, their muddy moraines, in order to comprehend both the height and the depth of the human mind in its searchings after the Infinite.'[23] It has been already stated that one of his motivations was 'to know, not their wisdom only, but their folly also.

But what were the other stimuli? Which publication took the responsibility of printing such an extensive series? To solve the problem and to help Max Mueller to achieve his dream, Oxford University Press came forward publishing the fifty volume set of Sacred Books of the East that took long thirty years. It is known that Oxford University Press is the largest University Press in the world that has been involved in print trade from around 1480 CE. It grew as a major printer of bibles, prayer books and scholarly works. However, the concern of this paper would be on CE 1867 onwards when the Press began its new line of works. Under the new scheme the Delegates of the Press (a group of fifteen academics appointed by the Vice-Chancellor of University of Oxford) approved the series, Sacred Books of the East, for publication in 1875. The Dean of Christ Church and the other Delegates of the Press initiated the necessary arrangements about the series. It was resolved that the expense was to be defrayed by the University Press and the Indian Government. This combined effort brought 'a vast range of religious thought to a wider readership'. Being assured, Max Mueller on his part opened a correspondence with the proposed translators[23-24]. He invited the renowned scholars of the age to contribute in the series, namely, Edward William West, Johann George Buehler, Hermann Jacobi, Hermann Oldenberg, James Dermesteter, James Legge, Johan Hendrik Caspar Kern, Hans Julius Eggeling, Julius Jolly, Thomas William Rhys Davids, Edward Henry Palmer, also Kashinath Trimbak Telang and the like.

If we go a little deeper into the subject, we have to examine the significance of the renowned translators invited by Max Mueller. Out of almost fifteen scholars, not less than five were Orientalists, the remarkable exception being Kashinath Trimbak Telang, the Indian Judge at Bombay High Court and the first Secretary of the Indian National congress. But who were these Orientalists? What was the ideology of these scholars? Why Max Mueller did became conscious, 'The time has come when the study of the ancient religions of mankind must be approached in a different, in a less enthusiastic, and more discriminating, in fact, in a more scholar like spirit.'[25]

Let us also scrutinize it in a fair frame of mind. According to Prof. Gyan Prakash,

> 'Orientalism was a European enterprise from the very beginning. The scholars were European; the audience was European; and the Indians figured as inert objects of knowledge. The Orientalists spoke for the Indian and represented the object in texts. It also made the colonial relationshipṭ the enabling condition of British Orientalismṭappear as if it was irrelevant to the production of knowledge. As a result, although colonial dominance produced the East-West construct, it looked as if this binary opposition not only predated the colonial relationship but also accounted for it. In other words, Orientalist textual and institutional practices created the spiritual and sensuous Indian as an opposite of the

> materialistic and rational British, and offered them as justifications for the British conquest.'[26]

On the other hand, Prof. Romila Thapar sharply criticizes them by saying, the Orientalists, by the middle of the nineteenth century, were not only the persons who had direct contact with India through the East India Company, but also condemns as –

> 'Some of the best known of such so-called Orientalists and Indologists had never even visited India, a case in point being Max Muller'[27].

Therefore, in reality, it can be alleged quietly that the Orientalists served the British supremacy in India by justifying the British occupation of the land. Max Mueller was himself an Orientalist. It is pathetic to say that as a matter of fact, the probability of his being otherwise in temperament is not viable. So, the question is, was it a pure academic interest that led him obviously to shoulder such a great responsibility of the fifty volume set of English translations of ancient religions of the East? If not, what could be the reason? Did he really love India and considered its benefit most important? Was his feeling towards this country was so genuine and tender? Was he a genuine benefactor of India? What exactly his real motive was? Let us look at the matter a little later.

It appears, apparently, that Max Mueller was an objective researcher who really admired India. Indian people also had great reverence for him. Early in April, 1886 Max Mueller received a curious letter from Calcutta (dated 16.03.1886) which had illustrated better than anything else the estimation in which he was held in India. The letter informed him about Babu Rakhal Sen, 'a medical man of this city', had offered him certain gifts on the occasion of the *Sraddh* Ceremony of his deceased father, usually distributed to the Brahman Pundits of India[28]. He tried to send gifts only to convince Max Mueller and his brethren in the West to assure what high estimation his services are held in this country. Not only to Babu Rakhal Sen, but possibly were more people to whom Max Mueller occupied a foremost place for his invaluable services in the cause of Sanskrit learning. For example, he received *Sraddh* presents on two other occasions also proving 'the Hindus ranked him with their most pious Brahmins'[29]. He had many stalwart Indian persons of the time as his close acquaintance, namely, Satyendranath Tagore, Keshab Chandra

Sen and so on. But alas! He was not in a position to pay attention to such emotional warmth. On July 13, 1883, he wrote a letter to W.E. Gladstone of Oxford,

> 'I have many friends among educated natives in India, and they speak and write to me, perhaps, more freely than to others. Nothing, I may say, has given me so much confidence in the future of India, as the thorough appreciation of Lord Ripon's sober government by the people of India. I am not thinking so much about the so-called Ilbert Bill, as about the preceding years when I felt very doubtful whether, after the rather Oriental regime of Lord Lytton, Lord Ripon's quiet industry, honesty, and far-seeing statesmanship would be appreciated. I believe there is a strong desire in India that Lord Ripon should remain, and, great as the sacrifice might be, it would, I believe, not be too great for the interests which are at stake'.[30]

To our dismay, his private letters (edited by his wife after his death) portray a completely different picture of Max Mueller. The person seems to be quite unfamiliar to us. Perhaps the impression of his private letters not only would upset the Indian readers, but also would make them able to estimate the person afresh.

On 25th August, 1856 he wrote a letter to Chevalier Bunsen where he clearly expressed his wish–

> 'After the last annexation the territorial conquest of India ceases–what follows next is the struggle in the realm of religion and of spirit, in which, of course, centres the interests of the nations. India is much riper for Christianity than Rome or Greece were at the time of St.Paul. The rotten tree has for some time had artificial supports, because its fall would have been inconvenient for the Government. But if the Englishman comes to see that the tree must fall, sooner or later, then the thing is done, and he will mind no sacrifice either of blood or of land. For the good of this struggle I should like to lay down my life, or at least to lend my hand to bring about this struggle. I do not at all like to go to India as a missionary, that makes one dependent on the parsons; nor do I care to go as a Civil Servant, as that would make me dependent on the Government. I should like to live for ten years quite quietly

and learn the language, try to make friends, and then see whether I was fit to take part in a work, by means of which the old mischief of Indian priestcraft could be overthrown and the way opened for the entrance of simple Christian teaching, that entrance which this teaching finds into every human heart, which is freed from the ensnaring powers of priests and from the obscuring influence of philosophers. Whatever finds root in India soon overshadows the whole of Asia, and nowhere could the vital power of Christianity more gloriously realize itself than if the world saw it spring up there for a second time, in a very different form from that in the West, but still essentially the same'[31].

Again in 1887 Max Mueller made it clear in a lecture at St. John's College –

'My own acquaintance with non-Christian religions is restricted to what are called in the East book-religions, that is, religions which are founded on some kind of sacred book. When I undertook to publish for the University Press a series of translations of the most important of these sacred books, one of my objects was to assist missionaries. What should we think of a missionary who came to convert us, and who had never read our Bible?'[32]

When Max Mueller decided to correspond with the celebrated Oriental scholars for translating the sacred books, he made it clear in the prospectus of the book, that it was primarily intended to help the missionaries to 'whom an accurate knowledge of them is as indispensable as a knowledge of the enemy's country is to a general'.[33]

On July 27,1879, Max Mueller made correspondence with Lady Welby,

'Of one thing I feel very certain, that this translation of the Sacred Books of the East, which some of the good people here consider most objectionable, will do a great deal towards lifting Christianity into its high historical position. I look forward to the time when those who objected to my including the Old and New Testaments among the Sacred Books of the East will implore me to do so[34].'

Hence his real motive was only to help the missionaries! As one would expect, to prepare the translation for the series, manuscripts were collected from many countries ṣIndia, China, Japan, Paris and so forth which require adequate hard work. But the way the manuscripts were brought together was not always acquired through just routes perhaps. For example, a letter of Max Mueller to Buehler (April 29, 1882) can be sited in this case, he wrote:

> '... I have sent, some time ago, a request to the Japanese Government, that my two Buddhists might be sent to India, Nepal, Tibet, and China, in order to look for MSS. They are quite prepared for this now, and, being priests, they hope to get admittance everywhere. But it must all be kept very secret'.[35]

Though the hope expressed here was never fulfilled, as Kasawara died soon after his return to Japan from ill health in same year and Bunyiu Nanjio (sent to India and Korea to look for MSS.), had not yet been sent to Tibet. But the manner of collecting the manuscripts, as it has been already said, was perhaps not so decent!

On the other hand, Mueller believed and hoped that increased funding for western education in India would help the English people to uphold a new country with new vision. He was looking forward to the day. In a letter to the Duke of Argyll in December 16, 1868, he regretted not being able to help actively in 'great work of educating and improving the natives'[36]. According to him, India could be and must be 'conquered' for a second time.

This standpoint of Mueller seems to be little shocking particularly when he was one of the persons who initiated Indology in the West! Indians revered him so much and academically he also had a close connection with India. Till date Max Mueller is considered one of the great Indologists in India. Therefore, it is of course painful for the Indians that a great scholar like him not only encouraged the policies of the British, but actively endorsed them and worked passionately for the interest of colonialism!

Nonetheless, Max Mueller's passion to see India's conversion to Christianity remained his dream only, but his effort was well acclaimed by the people of his 'adopted country', England. Dr. E.B. Pusey of Christ Church wrote to Max Mueller on 2nd June, 1860:

> 'Your work will form a new era in the efforts for the conversion of India, and Oxford will have reason to be thankful that, by giving you a home, it will have facilitated a work of such primary and lasting importance for the conversion of India, and which, by enabling us to compare that early false religion with the true, illustrates the more than blessedness of what we enjoy.'[37]

Therefore, it has now become apparent that the entire series was practically designed to hoist the colonial supremacy over the 'natives'– 'India has been conquered once, but India must be conquered again, and that second conquest should be a conquest by education' (Max Mueller to The Duke of Argyll, 1868). Strategy and hard labor for the collection of manuscripts, correspondence with the translators, translations of those manuscripts, the uphill struggle for preparing the series, long patience on the part of the Editor (for example, Burnell informed him about giving up his translation of the *Manu* after '*six years in uncertainty about it*') though it is hard to believe yet all were part of a big colonial game. In Asia, the academic aggression was not intended for India only; China was also under the same plan of action.

In the nineteenth century the age-old country had already gone under the sway of the European powers, among whom the British were leading. When the Chinese texts were first published by Oxford University Press under the name of The Sacred Books of China in 1879, China had already suffered awfully from a series of incidents, e.g, illegal Opium trade, First Opium War (1840), a series of treaties which made China semi-feudal and semi-colonial country, Second Opium War (1857), Treaty of Tientsin, and Convention of Peking in 1860. On the other hand, the Taiping Rebellion, The Restoration, and Self- Strengthening Movement made China weaker and very much prone to Western Powers. She almost lost her national independence. Moreover, missionary activities in China were unpleasantly terrible. At that time China not only was very anxious, but to some extent became traumatized for her future too. It was necessary to pacify her. The foreign powers, especially England, made an effort to know the root of the Chinese culture, and religion, indeed, would act as the foremost instrument to reach out to that goal.

For these reasons James Legge, a Protestant missionary and an unassuming Oxonian colleague of Max Mueller, was invited to take part in this endeavor by Max Mueller himself. He was conferred with the assignment for translating various Chinese religious texts. Though cordially invited, Legge had been alarmed also by Max Mueller in a letter written on March 10, 1876 of the difficult nature of the task,

> 'I ought to say that, as a rule, we intend to give translations of complete works only, not extracts. We must have what is tedious and bad as well as what is interesting and good, otherwise we shall be accused of misrepresenting the real character of the Sacred Books I mean of representing them in too favourable a light'[38].

The hard work of James Legge for Mueller's celebrated *Sacred Books of the East* series was published in six volumes between 1879 and 1891. But disappointingly enough despite the monumental productions of James Legge's *Chinese Classics* and *Sacred Books of China*, China had 'not been brought near to our hearts' as it has been estimated by Max Mueller in 1890 and also 'China is simply old, very oldṭthat is, remote and strange'[39]. Again in an address to the Royal Asiatic Society in the late nineteenth century, Max Mueller, the great Indologist and tireless promoter of Victorian Orientalism, expressed that the problem was having '*no intellectual bonds'* no linguistic, spiritual, or social kinshipṭthat could unite Europe and China[40].

However, it is ridiculous that such an old remote country without any linguistic, spiritual or social kinship would never prevent the Westerners from occupying China for their trade interests that gradually turned into political domination! Though long arguments can be formulated, yet on the whole, it can be suggested safely that Max Mueller and missionary James Legge both were concerned with their mutual involvement in the transformations of the missionary movement in China as well as India.

It is now perhaps the responsibility of young Indian scholars to evaluate properly and to formulate considered opinion about the entire series. Time has already come to acknowledge the problematique in this domain. The discrimination of the Oriental scholars, if necessary, be wiped out. If required, all the manuscripts on the basis of which the series was prepared should be brought together; perhaps an attempt to translate again the old scriptures would not be such a bad idea. If truth be told, the Europeans had different motive behind the publication of such monumental workṭto help the missionaries 'to whom an accurate knowledge of them (ancient texts) is as indispensable as a knowledge of the enemy's country is to a general', which had nothing to do with pure academic interest. Not only that, British Oriental scholars rejoiced 'governing and benefiting India'. Therefore, it is almost evident that the translation might have been influenced by the attitude of these translators. But now the moment has come to raise such question as to why we should consider the series as one of the most important works of Indology? It is necessary to corroborate the new translation with the ones of the Sacred Books of the East. Translations of Indian scholar may differ from that of the European scholars as firstly, an indigenous person knows the cultural nuances of the country better than an outsider; and secondly, the purpose will be thoroughly different from the great scholar Max Mueller, who was the editor of the series and who campaigned regularly for colonialism. It is comprehended that to arrange the entire scheme, such project will require lots of money and time. Also a lot of passion is essential in such an enterprise to prove ourselves. Perhaps Universities and various grants commissions will have to take the foremost responsibility to encourage as big a project like this one on the one hand; and on the other, it is also the task of Indian academia to be a part of such a venture. After sixty-six years of independence it would be a tribute to the Indians.

References

1. James, Lawrence (1994): *The Rise and Fall of the British Empire. London*: Little, Brown and Company (UK), pp-205-206.
2. Sharma, R.S. (2010): *India's Ancient Past.* New Delhi: OUP, p.6.
3. Prakash, Gyan (1996): Reason and its Postcolonial doubling, p-95.
4. Ibid, p-96.
5. Ibid, p-97.
6. Ibid, p-100.
7. Bandyopadhyay, Sekhar (2006): *From Plassey to Partition,* Orient Longman, Delhi, p-139.
8. Sharma, R.S. (2010): *India's Ancient Past,* p-6.
9. Thapar, Romila (1968) :Interpretations of Ancient Indian History, History and Theory, Vol.7, No.3, JSTOR, p-319; URL:http://www.jstor.org/stable/2504471 accessed on 06.05.2012.
10. URL:http://en.wikipedia.org/wiki/British_Empire#East_India_Company_in_Asia accessed on 21.04.13.

11. Ibid.
12. Kaul, Dr. Chandrika (2011): From Empire to Independence: The British Raj in India 1858-1947, URL: http://www.bbc.co.uk/history/british/modern/independence1947_01.shtml accessed on 21.04.2013.
13. Macaulay, T.B., *A Speech Delivered in theHouse of Commons* on 10.07.1833; URL: http://www.columbia.edu/itc/mealac/pritchett/00generallinks/macaulay/txt_commons_indiagovt_1833.html accessed on 09.06.2013
14. Hobsbawm, Eric (2009): *The Age of Empire 1875-1914*, London: (Little, Brown Book Group) Abacus, p-16.
15. Ibid, p-16.
16. Sharma, R.S. (2010): *India's Ancient Past*, p-7.
17. Minute by the Hon'ble T.B. Macaulay (02.02.1835); http://www.columbia.edu/itc/mealac/pritchett/00generallinks/macaulay/txt_minute_education_1835.html accessed on 26-04-2013.
18. Ibid.
19. Ibid.
20. http://www.sacred-texts.com/hin/sbe01/sbe01002.htm accessed on 12.04.13, Preface, p-xi.
21. Ibid, Preface, Vol.I, p-xvi.
22. Ibid, pp-xxiii-xxiv.
23. Ibid, p-xx.
24. Friedrich Max Muller(1902): *Life and Letters,* Ed. By His Wife, Vol.2, Longmans, Green, & Co., London, p-9.
25. SBE, Preface, Vol.I, p-x.
26. Prakash, Gyan (1990): *Writing Post-Orientalist Histories of the Third World: Perspectives from Indian Historiography, Comparative Studies in Society and History, Vol. 32, No. 2 (Apr., 1990)*, pp. 384-85,Cambridge University Press; URL: http://www.jstor.org/stable/178920.
27. Thapar, Romila (1968): *Interpretations of Ancient Indian History, History and Theory,* Vol.7, No.3, JSTOR, p-319.
28. Friedrich Max Muller (1902): *Life and Letters*, Ed. By His Wife, Vol.2, Chap-XXVIII, p-188: 'India Mirror' Office, March 16. 'A friend of mine, Babu Rakhal Sen, a medical man of this city, on occasion of the Shrad ceremony of his deceased father, made certain gifts to you as the first Sanskrit scholar in Europe. These gifts, consisting of articles usually distributed to the Brahman Pundits in our country on occasion of a Shrad, have been forwarded to you by my friend. I hope you have received them by this time. He has taken the liberty to make the presents to you, and he hopes that, though very trifling, they may be acceptable to you. He has only endeavoured

to render some honour to you, as one occupying a foremost place in the hearts of the Indians for his invaluable services in the cause of Sanskrit learning. The fact of a Hindu having on occasion of his father's Shrad made these gifts to you ought to convince you and our brethren in the West in what high estimation your services are held in this country. Yours faithfully, 'Nerendranath Sen.'

29. Ibid, Vol.2, Chap-XXVIII, p-189.
30. Ibid, Vol.2, Chap-XXV, pp-119-120.
31. Friedrich Max Muller (1902): *Life and Letters*, Ed. By His Wife, Vol.1, Longmans, Green & Co., London, pp-181-82.
32. Ibid, Vol.2, Appendix-D, p-454.
33. Ibid, Chapter-XXII, Correspondance on the S.B.E, Vol.2, pp-9-11: 'Apart from the interest which the Sacred Books of all religions possess in the eyes of the theologian, and, more particularly, of the missionary, to whom an accurate knowledge of them is as indispensable as a knowledge of the enemy's country is to a general, these works have of late assumed a new importance, as viewed in the character of ancient historical documents. In every country where Sacred Books have been preserved they are the oldest records, and mark the beginning of what may be called documentary, in opposition to purely traditional, history. A desire for a trustworthy translation of the Sacred Books of these six Eastern religions has often been expressed. Several have been translated into English, French, German, or Latin, but in some cases these translations are difficult to procure, in others they are loaded with notes and commentaries, which are intended for students by profession only. Oriental scholars have been blamed for not having as yet supplied a want so generally felt, of a complete, trustworthy, and readable translation of the principal Sacred Books of the Eastern Religions. The reasons, however, why hitherto they have shrunk from such an undertaking are clear enough. The difficulties in many cases of giving complete translations are very great. There is still much work to be done in a critical restoration of the original texts, and in determining the exact meaning of many words and passages. That kind of work is naturally far more attractive to scholars than a mere translation. ... ' It is clear, therefore, that a translation of the principal Sacred Books of the East can be carried out only at a certain sacrifice. Scholars must leave for a time their own special researches in order to render the general results already obtained accessible to the public at large....' 'Lastly, there was the most serious difficulty of all, a difficulty which no scholar could remove, viz. the difficulty of finding the funds necessary for carrying out so large an undertaking.... It would have been impossible to undertake a translation even of the most important only of the Sacred Books

of the East, without the support of an Academy or a University which recognizes the necessity of rendering these works more generally accessible....' 'Having been so fortunate as to secure that support, having also received promises of assistance from some of the best Oriental scholars in England and India, I hope I shall be able, after the necessary preparations are completed, to publish about three volumes of translations every year....'

34. Ibid, Chapter-XXIV, Vol.2, p-67.
35. Ibid, Chap-XXV, Vol.2, p-114.
36. Ibid, Chapter-XVI, p-357: To The Duke Of Argyll 0178 – "I have sometimes regretted that I am not an Englishman, and able to help more actively in the great work of educating and improving the natives. But I do rejoice that this great task of governing and benefiting India should have fallen to one who knows the greatness of that task and all its opportunities and responsibilities, who thinks not only of its political and financial bearings, but has a heart to feel for the moral welfare of those millions of human beings that are, more or less directly, committed to his charge. 'India has been conquered once, but India must be conquered again, and that second conquest should be a conquest by education. Much has been done for education of late, but if the funds were tripled and quadrupled, that would hardly be enough" Oxford, 16.12.1868.
37. Ibid, p-238.
38. Ibid, Chap-XXII, p-12.
39. Ibid, Introduction.
40. Ibid, Introduction.

15

Manuscripts: Reflection of Culture

– *Asok Kumar N.K.*

Generally any written document or manually recorded book or literary work is called a manuscript and the scientific study of manuscripts is called Manuscriptology. Though the science of manuscripts comprises topics related to writing materials, writing aids, scripts used, search, collection, cataloguing and preservation, it gives supreme importance to the edition and publishing of manuscripts. The word manuscript is derived from the *Latin* word *Manuscriptus/Manusriptum (hand-written) same as the word hastalikhita* in Sanskrit. It literally means a composition written by hand. As per another derivation *Manu-hand,* Scriptus-written (the Latin word Scriptus is the past participle form of scibere-to write) i.e. 'A manuscript is any document that is written by hand.' It may also be used to denote inscriptions that are not written but chiselled upon a hard material or scratched with a knife or with a stylus or are cuneiform writing of wet clay.

According to Archaeology 'A manuscript is any early writing on stone, metal, wood, clay, bark, leaves and prepared skins of animals such as goat, sheep and camels. *(The American Peoples Encyclopaedia)*. The most appropriate definition of a manuscript is -'A knowledge based hand written composition or text on papers, palm-leaves, birch-barks, cloths, metals or any other materials that has significant scientific, medicinal, historical, philosophical or aesthetic value.' Thus the definition itself proves the cultural value ofmanuscripts and its role in imparting knowledge and importance it has in the life style also. On a very critical study of its general and particular definitions, we may even say, it points to the human culture, his intellectual and circumstantial progress. His culture, aesthetic sense, skills, eagerness towards development, knowledge in arts and science etc are reflects in the selection of materials, tools, inks and preservation techniques of manuscripts. In India also Manuscripts have played a very significant role in the development, preservation and propagation of learning and literature, down the ages. Moreover, Sanskrit works, mostly recorded in the form of manuscripts, are the repository of the multifarious facets of knowledge i.e. in Vedic, scientific, medical, agricultural, mechanical, technical, architectural, aesthetic, mathematical and philosophical etc. Actually ancient manuscripts have a link between the past and the present and have revealed striking information in all the intellectual areas reflecting the scientific knowledge of the older generations in modern contexts.

Manuscripts represent an advanced stage in the history of language. Besides the best source material for linguists to study the history of language, manuscripts become authentic records for tracing the cultural, political, social and economical history of our ancestors. Changes such as the sound changes, grammatical changes, and change of forms at different stages of the development of a language are reflected in the manuscripts. The creative skills and endeavour of our ancestors on different branches of literature during the centuries are known to us with the help of manuscripts. Even at the age of super computers, information for the advancement of knowledge is provided by the manuscripts. Thus manuscripts pave the way to the entire world for the realization of our cultural heritage and knowledge treasure. Prof. Louis Renou has rightly pointed out, if India is loved and adored throughout the world, it is chiefly because of her being the repository of a long and venerable tradition, intellectual, moral and spiritual. *(Visalakshy., P. Dr. 2003)*. In olden days manuscripts were prepared for a variety of use; (1) for the use of the scribe himself, (2) for the use of someone else who would pay for or not for writing, 3) for the use of his own disciple or future generation, (4) for being gifted to some eminent person or the scribe's preceptor himself, and (5) for being kept as Royal/Official or family record. These uses also reflect our culture.

The different names like lekhya, pandugranth, matrka, pustika, parvajna, paavali, nuska, taliyola etc. used in the regional languages give clear evidence for the popularity and widespread use of manuscripts throughout our nation. According to the form and size of the manuscripts they are divided in to five viz. gudi, kacchapi, musti, samputephalaka, and cchivadi. Apart from this gutak, roll, illustrated, illuminated, patrakar and potho are other types of manuscripts. This also points to the cultural progress our ancestors had. It is also notable that the sizes were chosen for the easy conveyance of these to the different parts of the country.

Palm-leaves, birch-bark, leather, cloths etc. are some writing surfaces where the texts of the manuscripts are found written. They are called writing materials. The instruments to write on the manuscripts are called tools. Hard and soft materials are used in the form of both writing materials and tools. The different varieties of materials and tools themselves give clear evidence of our ancestors' progress, technological skills and enthusiasm in modernization. This reminds us of the old saying - 'Necessity is the mother of invention'. In olden day's manuscript were prepared on an auspicious day at a formal function. Whether a manuscript had copied another scribe was inducted and the duos were to compare the original with the copy. If the preparation or copying had been done for the nobility and the royalty, the new manuscripts are taken around the town in procession in a chariot and deposited in a public place or temple for its being read out ceremoniously for the public. Though the reading might extend for days together in case of longer texts it was done according to prescribed rules.

In addition to that, there was a custom to prepare and store several copies of the same texts in religious centres like Kasi, Banaras etc. for free distribution and for sale during religious festivals. The nobility and the royalty also got manuscripts prepared for themselves during their sojourns on pilgrimage. It may be noted that an effective motivation to the preparation of the gift of manuscripts in early India was the halo attached by Hindu religion and custom. 'The gift of knowledge was considered to be of paramount benefit in the present life and in the life hereafter. *(Kṛtyakalpataru)*.

The preservation itself proves skills and knowledge of our ancestors in science and technology. In the collection of manuscripts they conducted survey. Through this they show their skills in social sciences and techniques of business executives. For the preparation and conservation of manuscripts they depended upon Physics, Chemistry and Biology. Setting of manuscripts in the library and their cataloguing shows our forefathers knowledge in library science and information technology. In reading, re-writing, editing, and publishing of the manuscripts, we can see their awareness in Linguistics, Literature, Palaeography, History, Sociology and mastery of subjects dealt with in the text. Thus manuscripts and the science of manuscript have close affinity towards almost all the branches of knowledge and subjects like arts, language, literature, folklore, fine arts etc.

In many manuscripts we see some maṇgala or benediction. These were aimed to train the disciples to do as their Gurus did. These also show our culture of benediction. Colophon was a part attached to the manuscripts to shows for when that was written? By whom was that written? For who was that written etc. were usually attached in the beginning or at the end. Krotapatras are those pages added to certain page of the manuscripts were something was found omitted by the scribe knowingly or unknowingly. Also some wrote further extensions of the original texts supporting the originals. Some such were criticism of the originals. All these are the clear testimony of our culture of thinking and thinking over different topics.

It is proud, as an Indian, that no other world civilization has such a proliferation of hand-written literature as the Indian. It is a clear evidence that the listing of manuscripts of texts and authors engraved with the alphabet 'a' - 'अ'occupies one full volume of 505 pages of the New Catalogues Catalogorum: An Alphabetical Register of Sanskrit and allied Works and Authors. 'At present, there exist in India and outside of it some 1,00,000 manuscripts in various aspects of Jyotis-sastra. The majority of these texts were copied within the seventeenth, eighteenth and nineteenth centuries, for manuscripts cannot long survive in India except under exceptional circumstance'(David Pingree.1970) also point to the above fact.

Our forefathers' enormous contributions in various branches of knowledge like Astrology, Ayurveda, Pharmacology, etc are laid down in the unknown manuscripts. It is a fact that propagation and further development to the existing knowledge is possible definitely through some rare and hitherto unknown manuscripts. 'A good number of hitherto unknown scientific principles or even theories might be found in manuscripts and the discovery of such manuscripts can be helpful for further scientific discoveries or to make necessary amendments to the existing theories'. *(Visalakshy, P. Dr., 2003)*

In fact, as in other countries in the world, in India also a few of the available manuscripts are so far edited, studied and published and a large chunk of pioneering works, in the entire branches of knowledge, are still lying unnoticed even in this digital era. Only through the edition and study of such manuscripts we can throw light on the greatness of the people of yester years and their contributions. As the key to open the treasure-house of knowledge the manuscripts and the science of manuscripts can uplift our nation to a very high and unexcelled level.

Though the acquisition of knowledge through different ways to know the authenticity one should proceeds to the original source. Moreover the notion of originality is always vital for research. Even procuring manuscripts and studying them properly always remain challenging tasks, as far as Indian knowledge concern, no other source plays such an important role rather than manuscripts.

Any intellectual evolution could get explicit expression for the advancement of knowledge and induce intellectual thought among the people. After the advent of writing system, such knowledge was transformed into written records to serve as a permanent guide to the orally transmitted knowledge. It becomes a speciality to create a record of important subject information on a writing material. That way, a huge number of manuscripts were available to the new generations as written records. And as a link between the past and the present such ancient writings required to be studied extensively for a reconstruction of our Indian culture and tradition.

References

1. Visalakshy, P. (Dr.), *The Fundamentals of Manuscriptology*, DLA,Tvm,2003, p.6.
2. Visalakshy, P. (Dr.), *The Fundamentals of Manuscriptology*, DLA,Tvm,2003, p.6.
3. Bhandarkar, D.R., *The Origin of Indian Alphabet*, Sri Asutosh Mukherji Silver Jubilee Volume, Culcutta, 1922.

4. Bhowmik, S., *Conservation of Palm-leaf Manuscripts,* Baroda Museum and Picture Gallery Bulletin, 1996.
5. Buhler, G., *On the Origin of the Indian Brahmi Alphaet*, Strassburg,1998.
6. Pandey, Rajbali, *Indian Palaeography*, MLBD, Varanasi,1957.
7. Chatterji, Sunit Kumar, *Sanskrit and the Languages of Asia*, New India Book Pub. Pvt. Ltd, New Delhi,1986.
8. Chaubey, B.B., *Manuscriptology: Past and Present,* Hosiarpur, 2004.
9. Desuza, J & Kulkari, *Historiography in Indian Languages*, MLBD, New Delhi, 1972.
10. Jackson, D., *The Story of Writing,* London, 1981.
11. Mahaligam,T.V., *Early South Indian Palaeography*,University of Madras, 1974.
12. Ojha, Gaurisankar, *Pracina Bharatiya Lipimala*, Munshiram Manoharlal, New Delhi, 1918.
13. Paduragi, K.T., *The Wealth of Sanskrit Manuscripts in India and Abroad,* Banglore, 1978
14. Raghavan,V., *Search, Preservation and Publication of Sanskrit Manuscripts,* RamakrishnavMission Institute of Culture, Culcutta, 1978
15. Sarma, K.V., *Manuscriptology and Textual Criticism in Medieval India,* Adayar, Madras.
16. Sarma, S.R., *Writing Materials in Ancient India*,Vivek Pub., Aligarh, 1950.
17. Sastri, R.A., *On Old Mauscripts,* BRVRI, Trissur, 1981.
18. Sastri, Srikanta, S., *Bharatiya Samskriti*, University of Mysore, Mysore.1954.
19. Visalakshy, P., *Writing Systems*, DLA,Trivandrum, 2002.
20. Visalakshy, P., *Development of Sanskrit Language,* Pradeep Publications, Trivandrum, 1989.
21. Nair, K Maheswaran, *Manuscriptology*, Swatam Books, Trivandrum, 1998.

Secondary Source

- *The American Peoples Encyclopaedia, Vol.II*, p.390
- Sarma, K.V., *Research Indian Mathematics and Astronomy*, New Horizons, 1993.
- *Kṛtyakalpataru, Dānakhaṇḍa,* Baroda,1987, p.201
- New Catalogus Catalogorum,Vol.I, University of Madras, 1969.
- Pingre, David,*Census of Exact Sciences in Indian Sanskrit,* Philadelphia, 1970.

16

The Politics of Religion:
Reading Shri Chaitanya between Biographies

– *Jaydeep Chakrabarty*

This paper seeks to explore the politics of exclusion that attempts to make only one biography of the medieval Bengal saint Chaitanya Deb acceptable as the authentic representation of his life and philosophy. This is done by initiating an enquiry into the theological and practical reasons at work behind the production of Chaitanya's biographies, and more importantly, by reading the 'canonical' biography along with and against another not so canonical one.

The need for the biography of great men is central to the Gaudiya Vaishnava tradition in particular because according to them, only great men or *Avataras* have access to truth. Traditional Indian philosophies had emerged by way of finding out the fallacious nature of existing philosophy (purvapaksha) and giving more valid proofs and arguments. But Vaishnavite schools, being primarily based on 'faith,' tend to underestimate, if not reject altogether, other modes of finding truth valorized in the Indian epistemological traditionţlike inference *(anumana),* debates of various categories (*vada, vitanda and Jalpa)* etc. Krishnadas Kaviraj, the author of *Chaitanya-charitamrita,* for instance, rejects all the schools of philosophy as '*Param Karan Ishwar Keha Nahi Mane/Swa Swa mat sthape para matera khandane// Tahe chhay darshan hoite tattva nahi jani/ Mahajan jei kohe sei satya mani'* (quoted in Chakrabarty 69) (None of this schools of philosophies accept God as the prime cause or supreme truth, and are only interested in refuting each other's arguments

Thus, from the six systems of philosophy, we cannot know Truth, whatever the Great Men say can only lead us to truth). Though against the philosophical and epistemological schools, however, this idea of taking the ways of the 'great man' as authentic, or canonical, is not alien to Indian religious thought. One remembers the classic answer given by Yudhisthira to the query 'What is the way?– 'mahajano yena gatah sah pantha' (The road is that the great people have taken). In the *Bhagavadgeeta*, Krishna also foregrounds the role of the 'great' people in setting standards for society, as people tend to follow their betters – 'Yad yad acharati shresthas tattadevetaro janah (87)'. Following this, the most significant Vaishnavite text *Shrimadbhagavatm* postulates itself as the representative of Krishna, rather as Krishna Himsef: 'Now that the Lord is no longer on earth, who will give people knowledge? Verily, *Shrimadbhagavatam* itself' (1.4.43-4).

Obviously, what is happening in these cases is the conflation and confusion of discursive and textual representation with the real or empirical person. The problem becomes acute and gets implicated in the politics of canonicity in case of historical people like Chaitanya. Unlike Ramanuja, Madhva, Nimbarka and Ballabha, the founders of four 'canonical' Vaishnava orders, Chaitanya has not written any commentary of Vedantasutra, which is regarded as essential for establishing a new order in classical Hinduism. Neither has he composed anything in the vernacular languages, which was a practice common with his contemporary neo-Vaishnavites and Bhakti-preachers like Meerabai, Kabeer, Nanak, Surdas and Shankardev. His whole body of writing is contained in just eight couplets or slokas in Sanskrit, because his idea was to teach people by way of practicing – 'Ashtadasha varsha prabhu neelachale sthiti/apani achari jeeve shikhaila bhakati.' The problem becomes acute when such a person, with a wide following in Eastern India as well as in Vrindavana and Mathura, disappears. On what basis would his disciplinary succession or following continue? It must be through his biography. This is the reason why within just about 70 years of his death, eight major biographies were available in three languages – Sanskrit, Oriya and Bengali (Misra 56). Now, given that the biographies are humanly mediated accounts, there is no reason why their versions would match. But religious organizations cannot function on the basis of plurality of discourses and they need 'canons'. So, just as only four versions of Christ's life are included in the

New Testament as authentic, two biographies of Chaitanya got recognition and patronageţ*Chaitanyabhagavat* and *Chaitanyacharitamrita*ţamong the devotees in Bengal and Vrindavan and beyond. At a later stage, *Chaitanyacharitamrita*, given its wide range of reference, theological depth and representation of Chaitanya's 'religion' as distinct, different from and better than all other religions, came to be regarded as the authentic version of Chaitanya's life and philosophy. The Chaitanya with whom one is familiar today, especially due to the tireless preachings of Gaudiya Maths and ISKCON, is the one of *Chaitanyacharitamrita*. Interestingly and ironically perhaps, everyone except some scholars seems to have forgotten the fact that neither of the authors had any direct acquaintance with Chaitanya's life and philosophy.

The materials of *Chaitanyabhagavat* were supplied to its author mainly by Nityananda, the closest associate of Chaitanya who had stayed back in Bengal. The book was written in Bengal, shortly after Chaitanya's death, among people who knew Chaitanya personally. Brindavan Das's style is by and large of simple, factual and almost prosaic narration. One almost visualizes the early and middle part of Chaitanya's life in vivid details there. However, the last part, the most important eighteen years of Chaitanya's life in Puri, is presented by Brindavan Das in a hasty and somewhat sketchy manner. It appears that he was in did not have enough materials at his disposal. This is natural because there was nobody in Navadwip at that point of time who was an eye-witness to Chaitanya's life in Puri, not even Nityananda, whom Chaitanya had discouraged from staying at Puri (Sen 234). As Ramakanta Chakrabarty has indicated, it is obvious that Chaitanya was well accepted among the Oriya Vaishnavites which he reciprocated, something which his Gaudiya devotees did not seem to appreciate (47). It can be said that for the Bengal devotees Chaitnaya was a 'cultural capital' that they thought was being highjacked by the Oriyas. It is also possible, therefore, that Nityananda and his group were not interested to highlight the Puri or Orissa episode and did not commission its representation in details.

The author of *Chaitanyacharitamrita* takes advantage of the silences and absences in *Chaitanyabhagavat*. The scriptural basis of Chaitanya's religion is (read was) *Bhagavatam*, which preaches unconditional devotion and love for God. It presents the love and surrender of the Gopis (the milkmaids of Vrindavan) as one of the many ways of devotional practice and spirituality. However, by the time one comes to *Chaitanyacharitamrita*, known by various names as 'madhura bhava', 'kanta bhava', 'ujjwala rasa' etc, it has become the only privileged mode of worship and the goal of all other modes of worships. *Chaitanyacharitamrita* is a redefinition of both Chaitanya and Krishna. Brindaban Das had accepted the equivalence of Krishna and Vishnu, and had accepted Krishna as the incarnation of Vishnu. Krishnadas, by over interpreting certain couplets of *Bhagavatam* and with the help of a few other texts establishes Krishna as the original God, and Vishnu as the incarnation. Again, the Krishna that has been valorized as the Supreme entity, is the cowherd boy of Brindaban, not the King of Mathura or charioteer of Arjuna. Actually between the demise of Chaitanya and the writing of *Chaitanyacharitamrita*, a significant thing had happenedṭthe emergence and prominence of *shadgoswamis* or six goswamis in Brindabana. All of them were followers of Chaitanya and had been directed by him to stay in Brindabana, reinvent it as per scriptural descriptions and give sound scriptural basis to his Vaishnavism. They did all these very meticulously, and the last task extra-ordinarliy. Rup Goswami, Sanatana Goswami and Jiva Goswami reinterpreted and assimilated not only Vedic and Vaishnavite scriptures, but many things from Indian aesthetics as well as Shaiva-Shakta philosophy. The latter two need a female figure along with the male, and hence Vasudeva or Krishna of *Bhagavatam* was replaced by Radha-Krishna. In fact, the theological interpretation of Radha Krishna in Gaudiya Vaishnavism is a transliteration of Shiv-Shakti principle. Accordingly, Chaitanya was reimagined as the twin incarnation of Radha-Krishna. In doing justice to their scholarship and in their attempts to propound a theology that would be acceptable to the religious and philosophical elites of the country, the goswamis of Brindavan lost sight of the main focus of Chaitanya's mission—the common people. Chaitanya was at constant war with dogmatic religion and ritualized orthodoxies, and attempted to shun casteism by all means. He rejected existing Brahminical systems of worship and preached the chanting of God's name as the only religion, where there is no caste distinction or hierarchy. But at the hands of the Goswamis, Chaitanya's heresy became another orthodoxy. It also lost connection with its origins:

> The cultural ambience in Gaudiya Vaishnav theology was invented in Brindaban had almost no connection with the culture of Bengal.

> Gradually, the connection of Brindaban with Navadwip and Neelachal became very week. In these places, the basis of devotion was passion—But in the philosophy, aesthetic works and scriptures composed in Brindaban that passion is totally missing. (Chakrabarty 73)

This is evident in the complex imaginations of *Chaitanyacharitamrita*. By and large, the book is dedicated to establishing Chaitanya as Radha-Krishna incarnate, albeit not on the basis of miracles but theory. But this is something Chaitanya would have been the least interested in. Both these biographies have on record that Chaitanya vehemently opposed on several occasions the attempts of his devotees to showcase him as God or incarnation. The author constantly tries, however, to establish Radha-Krishna incarnated as Chaitanya as the ultimate reality. It is, however, not the Krishna as the prophet of ethical action or epistemological tradition, but an erotic-pastoral Krishna who is to be the ideal of worship— *'Brindabane aprakrita nabin madan/Kam gayatri kambeeje jar upasan'* (244). Backed by the theology of the Goswamis, Krishnadas replaces the Krishna-Vishnu worshipped in the Vedic-Puranic tradition with the worship of Krishna as Kaamdeb or God of erotic love, more in sync with Tantric Vaishnavism. Radha, who finds no mention in *Bhagavatam* comes as Krishna's consort. However, this cannot be said to be a sudden change or arbitrary decision or just 'romantic imagination'. Post-vedic Hinduism has always nurtured Tantric worship as a parallel tradition, and the two most important centres of Chaitany's religion—Bengal and Orissa—had pronounced Tantric bias. It is possible that the Goswamis thought the introduction of a supreme Goddess, i.e. Radha and the recasting of Vasudev-Krishna as Radha-Krishna will be instrumental in affiliating the large mass of Shakta people, the dominant community in Bengal, whose God is imagined as 'Shiv-Shakti'. This will also make the neo-converts more comfortable. It is interesting to note here that a similar thing happened with the core Vedic prayer, Gayatri mantra. In order to appropriate the Tantric tradition within the Vedic, the God of Gaytri mantra, that is Sun, had to be reimagined as a female deity with three forms. It is probably only in India that female deities have often compelled the male deities to give them 'a room of their own', and have at times almost replaced them.

In addition, in case of Gaudiya Vaishnavism, the worship of Radha got strong support from the appearance of female gurus and ideologues. Wives of Nityananda and Advaita had emerged as gurus on their own right. Nityananda's wife Jahnaba Devi sent especially made idols of Radha to Brindaban to be worshipped along with the Krishna idols there (Sen 321). It is also a fact that in both court and folk literature of eastern India, Radha-Krishna love story was a common motif during that age, as may be seen from the compositions Jaydeb, Chandidas, Vidyapati and others. All these inspired or compelled Krishnadas to reimagine Chaitany as the incarnation of Radha-Krishna instead of Krishna. This is a classic example of how biographies or hagiographies posthumously redefine and reproduce saints. However, to avoid contradictions with the earlier biography, Krishnadas introduces the Radha-bhava of Chaitanya in his later life, which, as has been suggested, is underrepresented in Brindaban Das. Moreover, he shows this to have come from Ray Ramananda, the meeting with whom was a turning point for Chaitanya' theology.

Chaitanyabhagavat's Chaitanya admits of no intermediary between devotee and God. A person attains God by genuine devotion and chanting:

> O dear Mishra! In this age of Kali, there is no sacrifice, no austerity, no rituals. He who dedicates himself to Krishna is very lucky. Hence, you go home and devote yourself to Krishna, leaving all ritualistic details. Hare Krishna...Hare Krishna...Krishna Krishna...Hare Hare/Hare Rama...Hare Rama...Rama Rama...Hare Hare—just keep chanting this, all theories and mysteries will automatically be revealed to you and you will attain unflinching love of God. (77-8, translation done by me).

Same is the case of the eight slokas that he composed. In contrast, *Chaitanyacharitamrita* has made the position of Guru and disciplinary succession central for God or self realization, albeit Guru is reimagined as 'sakhi' or female-friend of Radha and Krishna. Without his or her help, it is impossible to for one to attain God in what is postulated as their real form:

> The divine pastimes of Radha and Krishna are the supreme mystery, unattainable by *dasya* or *batsalya*. Only the *sakhis* have the right to access this, and it is through them that this leela spreads. This leela is nurtured by the sakhis, and they enjoy this

> leela by proliferating it. Hence, without the sakhis' approval, nobody will be able to enter this world of supreme bliss, and whoever adopts the nature of Sakhis, will have this mysterious world open to them. The supreme target of all worship, that is serving the divine couple in their bower of bliss, can only be achieved by the blessings of sakhis. (251, my translation).

However, Krishnadas is anxious to point out that the love of Gopis or Sakhis is not the sexual love of human world. However, due to its apparent similarity to sex or sexual love, it has been termed Kaama: 'Sahaje Gopir prem nahe prakrita kaam/ Kaamkreerar samye tare kahi kaam naam' (252).

Thus, *Chaitanyacharitamrita* presents a new theology and philosophy in a systematic order, which is not just a copy of *Bhagavatam* and can be distinctively marked as 'Gaudiya' or 'Chaitanyaite'. Naturally then, to found and continue sects and disciplinary tradition or *shishyaparampara*, it is *Chaitanyacharitamrita* which would be much more help than *Chaitanyabhagavat*. Thus, *Chaitanyacharitamrita* became important not because it is an authentic representation of Chaitanya's life, but due to the fact that it has started a discursive field. To use a Foucauldian concept, while Brindaban Das is more of an 'author', Krishnadas Kabiraj as well as the goswamis of Brindaban are more like 'founders of discursivity' (Foucault 183).

Having said that, it would be appropriate to conclude by indicating that a more objective and inclusive idea about Chaitanya can be formed only by reading his other biographies, as well as biographies in other languages like Oriya. To use two Saidian tropes, in the place of reading *Chaitanyacharitamrita* as the canonical text and other biographies as apocryphal, it is time one read these biographies contrapuntally, pitting each against the other/s.

Bibliography

- Chakrabarty, Ramakanta. *Bonge Vaishnav Dharma: Ekti Oitihasik ebam Samajtattvik Adhyayan*. Kolkata: Ananda Publishers, 2009.
- Das, Brindaban. *Chaitanyabhagavat*.1548. Kolkata: Reflect, 1994.
- Foucault, Michel. 'What is an author?' *Modern Criticism and Theory*. Ed. David Lodge. Delhi: Pearson, 2003.

- Kabiraj, Krishnadas. *Chaitanyacharitamrita.* Gorakhpur: Geeta Press, 2007.
- Misra, Baniprasanna. Unmochita Dhakadakshin: Shrihatta Thakurbarir Khandchitra (*Dhakadakshin Unveiled: Portrait of Shrihatta Thakurbari*) Silchar: Srijan, 2011.
- Said, Edward W. *Culture and Imperialism.* New York: Alfred A. Knopf, 1993.
- Sen, Sukumar. *Bangala Sahityer Itihas.* Vol I. 1940. Kolkata: Ananda, 2009.
- Vedavyas, Krishnadvaipayan. *Shrimadbhagavadgeeta.* Trans. Jagadeeshwarananda. 1961, Kolkata: Udbodhan, 2009.
- -- *Shrimadbhagavatam.* Trans. Adhikari, Pranab et. al., Vol. I & II Gorakhpur: Geeta Press, 2005.

17

Puya: The Ancient Manuscript Tradition of Manipur

– *Ruma Sarma*

Manipur has been called by different names -*Kathe* by Burmese; *Moglei* by people of Cachar, *Mekhlee* by Assamese and *Cassay* by Shans.[1] Her indigenous names are '*Kanglei' (pak), 'Poirei' (pak*) and '*Meitrabak*'.[2]

In the ancient Manipur, there were seven salais or clans namely, *Angom, Khuman, Khaba, Nganba, Ningthouja, Moirang, Luwang* and *Chenglei Sarang Leisangthem*. During the reign of *Meidingue Charairongba* (17th CE), the Meitei became the common name of all the seven *salais*.[3] The account of the coming of the Brahmans as early as the 15th century is described in a *puya*/ancient manuscript called '*Bamon Khunthoklon*.[4]

There are several ancient puyas or hand written manuscripts written in archaic Meitei script that record the history of Manipur since ancient time's. Originally written on small,thin, rectangular boards of the sap of a tree called *Agaru* or *Agar (Aquilariaagallocha)* with the pens made up of fully matured and seasoned bamboo.The ink used was made up of lamp black and gall.The manuscript were preservedby means of sandwiching betweenwood and secured by a string.Then they were securely kept inside a *Lubak* (bamboo basket) which was kept on a *Lap* (a bamboo rack)to prevent any seepage of moisture.[5]

The '*Cheitharol Kumbaba'* of 1st CE gives us a list of more than forty eight rulers from 1st CE century till 19th century. It sets out briefly in a solemn diction, important events, eclipse of the sun, the moon, the earthquake, the epidemics etc. The worship of many indigenous deities as *Marjing, Koubaren, Koubru, Nongsaba, Laikasa, Lai Punthiba, Panthoibi, Yimthelai, Leisembi, Pakhangba, and Sanamahi*, prior to the adoption of Hinduism as state religion by king *Garbiniwaz* in 17th century is also mentioned here.

According to *Cheitharol Kumbaba, Pakhangba* was the first, historic king to ascend the throne in 33rd century CE. He was succeeded by *Khuyoi Tompok* in 154 CE.

Puyas 'Chakparol' and *'Chakpakunda Khunthok'* gives account of the use of word '*Chaphu*' (a pot used for cooking rice) originating from the word '*Chakpas*'.[6] *Chakpas* are indigenous tribe of Manipur who reside in the villages of *Andro, Chairen* and *Leimaram*. They also bespeak of the pottery making as an ancestral profession of the Andros which is the most famous site of ancient pottery in Manipur.

The presentation of various kinds of pots and implements like the beater-*phuyeichei,* wooden platform – *Leisuphal*, pestle-*suk*etc, by the Andros to the Meitei king, on important occasions, for ritualistic and related purposes is also mentioned here. According to manuscript *Tampak Loimasil*, the Andros used to offer twenty six pots annually as rite-depassage.[7] Similarly, ancient manuscript *Loiyumbashilyen* describes that appliquê or *Leeba* was essential for the artistic embellishment of any cloth.

*Ningthourol Lambuba*gives the reference of *Khagee Khulellei* (the Chinese town or the big Chinese village) invaded by a Manipuri king in 1631 who also conquered it and assumed the reign name *Khagemba* (the conqueror of the Chinese). This fact is also supported by *Cheitharol Kumbaba*.

During the reign of *Meidingu Loiyumba*, (1074-1122 A.D.) a treatise on distribution of occupations was written. The *'Loiyumba Shilyen'* distributes the occupational arts to certain lineage as follows:[8]

Name of Lineage	Occupational art
Thingucham	*Mungphi*
Lairellakpam	*Laiphi*

contd...

Kaswam	*Wanakatangphi*
Chakpa Thiyam	*LaiphiTonkap*
Chakpa Lampam	*Phiren*
Kongpacham	*Langtomphi*
Thongkabam	*Yarongphi*
Khumallabam	*Chamiphi*
Haokhom	*Tungkapphi*
Laikhuram	*Sarongphi*
Salchiram	*Leirumphi*
Wahengbam	*Dolaikup phi*
Kabacham	*Dolai Thanaba phi*
Apucham	*Phiroi phi*
Haodijam	*Heikoi phi*
Thodingcham	*Singkap phi*
Thongpam	*Laiyek phi*
Kongbam	*Purum phi*
Chingkhalpam	*Tarao phi*
Thinpam	*PumthitPhanek*
Taibangcham	*PhimuYekpa phi*
Yumlenpam	*Nongphi*
Wokthiyambam	*KhunungMusum phi*
Chakpram	*Phiren*
Thoudam	*Phagang phi*
Nongthombam	*Ningthouphi*
Ahongsangbam	*Embroidery work*
Ningthoujam	*Chinphi*
Khoiri Sumbam	*Khunung Chumkan phi*
YumnakSangbam	*Chingkhong phi*
Khoisnam	*PhimuLanphi*
Sing Khangbam	*KhunungMathang phi*
Chingkhawapam	*Korou phi phingang*
Wangpacham	*ShangmiLanmu phi*

Ningthou phi Shabane[6] (kings royal both made), the traditional Meitei manuscript mentions that the woven clothes with patterns made ofkabrangwere made during his reign.The manuscript says, *'Laireng Mateng … Phimank kina Phiroikhiye'.*

Laireen Mateng-ngu Khuyoi Tompopkta | | *Matairem Laikoksu Charei Phisahabana* | | *Lairel Hangkok Unyek Tam* | | *Tupi Haina Mami Lakna* | | *Langla Langkhan Tei* | | *Kabrangja Chulangna* | | *Lairel*

Hangkok Mami Louke || Haipaki || LoitamMeratha ||... Puknungwalpha phi Haona || Charei Phisa Tamye || Lairel Haikok Thok || Tupi Yekpu Yeksoitas Loitam Thapum Suna || Charei Phi Sarapaki SangtingPhiroi Tam || Matairem Khoriyan Phisabana || Nauwa Khoirel Thangpu || Samu Khutna Paiyna || Punungphi Koilen || ChareiPhimank Kina || Phiroikhiye ||

Its literal meaning is: 'The faithful servant *Laikoksu*, the seniormost skillful weaver, visualizing the image of *Lairel Hangkok* and adopting this skin pattern wore a *kabrang* cloth in the month of *Mera* (Sept-Oct) and presented it to *Lairen Meidingu Khuyoi Tompok* .... Weaving of *Puaknungwalphakphi* was also begun. Adopting the skin pattern from the python without making any error, the cloth was woven within seven months, the faithful servant *Khoiyah* the weaver carefully measured the length of cloth and holding a *Khoirel-thang* (knife used for cutting umbilical cord of a newborn) cut out the ready cloth.'[9]

Manaphi (royal cloth) made of silk was bestowed upon the nobles and warriors as a reward. *Ningthouphi (Ningthou-* king, phi-cloth) was also used for rewarding. Both are made of silk. The manuscript *'Ningthousaba'* states that a second type of Ningthouphi was made in the reign of *Meidingue Naokhongba* (428-518 CE)

Ancient *puya Lasing Meihourol* mentions the use of cotton (*Lasing*) by goddess *Leisembi*. She produced cotton yarn by pulling out fibers from the cotton ball and by rolling fiber, on the thigh with the palm of her right hand while the left hand pulled the cotton ball away thereby twisting the cotton fiber strands into twisted yarn.

Again, *Loiyumba Shil-yen* speaks of the tribute paid by the dependencies of Manipur. The Shan principalities paid silk as tribute, the western hills paid conchs and areca nuts.[10]

In ancient texts like *Numit Kappa, Poreitonkhuntok, Loiyumba, Shilyen, Cheitharol Kumbaba*, the methods and materials of metal casting is discussed.

According to ancient manuscript or *puya Ningthourol Lambuba*, ancient Manipuris collected beeswax and honey of wild bee from woods. Again, during the reign *Meidingu Chandrakirti* (1850-1866) a metal image of Lord Vishnu which was lost was recast. This statement is recorded in *Cheitharol Kumbaba* are as follows. *'Kumbi Khunnathabagikum. Sakabda*

1773 ... Phairanthadi Sagolsennahanle ... Thaninnong Sagolsen da Lainingthou Sana mahi da Mamangei Vishnu thamlambabu mangle Haiduna Mahavishnu Aamaheiyeh' (L. Ibungohal Singh, N. Khelchandra 1989 : 311).

Its literal meaning in English is that an image of lord Visnu which was kept at *Laiengthou Sanamahi* was lost. Hence an image of same was cast on Thursday, in February *(Phairen)* in *Sakabda* 1773.[11] This statement does not mention the time of making and installation of that lost image. But from this passage it can be safely concluded that a tradition of metal casting had started since ancient times in Manipur.

The ancient *puya 'Paaphallambuba'* is dedicated to *Paaphal*, the symbolic diagrammatic illustration of the indigenous serpent deity of *Meiteis*. It illustrates 364 designs of *Paaphal* (Pl.17.1-Pl.17.3) in various animals as birds, tiger, duck, cat, python and the dragon. Some forms symbolize evil, and others symbolize the bad or ill omen. The basic form of *Paaphal* is the intertwined body ending in the head biting the tail. Sometimes they are depicted separate. According to scholars, this from is not merely peripheral but highly symbolic and means ill omen, danger and inauspicious in opposition to the former aspect which defines the benevolent, good omen and male and female evolution. The upper overlapping part of the body is male part are *Pangabung*. The overlapped part is female part and hence is called the *Nupa-Nupi* concept. Traits of Astroloid culture which came into contact with the old *Meitei* Manipuri culture through the Mon culture of Burma can be seen in various *Paaphal* illustrations. The Mons came to settle in Manipuri around two thousand years B.C. After their settlement their ways of life were mixed up with the old ways of the *Meiteis*. They in their turn, added some more *Paaphals* to the existing ones of the *Meteis*. The additions were characterized by the more and more intertwining of the body of the shape.[12]

Most of these illustrations in the manuscript or puyas have no or little relation to the text. Very few are actually drawn to illustrate the meaning of the text. Usually, these are placed in a consequential manner. On top, corners, bottom or even to disguise the spilled ink. Colour is used sparingly and applied in flat tones with no dimension, light and shade in the western sense. What often results is a mêlange of pictures of animals, buildings, people, flowers, cosmic symbols which does not contribute to the appreciation of the text.

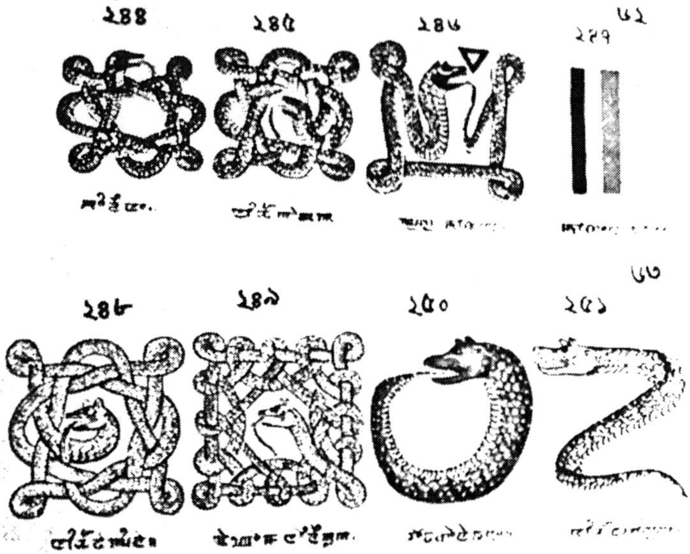

Pl.17.1: Pakhangba forms

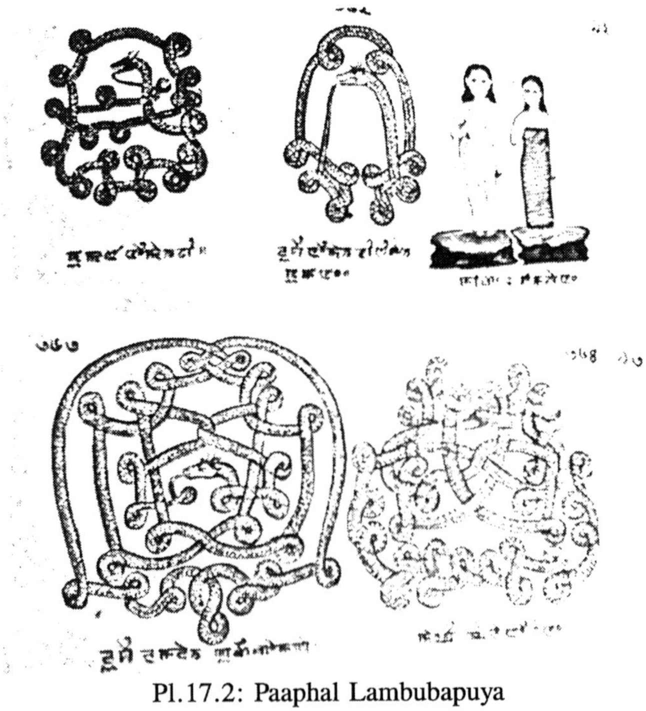

Pl.17.2: Paaphal Lambubapuya

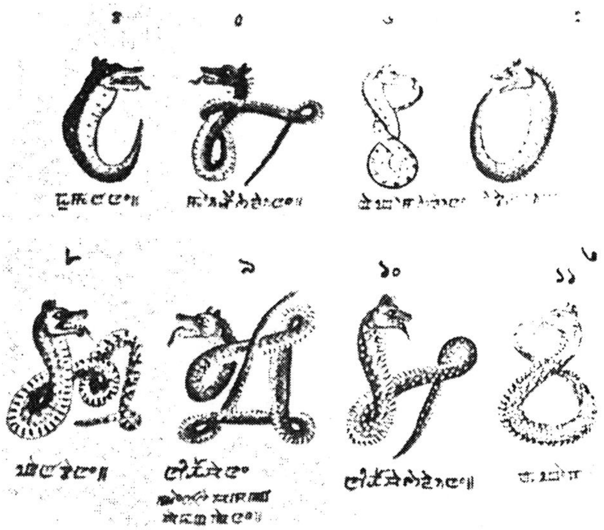

Pl.17.3: Pakhangba forms

An important feature of these paintings is those scribes who write the text were usually the artists of these paintings unlike the paintings executed by professional *karigars* under guild in most parts of India. The most deviating factor is the fundamental change in aim and aesthetics.

Emphasizing simplicity and tight control in design and form, these illustrations are depicted in the simplest terms with no excessive decoration. As in the world of myths, where the events do not follow a realistic sequence but create a parallel reality, so is the case with the artist of these paintings.

Like a child and naive painter, he strives to shape and interpret their experience of world in images. Their disregard for anatomy and perspective are not the result of a deliberate choice of style, rather the stamp of a less developed level of consciousness. This perceptual limitation at the same time favors the presentation or total expressiveness and originality of image[13]. Manipuri manuscript painting, though derives its substances from nature, does not render is in the naturalistic manner.

These manuscript paintings in the right sense represent the folk art of Manipur and are free from influences from Hinduism in the early period. Intercourse with neighboring countries like China, Burma and Thailand is evident by representations of dragons, peacocks and lion.

With the advent of Hinduism in late 16th century many Hindu elements were incorporated into the local idiom. One manuscript painting depicts the monkey god, Hanuman is in red colour. The masculine body shows small spike like hair done in back lines. The face sports a larger moustache and spiky beard. His tail curls over head towards right. The right hand holds mountain symbolized by a tree and left hand holds a decoratively done *gada*.

The Manipuri manuscript painting, like the Manipuri sculpture, was characterized by a two dimensional approach devoid of perspective in western sense, and without a vanishing point. The figures were rendered without modeling or light and shade that would give them an overall sense of depth. There was an economy of line and a tendency to use colours flatly and in blocks rather than those in graduated tones between one hue and the next. In fact they are products of craftsmanship rather than true artistry. Even though, manuscripts are an important cultural achievement. What emerged were an aesthetically pleasing, revealing of the culture in its portrayal of the entire spectrum of Manipuri society since ancient times.[14]

Notes & References

1. Hodson, T.C., T*he Meitheis*, Delhi, 1908, pp. 95-119.
2. Sanajaoba, Naorem (ed), *Manipur Past & Present, Vol. I,* New Delhi, 1998.
3. Devi, K. Sobita, *Traditional Dress of the Meiteis*, Imphal, 1998. p.1
4. Singh, M.K., *Religious Developments in Manipur in 18th-19th Centuries*, MSKA,1980.
5. Laisram, Rena, *Early Meitei History: Religion, Society and the Manipur Puyas*, Delhi, 2009, p. 11.
6. Chakpas are an aborigine of Manipur. A belief traces the meaning of Chaphu (Chak plus phu) is the earthen vessel of the Chakpas as they were treated as innovator of pottery and are still regarded as potter community. Imoba, Dr. L., Rabikanta, T., and Rajketan, C., '*Pottery in Manipur*,' Mutuwa Museum, Imphal, 1999, p. 44.
7. Imoba, L., Rabikanta, T., Rajketan, C., *Pottery in Manipur*, Mutua Museum, Imphal, 1999, p.10.
8. Devi, K. Sobita, *Traditional Dress of the Meiteis*, Imphal, 1998.
9. Bahadur, Mutua, *Traditional Textiles of Manipur*, Mutua Museum, Imphal,1997, p.10.

10. Devi, K. Sobita, *Traditional Dress of the Meiteis*, Imphal, 1998.
11. Singh, L. Ibungohal, Khelchandra, N., (ed), *Cheitharol Kumbaba*, Manipuri Sahitya Parishad, Imphal, 1989.
12. Bahadur, Mutua, *Illustrated Manuscripts of Manipur*, Mutua Museum, Imphal, 2005, p. 10.
13. Merin, Oto Bihalji, *'Masters of Native art'* New York, 1970, p. 21-22.
14. Sharma, B. Ruma, Manuscript Paintings of Manipur (Chheda Yekpashing), *Art & Deal*, Delhi, Issue 48/Vol.8 No.18/Apr-May, 2012, pp.50-53.

18

Gaoseng Faxian Zhuan 高僧法显传: The Earliest Extant Chinese Manuscript on Indian Kingdoms- A Critical Study

– *Dhriti Roy*

China, perhaps, is one of the very few countries in the world, which has paid enormous attention to meticulously recording historical events and carefully preserving historical records through official endeavour. Chinese cartographic and historiographic tradition dates as far back in time as the Han dynasty (206 BCE-220 CE). From historical records like the *Shiji* 史记, the *Hanshu* 汉书, the *Hou Hanshu* 后汉书, to mention but a few, compiled under imperial orders down to Buddhist bibliographical and biographical literature, each of these extant pieces of literature reflect some of pre-modern China's social and intellectual consciousness, and political tendencies. Whether Buddhist or secular, such documents preserved over centuries help reframe history.

One such epochal event in world history, the transmission of Buddhism from India into the foreign land of China, an event which subsequently closely influenced the religious, cultural, and intellectual perception of the peoples of this ancient geographical and cultural space, remains captured in some of China's early extant historical records. The study of the history of this transmission of the *dharma*, as well as events related to its adaptation, reorientation and assimilation, is full of unconceivable complexities. In order to be able to develop a comprehensive understanding of this complex dynamics of transmission of Buddhism into China, we rely upon sources in Chinese, dating across over a millennium.

From the mid-second century onwards, hundreds of Indian Buddhist scriptures were rendered into Chinese. While most of them are either lost or have been subject to subsequent revision, there remain extant quite a few as well, dating from the Eastern Han (东汉 25-220 C.E.) and the Three Kingdoms period (三国 220-265 C.E.). Some of these unrefined earliest translated versions of Indian Buddhist scriptures included *Mahāyāna* and non-*Mahāyāna sūtras*, *jātaka* tales (birth stories of the Buddha), *abhidharma* texts (scholastic treatises), biographies of the Buddha, didactic verses as well as basic texts on simple meditation.[1]

Even though the aforementioned sources offer glimpses into the complex processes of Buddhist transmission and assimilation, they need to be used with a lot of caution. First, on account of them being fragmentary in nature, and second, on view that they deal with diverse time lines associated with different phases in the formation and evolution of the Buddhist monastic community in China. The first three centuries of the Common Era witnessed the gradual penetration of Buddhism into China while the period between the third and the fifth marked the consolidation of the *dharma*. In the aforementioned Chinese renditions of the Indian Buddhist *sūtras*, Chinese perception of India does not feature at all, athough a genuine understanding of the Indian Buddhist theories are attempted there. While some of the earliest Chinese translations of the Buddhist scriptures were in circulation, the Chinese audience was still associating magical feats with Indian monks, believing them to be engaged in activities as rainmaking, healing, and the prognostication of fate.[2] India came to be depicted through eye witness accounts, only a few centuries later, in the travel diaries of itinerant monks. One such account is of interest to us here and forms the subject of this study.

Here we concern ourselves with a particular piece of Buddhist literature, identified as a travel narrative, composed by a distinguished fifth century Chinese pilgrim-monk-scholar Shi Faxian[3], while travelling through the kingdoms across the trans-continental Silk Route to reach India in search of authentic Indian Buddhist scriptures on monastic discipline (*vinaya*). This is one of the first such extant manuscripts in Chinese language on fifth century Indian social customs and religious (mainly Buddhist) tradition. It should be taken note of the fact that this particular Chinese manuscript predates any Indian extant source on the geography, topography, culture and custom of the northwest, north and east of India.

Shi Faxian's Chinese Buddhist manuscript is significant for two reasons. First, it is so, owing to the fact that scholars across the globe attach immense importance to this travel narrative as being a key textual evidence available at our disposal that could be utilized for extracting detailed information on the state of Buddhism prevalent in the Indian subcontinent and the Central Asian oasis states, a feature which beyond doubt makes it priceless. And second, more so because of the fact that Shi Faxian's travel account introduced for the first time to Buddhist scholars, glimpses of the nature of Buddhist monasticism as prevalent in fifth century China. The manuscript therefore highlights the factors back in China which were responsible for triggering such a travel rather than just focusing on the epic journey itself.

Chinese Buddhist bibliographical, biographical and canonical literature have unanimously testified to the fact that Eastern Jin Dynasty 东晋朝 pilgrim-scholar-monk Shi Faxian 法显 left behind for posterity, a written narrative, based on his sojourn across the world's most inhospitable terrains, braving way through the most perilous environmental and topographical conditions and introducing to the community (both clergy and laity) in fifth century China, a firsthand eye witness account of the topography, climate, flora and fauna of over thirty kingdoms that he traversed, alongside providing a detailed depiction of Buddhist customs, ritualistic practices and legends associated with the lands he set foot upon.

Earliest Documentation of Faxian's Travel Narrative in Chinese Sources

Shi Faxian's travelogue is most popularly titled as *Faxian zhuan*. The earliest Chinese textual document that testifies to the composition of *Faxian zhuan* 法显传 is the earliest extant Buddhist catalogue in Chinese that we have at our disposition, Sengyou's *Chu sanzang ji ji* 僧祐出三藏记集.[4] The travel account is mentioned there under the title *Faxian zhuan*. All of the later catalogues, namely Sui Fajing's *Zhongjing mulu* 隋法经衆经目录,[5] Fei Zhangfang's *Lidai san bao ji* 费長房歷代三寶纪[6] have all certainly had the travelogue recorded in their collection. This is evidence enough to contend that such a piece of travel diary was actually composed by Shi

Faxian 释法显. The earliest recorded secular document, to have mentioned Faxian's itinerary, was *Jing ji zhi* 经籍志 of *Sui Shu* 隋书, which was a piece of literature of the genre of biographical history *zheng shi*, history books written in biographical style.

Faxian zhuan 法显传 Oremains the original composition of our protagonist dating back to the twelfth year of the Yixi reign period of the Eastern Jin dynasty 东晋義熙十二年 corresponding to the year 416 C.E. This was written down as a first-hand travel account, after Faxian's return to his homeland during the eighth year of the Yixi reign period, which was somewhere around 412 C.E.[7] The narrative depicts facts related to regions that had always remained far distanced, both geographically and perceptually from the understanding of the people of a land, to who this historical and geographical treatise was directed to. Soon after its composition, it was rather widely circulated, with readers mostly belonging to the Buddhist monastic community. Its contribution towards Chinese society can be acknowledged from the fact that it was a fine piece of creation, produced just during a time when the 'look west policy', initiated by the Chinese Buddhist master Shi Daoan 释道安 was at its zenith and there was a rising tide of embarking upon the westward bound sojourn in search of the *dharma*, in its true, unadulterated form. While India had for long been a kind of mystic land in the perception of the common Chinese masses, with Buddhist monks there, being seen as rain makers or magic healers,[8] Faxian's travelogue for the first time broke this myth and presented to the readers a real picture of the country that was venerated by thousands of Chinese monks and laity for being the fountain head of the *dharma*. From the kind of detailed depiction that the travel narrative puts forth in relation to the location of the kingdoms set foot upon, their distances from each other, the direction of trek, the climate, topography, flora and fauna, the Buddhist practices, the rituals and customs, the relic veneration ceremony and the imperial connection, it might be discerned that it could never have been a modest piece of reminiscence only, but created more under the motive of leaving behind a strong piece of reference for posterity.

Faxian Zhuan in Modern Western Scholarship

To have been held in high esteem by scholars outside of the Chinese Buddhist monastic fraternity, is also a fact in itself that has rendered one of the highest acknowledgements to this travel narrative. Together with Tang dynasty scholar-monk Xuanzang's travel account, *Da Tang Xiyu Ji* 大唐西域记, Faxian's travel narrative remained as one of the two most distinguished historical narratives, which got included in the famous collection termed *Complete Collection in Four Treasuries*, *Si ku quan shu* 四库全书 under the category of 'historical and geographical treatises'.[9]

Towards the end of the nineteenth century and the beginning of the twentieth, western scholarship was focusing attention on research on Asia, its cultures and peoples. Religion and philosophy of the Orient was emerging as a new field of academic exploration. Among few of the most distinguished scholars of the west who engaged in the study of Faxian's travel narrative, there were Abel Remuśat, the first professor of Sinology, at the Institute of France, Samuel Beal, an English missionary to Qing China, Herbert A Giles, a diplomat by profession, having been deputed by the Royal House of England to China, Thomas Watters, a distinguished scholar and James Legge, a noted Scottish Sinologist and the first professor of Chinese at Oxford University.

Wang Bangwei, in his appraisal of all extant research work on Faxian's travelogue, suggests that the western scholarly world's interest on *Faxian zhuan* in the nineteenth century, was neither accidental nor casual. This interest stemmed out of the opening up of western academia to the study of history, culture, archaeology and geography of India and of Central Asia.[10] Systematic study in this regard meant complete dependence on authentic sources, and it was coincidentally during this period in time, that western scholars found access to Classical Chinese documents, serving as a rich repertoire of information on almost all aspects of society, religion, customs and tradition of China as well as her neighbours.

Chinese pilgrim-monk-scholars' first hand travel accounts were held in high esteem as they served as primary sources on all kinds of Buddhist practices, rituals, ceremonies prevalent in the visiting kingdoms, now lost into antiquity, beneath the shifting sand dunes, as well as on the topography, climate, flora and fauna of the regions. Faxian's travel narrative was followed by Xuanzang's *Da Tang Xiyu Ji* 大唐西游記, and Yijing's *Nanhai Ji Gui Nei Fa Zhuan* 南海寄规内法傳, both closely styled much upon Faxian's work.

Modern China's Approach to Faxian's Travel Narrative

Late nineteenth and early twentieth century China also witnessed opening up, in regard to an increased influx of information on Western science, medicine, philosophy and the like. From the Chinese perspective, for scholars, the way of looking at their country, their civilization, as well as the way of studying about their very own people also underwent metamorphosis. Critical, analytical, research based studies gradually emerged out of the cocoon of subjectivity and such related biases. During the early years of the Republic, there was a scholar, Li Guang Ting 李光廷, who wrote an article titled, *Jielu Jin Shi Faxian Fo Guo Ji* 节录晋释法显佛国记 under fascicle/juan number seven of the *Han Xi Yu Tu Kao* 汉西域图考. There was also a work by Ding Qian 丁谦, titled, *Jin Shi Faxian Fo Guo Ji Dili Kao Zheng* 晋释法显佛国记地理考证. There was a final work dating from this period, titled, *Fo You Tian Zhu Ji Kao Shi* 佛游天竺记考释, by Cen Zhongmian 岑仲勉.[11]

Focus on Historical Travel Narratives in Contemporary China

The reform and opening up policy, initiated in China from 1979 onwards heralded a new era of globalization, more so as it was triggered by China's domestic front. Academic research in this period on contemporary Chinese history witnessed unprecedented progress. The study of China's own history and culture was rejuvenated. The year 1985 featured as an important turning point in this regard. Reason being two of the most significant historical travel accounts, were again brought to light and researched upon, with more objectivity, rationalism and analysis.

Beijing zhonghua shuju 北京中华书局 (China Book Agency, Beijing) had Ji Xianlin's *Da Tang xiyu ji jiaozhu* 大唐西域记校注 published while Shanghai Guji chubanshe 上海古籍出版社 (Shanghai ancient records publishing house) had Zhang Xun's 章巽 *Faxian zhuan jiaozhu* 法显传校注 published. Zhang Xun's work on Faxian in fact has for long now been held in high esteem. The work performs a critical analysis of the innumerable editions that were in circulation, the collation and annotation has also been applauded by many a distinguished Chinese and western scholar.

After Zhang Xun, it was Li Rongxi 李荣熙, belonging to the Buddhist Association of China 中国佛教协会, who brought out a fresh translation of the travelogue in English, somewhere in the 1980s. Mainland China and Taiwan, then again in the 1990s, published quite a few articles, related to the composition *Faxian zhuan*.

Earliest Block-Printed Editions of the *Faxian zhuan*

From China's Song dynasty (960-1127) onwards, block printed editions of Chinese Buddhist Canon (*Tripimaka*) were made available for large scale circulation among Chinese audience. These block printed editions in fact were the earliest editions available, all of which had Faxian's travel diary contained in them. The first printed edition of the canon dates back to the time of Emperor Taizong of the Song Dynasty 宋太宗, when the emperor deputed some important officials to go to Chengdu in Sichuan in 971 C.E. to print the canon by means of wooden blocks. The order was successfully carried out in 972 CE, and different editions of the canon were printed in gold and silver. These editions, five in number, have survived under specific titles, depending upon the period in Chinese history to which they belonged. These were as follows, the *Chongning wanshou dazang* 崇宁万寿大藏, printed during the Northern Song dynasty, the *Pilu dazang* 毗卢大藏, printed between the Northern and the Southern Song dynasty, and the *Tripimaka* Collection titled *Sixi yuanjue zang* 思溪圆觉藏, *Sixi zifu zang* 思溪资福藏 and *Qi sha*[12] *zang* 碛砂藏, all of the three printed during the Southern Song dynasty. However the five different editions of *Faxian zhuan* preserved in the five aforementioned editions of the Chinese Buddhist Canon were finally compiled into a final version that got preserved into the *Zhaocheng zang* 趙城藏 edition of the *Tripimaka,* printed during the Jin dynasty.

The *Chongning wanshou* edition of the Chinese Buddhist Tripimaka started to be printed during the third year of the Yuanfeng 元丰 reign period of the Northern Song dynasty, corresponding to 1080 C.E. in the Dongchan monastery (Dongchan si) of Fuzhou 福州东禅寺. The *Faxian zhuan* contained in this Tripimaka edition was printed around 1104 C.E, during the third year of the Chongning 崇宁 reign period and stands abbreviated under the title Dongben 东本.[13]

The *Pilu dazang*, titled as so, is a Chinese Tripimaka that was printed around the second year of the Zhenghe 政和 reign period, in 1112 C.E. at the Kaiyuan chansi (Kaiyuan chan monastery) in Fuzhou 福州开元禅寺. The *Faxian zhuan* therein was printed around 1148 C.E., during the eighteenth year of the Shaoxing 绍兴 reign period. It has the abbreviated title *Kaiben* 开本.[14]

The travel account of *Faxian zhuan* as the Dongben edition in the Chinese *Tripimaka* is the one that is preserved in the Japanese edition of the Buddhist Canon, titled *Riben jingdu shi dagong xijiu tiao dong si* 日本京都市大宫西九条东寺 and *Jingdu fuyu zhijun tihu si* 京都府于治郡醍醐寺. The Kaiben edition of *Faxian zhuan* is the one that has been preserved in the Japanese edition of *Riben gong nei tingshu lingbu tushu liao* 日本宫内厅书陵部图书寮 and also ones titled *jingdu shi zhien yuan jingcang* 京都市知恩院 and *jiu jin zewen ku* 旧金泽文.[15] Since both the *Dongben* and the *Kaiben* editions have been preserved in the Japanese edition of the Canon, these have also all along served as the most reliable manuscripts that Japanese scholars have depended upon. The *Dongben* edition of *Faxian zhuan* dates from around the time of the Northern Song period, it still survives as the earliest extant printed edition of *Faxian zhuan*. The *Kaiben* edition of *Faxian zhuan* dates to a later period, having been spanned from the *Dongben* edition by forty four years or so. While preparing a collated translation of *Faxian zhuan*, Adachi Kiroku (Zuli Xiliu) had discovered that both the *Dongben* and the *Kaiben* editions of *Faxian zhuan* were more than identical in every way, with only minor differences confining to a few characters. Most importantly the contents portrayed in each of the two editions have also been seen as being identical. The format of the two texts also remain very similar, each begins with six lines, and each of the six lines bear seventeen characters each.

Sixi yuanjue zang edition of the Chinese Buddhist *Tripimaka* was printed during the second year of the Shaoxing 绍兴 reign period, around 1132 C.E. at the Sixi yuanjue chanyuan 思溪圆觉禅院. The *Faxian zhuan* contained therein is titled *Yuanben* in abbreviated version. In 1955, this edition was printed by Wenxue guji kanxingshe. The Chinese Tripimaka *Sixi zifu zang* edition is generally believed to have been printed during the second year of the Chunxi 淳熙 reign period, corresponding to the year 1175 C.E. at the Sixi fabao zifu chan si 思溪法寶资福禅寺 in Huzhou. The *Faxian zhuan* present therein is suggested to have been printed in 1239 C.E., it being the third year of the Jiaxi 嘉熙 reign period. It has the abbreviated title of *Ziben* 资本.[16] Also printed around the Southern Song dynasty, like the *Yuanben* and *Ziben*, the *Qisha zang* edition of the Canon got printed during the beginning year of the Baoqing reign period (between 1225-1227 C.E.) at Qisha yansheng yuan in Ping jiang fu 平江府. The printing project got completed only with the advent of the Yuan dynasty. The *Faxian zhuan* edition contained therein did not have any specific date of printing mentioned in it. It is often referred to as the *Qiben* 碛本 edition.[17]

The *Zhaocheng zang* edition of the Chinese Buddhist *Tripimaka*, was printed between the eighth year of the Huangtong reign period and the thirteenth year of the Dading reign period, ideally between 1148 and 1173 C.E. It originally survived in the Shanxi zhaocheng xian guangsheng si, as the only extant copy in the world. It has been shifted to Beijing Tushuguan (National Library of Beijing). The *Faxian zhuan* preserved therein stands abbreviated under the title *Jinben*. It is also preserved in the Historical and Language Research Institute of Taiwan.

Adachi is of the opinion that the *Ziben* edition of the Southern Song edition of the Chinese Buddhist *Tripimaka* might have served as the original text of *Faxian zhuan* of the Yuan and Ming editions of later years. There might be noted a certain coherence there. Zhang Xun also while amidst his task of collating the manuscripts of *Faxian zhuan* from the Grand *Tripimaka* Collection of *Da zheng xin xiu* of Japan, also suggested a continuum between the contents of Southern Song (Nan song), Yuan and Ming editions. Therefore from the *Dongben* edition of the Northern Song (Bei Song Ban de Dongben) to its embodiment into the *Kaiben* edition, it was passed on to be the *Yuanben* edition of the Southern Song and later finally embodied into *Ziben*. This was again later passed on to become *Qiben*, which later got disseminated as both the Yuan and Ming editions. This then happens to be the southern lineage of transmission of the block printed edition of *Faxian zhuan*. The northern line of dissemination of *Faxian zhuan* seems to have originated from the *Jinben* and passed on to the *Gaoli zangben*.[18]

Variant Titles of Faxian's Travelogue

Faxian's travelogue, has over centuries now, been referred to by variant titles, most of which remain preserved in the various biographical and bibliographical sources.

- Sengyou's *Chu sang jiji* (in two fascicles) 僧祐出三藏记集 mentions the travel diary as *Fo you tianzhu ji* (in one fascicle) 佛游天竺记一卷.
- *Shuijing zhu* (fascicle one and two) 水经注卷一, 二 mentions the travelogue by the title Faxian zhuan 法显传. Fascicle sixteen refers to it as *Shi Faxian xing zhuan* 释法显行传.
- Catalogues like Fajing and others in their *Zhongjing mulu* (fascicle six) 法经等衆经目录卷六 has it mentioned as *Fo you tianzhu ji* 佛游天竺记一传 (one fascicle), it was later compiled in *Xiyu sheng xian zhuan ji* 西域聖賢傳记, having been renamed as *Xiyu shengxian suo zhuan* 西域聖賢所撰.
- There was also *Faxian zhuan* 法显传一传 (scroll one), with Faxian's own narration of his westward sojourn, included in *Ci fang zhu de zhuan ji* 此方诸德傳记.
- *Lidai sanbao ji* (in seven juans) 歷代三寶纪 puts into record, Faxian's travel diary under the title, *Li you tianzhu ji zhuan* (in one juan/roll) 歷游天竺记传一卷.
- Scroll number thirty three, of *Sui shu* 隋書, bearing the title *Jing ji zhi shinbu za zhuan lei* 隋书卷三十三经籍志史部雜传类, mentions the itinerary as *Faxian zhuan* (in two rolls) 法显传二卷. There is yet another text, also *Faxian xing zhuan* (in one fascicle) 法显行传.
- Secular texts on geography and cartography, *Dililei* 地理类, also preserves Faxian's travel account as *Fo guo ji* (in one juan) 佛国记, the original note that follows, reads, *Shamen shi Faxian zhuan* 沙门释法显撰.
- Daoxuan's *Ji shen zhou sanbao gantong lu* 道宣集神州三寶感通録, has in the scroll, a section titled, *Liang jing zhou yu tian wang zhantan xiang yuan* (in twenty eight scrolls) 梁荆州優填王栴檀像缘, which refers to the travel narrative as *Fo you tianzhu ji* 佛游天竺记.
- *Da Tang neidian lu* (scroll three) 大唐内典録, has the title of the itinerary mentioned as *Li you tianzhu ji zhuan* 歷游天竺记传.

- *Daoshi Fayuan zhulin zhuan jipian* 道世法苑珠林 has it as *Li you tianzhu ji zhuan* (in one fascicle) 歷游天竺记传一卷, on the right hand side, it has mentioned Dong jin pingyang shamen shi Faxian zhuan 东晋平阳沙门释法显撰.
- Li Xian's note in *Hou Hanshu Xiyu zhuan* 后汉书西域传 titles the travel account as *Shi Faxian you tianzhu ji* 释法显游天竺记.
- *Kaiyuan shijiao lu* (Scroll/fascicle number three) 开元释教录 bears the title for the itinerary as *Li you tianzhu ji zhuan* (one juan) 歷游天竺记传一卷, the original note reads it also as *Faxian zhuan* 法显传.
- Faxian's own narration of his sojourn across Tianzhu can also been seen in *Zhang fang lu* 張房録.
- There was also a *Fo you tianzhu ji* (in one scroll/fascicle) 佛游天竺记, the original annotation of which can be seen in Sengyou's catalogue 僧祐出三藏记集.
- Scroll numbers thirteen, seventeen and twenty have the travelogue titled as *Faxian zhuan* (in one scroll) 法显传一卷, moreover the annotation has it mentioned also as *Li you tianzhu ji zhuan* 歷游天竺记传.
- Duyou 杜佑, in the one hundred and seventy fourth fascicle in Tongdian 通典 refers to the travel diary as *Faming you tianzhu ji* 法名游天竺记 (Faming has been employed due to state prohibition against using Xian) as mentioned in the one hundred and ninety first scroll. The change in reference in *Tongdian* from Faxian to Faming has been attested in the synopsis of the general table of contents of the Complete Collection in Four Libraries. Owing to a prohibition issued against the usage of certain names, and 'xian' supposedly being one of them, the Tang dynasty people used 'ming' to replace 'xian'. This is how the itinerary witnessed a shift in the name of it's composer from Faxian to Faming.
- Yuanzhao's *Zhen yuan xinding shijiao mulu* 圆照贞元新定释教目録, scroll five has the travelogue titled, *Li you tianzhu ji zhuan* 歷游天竺记传 (scroll one). The annotation therein mentions the travel diary as *Faxian zhuan* 法显传. Following this, scrolls twenty three, twenty seven and thirty, in general has the travel diary

mentioned as *Faxian zhuan* (in one juan) 法显传, the annotation is also mentioned *Li you tianzhu ji zhuan* 歷游天竺记传.

- *Taiping yu lan* 太平御覧 in fascicle number six hundred and fifty three as well as in fascicle number six hundred and fifty seven mention the travel diary as *Faxian ji* 法显记.
- From the Northern Song dynasty down the centuries, through history, the Chinese Buddhist Tripimaka on several occasions have had the travel narrative mentioned as *Faxian zhuan* (in one scroll/fascicle) 法显传. It is only the *Zhaocheng* edition compiled during the Jin dynasty that has the travel account mentioned as *Xi daoren faxian cong changan xing xi zhi tianzhu zhuan* (in one juan/fascicle) 昔道人法显从長安行西至天竺传. The Gaoli *Tripimaka* edition records the travel narrative under the title *Gaoseng Faxian zhuan* (in one roll) 高僧法显传.
- Since the Ming dynasty onwards, the entire collection of books and block printed editions like the *Mice hui han* 祕冊彙函, *Jindai mishu* 津逮祕书, *Tang song congshu* 唐宋叢书, *Zengding hanwei cong shu* 增訂漢魏叢书, *Xue jin tao yuan* 學津討原 and so on had the itinerary depicted under the title of *Fo guo ji* 佛国记. It was only Baicheng that titled Faxian's travel account as *sanshi guo ji* 三十国记.
- The printed edition of shuofu 説浮 (in four fascicles), raised in the handwritten copy of the Ming edition by Zhang Zongxiang 張宗祥 also mentions Faxian's travel account as *Faxian ji* 法显记.[19]

All the aforementioned variant titles refer to the same historical work. *Fo guo ji* is first seen being mentioned in the *Suizhi* 隋志 (the sui annals), however the original annotation of *Suizhi* has already illustrated the fact that this particular travelogue was known under the title, *Shamen shi Faxian zhuan* 沙门释法显撰. At present the edition of *Fo guo ji* that is available across the world, is the same as *Faxian zhuan*. *Li you tianzhu ji zhuan* 歷游天竺记传 is also *Faxian zhuan* 法显传. Therefore scholars have now reached a consensus that although the travel diary bears variant titles like *Faxian zhuan*, *Fo guo ji*, and *Li you tianzhu ji zhuan*, they refer to the same biographical treatise on Central Asian, Indian, and Sri Lankan history, culture and geography, authored by Shi Faxian, the once distinguished Eastern Jin dynasty pilgrim-monk-scholar, around the fifth century C.E.

General Structure of Shi Faxian's Travelogue

The travel account is not homogeneous in structure and therefore cannot be treated as a unitary whole. It is a repertoire of information on diverse issues, related directly to fifth century Buddhist culture in China, physical geography, tradition and practices, as was prevalent in some parts of the Central Asian oasis states, kingdoms in India and Sri Lanka. The travel diary is multilayered and the facts presented therein, multi-dimensional.

Faxian Zhuan's Direct Influence on Chinese Buddhist Society

It is difficult to discern who had been the targeted audience of Faxian's travel diary. It is equally difficult to make a conclusive statement that Faxian's travel diary was meant to cater to the inquisitiveness of the Chinese Buddhist followers. However when the structure of the travel diary as well as the depicted facts therein are studied carefully, we do arrive at a fair idea, of what impact Faxian's travel account might have exerted on to posterity.

First and foremost the writing style followed in the travel narrative is lucid. The narration carries the feel of contemporary field diary writing, something that is worthy of note. The most striking feature in the travel diary is the depiction of Buddhist rituals performed by respective royal families in the kingdoms visited by Shi Faxian and his fellow travellers which succeeded in creating for the first time in China around the fifth century, a legitimate connection between the aristocracy and the monastic community, suggesting somewhere passively, a symbiotic relation between the two. Though there have already been instances of non-Chinese ruling houses, especially under the northern Wei (Toba/Tuoba) dynasty, of having patronized the Buddhist movement in the north, it might still be assumed to have been an isolated event, and not really one that could be cited as the common spirit of the times. With Faxian's travel diary explicitly portraying rulers of Buddhist kingdoms engaging in lavish ceremonies and granting rich endowments to monasteries, marked the first legitimate beginning of imperial intervention in Chinese monastic life.

Alongside this, the travel account mentioned Buddhist legends associated with each of the sites visited, in such great details, that it perhaps played a role in reinvigorating the knowledge of relic veneration in China. Knowledge of the entire tradition of relic veneration had been prevalent in second and third century China, through the translation and circulation of the *MahāparinirvāGa Sūtra*. However, for relic veneration to emerge as a cult, Faxian's description of the same, in Central Asia, northwest and Central India can beyond doubt be said to have played a major role in here. From this very point again, through the spontaneous discovery of Buddhist relics in almost all places in China, on account of it being considered to be a part of *Jambudvïpa*, and therefore a legitimate part of the Aśokan empire, China was finally transformed from a border land into a legitimate realm of Buddhism. The rise of indigenous Buddhist schools, an increase in the arrival of Buddhist itinerant monks from East Asia as well as from India and finally China becoming the abode of distinguished Bodhisattvas, all owe it to Faxian's distinguished travel narrative.

Influence of *Faxian zhuan* on posterity

It is difficult to discern who the targeted audience were for Shi Faxian's travel notes. It was also not the case that Faxian's travelogue remained confined only within the Chinese Buddhist monastic community members. In fact, this piece of Buddhist literature was also referred to by scholars and writers from the secular world.

Shujing zhu, a fifth century commentary by Li Daoyuan 酈道元 (d. 527), an official of the Southern Qi and Liang dynasties, on *Shuijing* (Water Classic), a work attributed to the Three Kingdoms Period, and also arguably sometimes to the Han Dynasty, is perhaps the most explicit exemplary, in the Chinese literary archive, which has directly borne the influence of Faxian's travelogue. A distinguished desk geographer of his times, Li Daoyuan, was keen to survey the courses of rivers and explore their origins. Amongst the chief sources of his work, Faxian's itinerary stands out most prominently as the most important reference work, having been quoted on twenty different occasions. Not only was Li Daoyuan's work a piece of hydrographical investigation, but the same was also reflective of his interest in engaging himself with historical facts, strange customs and traditions of holy places, sometimes some of which bore a certain Buddhist overtone. Faxian's travelogue is referred to, in context of regions lying south of the Hindukush and central India. The passages in the *Shujing zhu* on rock-cut stairs on steep mountainous cliffs past the

Congling mountain ranges, on the flow of the River Xintou, meandering its way through the kingdom of Wuchang with Lord Buddha's footprints therein, and then curving south westward directly through the plains of central India, echo complete dependence on Faxian's portrayal of the same.[20]

It is perhaps possible to claim that every other itinerant monk-scholar who came later in history, the most prominent ones being Xuanzang and Yijing, did draw inspiration from Faxian's work. Travel diary writing became a popular genre of sharing facts, seen and heard, as is suggestive from the travel accounts of Xuanzang, Yijing, Songyun, Ennin and quite a few that followed down the line of history. Faxian's itinerary will remain in the centuries to come, an exquisite piece of Buddhist literature, commendable as a modern day travel narrative as well as a repertoire of lost information on lost Buddhist regions. It will all along carry the essence of the sojourn, undertaken way back in the fifth century, as much as it does today, and present it to the reader of this contemporary world.

Faxian's Portrayal of Religion and Culture in Fifth Century Indian Kingdoms

In the final section of the paper we bring to light some relevant sections on India as was portrayed by Shi Faxian in his travelogue in English translation.[21] The Korean recension of Faxian's travelogue 法显传 *Faxian zhuan* as appended in the annotated, translated, English rendition authored by James Legge has been used here as the primary source material. The original unpunctuated text runs without a break, but the aforementioned Korean version of *Faxian zhuan* was divided into forty chapters and accordingly punctuated by James Legge.

The first passage is from **chapter one**, where Shi Faxian along with his fellow companions, 慧景 Huijing, 道整 Daozheng, 慧應 Huiying, and 慧嵬 Huiwei set out from the Chinese city of Chang'an and reached the commandery of Dunhuang, the latter then a military outpost of the Chinese empire in the modern Xinjiang Uyghur Autonomous Region. The following information was put to record about the place.

"A border garrison or a commandery (as *Dunhuang* had been), stretched for about eighty li from east to west and forty li from north to south. The (group) stayed on at *Dunhuang*[22] for a little over a month, following which all five travelers, including Faxian, took leave of 寶雲 Baoyun and the rest. 李暠 Li Gao, the Prefect of *Dunhuang*, supplied them (all necessary provisions required) for crossing the 'sea of shifting sand'.[23]

In the midst of the 'River of Sand' lived innumerable evil spirits, while scorching winds blew on...anyone encountering these, were left to perish...none were able to survive whole. There were no flying birds above....no walking beasts below...looking far in the distance, as far as the eye could see, one would only wish to cross (this vast expanse of land)...knowing not however (where to begin from)Ṁonly withered human bones served as markers."

Chapter eight depicts Shi Faxian and his group arriving at the kingdom of 烏長 Wuchang[24]. The passage reads as follows... "The country of *Wuchang* was precisely located in North India. The central Indian dialect was spoken by the entire population of the region. Central India in particular was the region that could be called 中国 '*Zhongguo*'[25] (Madyadeśa, Middle Kingdom). The dress and food habits of the people also resembled those of the people of belonging to the Middle kingdom. The Dharma greatly prospered within the country. The place where the monastic community resided was called a 僧伽藍 *Sengjialan* (Saṃghārāma, monastery). There were a total number of about five hundred monasteries, all of which professed faith in the Hïnayāna. If there ever happened to arrive travelling Buddhist monks from afar, they would all be provided with food and drink for three days, after which, they would be asked to seek their own accommodation."

Having traveled through the kingdoms in northwest India in what is present-day Afghanistan and Pakistan, Shi Faxian reached north India and depicted the following facts. ṢAfter having travelled through all of these places, they arrived at a kingdom, 摩頭羅 Motouluo[26] by name. Once again they crossed the river 捕那 Buna[27], both the banks of the river, on the right and the left were dotted with about twenty saṃghārāmas, housing about three thousand Buddhist monks. The Dharma was gradually prospering in this region. In all of the kingdoms of 天竺 Tianzhu (India), situated to the west of the rivers of sand, there were sincere reverential believers of the Dharma, who would be making offerings to the monastic community. At times the ruler would cast away his imperial crown and in accompaniment with the members of his clan and with his group of ministers would himself go to every other place and beg for alms. After having begged for alms, the king would spread felt on the ground and be seated in front of the assembled monks, facing the 上坐 Sthavira /seat of honour. He would not dare to sit on the main seat or bed. From the lifetime of Tathāgata Buddha down to the present times, the manner in which the rulers of every kingdom would pay obeisance to the Lord remained just the same. The region further down south was termed the Middle Kingdom. Climate in the Middle Kingdom was moderate and favourable, both during the summer and the winter months with neither frost or snow. The masses were prosperous, peaceful and happy."

"The system of registering the population was not prevalent nor did there exist a definitive judicial system under the administration of officials. However the cultivators of the royal land were supposed to hand over the profit derived from the soil. If they desired to leave they could leave, if they wished to stay, they were free to do so. While governing the country, the ruler did not impose punishment of any kind, all the offenders were supposed to pay the ruler, penalty, the amount being determined by the severity or leniency of the matter, although recurrence of any conduct of misdeed would result in severing of the right hand. Nearly all imperial body guards of the ruler received official emoluments. None of the citizens of the nation killed living animals, none consumed alcohol or even garlic and onions, exception being the people belonging to the caste of *Chanḍāla*. The *Chanḍāla* were looked down upon as evil persons, they did not reside with the common people. If they entered the city they were supposed to rap a piece of wood in order to express their class distinction that made them different from the others..."

The ancient kingdom of Pataliputra comes to light in chapter twenty-seven through the following depiction. "Having crossed the river and travelling down south for a yojana, they came over to the city of 巴连弗邑 Balianfuyi[28] in the kingdom of 摩竭提 Mojieti[29]. Balianfuyi was a city ruled by King Aśoka. The imperial palace together with its halls and temples, built of stones, having been the handiwork of divine powers and deities. The rich engravings of decorative patterns were not the creation of the mortal world. All of these exist till date. King Aśoka's younger brother having cultivated the path of Arhatship, would often reside at

耆闍崛山 Gṛdhrakūta, desiring to derive pleasure amidst the peace and tranquility of the tranquil atmosphere during leisure hours."

Chapter twenty-eight portrays the city of Rājagṛha as follows. "The new city of Wang she cheng[30] was said to have been built by King Ajātaúatru. The city housed saṃgharāmas. Three hundred paces ahead of the west city gate was the site where King Ajātaúatru after having received a relic of the Buddha, raised a stūpa in order to make offerings. The stūpa was magnificent and resplendent. Walking four lis away from the city, keeping to the south, they entered a valley of five hills. The five hills surrounding the city resembled the inner and the outer city walls. It was the ancient city of King Bimbisāra. The east-west extent of the city would be about seven or eight lis. The city housed some important sites like the ones where Śariputra and Maudgalyāyana for the very first time met Upasena, and where 尼犍子 Nigrantha dug a pit of fire and invited Buddha to have a poisonous meal, and also Ajātaúatru intoxicated a black elephant and instigated him to harm the Buddha. The north eastern corner of the city, beyond the bent, also carried reminiscences of the spot where Jïvaka raised a vihāra at āmrapāli's garden, inviting Lord Buddha together with one thousand and two fifty disciples to accept his offerings. All these places existed even then. The city however wore a desolate look with no trace of human population.

In the last phase of his journey across India, Shi Faxian came over to the kingdom of Duomolidi.[31] This has been recorded in chapter thirty-seven in the following words. "It was apparently a seaport or an estuary. The aforementioned kingdom housed twenty four samgharamas, each of which had residential quarters for monks. The Dharma was also in a state of prosperity. Faxian stayed back here for over two years, copying Buddhist scriptures and painting Buddhist images. Thereupon having boarded an ocean bound large merchant vessel, Faxian set sail in a south westerly direction, relying on the trade winds of the of the early winter months. Sailing on for fourteen days and nights together, he finally arrived at the kingdom of Simhaladvïpa (Ceylon)."

Conclusion

The above study testifies to the fact that Faxian's travel narrative still stands out today as one of the earliest preserved Chinese records on the state of Buddhism in various kingdoms in India, Central Asia, and Sri Lanka. This fact has for long been acknowledged by historians. But the fact which adds value to Shi Faxian's work and which has been understated by scholars is that it serves as a rich repertoire of information on the state of Buddhism, especially with regard to bringing to light the deficiency of Buddhist disciplinary rules (*vinaya*) as prevalent in fifth century China, thereby putting to question the legitimacy of the Buddhist monastic tradition in fifth century China. There were other travel accounts written or recorded by pilgrim-monk-scholars of later centuries, the most celebrated ones being Xuanzang's *Da Tang Xiyu Ji*, and Yijing's *Nanhai Jigui Neifa Zhuan*. Indian kingdoms during the seventh century also came into life through the narratives in these travel diaries. *Faxian zhuan* introduced many more issues which eventually shaped Chinese Buddhism into a specific mould. The introduction of the relic veneration cult, the granting of imperial patronage to Buddhist monastic community, the rise of apologetic literature, the virtual transformation of China into a legitimate realm of Buddhism owed much of their origin to Faxian's travel narrative, as there are subdued hints on each of these issues in the travel narrative. Shi Faxian although so far remembered only as one of the first Chinese pilgrims, certainly deserves greater scholarly attention. He should be remembered as not one among many but rather as the first one without whom, the tide of Chinese Buddhism would have flown in a very different direction and his *Faxian zhuan* brings this fact to light.

References

- *Gaoseng Faxian zhuan, Dong Jin Shamen Shi Faxian Ziji You Tianzhu Shi* (高僧法顯傳, 東晋沙門釋法顯自記遊天竺事), as an appended text in Legge, James. 1971. *A Record of Buddhistic Kingdoms, Being an Account by the Chinese Monk Fa-hien of His Travels in India and Ceylon* (A.D. 399-414), *In Search of the Buddhist Books of Discipline*. Delhi: Oriental Publishers.
- *Gaoseng Faxian zhuan* (高僧法顯傳), T. 2085.
- Sengyou (僧祐). *Chu sanzang jiji* (出三藏記集), T. 2145.
- Bagchi, P.C. 1981. *India and China, A Thousand Years of Cultural Relations*. Calcutta: Saraswat Library.
- Beal, Samuel. 1964. *Travels of Fah-hian and Sung-Yun, Buddhist Pilgrims, from China to India (400 A.D.and 518 A.D.)*.
- Legge, James. 1971. *A Record of Buddhistic Kingdoms, Being an Account by the Chinese Monk Fa-hien of His Travels in India and Ceylon* (A.D.

399-414), *In Search of the Buddhist Books of Discipline*. Delhi: Oriental Publishers.

- Nattier, Jan. 2008. *A Guide to the Earliest Chinese Buddhist Translations, Texts from the Eastern Han* 东汉 *and Three Kingdoms* 三国 *Periods*. Tokyo: Soka University.
- Ray, Haraprasad. 2006. *Chinese Sources of South Asian History in Translation: Data for Study of India-China Relations through Ages, Volume II*. Kolkata: The Asiatic Society.
- Sen, Tansen. 2004. *Buddhism, Diplomacy, and Trade, The Realignment of Sino-Indian Relations 600-1400*. New Delhi: Manohar.
- Wang, Bangwei (王邦维). 2003. *Faxian yu Faxian zhuan, yanjiushi de kaocha* (法显与法显传：研究史的考察) [A Survey of the History of Research on Faxian and Faxian zhuan].
- Zhang, Xun (章巽). 2008. *Faxian zhuan jiaozhu* (法显传校注) [Collated and Annotated Version of Faxian zhuan]. Beijing: Zhonghua shuju.

Footnotes

1. See Jan Nattier, *A Guide to the Earliest Chinese Buddhist Translations, Texts from the Eastern HanṢNIland Three Kingdoms* 三国 *Periods* (Tokyo: Soka University, 2008), p. 3.
2. Tansen Sen. *Buddhism, Diplomacy, and Trade, The Realignment of Sino-Indian Relations* 600-1400, (Manohar: 2004), p. 7-8.
3. Faxian is the modern pinyin romanized name of our protagonist. He has been known in history as Fa-hien.
4. See Sengyou, *Chu sanzang jiji*, T.2145.
5. See Fajing, *Zhongjing mulu*, T. 2146.
6. See Fei Changfang, *Lidai sanbao ji*, T. 2034.
7. See Bangwei, *Faxian yu Faxian zhuan : Yanjiushi de kaocha*, 2003, p. 20.
8. See Tansen Sen, *Buddhism, Diplomacy, and Trade, The Realignment of Sino-Indian Relations* 600-1400, (Manohar: 2004), p. 8.
9. See Bangwei, *Faxian yu Faxian zhuan:yuanjiu de kaocha* 2003, p. 21.
10. See Bangwei, 2003, p.22-24.
11. Cf. Bangwei, 2003, p. 23-24.
12. See P.C. Bagchi ,*India and China* (Saraswat), p.133-134.
13. See Zhang Xun, *Faxian zhuan jiaozhu*, 2008, p. 13.
14. See Zhang Xun, 2008, p. 13.
15. See Zhang Xun, 2008, p. 14
16. See Zhang Xun, 2008, p. 19-20.
17. See Zhang Xun, 2008, p. 21-22.

19. See Zhang Xun, 2008, p.6-8.
20. See H.P. Ray, *Chinese Sources of South Asian History in Translation, Volume Two*, 2006, p.39-54.
21. The English rendering of the passages here is credited to the author.
22. 燉煌 Dunhuang during Faxian's time around fifth century did not figure out as prominently as in a few decades that followed. The Mogao caves were just being hewn around 365 C.E. The frescoes and grottoes were on their way to being depicted. Dunhuang was still far from its later period of glorious history.
23. Sea of drifting sand or ocean of shifting sanddunes, 沙河 *Sha he*, as has been literally translated in the text, refers to the wide expanse of desert land that lies between the region, west of Dunhuang and the kingdom of Shanshan. The *Hanshu Dili zhi* records, "On the extreme west of the Dunhuang prefecture lies the white dragon sand mounds." James Legge identifies it with the Gobi Desert. Samuel Beal also refers to it as the Gobi Desert, called by Marco Polo the desert of Lop. We beg to differ here. The point of departure for the itinerant monks being Dunhuang and the next destination being the kingdom of Loulan/Shanshan, we identify it with the Taklamakan Desert, close to the Tarim Basin. Gobi desert would be further north of Dunhuang, and was therefore on Xuanzang's itinerary.
24. 烏長 Wuchang has been identified with Udyāna, the former being a transliteration of the Sanskrit name. The ancient site of Wuchang guo corresponds to the drainage basin of River Swat, to the north of modern day Pakistan. Legge and Beal both refer it to Swat, north of Punjab. Cf. Legge. 1971, p. 28. See Beal. 1964, p. 26.
25. Here 'zhongguo' refers to Madhyadeśa. China in history has perceived itself as the Middle Kingdom, but here Faxian refers to India as the Middle Kingdom and hints at China being the Buddhist borderland state.
26. 摩頭羅 Motouluo in *Faxian zhuan* is the same as 秣兔羅 Motuluo in Xuanzang's *Da Tang Xiyu Ji* (Fascicle no.4), being the Chinese transliteration for the Sanskrit name Mathura. There is also unanimity among all other scholars in identifying the place with Mathura, be it Legge, Beal and Giles.
27. 捕那河 *Buna He* has been identified as the River Yamuna or Jumna, as Legge puts it. There is a close resemblance between the sounds Buna and Yamuna though it has not yet been proven by linguistic study in the recent times.
28. Balianfuyi has been identified as Pāmaliputra.
29. Mojieti stands for Magadha.
30. Wang she cheng has been identified as Rājagṛha.
31. Tāmralipti, present-day Tamluk in Bengal is the kingdom of Duomolidi.

19

Manuscript: Language Study of *Lalitavistara Sūtra*

– *Buddhadev Bhattacharya*

The English Word 'Manuscript' (Ms.) has two components. Latin Word '*manus*' means by hand and 'Script' refers to a scribled document. The Sanskrit term '*pāndulipi*' signifies scribbled on a yellowish material like dried processed palm leaves or papers. Another term generally found used in ancient Jaina-text is *mātṛkā*.

Birch-bark (*bhurja-patra*)' Cotton cloth (*karpāsa-palika*). Wooden boards (*kāṣṭha-phalaka*), Palm leaves (*tāla-patra*), Skin (*carma*), Matals (*dhātaba*), Stones (*śila*) Bricks were used for writing the manuscripts (*iṣṭaka*) and Paper (*patra*) were used for writing by human beings in the different parts of the world. Since Buddhism had once crossed the boundary of India in the Ashokan period after the 3rd century, Buddhist Mss. are available in almost all varieties of writing material. For instance, *Gāndhār Prākṛt Dharmapada* discovered by Manson Petroffsky in Stupas of Afghanistan and J.L. Dutreuil de Rhins. Also inscription of Ksatrapamahapana in wooden block kept in the Guild Hall regarding a lone agreement is important. Old fragments of palm leaves belonging to Khāsgar Buddhist (circa 4th Century A.D.) and palm leaves Mss. of 6th Century A.D. preserved in the Horiuzi monastery in Japan which is attributed to a Kashyapa in Siddham script deserved mention. Similarly Sir Aurel Stein discovered Kharosti official documents written on leather (*carma*) at Niya at Chinese Tārkisṭhan.

Specimen of Buddhist inscribing on gold and silver plates and urns in the Stupas at Ganga(n) and at Bhattiprolu near Taxila. Names of the Venerable śaramaṇas focus the spread of Buddhism in North-West. Very few ancient Buddhist Mss. on stone, bricks etc. other than edicts issued by the rules like Ashoka has come down to us. Buddhist texts written on coarse paper with gypsum pigment are discovered from Central Asia like Khotan, Kuchea, Kāshgar etc.

Tibetan Mss. are written on hand made paper which is properly known ***shokpu***. As a section of Tibetans have made paper making a trade, Tibetan paper is now mostly available in Nepal and even in the hand of Kagate those residing in Darjeeling district and eastern Sikkim. In spite of xylographs wooden block printed, hand written *pothi* in Tibetan are available with learned lamas. The writing materials may be secondary in the contents of Mss., their languages particularly scripts (Brāhmi, Kharoṣ it, Newari, Nagari etc.) being of primary importance.

Birch-bark (*bhurja-patra*): '*Kharosṭhi Dhamma-pada*' from Khotan in 1892 discovered by Manson Petroffsky. J. L. Dutreuil de Rhinsinalso found out a Ms. from Stupas of Afghanistan is also called *Prakṛt Dhammapada*, dated C. 200 A.D. edited by Senart in Journal Asialique, 1898 and again by Benimadhab Barua and Sailendra Nath Mitra in Calcutta, 1921.

Fragments of Ms. (56 leaves) the S.H. Godfrey Collections, partly reproduced by Hoernle in journal of Royal Asiatic Society, London in 1897.

Birch-bark is the inner back of the Bhurja trees which grow abundantly in the Himalayas.

Birch-back was used as writing materials at the time of Alexander's invasion. It is an inference that all of these manuscripts were written after 15th Century A.D.

Cotton Cloth (*kārpāsa-palika*): Cotton cloth was used as writing materials as mentioned by (a) Nearchos (b) some metrical smrtis and numerous inscriptions of the non Buddhists a Ms. is available with the material of Sātavāhana period, where it was called '*paṭa*', *Paṭika* or *Kārpāsikāpaṭa*.

Buhler discovered a silk band Jain Sātras inscribed in ink. Peterson found a cloth Ms. dated back to Vikrama Samvat 1418 (AD 1351-52) at Anahilvad Paṭam.

Burnell and Rice who state that Kanarese merchants to write with chalk or stravite pencil on type of cloth banned Kadatam, coloured with tamarind seed paste and bleached with charcoal.

Wooden Boards (*Kāṣṭha-Phalaka*): The wooden boards used as writing materials is mentioned in the (a) Vinayapiṭaka, (b) Jātakas and (c) an inscription of the western India '*Ksatrapa-mahapana*' which stated of a '*phalaka*' or board was kept in the Guild hall and agreements concerning loans were noted on it. The Bodlian Library of Oxford University has preserved a manuscript written on wooden board is of Assamese origin.

Palm Leaves (*tāla-patra*): Hoernle established the fact that all the early palm leaf Mss. used the leaves of corphya Umbraculifera, (a) A few fragments of the S.H. God-Frey collection of Kāshgar belonging to the 4th Century A.D. (b). The Horiuzi Palm leaf Mss. of the 6th century which was edited by Jakumio in 1727 had been brought to Japan in providence of Yamato in 609 A.D. attributed to Kasyapa, G. Buhler, remarked that 'palm-leaves were used as writing materials as also mentioned by Hiuen Chuang in the 7th Century A.D.'.

Indian palm-leaf manuscripts were made either from the leaves of 1. Corypha Umbraculifera (*taditali*), 2. Borassus Flabellifera (*tadatala*).

Skin (*carma*): Skin was sometime used as writing material. This is mentioned by (a) Subandhu'sVasavadatta and (b) Sir Aurel Stein who found Kharaṣthi official documents written on leather at Niya during his visit to Chinese Turkisthan. The European collections also claim to have pieces of leather from Kāshgar imprinted with Indian characters.

Metals (*dhātaba*): The metals like gold, silver copper were commonly used. Specimens of gold and silver plates bearing inscriptions on them have been discovered in the stāpas at Gangānear Texila and at Bhattipolu. Copper plates (*tamrapatra*) are much more in number than gold and silver. Copper plates were used as documents for land grants and so on.

Stones (*śila*): Stones were used as writing materials for a wide variety of purposes like as (a) official documents (b) as private documents (c) to record works of literature, plays, poems. Numerous pieces of plays written by a Vigraha IV, the Cahamana king and his poet Somadeva, are discovered at Ajmer. A huge Jain Sthalapurana in a number Sargas (cants) at Bijholli.

Bricks (*Isṭaka*): Bricks containing the Buddhist Sātras written on them were discovered in the North-western providences.

Paper Manuscripts: A large number of Mss. written on hard papers covered with a layer of Gypsum, originating from Kāshgar are believed by Hoernle to be of Central Asia and not from India.

Many Mss. are found damaged or in a deteriorated conditions. Mss. may be good or bad. That is readable and obscure. Some reasons about the bad Mss. are sorted. Such as:

(a) Fading of the written materials,

(b) Wear and tear due to continuous handling,

(c) Damaged by insects or using pests,

(d) Self-decoposition (Crumbling) of the written material or prolonged exposure to air.

In this connection Sarat Chandra Das has informed that the cheap edition of Kanjur and Tanjurœ were brought to the Lhasa market for sale. Those papers are so then that sometimes the writings on both sides of the paper create blurred impression. So it is very difficult to recover from these Tibetan xylographs like as ārya *Lalitavistara Nāma Mahāyāna Sātra,* (Tib. *'Phags pa rgya cher rol pa shes bya ba theg pa chen po'i mdo*).

Lalitavistara Sātra is the first Bi-lingual Critical Edition by me. In fact, it is the first attempt at doing this research work by using Tibetan source material which was originally translated from Sanskrit in the 9th century A.D. The study has been done based on three Tibetan Xylographs, three Sanskrit Manuscripts belonging to the Asiatic Society, Kolkata. In this article, I would like to focus its language study.

Language Study on ārya Lalitavistara Sātra Manuscript

Ārya Lalitavistara Sātra has two recessions, one in *Gāthā*– and other in prose. In the Asiatic Society, Kolkata, ārya *Lalitavistara Sātra* in mixed form is available vide manuscripts no. Government Collection 9975 (A), 4735 (B), 4725 (C), 9975 (D) and the Asiatic Society Collection Ms. No.

815 for reference. In Nepal however, various recessions are available. Here for examining of the language status of Mixed Sanskrit a few verses from the ārya *Lalitavistara Sūtra* are examined. It may be noted that the Sanskrit manuscripts in the Asiatic Society, Kolkata, appeared to be of the later versions, because in many cases the Mixed Sanskrit means irregular Pāṇinian forms have been omitted and corrected according to the grammatical rules. Despite that some Mixed Sanskrit forms may be traced.

It is said that *ārya Lalitavistara Sūtra* in *Gāthā*— form had existed. Impact of that may be traceable from the following:

यथ[1] पूरित एष[2] धनुमुंनिना न च उत्थितु[3] आसनि नो च भूमी।
निःसशयु पूर्णमभप्रायु मुनिर लधु भेष्यति जित्व च मारचमुं।।

Translation

Since the Sage strung the bow without rising from his seat of the ground, there is no doubt that the Sage will achieve his purpose after defeating the army of Māra.

1. यथ a corrupt form according to Pāṇini. Panini explains यथ + थाल (थाल प्रकारे) तद्धित प्रत्यय। In Pkt. And Apbs. यथ is used for यथा।
2. एष a case and derived from Pāṇini Sandhi rule. एष in Pkt. is not used here it suggest that the gāthāmeter does not permit, षो as a long verb.
3. Pkt. ठा (to exist, to set etc.) उत् is a Skt. उपसर्ग is irregularly combined with ठा। The form becomes उड्डा। Pkt. grammarian notes the change उड्डित for उत्थित। Cerebralization of dental ड्ड is supported by Pkt. grammarian.

त्यजि[1] त्वयि[2] पुरि[3] भवि धनमणिकनका सखि प्रियसुत महि सनगरनिगमा।
शिरमणि त्यजि स्वकु[4] करवरनयना जगति य हितकरु[5] जिनगुणनिरता।।

Translation

In your previous births, you renounced wealth, jewels, gold, your friends, dear ones, and sons on this earth, along with its numerous cities. You even renounced your own head, your hands, feet and eyes, engaged as you were in the Jina virtues, doing well to the world.

1. त्यजि for त्यकत्वा।
2. त्वयि for त्वया।
3. पुरि Pkt. 2p.s.?
4. यवि note the use of भु instate of भइ। The rhythmic balance त्विज त्वयि पुरि पेरि भोवि note here.
5. स्वक. Ip.s. हितकरु is same.

पुरि[1] तुम[2] नरवर सुतु[3] नपु[4] यदभु[5] नरु[6] तव अभमुख इम[7] गिरमवची[8]।
दद मम इम[9] महि[10] सनगरनिगमां त्यजि तद[11] प्रमुदितु[12] न च मुन श्रुभिती।।

Translation

Previously, when you were a king and the son of a king, men before you spoke these words "Give me this earth along with its numerous cities"; you gave them away, untroubled in mind. B. Goswami. p.155.

1. Apbs. पुरि, Māgadhi पुरे = पुर = पुरा (p.348 BHS).
2. तुम for Roe in Pkt. तुमं in Apbs. तुम।

3/4/6/11. In Apbs. I.s. of सुत (son), नृप (king), नर, मन (मानव)।

5. In Pkt. and Apbs. हलन्त letter omitted.
7. The conjugation of वच is limited in Skt. अवोची might be and old form.
8. इम Apbs. for इमम।
9. An alternative form मही in Pkt., Apbs.
10. तद for तदा।
12. The gāthāmeter with alteration of word शब्दानुप्रास makes the verse elegant.

पुरि[2] तुम[2] नरपति स्वकु[3] द्विज यदभू[4] गुरुजनि[5] परिचरि[6] न च दुहि[7] परतो।
स्थपयिसु[8] द्विजवर बहु।। जन कुशले च्युतु तुतु[9] भवगतु मरुपुरनिलयं

Translation

Previously, O Lord of men, when you were born a Brāhma, you saved your elders and harmed no other. O supreme Brāhma! You established the good of many. Depart, therefore, for the home of the gods, O Lord! B. Goswami. p-155.

1. See above note पुरि।
2. See above note तुम।
3. स्वकु, च्युनु, भवगतु I.s in Apbs. of the words स्वकं, च्यतं, भगवतुं in Skt. respectively.
4. See above note यदमू।

5.6. गुरजनान परिचर्य in Skt. Here is a case of rhythmic simplification.

7. दुहि from the verb root दुह, to bear malice or hatred लोट हि BHS for दुहा।
8. Root स्था + निच–लो ट? मरु suggested the पुरनिलय is like a desert.
9. ततु, ततःनत्त+उ = ततु।

यद नारिगण प्रहर्पितो वाधेयती तुरिय[1] र्महामुनिं।
तद गाथ विचित्र निश्चारी तुर्यशव्दात् सुगतानुभवतः[2]।।

Translation

When the joyous women awakened the Great Sage with *tāryas*, these wonderful gāthās emanated from the notes of the *tāryas*, by *Sugards* power. B. Goswami. P-164.

1. BHS Dic. Suggest तुर्योः। Probably the form is तुरीयै means excellency understood.
2. सुगतानु भावन suggest could understood conveniently.

लधु तद्ध जति सर्वसंस्कृतं, अचिरस्थायि[1] नभेव[2] विद्युतः।
अयु कालु[3] तवा[4] उपस्थितः, समयो निष्क्रमणय सुव्रत।।

Translation

All conditioned things break easily, they are momentary like the lightning in the sky. Your moment has arrived; this is the time for your departure, O Suvrata!

1. A case when the general rule of co-relation between noun and adjective is ignored. विशोष्यस्य हि यल्लिङं विभक्ति–वचन च ये। तानि सर्व्वाणि याज्यानि विशेषणपदेष्वपि।। Here विद्युतः I.p but अचिरस्थायि 1.s.

2. In Pkt. usually हलन्त words are omitted. नभ+इव = नभेव for नभसीव (नभसि–इव)।
3. Apbs. form 1.s. for अयं कालः।
4. For तव occasional lengthening in Apbs. may be for sake of meter.

एषो हि देव पुरुषाो मृतु[1] जम्बद्वीपे नहि भूयु[2] मात्पित् द्रक्ष्यति पुवदारं।
उपहाय भोगगृह मित्रज्ञतिसधं परलोकप्राप्तु[3] नहि द्रक्ष्यति भूयु[4] ज्ञाती[5]।।

Translation

Sir! This is not the peculiarity of this family, of this country, (Jamudvipa). Old age attacks the youth of all worlds. You too, along with your mother, father, friends, relatives and clan are not free from old age. There is no other way for man.

1. Apbs. 1.s. मृत for मृतु।
2. मूयु = नियात Apbs.
3. परलोकप्राप्त Apbs. 1.s.
4. मूयु = नियात Apbs.
5. ज्ञाती Apbs. 2.p. The Skt. form ज्ञातीन्।

   It is to be noted that Sārathi speaks in local dialect, presumably in Apbs, while Bodhisattva speaks in Sanskrit in their conversation.

यन्ते गोये चित्तीकारं[1] करोषी नित्यं पूजां गौरवेन्तमेणोन।
नास्ती[2] तुभ्यं[3] दुर्गकः नवै शोकः क्षिप्रं भोही[4] प्रीतिप्रमाधेलब्धा।।

Translation

As you, O Gopā, hold me in reverence and worship regularly with great respect, neither misfortune, nor grief will come to you and you will soon attain happiness and joy. B. Goswami. P-187.

1. चित्तीकारं करोषी do recollect in mind. चित्तीकार चित्त+कर in Pkt. construction the augmentation of short i (इ) कर is peculiar form. It may corresponds to चित्तीकार करोषी। The lengthen of करोषी may be for meter sake for gāthā.
2. दुर्गती Apbs. (स्त्रीः) 1.s. विकल्प। Here दुर्गती and नास्ती are rhythmic semblance.

3. तुभ्यं (4th case-ending) peculiar change of case-ending for त्वा (2nd case-ending), rs (6th case-ending).

4. भोही। for भवति in Skt. भो for भू in Skt. भो + हि = भोहि। Again the rhythmic semblance.

   छन्दको चपलु[2] मा विलाम्बहे[3] अश्वराज दद[4] में अलंकृतं।
   सर्वसिद्धिमम एति मंगला अर्थसिद्धि ध्रुवमद्ध भेष्यते।।

Translation

Hurry, Chādaka, do not delay! Fetch me the lordly horse ornamented. Auspicious success in everything approaches me; I will certainly achieve my purpose today. B. Goswami. p-198.

1. संबोधने एकवचन। In Pkt. alternative form हे छन्दक, हे छन्दका। The lengthening in vocation is common in Pkt. Apbs. and Skt.

2. Adverbial phase क्रिया विशेषण such as भुयु above.

3. In Pkt. verb तिनन्न विधि कर्मवाच्य।

4. दद in Pkt., दद for Skt. दा to give, e.g. Pāini.

   ध्वसोरद्धावभ्यासलायश्च। (धु + असोः + एत + हौ + अभ्यासलापेः + च, दा for दहि in place of दद)

   साधु तव सुद्दष्टदर्शनं ते, यनु[1] तव जन्म वयं पि[2] तस्स शिष्याः।
   अपि च मम क्षमस्व आश्येनाः[3] यमपि निमन्त्रितु[4] कामवीतरागी।।

Translation

Good for you, I am fortune to see you. At the place of your birth, we are also his (Suddhodana's) disciples. Moreover, forgive me for that wish, through which I invited you, the dispassionate, to (enjoy) desires. B. Goswami. P-227.

1. यनु – a peculiar usage. Rhys Davias refers be an archaic usages (Ed. 2003: 543). Edgarton (Ed. 1953: 444) suggest यनतु in syncope. Is it a case of synocope?

2. पि Pkt. निपात।

3. आशयेना for आशयेन।

4. निमन्त्रितु Pkt. form निमन्त्र + तु (for तुमन) Note निमन्त्र is a sound simplification, निमन्त्त in Skt.

यदि त्वये[1] अनुप्राप्त[2] भीति[3] बोधिः तद मम सेति भोति[4] धर्मस्वामिं[5]।
अपि च मम पुरा सुलब्ध लाभा[6] मम विजिते वससीह[7] यत्स्वयंभों[8]।।

Translation

If you attain Bodhi, it will be mine, O Lord of Dhamma! Moreover, I have gained a great gain, you will live in my kingdom, O Self-born! B. Goswami. p.227.

1. A case of elision त्वय for त्वया।
2. Already discussed I.s.
3. In Pkt. भोति for भवति। तद for तदा। Rhythmic semblance in gāthā for meter.
4. सेते, Rhys Davias concurs Vedic ओनो Avasta *Saiti* to put to sleep. Pāli धातु reads से for शय to lie down to sleep. The context however sugges सोति भोति to be relaxed. PED 2003: 722.
5. धर्मस्वामि – a Pkt. form.
6. Lengthening लाभा for meer sake.
7. वससि + इह a Sandhi.
8. A case of mis-analogy for स्वयंभो (सम्भु, स्वयंबाधेन–एकवचन), सं + भु (संबाधेन–एकवचन) in Skt.

प्रज्ञबलं[1] च उपायबलं ऋद्धिम[2] संगतमैत्रिबलं च।
प्रतिसंविदपरिसत्यबलं च तेस[3] मिं[4] निष्पदि[5] भेष्यति अद।।

Translation

Prajñābala, *Upāyabala*, miracles and the powers of unity and amity, special knowledge and truth will be accomplished today.

1. प्रज्ञबलं for प्रज्ञाबलं for sake of meter – (shortening the second syllable).
2. ऋद्धिम a Pkt. suffix म for Sanskrit मतु।
3. तेष for Pkt. and Pāli तेष।
4 मि an absolute monosyllabic Pkt. from for मं।
5. Edgartan suggest Pkt. *Nippaddi* ? p.308.

पुण्यबलं च तवापि अनन्तं, यन्मम दास्वसि अद्य तृणानि।
नद्यपरं तव एतु[1] निमिन्तं, त्वं पि[2] अनुत्तरु[3] मे भयसि शास्ता।।

Translation

You will acquire endless virtuous power that you give me this grass today. You need no other sing. You, you, will be the Supreme Instructor.

1. Already discussed एतु for एत्
2. पि Pkt. निपात अपि।
3. अनुत्तरु I.s.

श्रृतु[1] ति[2] धरणिपालः शाकियानां कपिलपुरं परमं सुत्रऋद्धिस्फीतं।
दने पितु[4] मम शुद्धोति[5] नाम्ना तनु अहु प्रव्रजितो गुणाभिलाषी।।

Translation

You have heard, you're Majesty, of Kapila, the city of the Īākyas, prosperous and flourishing. My father is named śuddhodana. From there, I have become an ascetic, desirous of merit.

1.4.7. Apbs. form I.s of श्रृतु, पितु and अहु for श्रृतः, पिता and अहं in Skt. Rerely पितु in Pkt. is found.

2. ति for इति in Pkt. and Apbs.

3. Māgadhi Pkt. form for शक्यानम्। In Pāli also शकिय for शक्य। However शकिया with palatal श from the above examples, it may be pointed out that gāthās had been closed to the Pure Sanskrit.

5. Irregular in *Sandhi*. (शुद्धदोनः+इति) according to Shaklya. भोभगोअधोअपुर्व्वस्य योहशि। लापेः शाकल्यस्स। हलि सव्वेणामे। (व्या० कौ०)। In Pkt. विसर्ग change into ओ in I.s or dropped. Hence शुद्धदन + इति (अ+इ = ए)।

6. Irrgular in *Sandhi*.

From the above examples, if may be pointed out that *Gāthās* had been closed to the Pure Sanskrit. In fact, the normal growth of *Gāthā* Sanskrit towards Pure Sanskrit developed in course of transformation in language. It has been already stated the *Gāthā* Sanskrit developed during the *Mahāyāna* who required relating the account of the merits of the Buddha in Sanskrit to the IA speakers of Parthia, Anatolia and Bactria by the 4th century BCE. Those he IA borrowings in Anatolian documents also are more comparable to Middle Indo Arian than Old Indo Aryan. They might have belonged to a dialect like Buddhist Hybrid Sanskrit appearing somewhat like a transitional stage between Old Indo Aryan and Middle Indo Arian.

Some special linguistic features which appear as the source language of Anatolia borrow words which appeared in the transitional stage between Old Indo Aryan and Middle Indo Arian languages like proto Buddhist Hybrid Sanskrit.

1. Dissimilar plosives have been assimilated, e.g. *Sapta satta.*
2. Conjuncts in semi-vowels and liquids are not assimilated like first Middle Indo Arian, e.g. *Vartana/wartana, rathya/aratiya, virya/birya*, and *vatdhasva/bardasava.*
3. Conjuncts in nasals are not assimilated unlike first Middle Indo Arian and like Old Indo Aryan which places this dialect closer to Old Indo Aryan, e.g. *Rukma nurukna, ṛtamna/artamna.*
4. Anaptyxis is quite frequent, e.g. *indra/indara, smara/sumara.*
5. Often verb, e.g. *virya birya, vṛdhasva.*

The above specimens cited from the text *ārya Lalitavistara Sātra* may focus a new light on the growth of the Pure Sanskrit from the *Gāthā* Sanskrit or Mixed Sanskrit. Thus it may be deducted:

1. In the history of the growth of Sanskrit from the Vedic language, several stages have already been determined by linguistics.

   For the growth of languages from Vedic speeches to Sanskrit, the *Sātra* text including the *āraṇyaka*, *Brāhamaṇa* and *Upaniṣads* played an important role and it may require a separate study as to how Pāṇini and others enunciated grammatical formula.
2. The specimen take under review seem to suggest that various Prākṛts and Apabhraṃśa had been in common use by the local inhabitants of the said areas.
3. The irregular forms, according to Pāṇini's Grammar *Aṣṭādhyāyi Vyākaraṇa*, occasionally perturb the Sanskrit-knowing scholar for non-Sanskrit usages in the Buddhist Sātra literature.

4. It may be further shown that many Prākṛt forms and occasionally Apabhraṃśa words have been is use to enrich the *gāthā* with sonorous rhythm. It is reasonable use to hold that a major portion of the *gāthās* in the Mixed Sanskrit and covered Uddiyana and adjacent areas of Central Asia.
5. Many Pali words are also traces and these many open a new relationship between the *Therāvadin*, *Sarbāstibadin* and *Sthavaras*.
6. It may be added that in the *gāthā* language may be traced in some of the Ṛk-Veda hymns in which peculiarities of *gāthā* Sanskrit are observed.
7. Critically speaking it may be observed that the *gāthā* singers in praise of the Buddha and the Bodhisattvas contributed verses in melodious rhythm sonorously in the Mixed Sanskrit having many Prākṛt words and occasional Apanbharmśa expressions which had been in common usage locally in those days.

Notes and References

1. **Kānjur** (*bka 'gyur*) and **Tānjur** (*Bstan'jyur*) **:** The literary history of Tibet goes back to the 7th Century with the translation of a few Indian canonical texts. Later on the translation literature in Tibetan is divided under two broad heads. One is Kānjur (Bka'gyur) comprising the canonical that is *Buddhavacana* and other is Tānjur (Bstan'jyur) comprising the non-canonical literature like commentaries on the Kānjur Texts, lexicon, poetry, drama, philosophical works etc. The two collections comprise 4,569 titles according to the sde-dge edition. An eminent Tibetan scholar Bu Ston (A.D. 1290-1364) collected the translated Indian texts which were scattered throughout the country with the help of monk scholar Tshal pa Kumdga¿ rdo-rje. Generally Kānjur have nine resonations and Tānjur have four, they are follows:

   Kānjur (bka 'gyur) Edition:

   1. Cone (co ne) edition
   2. Dege (sdeege) edition
   3. Phug brag edition
   4. Lhasa (lhasa) edition
   5. Lithang (li thang) edition
   6. Peking edition

7. Narthang (snarthang) edition
8. Orgyanghing or Tawang edition
9. Stog (stog) palace edition

Tānjur (bstan 'gyur) Edition:

1. Cone (co ne) edition
2. Derge (sdedge) edition
3. Peking edition
4. Ganden (dga 'ldan), 'Golden Manuscript' edition.

2. Etymologically *gāthā*is derived from root *gāth*; Prākṛt root presumably *gāa*, alternative *gāy* referring to a Prākṛt dialect presented in tunes. In Sanskrit *gāthā* means a song or singing. Therefore *gāthāka* is a singer. Again *gāthākāra* is a writer of Prākṛt verses. Its leaves a room to presuppose that *gāthā* had been in vogue either non-Vedic speaker who was probably named as *gāthāka*, singer of songs popularly performed in context of the Vedic.
3. In this regard *gāthā* is mostly used in *Prākṛt Jātaka* legends in stanza style. Regarding the *Jātaka* stories as they have come in the present form might not be always in verse or *gāthā*. M. Monier Williams however shows that *gāthā* as a song. It may be mentioned that the many Buddhist *sātras* are written entirely in verses. Although the present form of the *Sutta Pitaka*, particularly, *Dighanikāya*, *Majjhimanikāya* and *Samyuttanikāya* are in admixture of prose and verse.

Abbreviation used in this article:

Pkt = Prākṛt, Apbs = ApabhraAśa, Skt = Sanskrit, 1.s. = First Person Sing.

1. p. = First Person Plu. Num., BHS = Buddhist Hybrid Sanskrit, BHSD = Buddhist Hybrid Sanskrit Dictionary, ALVS = ārya Lalitavistara Mahāyāna Sātra

Selected Bibliography

1. Katre Sumitra Mangesh (1941): An Introduction to Indian Textual Criticism, Karnatak Publishing, Bombay.
2. Buhler Georg, Indian Paleography (1959): (from about B.C. 350 to about Ad 1300) Tr. by J.F. Fleet, D.P. Chattopadhyaya, Calcutta.
3. Theodor Aufreeht, Catalogus Calalogrum(1962): Part I and II, Franz Steiner Verlag Grah, Wiesbaden Germany.
4. Pathak, S.K. (1990): Classification of The Buddhist Literature in Tibetan (In Principles of Editing and Instrumentation ed., Dwivedi and Samtani, Sarnath), pp. 434-448.

5. Sharma, K.V.(1990): Variant Reading and Text Reconstruction in Indian Manuscriptology (Principles of Editing and Instrumentation Ed., Dwivedi and Samtani, Sarnath), pp. 134-148.
6. Sharma, K.V (1990): Novel Techniques in Collecting Manuscripts and Editing Texts, pp. 313-320.
7. Santani. N.H., Some Problems in Editing Buddhist Texts (in same above book), pp. 237-245.
8. Pandeya Janardan, Indian Scripts and their Problms (*Bharatiy Lipiyan Aur Unki Samsyaen,* Hindi), Sampadana De SiddhantaAurUpadana ed., Dwive and Samtani, 1990, Sarnath), pp. 35-124.
9. Bahulkar, S.S., Problem of Variants (with special reference to GuhyasamajaTantra) (in same above book), pp. 158-169.
10. Sankrityayan, Rahul, Sanskrit Palm Leaf Manuscripts in Tibet, Journal of Bihar and Orissa Research Society, Vol. XXI, pp. 21-43.
11. Sarma, B.R. (1996): Text Editing and Text Critical Study, RabindraBharati University, Calcutta.

Sanskrit Ms.

(a) Govt, collection No. 9974 (MS. A), unseasoned plam leaf. 15 x 2 inches, Folio-58, Script, Newari, Date-713 (N.S.) 1593 (A.D.).
(b) Govt, collection No. 4735 (MS.B.), Nepalese paper 11x3 inches, Folio-99, Script-Newari, Date-773 (N.S.).
(c) Govt, collection No. 4725 (MS. C), seasoned palm leaf 13 x *Wi*inches, Folio-77, Script-Newari, Date-515 (N.S.).
(d) Govt, collection No. 9975 (MS.D.), unseasoned leaf 16x2 inches, Folio-96, Scripto-Newari, Date-744 (N.S.).

Tibetan Xylographs

(a) Lhasa Edition (MS. L.), Script-dbu-chan (Tibetan), Volume No. 'E' (Ja), Recession Lhasa Shol. Machine Made Paper 50 x 10.2 cms. Folio.314b2 to 388a5. Date-7th Century, Translators-Jina Mitra, Dana Sila and Tibetan lo tsaba, ye ses sde.
(b) Peeking Edition (MS. Pkg), Ms Call No. 784-91-5-7, Volume No. 30, Script-dbuchan (Tibetan), Folio-224a7-274b4.
(c) The Asiatic Society (Calcutta) Collection (MS. AS), Script: dbu-chan (Tibetan), Volume No. 'E' (Ja), Hand Made Paper, Translators-Sakyapraba, Santa Raksita 68 X 20.2 cms., Folio-313a6 to 382al. lb. ārya Lalitavistara Nāma Mahāyāna Sātra (ALV), (*Phags pa rgyachenrol pa shesbyabatheg pa chenpo'imdo*). Tibetan

(a) Peking Edition, Vol. 27 (763), Folios No. 153-271, dbu-chen script.

(b) The Asiatic Society Collection, Vol. 'kha', Folioes No. Ibl-216b7, dbu-chen script.

(c) Lhasa edition. Vol. 'kha' (37), Folios No. Ia-352a6. dbuchen script.

Sanskrit Mss.

(a) The Asiatic Society, Collection Ms. No. 785, Folio-246, Newari script, Appearance, old.

(b) College of Fort-William Collection (1825), Manuscript is uncatalogued in The Asiatic Society. (c) Lalita-vistara Ed. by Dr. P.L. Vaidya. Puboished in the Mithila Institute of post Graduate Studies and Research in Sanskrit learning, Darbhanga 1958. (d) Lalitavistara Ed. by Dr. S. Lefmann, Halle 1902. (e) Asiatic Society, Collection Ms. No. B. 14. (f) Lalitavistara (translated from original Sanskrit) by Rajendralala Mitra, Calcutta, 1881. (g) The Asiatic Society, Collection Ms. No. 61, New Script.

20

The World of Western Indian Manuscript Painting in the 15th-16th Century India

– *Swati Biswas*

The history of manuscript production is a significant literary and art activity of the medieval times in the subcontinent. The history of it is not much known in the ancient times or before 11th -12th century. This is all the more true for Western Indian style manuscript or what is popularly known as Jaina manuscript. The manuscript illustration of this type had a large geographical extent. It is tru e that it started in Gujarat as it had the largest concentration of Jaina Bhandaras or monasteries. The scholastic activity in the Bhandaras led to the production of huge amount of manuscript. The zeal to preserve the religion and the attempt to spread the religion made manuscript production a religious mission and a successful one. Soon it spread to other parts of north India

It is important to look in to the history of the period to understand the real affair that led to the production of this style of manuscripts.

It started during the time when Muslim rulers were at their helm in north Indian politics. It flourished during the time when Delhi saw two empires back to back led by the rulers who were followers of Islam and also the intermediate period.

The advent of Islam in the political sphere brought India closer to the larger rubric of Islamic civilization. Inspite of this fact India became the safe haven for people of West Asia and Central Asia who wanted to get a refuge from the neo-Islamists namely the Mongols first and then the

Timurids. The political leaders and the sword bearers of Islam as sometimes they have been wrongly branded never wanted to try their fortune in the west but settled in India along with the large section of non Muslim subjects and never intended to convert them categorically because their aspiration was purely political and not religious. The turbulent time of Asia inculcated many changes within the socio economic cultural sphere of India which never had any uniform cultural code and was always exposed to different socio- political, cultural and religious upheavals in Asia.

The period thus has to be seen and understood on the basis of this understanding. Art and culture of the period also canvassed the above reality. It gave the period a kind of flexibility to adopt different cultural norms on one hand and also the passion to preserve the indigenous identity. Thus the Jains produced the religious manuscripts with strict iconography whereas flexible enough to incorporate new technique, colour and skill. This in turn gave the form of painting a popularity in which other subjects apart from Jaina themes were hence illustrated.

The norm of book illustration of Iran in the 14th century was essentially influencing the whole of Asia and India was no exception. During this period the art of calligraphy and illustration was very popular in Persia and it was essentially pursued as a pious mission. The story of calligraphy and illustration in India likewise also started in the hands of the Buddhist, Jain and to some extent the Hindus in the same way. The Sultanate rule of the Muslims in India and their relation with Central and West Asia opened the market of India for this art form to creep in. The artists in India were receptive enough to inculcate the new technique in to their own practice.

On the other hand the advent of the Mughals to the Indian subcontinent was not a mere accident. Babur, the founder of the Mughal Empire made very calculated move to enter the land and waited outside the land for considerable number of years. The Mughals brought with them the legacy of the west Asian and central Asian art and culture. The land to which they arrived also went through significant change in the previous century and the culmination of that change in the 16th century opened new vistas for different art forms. The legacy of its history continued along with significant change that was in evident. Thus when the Mughals arrived to this land the cultural milieu was expecting a leadership that was well served by the Mughals.

In between the period of Delhi Sultanate and Mughal empire was a period of political activity which created the space for regional identity. This itself led to the flourishing of different art activity which in turn created authentic regional art forms.

The western Indian painting style started in the region of Gujarat as mentioned earlier and then moved on to flourish in Jaunpur, Mandu, Malwa and the Delhi Palam region. It is thus important to grasp the history of the region to understand the milieu in which over centuries this style developed.

The changes in India starting from the 12th century was part of a trend of Asia where the nomadic people of the steppes of Inner Asia migrated and became politically dominant over sedentary agrarian societies. The entire West and South Asia in this era was transformed due to the superior military technologies of the new conquerors. In the Indian subcontinent this changes interestingly made the arid zone of the Indus Valley through Rajasthan and into the central India and Deccan very active. This zone became the decisive factor in Indian history due to improvements in livestock, advances in horse-riding technology, and the greater political influence of these people. Thus the inner frontier of this scorched zone was a place of social dynamism and fluidity. The cultural upheaval in this region again is just another manifestation of this dynamism.[1]

The establishment of the Delhi Sultanate paved the way for the incorporation of South Asia into the growing geographic sphere of Islam. The initial Mongol incursions into Iran led to an even greater cultural link between north India and the lands to the west. Islam was transmitted by maritime routes as well and gradually spread into Southeast Asia by the fourteenth century. India on the other hand due to this trend became a very cosmopolitan place. Thus Delhi Sultanate drew India firmly into the networks and in to the multicultural and pluralistic society that had been created by these Islamist rulers. It was an era of escalating circulation of goods, people, technologies and ideas.

North India between empires and the growth of regional identity: The period of fifteenth century saw the weakening of the Delhi Sultanate and the rise of number of regional powers with strong local identity in north India. Irrespective of religion the local powers were able to establish political zones with very strong regional identity. The cultural ethos of these political zones had very strong local cultural fervor as a result of which regional languages and local art and architecture flourished within the rubric of the greater Islamic aesthetics.

Gujarat in the western region took longer time to get out of the clutches of Delhi Sultanate. In 1407 CE Zafar Khan assumed the title of Muzaffar Khan and claimed independence. Gujarat Sultanate came to be known after his grandson Ahmad Shah who founded the city of Ahmedabad in 1411 CE and it lasted until the Mughals incorporated Gujarat as part of their ever expanding empire in 1573 CE. The Sultanate of Gujarat had much of similar history of Bengal Sultanate only that its foes were more and had to be more alert. They had to combat Malwa Sultanate, Rajput Rajas of north Gujarat and Rajasthan and at the near end the Portuguese. Gujarat in the fifteenth century traded in teak wood, bamboo, spices, pearl, gold, silver, carnelian and woven cotton and camel to South East Asia, Africa, Middle East and Europe. To the travelers and merchants Ahmedabad and Champaner were considered model urban centers. Usmanpur, a suburb of Ahmedabad was a leading Sufi centre.

The Gujarat sultans like their contemporaries elsewhere in north India did not make or break political agreements in terms of religion. Gujarat's bardic traditions claim that the Hindus held high position in the political sphere in Ahmad Shah's administration and the ruling elite often married Hindu Rajput women as a means of maintaining good relations with local populations. The sultanate architecture of Gujarat is deemed by many to be the most elegant of all pre- Mughal regional styles. They are very unique and has strong regional characteristic which later inspired Mughal architecture. The capital cities of Ahmedabad and Champaner as it exists today can claim high end planning which was unique.

The Sufi cult here also played a very important role in the social and cultural sphere of Gujarat. The site of Ahmedabad for instance was chosen by the famous saint Makhdum Shaikh Ahmad Khattu [1336-1445 CE] and laid its foundation stone. Muhammad Shah, the successor of Ahmad Shah, as his homage to the saint constructed a *khanqa*.

The multi cultural ambience that was created by the Gujarat Sultanate was undoubtedly unique. It was this milieu in which the western Indian painting style developed, flourished and spread to other parts of north India.

The next important regional zone is Jaunpur. Jaunpur within its very short span of independent history should be remembered for its unique excellence in art and culture.

Jaunpur broke official ties with Delhi Sultanate in 1396 CE. It was the region between Delhi and Bengal and continued its hostility throughout its existence with Delhi. It deprived the Tughluqs, Sayyid and the Lodis of a large chunk of their crown land. The Jaunpur army entered Delhi twice but was ultimately crushed by Sikandar Lodi in 1494 CE. The Sultanate of Jaunpur also known as the Sharqi rulers had to combat the power in Orissa. Inspite of all this hostility Jaunpur became the cultural hub of the Islamic world for a brief period attracting artists, masons, poets and intellectuals of all fields to its court. Jaunpur claimed its fame due to its superb architecture which was much copied by the Lodis in Delhi. The architecture of the time proved that the Sharqis were aware of both Indian and Islamic tradition when it came to designs. The literature of the time does give an idea of the harmonious relationship between the communities of Hindu and Muslims throughout the Sharqi period. The merchants essentially Jain also had their share of contribution to the cultural life of the region.

Malwa claimed its independence from the Tughluqs in the early fifteenth century. Malwa's biggest rivals were the Bahmani sultans of the Deccan, the sultans of Gujarat and the rulers of Mewar. The hill fort Mandu, embellished with palaces, mosques, tombs and gardens, was the capital of Malwa. The Jain merchants played an essential role in the economic sphere as well as in the cultural sphere in Malwa as in Jaunpur and Mandu. It is this group of Jain merchants who significantly was responsible for the development of western Indian manuscript style. They commissioned various artists and scribes to create these manuscripts as a part of the religious pursuit.

The Rajput painting style also owes a lot to the western Indian painting style. The style was largely followed in the areas of western India ruled by the various Rajput clans. The style supplied skilled artist for the Rajput painting style which started developing within this milieu and flourished in the different Rajput houses later.

The term Rajput is a broad label to the warrior clans of western India today whose presence in the medieval age was very much felt in the central and northern India along with west. The first major Rajput kingdom was Sisodiyas of Mewar. Mewar is in the south eastern Rajasthan and receives more rainfall and has better soil than any other localities within the region. It was strategically located on the trade routes from Delhi and the Yamuna-Ganges doab down to Gujarat. The Sisodiya base, Chitor fortress was situated on an isolated plateau rising abruptly above the surrounding plain and so was easily defensible. Under the rule of Rana Kumbha who ruled from 1433 CE to 1468 CE Mewar became the most powerful states. Malwa and Gujarat were the hostile kingdoms he had to reconcile with. He was able to capture Sultan of Malwa in 1437 CE but released in true Rajput chivalrous gesture. The incident was commemorated again by building different architectures. Thus architecture was the marker of personal victories of the rulers throughout this period in North India. He was also acclaimed in history for constructing massive forts like the one in Kumbhalgarh. His palace gives an idea of the fifteenth century view of the domestic and administrative life under the Rajputs. Gwalior was the other kingdom of the Rajputs which acclaimed fame for cultural distinction. Under the Tomars it reached its pinnacle in cultural and architectural brilliance. Babur, the first Mughal ruler of India was very impressed by Raja Man Singh Tomars palace.

It could be rightly said that the period saw dynamism in politics and religion. This on the other hand had tremendous effect on the social life of all strata of people and their culture. The volatile dynamism paved the ground for the Mughals to build an empire so diverse in nature with this magnum opus of regional culture. Delhi Sultanate gave the region the legitimacy it needed to be within the ambit of the newly Islamic world. India not only became strategically important but culturally attractive to the world and a land of peace and prosperity.

Within this political milieu many art forms flourished. The history of western Indian painting started in this area as a religious pursuit and soon became an art form in which secular and foreign themes were illustrated. This significantly proves the potential of the form which was flexible enough to incorporate new techniques and was rigid enough to stick to its iconographic representation. It supplied trained artist to the grand Mughal atelier who could promptly adapt themselves in the camp with very strong Persian influence and which in turn was trying to form consciously as an independent art form.

The Story of Western Indian Painting School[2]

Western Indian Art as a term does not only cater to the Jaina miniatures only but encompasses a style that was prevalent in North India from 13th century and developed to form other painting styles as mentioned earlier.

The manuscripts that have been available till date suggest that the first half of 15th century was the formative period of this school. From 14th centuries monotony it progressed fast to improve the quality of the drawing and colours and the painters did enjoy some freedom of expression. Patan, Ahmedabad, Gandhar, Vadnagar, Champaner were important centers in Gujarat. Mandu with its *Kalpasutra* [now at National Museum] stands out as another important centre during this period.

Based on strict iconography it was started by the monks in the *Bhandaras* to preserve the religious tenants of Jainism. It moved from palm leaf illustration to paper illustration in the 13th century giving more scope to the artist to experiment. The *pothi* format remained intact throughout. It conformed to the one hole two column pattern with margins in red and red roundels marking the hole. In the paper format the numerals were written in the bottom right hand corner. This format continued till 17th century.

The iconography of the Jainas gave little scope to experiment with the narrative tradition of illustration initially. The 14th century illustrations were though of high quality but from 1400 CE there was an increasing tendency towards rigidity and distortion. The protrusion of chest, bust and hips along with the exaggeration of the further eye became the marker of this artistic style. The tilt of the Ajanta frescos in which the further eye was stylistically used now became so exaggerated that it almost appeared to be in the space. From 15th century the progressive Jaina and Hindu miniatures tried to keep the figures in strict profile.[3]

The paper miniatures abandoned the habit of colour modeling a prevalent style of the palm leaf illustration and the outlines were now in flat planes of colour in brittle line. Costly colours were used along with gold and silver.

Apart from the change in profile and colour there were other changes which made significant transformation in the illustration of Western Indian Painting style in the 15th and 16th centuries. The rigidity in the 15th and

16th century diminished in some of the high quality manuscripts. The linear format was still used but changes soon progressed in the areas outside Gujarat. The non Jaina professional artists initiated such move sometimes unknowingly. The Persian motifs soon became popular.

The Jaina miniature progress had been slow holistically. There were few exceptional manuscripts which gave the hint of the changes that was taking place. Some of the Jaina miniatures had a curious central medallion along with small four medallions and it reminded us of the contemporary Korans in *Behari* script.[4]

This art form became a bridge between the Mughal style and the indigenous schools of India.

Incidentally Mughals came to India at a time when the Jaina school of painting reached an interesting phase. It had gone through a matured painting phase with serious painters and patrons in west and central India. It was this group of painters who flocked to Mughal atelier and adopted themselves to the Mughal painting culture in large numbers. Highly skilled and efficient they were accepted and became invincible for the Mughal atelier. Though difficult to trace but they also had their own influence in the Mughal atelier. Thus it was very important to understand the history and cultural milieu in which this art form developed and how this contributed to the Mughal culture.

The Journey in the 15th century

The 15th century could be considered a time of maturity of the western Indian painting style which incorporated many changes responding to the contemporary painting scenario.

The 15th century significantly was a period when the Indian painting style was highly influenced by the Persian element. In spite of hieratic rigidity it struggled to reach that natural form in the hands of the painters. The pictorial effect was enhanced by the judicious use of colours and metallic effects of gold and mica. The tendency was to hire essential Persian style out of necessity. With time it also became a marker for the Jaina expressions as evident from the *Shahi* figures of *Kalakacharyakatha*. Interesting was that the *Shahi* king and his followers were all in full or three quarter profile without the protruding eyes. The inspiration could well be the pottery and carpet designs available in the market.

The earliest paper manuscript *Supasanahachariyam* of 1413AD in the Sri Hemachandracharya Jain Mandir, Patan incorporated all the changes of the late fourteenth century. Full illustrations appear. The draughtmanship become judicious and neat. The composition was more elaborate and scope for landscape was enhanced. The use of ultramarine blue was very obvious.

The *Kalakacharya Kathas* of Mandu in the collections of Muni Sri Punyavijjayaji [published by Pramod Chandra in Bulletin of The American Academy of Banaras, No1] was distinct for its draughtmanship. This was much comparable to the Mandu *Kalpasutra* of 1439AD. The use of orpiment for the colour of the human body was very prominent.

The landscape was a distinguishing feature here. The trees had been curiously treated in the foreground. The clouds had also been treated dramatically using greenish blue shade along with grey and pink bordered by white. The yellow sky with white and black curly clouds with nail like projection had resemblance with Chinese clouds represented in certain Persian manuscripts of the fifteenth century. This gave an idea that the artist could now go beyond the convention and tried different means to express his ideas which was very rare compared to the time.

The 1414 CE *Kalakacharya Katha* of Patan proved how draughtmanship, detail and the use of ultramarine and gold became important to this genre of painting style.

The manuscript *Kalpasutra* and *Kalakacharyakatha* at the Chhatrapati Sivaji Maharaj Vastu Sangrahalay, Mumbai is the best example of the change that was heralding. It has forty three illustrations among one hundred and eight folios. Distortion of the later period was absent with protruding eyes remaining just as a part of tradition. The human figure was marked by fine draughtmanship. Exaggeration of the body parts had also been avoided. The female figures were artistically drawn. Aesthetics won over clichê iconography.

The surface was divided in panels. Each panel depicts a story. The textile patterns were intricately visible. The vegetation and animal figures inspite of its decorative use had a charm which was very different from the earlier form.

The Jaina bankers took immense interest in the project of manuscript illustration and the use of rich material started. The austerity thus diminished. The best example may be that of the 1475 CE *Devasano Pado Kalpasutra* of Gandhara port [near Broach]. The patterns were drawn from architecture, textiles and carpets. Persian elements were included in the new style. This was definitely a significant change in the art form. The illustrator understood the landscape more and attempted to include social life of the people in the subject.

The Jamnagar manuscript painted at Patan in 1501 CE also showed the same trend. These efforts prove that the subject matter was treated differently during this time which brought about a significant change in the style.

These trends were adopted by the Vaisnava paining like *Balagopalstuti* and *Gitagovinda* and they further enhanced by improving the emotional understanding and added movement. The earliest document of this new movement was the secular scroll painting of *Vasanta Vilasa* of 1451 CE.

This aspect moved from the boundaries of Gujarat, Malwa and Rajasthan and reached Jaunpur as evident from the *Kalpasutra* of 1465 CE.

The story of Western Indian Painting will remain incomplete without the analysis of the two brilliant pieces of Jaina manuscripts from Mandu.

Jainism flourished during this period and the period before that is during the Paramaras in Mandu. Interestingly the pictorial art of Malwa is few. After the frescos of Bagh in the 5th century the two illustrated Jaina Manuscript appears.

The first *Kalpasutra* was published by Sarabhai Nawab. The manuscript is in the collection of Sri Kantivijayaji, now deposited in the Atmananda Jnana Bhandara, Baroda.[5]

The manuscript though not datable mentioned two names the chief minister Kala of the Pragvata family and his son Haridasa and thus could be safely said that it belonged to the 15th century. The ultramarine was used in substantial amount and the draughtmanship is of high quality. The marriage procession of Neminath is a full page illustration which is very unlikely of Jaina illustrations.

There were other illustrated manuscripts also probably illustrated here at this time.

The second *Kalpasutra* manuscript was presented to the National Museum by Acharya Vijayendra Suri.[6]

The manuscript prepared in the year 1439 CE for one Kshemahamsagani as per its colophon during the time of Mahmud Shah Khalji was of great importance for the understanding of the evolved painting style of 15th century and the influence of the Persian painting style on the contemporary painting schools of India. The Jaina School did not deviate from its root but perhaps due to the availability of Persian paintings in the market especially the Turkoman style of Shiraz influenced the artist greatly.

The format is in oblong form. The page was divided in the middle by floral motifs [three types of motifs]. The script is written in gold. There were seventy three folios of which folios 5, 31, 36 and 39 are missing. The folios measure 29X10.1cm. The area covered by the text is 24.5X7.5cm. The rest of the folio is occupied by vertical floral or geometrical band. The text runs to seven lines per folio, is written in gold letters on a crimson ground. The paintings are usually in the right hand side and of very high quality compared to the contemporary painting style of western India.

The colophon is inscribed in black ink on a crimson ground.

The draughtmanship is of excellent quality without any change in the iconography. The *Kalpasutra* suggest that at that juncture aesthetics was more valuable than hieratic to the artist and their patron.

The human figures were carefully drawn with the narrowness of the waist much minimized. The nails were indicated by dots. The female figures reached an aesthetic fullness. The seated figures had similarity with the *Mahapurana of 1540*. Thus this *Kalpasutra* was a trend setter.

The colours used were red, carmine, blue [azurite], green [copper sulphate], yellow ochre mauve, purple, pink and white. The use of gold was limited to the ornaments and certain furniture. This gave a rare balance to the pictorial aesthetics. Sandalwood colour was often used for the body. The traditional colours of green and blue were used for the *jinas*. Sometimes gold was also used for *jinas* to indicate the metallic nature and create a sense of detachment.

The landscape was mostly confined to 'variegated cloud treated dramatically'. The clouds were black with white borders. The depiction of the trees here continued in the early Rajasthani painting.

Architectural detail was reduced to minimum. The two storied building in one of the illustration showed the detail of the wooden work of the period.

The arch horses had traces of Persian influence. Apart from this not much Persian influence could be found in this manuscript. The treatment of the horses continued even in the *Mahapurana* of 1540AD and in early Rajasthani painting. The treatment of the elephants followed the decorative style of the contemporary Western Indian style. The bulls on the other hand were depicted much naturally.

Seventy years later *Ni'mat-nâma* from Mandu had stray similarity with it hinting to the fact that this *Kalpasutra* perhaps was the beginning of a new form that evolved in the later years in Mandu. The architectural settings like domed pavilion were found in both the manuscripts and were very much a feature typical to the Mandu style. The clothing of the female figures and treatment of the postures also had similarities.

The artist matured themselves to the height of excellence in the coming years and was thus later able to grasp the activities of the Mughal School.

The *Jaunpur Kalpasutra of 1465 CE* [now at Baroda at the Narasimhaji Pol na Jnanabhandara] and the *Devasano Pado Kalpasutra of 1475 CE* also have certain similarities with the above *Kalpasutra*. The finish can well be compared to the Jaunpur *Kalpasutra*. The cultural proximity of Malwa and Jaunpur may be the reason for this similarity. The influence of all this to the Mughal School is not easy to draw but scholars like Robert Skelton hinted to the trace of this school to the Rajasthani painting of 17th century. Karl Khandalavala was also of opinion that the Rajasthani painting school of 17th century was not any independent feature but definitely a continuity of the past traditions. Mandu had close cultural proximity with Rajasthan.

Glimpses of the other Manuscripts of 15th century

The *Kalpasutra* in the collection of Muni Kanti Vijayaji in the Atmanan Jnana Mandir, Baroda was also painted in Mandu. The colophon is incomplete. Stylistically this manuscript belonged to the 15th century. The refinement here also is mention worthy. The composition is elaborate. The Persian influence is limited to the use of ultramarine, carmine and gold. The floral spray also has Persian lineage.

The *Vasanta Vilasa* at the Freer Gallery of 1415 CE[7] gave a new direction to the western Indian Painting. It is an old love poem of Gujarat. The subject itself gave scope to treat the human figures with new life in the backdrop of a different landscape far removed from the Jaina hieratic of the time. The scroll originally had eighty four paintings of which five have been lost. It was done for one Chandrapala of Ahmedabad.

The text was done first with spaces left for illustrations. The background was done in red, yellow and gold. The angular draughtmanship and further eye remained as the marker of the time. Inspite of this the figures gained some mobility. The costume used certain ripple to break the monotony. The 16th century feature of narrow waist was found here. The action took place in the same plane without leaving any place for perspective.

Landscape has been very interestingly treated. It corroborated the theme with green trees, gardens, lotus pool and black bee. The new trend gave life to the rigid draughtmanship of the time. The treatment of the sky was also given a new look with the use of blue, white, red and grey asymmetrical stripes. The *Devasano Pado Kalpasutra* style curly clouds appear once. The lotus pool and brick steps found here came to be a common feature in the later illustrations.

The *Damayanti Katha campu* composed by Trivikrama can be dated to 1450 CE[8] or sometimes earlier. The illustrations though in bad condition reveal the painter through his draughtmanship was able to use his lines confidently to define not only the body contour but details of the costumes and how it was worn. This definitely proves that a new movement started in the middle of the fifteenth century in Gujarat. The colour scheme had red in the background and yellow for carnation keeping with the tradition.

The *Jaunpur Kalpasutra of 1465 CE*[9] written during the time Hûsayn Shah Shârqi is another excellent piece of work which speaks loads about the brilliance of painting during this period. It is now with the Narasimhaji ni polna Jnana Bhandar, Baroda. The marginal decorations have definite influence of the Persian carpet and the contemporary tile decoration of the architecture.

The use of gold, ultramarine, carmine and green dominated over the usual red.

The figure composition deviated from the linear composition of Devasano Pado *Kalpasutra* and was much closer to the *Kalpasutra* of 1469 CE. The further eye did not have any organic character. The figures had close proximity with the early Rajasthani painting if the further eye was eliminated. The curly clouds were similar to the Mandu *Kalpasutra* of 1439 CE.

The Devasano Pado *Kalpasutra* and *Kalakakatha*[10] of 1475 CE revealed how the *Jainas* in spite of their rigidity were able to add to the extravagance of book illumination.

The paper manuscript originally had two hundred folios of which one hundred and forty five were dedicated to the *Kalpasutra* and the rest fourteen to *Kalakacharyakatha.* Of the one hundred and forty five folios, forty five including the colophon had been lost. The folios each measure 26x11.5cm with seven lines of text in Jain *Nagari* script. The script was written in gold on even ground. The background was usually deep red or ultramarine blue and occasionally black or pale yellow. The style of the manuscript conformed to the manuscript illustration of 1470 CE-1510 CE.

The border of the manuscript was extremely elaborate and depicted unusual detail of social life. According to Sarabhai Nawab the manuscript illustrate seven very rare incidents which were never illustrated before like the wedding of Vardhamana or Mahavira, Kalputana's attack and Rishaba receiving his first alms. The illustrations were devoid of landscape and architecture.

The painter used motifs from Hindu themes as well as carpets and textile of Persian origin. In the border decoration contemporary soldiers were depicted. The full page illustrations proved that the painter was in a position to paint elaborate themes and costly colours such as gold, ultramarine and carmine.

The border decorations had very strong Persian influence of the human figures though. This aspect remained intact toeing the Western Indian tradition.

The *Kalpasutra* of 1490 CE copied at Vadnagar[11] was mass produced type and lacks the finesse. The use of gold and blue are in opulence hindering the aesthetic value. Interestingly this manuscript was commissioned by one Nagara Brahmana of Vadnagar and copied by one Vachhaka of Patan. The religious differences did not restrict one from commissioning a piece of art during this period.

Patan along with Delhi-Gwalior-Agra region were very important areas of book illustration during this period.

The *Uttaradhayana Sutra* of 1492 CE[12] painted at Patan was stereotyped but in spite of that the painter attempted to give certain elaborations. The decorative element gave detail which was significant. Use of gold was minimal. Mica was used for the garments of the Jaina *Acharya*. The composition went beyond the limit of two or three figures. The illustrations could go beyond hieratic and animals, birds and trees were seen in the background.

The *Madhavanta-Kamakandvala-katha*[13] was illustrated in 1493 CE at Patan. The story of Madhavanta and Kamakandvala was a popular theme in the seventeenth century Popular Mughal School and in Pahari paintings. The 15th century illustration tried to keep up to the trend of movement in the figures that was done by *Vasanta Vilasa*. This extended the scope of secular subjects which hence flourished.

This new trend had a folk orientation. The attempt was to simplify the composition and colours. The focus of the illustration was always the story and the composition very simple. The attempt was to bring certain movement in the illustration. It deviated from the Jaina rigidity. The monotonous colour scheme of the background remained unchanged with the use of red and white. The story did not have much scope for landscape illustration yet it used clouds and room decorations to break the monotony.

Chandraprabhacharita[14] was illustrated again at Patan in 1498 CE. This manuscript proved how even a conservative subject could be given certain movement. Mica was used to paint the clothes. To break the monotony of colour scheme the painter used peacocks and decorative trees. Even a panel of faces appears in the background.

Delhi-Gwalior-Agra also produced excellent illustrated manuscripts during this time.

By the end of 15th century the art of Western India took a new direction after two hundred years of experimentation. The convention of further eye was now just a decorative feature. By 1500 CE this feature was eliminated. The Persian elements were simplified. On the other hand in Uttar Pradesh the heroic lore found expression in western Indian form with the use of these changes. This changed western Indian form had become the trend in whole of North India. This fact can be emphasized by the Buddhist wooden *pata* illustrated in 1446 CE at Arrah in Eastern India.

The observation will remain incomplete without the mentioning of the *Shahnâma* discussed elaborately by B N Goswamy[15]

The manuscript was probably done in the middle of the 15th century. The name of the painter or provenance or its patron was not known. It is 'fresh in vision, bold in execution and remarkably innovative'. The artist tried to break the trend by illustrating a Persian epic with the indigenous skill of the Western Indian Painting. He was thus able to open new vista for the future. This manuscript opened a new chapter in understanding of the painting style of the period. At one hand we have a mixed group of Sultanate painting incoherent in nature and on the other hand the period witnessed the rich development of conservative rigid Jaina painting style and to some extent less rigid Hindu painting style and the folk painting group.

The analysis of the style made one believe that the manuscript was done in mid 15th century in North India probably in Gujarat, Malwa or Bundelkhand. John Syller proposed a date of around 1425 CE[16] and opined that it had connection to the *Kalpasutra* of 1422 CE and was probably illustrated at Mandu. The fine Persian in the borders suggests that it was prepared for a well read patron. Firdausi's *Shahnâma* was very popular at that time among the Muslim elites.

The manuscript surfaced in 1988 CE in bound cover with three hundred and fifty folios. It is incomplete in nature. It had no *unwan* or *sarlavh*. It had a decorated panel before two sections. The fly leaf has no information except for three seals in Persian, two circular and one oval. It belonged to one person named Muhammad Fazil bearing two different dates of 1696 CE and 1718 CE. Thus the name of the original patron was not known. There was no colophon either. The manuscript folio measured 32×25cm. It was in the usual Islamic vertical codex format. The original text was in *Naskhi* but the damaged portions were retouched in *Nastaliq*. The text was written in four columns each with thin double rules. Some places were left blank. There was a long preface written in verse and prose a mixed technique very common for epic.

Paintings were sixty-six in number. The paintings were horizontal in format. The paintings stretched over the whole page. The text in four columns was only a part of it. The painter thus was still thinking in the format of *pothi* of Western India which was very popular in contemporary India.

The painter must have been narrated with the story. He used his indigenous skill to depict a foreign land and the characters of its epic with his skill and this resulted in this brilliant depiction. The style, the colouring, the vocabulary of conventions and the iconography remained pronouncedly Indian. The background was a flat vermillion red, the rocks and trees were depicted much like one found in the Jaina manuscripts. The sky also imitated the Chinese format that the Western India tried to grasp and then landed into its own format of lining in white. The depiction of the demon had all the insignia of an Indian mendicant while the protagonist Rustam had that foreign look that was well in vogue in the Western Indian Painting. Thus the figures had nothing to claim Persian for that matter. The depiction of women was grossly Indian. They were all feminine like the Western Indian style with full busts and narrow waist. The general clothing was differently done to give a foreign look but the lain cloth or *orhni* was significant. The jewelry like the *Hnasli* neck lets; anklets of gold and pearls, *Chhanavira* like cross garlands, and the pearls along the side of the head were in close proximity to the women of *Kalpasutra* or *Vasanta Vilasa* scroll discussed later in the chapter.

The interior decors like *toron* or furniture were all of Indian origin. The projecting eye was used with ease keeping the format of the Indian painting style of the period. The postures of the figures with the bulging chest, the absence of pupil in the eyes of the dead were the traits of the Indian counterparts of Gujarat. The spiky fire flames and the basket form of water with fish also reminded us of the Indian mannerism of the period. In one of the folios the appearance of the same figure twice for the narration of the story was found like the Jaina manuscripts [Death of *Siyavash*]. The detail was carefully repeated.

This was a 'Jainesque' work and not a painting done by a provincial painter for a Muslim patron who incorporated certain Indian elements with which he was familiar. 'It is a Ṣbridgeṣwork¿ that raised questions wholly relevant to the disparity that existed between style and subject matter'.

The painter was aware of the epic narration and perhaps the market had different versions of this Persian epic drama. The painter did not imitate the provincial style may be due to his own limitations. On the contrary he chose a style relying on his own skill by incorporating the depiction of the foreign elements as in *Kalakacharyakatha* of the time and gallantly depicted in a new format unknown before or after. It was very difficult to think that this style was repeated or existed before as no other evidence had been found.

This new approach gave the particular *Shahnâma* 'the air of freshness and of released energy'. The characters wore different dresses and carried different weapons keeping in view the cultural context from where they came. The vitality of the narration could be noticed in spite of the pictures not being burnished. The flat rich and saturated colour gave it a peculiar interesting look.

The combination of simplicity along with sophistication reminded us one of the early Rajput painting ushered by illustrations of Palam *Bhagavata Purana*. Interestingly the artist was able to bring the emotions of the characters in their joy and sorrow which was very rare in the contemporary world. The painter was able to grasp the storyline well and could react to the emotions of the foreign land with his Indian skill. Thus this manuscript remained one of the fascinating riddle of the age and well linked the Western Indian format with the Persian sentiment of the time.

16th century and the story continues

The *Kalka-Katha* and *Kalpasutra* of 1501 CE[17] from Patan revealed how the Jaina painting could get out of the clutches of rigidity and gallantly depict the richly decorated borders. This manuscript uses decorative motifs of the Devasano Pado *Kalpasutra*. This richly decorated manuscript has patterns drawn from textiles and calico painting. Geometrical figures and birds play an important part in its decoration.

The constant source of inspiration for these manuscript illustrations was the Wood work of Gujarat and the temple sculpture. Added to these was the influence of the Persian culture which the Muslim rulers of Gujarat imbibed.

Again scholars like Motichandra and U.P. Shah[18] opined that the synthesis of the Persian element with indigenous elements occurred perhaps hundred years before the Mughal School was established. This conclusion was made by them with the varied manuscripts from western India that they studied.

The *Mahapurana* of the Digambaras were now illustrated with grandeur. Delhi was the main centre. The *Mahapurana* of 1540 CE[19] painted at Palam is mention worthy. Here interestingly the further eye was eliminated. On the other hand the colour scheme and the representation of human figure followed the earlier tradition. *Mahapurana* of the Sagar Bhandara is interesting. It is very close to *Chaurâpanchâsikâ* and belonged to the same period. It was illustrated by two groups of painters. The first group is more related towards Western Indian style while the other group was close to the *Chaurâpanchâsikâ* style. The juxtaposition of these two groups gave the work a unique vitality. The Palam *Mahapurana* on the other hand is stylistically simple. It is believed to be the precursor of *Chaurâpanchâsikâ* style by some scholars. The *Chakdar jamâ* is absent in this manuscript like the *Aranyaka Parvan* of 1516 CE. The short squat figures in the manuscript are reminder of the Mandu *Kalpasutra*. Thus the development of the style in the manuscripts of the 15th and 16th century was definitely interrelated.

The last quarter of the 16th century saw the advent of the artists from Mughal atelier to Gujarat who failed to seek position there. The traditional painters worked in Gujarat and to divert them from their acquired skill and conservatism was not an easy task. The patrons were also conservative. Inspite of this attitude Mughal technique was steadily gaining grounds in Gujarat. The new technique also had to compromise with indigenous elements and thus the monochrome background and enamel like colours continued for a long time in Gujarat and Malwa. Later Mughal landscape was adopted. The compromise of these two elements gave birth to the Rajasthani School.[20] This term was also used for convenience as the earlier version came from Rajasthan. This form of painting style was found in Gujarat, Malwa, Uttar Pradesh, Bundelkhand and many other places.

Agra, Delhi and Jaunpur were the centers of the Popular Mughal style as evident from the manuscripts of *Meghaduta* and *Kumarasambhava* [near Jaunpur painted at Asanikotta and Nautanpur [near Agra] respectively.[21]

The colophons of the Jaina School which mark the names of the scribe indicate that they were mostly monks in the initial phase. The illustrators perhaps were also monks. In the 15th century there were the new group of professionals who functioned alone or with groups of assistants or in family as scribes and professionals. The 15th and 16th century miniatures at least gave enough evidence to prove such a claim. The Jaunpur *Kalpasutra* of 1465 CE, the Mahapurana of 1540 CE, the *Aranyaka Parvan* of 1516 CE and the Buddhist manuscript from Bihar of 1446 CE were all done by *Kayastha* scribes. Thus a group of professional artists were there who were trained enough to illustrate miniatures of different religion. They were definitely recruited in different areas and moved to different parts of the subcontinent in search of work. They were receptive enough and were influenced by contemporary Persian painting style and other indigenous styles. They were thus responsible enough to bring about changes in techniques and new style evolved with their initiative.

References

1. Catherine B. Asher and Cynthia Talbot, *India before Europe,* Cambridge University Press, 2006.
2. The section has referred the following books along with other essays to be mentioned in the section:
    i. Moti Chandra, *Studies in Early Indian Painting,* Tagore Lectures, Bombay, Asia Publishing House, 1970.
    ii. Saryu Doshi, *Masterpieces of Jaina Painting*, Marg Publication, 1988.
    iii. Moti Chandra, *Jain Miniature Paintings from Western India*, Ahmedabad, 1949.
    iv. Moti Chandra and Karl Khandalavala, *New Documents of Indian Painting*, a Reappraisal, Bombay, 1969.
    v. Moti Chandra and U P Shah, *New Documents of Jaina Paintings*, Sri Mahavir Jaina Vidyalaya Golden Jubilee Volume (edited by A. N Upadhye and others), Vol I, Bombay 1968.
    vi. Jeremiah P. Losty, The Art of the Book in India, The British Library, 1982.

3. Moti Chandra, *Studies in Early Indian Painting,* Tagore Lectures, Bombay, Asia Publishing House, 1970, pp. 340-373.
4. Losty, 1982, pp. 37-54.
5. Chandra and Shah, Bombay 1968, pp. 348-373.
6. i. *Ibid.*
   ii. Pramod Chandra, Notes On Mandu Kalpasutra of AD 1439, in *Marg*, Vol XII, No 3, Bombay 1959, pp. 51-54.
   iii. Moti Chandra, Karl Khandalavala, Pramod Chandra and PL Gupta, A New Document of Indian Painting, *Lalit Kala*, No 10, New Delhi 1961, pp. 45-54.
   iv. Moti Chandra and Karl Khandalavala, A Consideration of an illustrated MS from Mandapadurga (Mandu) dated 1439 AD, *Lalitkala,* No 6, New Delhi 1959, pp. 8-29.
7. W Norman Brown, *The Vasanta Vilasa,* Connecticut, 1962 and Moti Chandra, *Studies in Early Indian Painting,* Tagore Lectures, Bombay, Asia Publishing House, 1970, pp. 59-113.
8. Chandra and Shah, 1968, pp. 348-373.
9. Chandra, 1970, pp. 59-113 and Losty, 1982, pp. 37-54.
10. Saryu Doshi, 'The Master of the Devasano Pado Kalpasutra and Kalakacharya Katha' in *Masters of Indian Painting, 1100-1650,* edited by Milo C Beach, Eberhard Fischer, B N Goswamy, Project Director-Jorrit Britschgi, Artibur Asiae Publishers, 2011, pp. 53-66.
11. Chandra and Shah, 1968, pp. 348-373.
12. *Ibid.*
13. *Ibid.*
14. *Ibid.*
15. a. B N Goswamy, *A Jainesque Sultanate Shahnama and the Context of pre-Mughal Panting,* Museum Rielberg Zurich,1988, pp. 5-34.
    b. B N Goswamy in , 'The Master of the Jainesque Sultanate Shahnama', *Masters of Indian Painting, 1100-1650,* edited by Milo C Beach, Eberhard Fischer, B N Goswamy, Project Director-Jorrit Britschgi, Artibur Asiae Publishers, 2011 pp. 41-52.
16. Goswamy, 2011, pp. 41-52.
17. *Ibid.*
18. *Ibid.*
19. Chandra, 1970, pp. 59-113.
20. Losty, 1982, pp. 37-54.
21. Chandra, 1970, pp. 59-113.

21

Yogsangram:
The 17th Century Marathi Manuscript

– *Ravi Khangai*

Name of Sheikh Mahammad's father was Raje Mohammad and mother's name was Fuali. Raje Mohammad was also a person of spiritual inclination. He was a disciple of Sufi Mohammad Gaus. Mohammad Gaus was the first person of Kadri branch of Sufis, who came to India and established his center at Gwalior in early 16th century. Raje Mohammad had a disciple named Chand Bodhle, who later became the spiritual mentor of Sheikh Mahammad. The centuries of coexistence of Hindus and Muslims had led to the atmosphere of mutual tolerance and acceptance. It was common for many Hindus to have a Sufi spiritual mentor.

Tough Chand Bodhle was a Hindu, his spiritual linage was Sufi. As per tradition Chand Bodle gave a copy of *'Jnaneshwari'*[2] to Sheikh Mohammad. Influence of *Jnaneshwari* on *Yogsangram* is clearly traceable. Ekanataha (16-17th century) the famous saint of *Bhakti* movement of Maharashtra also traces his spiritual linage to Chand Bodhale. Eknataha's guru Janardhana was also a disciple of Chand Bodhle. Thus Eknatha and Sheikh Mahammad, both belong to same spiritual tradition.

Maloji Bhonsle, the ancestor of Shivaji became the disciple of Sheikh Mahammad. He constructed a *'Matha'* for Sheikh Mahammad at Srigonde, in Ahmadnagar district of Maharashtra. This took place around 1595 CE. After this Sheikh Mahammad continued to reside at this place for next fifty years and died in CE 1660. In 1645, he composed *Yogsangram*.

Subject matter of the manuscript

Through this long poem Sheikh Mahammad metaphorically explains the struggle of soul against the temptations of the material world. In this the soul is a warrior, who subdues the mind (which is represented as steed) and riding over it wages war against ego. This ego is having an army comprising of desire, anger and laziness etc. This struggle is termed as *Yogsangram.* In the 17th chapter the poet describes this struggle of soul against enemies like pride, desire, anger, conceit and jealousy.

Similar metaphor is also used by Jnaneshwara in *Jnaneshwari* (9th and 12th chapter). Eknatha also uses a similar kind of metaphor in the 9th chapter of his Marathi commentary on the 11th chapter of the *Bhagavata Mahapurana*.

Apart from the metaphor mentioned above, Sheikh Mahammad also narrates the deplorable socio-religious conditions of contemporary Maharashtra. He is very critical of the hypocrisy that exists in the society under the guise of religion. The detailed analysis of the different topics commented in the manuscript is given below.

Concept of God

Medieval Bhakti movement is classified in two broad category; *Saguna* and *Nirguna*[3]. Usually the *Nirgunapanthi* saints like Kabir treats *Saguna* form of worship with contempt. But in the compositions of many *Saguna* poets we find a belief that *Saguna* is a stage towards the realization of *Nirguna*. This kind of belief we find in the compositions of the Marathi Bhakti saints like Jnaneshwara and Eknatha. We find the similar kind of belief reflected in '*Yogsangram*'

The poet explains the unity between *Saguna* and *Nirguna* in the simple words. He says that as the wall paintings are supported by wall, similarly *Saguna* worship is supported by *Nirguna*. If one wipes out the wall paintings, what will remain is wall. So similarly if we try to rise above *Saguna, Nirguna* will emerge. (9;64, 65)[4]

Though Sheikh Mahammad believed that the real nature of supreme is *Nirguna*, he also says that *Saguna* worship is a beginning and a devotee who starts at *Saguna* will eventually reach *Nirguna*. These are only different stages towards self realization. Sheikh Mahammad also says that though the God is *Nirguna;* it is devotee who had given him form.

"*Amhi Bhaktani Kela Sasjira*" (7;89)
(We devotes have given attributes to God.)

We find the Marathi Bhakti saints like Eknatha saying that though the God is *Nirguna*, it is to enjoy the Bhakti that he had assumed the *Saguna* form, like he acquired hands so that he can embrace the devotee.

Influence of '*Adwita*'[5] is visible on '*Yogsangram*' at many places. The poet writes that if somebody can kill his ego, he himself will become like a God. (5;106). He also uses adjectives like '*Awyakta*' (which cannot be explained). '*Avinash*' (which do not get destroyed) to describe the God, but though tending towards '*Nirguna*', he is not totally free from the use of symbolism that is used by *Saguna* poets. He calls the God *Awyakta* Rama, i.e. Rama, who cannot be explained.

God is so mysterious that whatever attempts that are made by scriptures to describe the God have failed to do so. Sheikh Mohammad says,

"*Tethe Vedbhed Shastracha Vicharu Pau Na Shake*" (1;2)

(*Vedic* debate and thoughts in *Shastras* cannot reach up to there)

He further says that while trying to describe the God, the Vedas and *Shruti* have got tired. Vedas and *Shruti* says, '*Not this, Not this*' as they try to describe the God. Sacred literature of the Hindus at many places takes stand that the real nature of divinity is difficult to comprehend and explain. While addressing God, the poet calls him '*Alakshya*'; that cannot be achieved and '*Agayma';* that cannot be comprehended. (8;1)

Sheikh Mahammad is critical of devotees who worship different Gods due to false belief in polytheism. He says that there is no difference between Shiva and Vishnu. He mocks those Hindus who not only worship different Gods on different days but also worship Muslim *Pirs* with selfish motives of getting something in return. This belief in polytheism is criticized by Sheikh Mahammad. (Ch.12)

"*Eka Hari Allaha Jari Don Aste*
Tari Te Bhandbhnadoch Marate
Volkha Kahi Thav Uro Na Dete
Arun Aracha Pai" (11;95)

(If Hari and Allaha had been different, they would have died fighting with each others and would have left no trace of each others)

Sheikh Mahammad criticizes the apparent polytheism prevalent among the common masses. Some people do not tolerate other Gods than their own. In Ancient times there was a rivalry between the *Vaishnavites* and *Shaviaties*. In medieval Maharashtra also some traces of this conflict could be traced. Sheikh Mahammad says that People belonging to *Vaishnava* cult never utter the name of Shiva. (12; 31). But Shiva and Vishnu are not different.

> "*Shivache Hridayi Vishnu Vyapun*
> *Vishnu Dhaytase Shivalagun*
> *Aise Ase Dohoche Sandhan*
> *Te Chanchal Bhatktas Na kale*" (12;33)
>
> (Vishnu occupies the heart of Shiva
> Vishnu also always remember Shiva
> Thus both are connected
> But a restless devotee does not understand this)

Hinduism is like an umbrella under which different religious beliefs and practices co exist. Along with the prominent Gods of Brahminical religion, people still continues to worship many deities which were probably worshipped even before the Brahiminical religion spread over the major part of the country. During Sheikh Mahammad's time also worship of these Gods was prevalent at many places. Worship of these Gods involved relatively primitive practices like animal sacrifice. These types of practices are looked down upon by those who practiced relatively refined form of Hinduism.

The poet says,

> "*Satvichi Bhaktin Mangin Ase*
> *Tayechya Charnala Brahmin Viswase*
> *Adik Adik Navas Puse, Kakulti Yeyuni*" (13;19)
>
> (Goddess *Satvi* is worshipped by a *Mangin*. A Brahmin also keeps faith at her feet and repeatedly, eagerly asks what he should offer to the goddess to have his wish fulfilled.)

Satvi is a goddess which is feared among the people of Maharashtra. It is believed that if she is angry, she troubles small children. As narrated by the poet, a Brahmin, who is supposed to be an apostle of refined Brahminical religion, also worships her. The *Bhaktin*, the chief devotee of that goddess is a woman from *Mang* community called *Mangin*. Mang is an *Antyaj*[6] community in Maharashtra. So here we see a Brahmin through a *Mangin* seeking favor of goddess *Satvi*.

Obviously it reflects eagerness of ignorant, superstitious mind to get the work done from any God. But a Brahmin seeking favor through *Mangin*? Does it indicate that caste stratification was not as strict during those days as it became later. Maharashtra is far away from the Ganga-Yamuna Doab, the main cradle of orthodox Brahminical religion. Maharashtra is also a mountainous state. The percolation of the orthodox Brahminical ideas must have taken a lot of time. It appears that the society in Maharashtra did not become very rigid about caste stratification till 17th century. It was due to relatively less orthodox atmosphere that *Bhakti* movement of Maharashtra found it easier to accommodate the lower caste saints like Chokhamela, maid Janabai and also a Muslim like Mahammad.

About Caste

The poet says that one should not judge a person by the circumstances of his birth. He gives numerous examples to prove his point. Sage Parashara had an illicit relation with Satyavati but out of that Vyasa was born and Vidura was born from the womb of slave. (2;27,28).

He says,

"*Jyala Navajita Eshwar, Tayacha Shodhu Naye Kulachar*" (16;67)

(If a person had realized God, His linage is not to be looked into)

His definition of a Brahmin is different. He says,

'*Brahma Jane Tochi Sovala Brahman*'(17;185)

(Anyone who knows *Brahma* is a pure Brahmin)

Caste and linage is not important for *Bhakti,* says the poet. He gives numerous examples from Hindu scriptures and Mythology. He narrates the whole episode of Prahalada and says that though born to demon, he could achieve Hari due to devotion.

He criticizes those Brahmins, who though takes bath and do *Pranayama* as rituals of Brahminhood, but have illicit relationship with a *Shudra* woman (5;20)

Many Bhakti saints though liberal as compared to orthodox Brahminical religion, were not able to completely rise above the psychological conditioning that came from conservative society. The poet while highlighting the moral degradation of a Brahmin says that he is having an illicit relation with a *Shudra* woman. Illicit relation with other woman irrespective of caste would have been equally degrading, but an illicit relation between a Brahmin male and a *Shudra* female brings out a contrast. And the poet mentions that it as a degradation of a Brahmin. Is it not degradation for a *Shudra* woman as well? But the poet does not mention it. Gender and Caste bias is obvious in this statement.

Sheikh Mahammad must have faced non-acceptance and criticism from the orthodox Hindus. He narrates his experience,

> "*Ek Mahanati Ha Yaticha Mlenchha*
> *Mahnwuni Nikhandito Amachya Devtas*
> *Yacha Manu Na Amhi Viswas*
> *Pratima Nikhandilya*" (16;62)
>
> (Somebody said that he is a *Mlenchha*[7]
> That is the reason he is criticizing our Gods
> We will not trust him
> He is an idol breaker)

The poet complains to God,

> "O God, you made me *Mlenchha*.
> The pure Brahmins consider me impure
> And call me *Avindha*[8]" (8;83)

He also tries to explain it to the people that there is no difference between Hindus and Muslims.

> "*Saccha Pir Kahe Muslaman*
> *Marathe Mahanviti Sadguru Purna*
> *Pari Dohnit Nahi Bhinnatvapan*
> *Akhi Khol Dekho Bhai*" (17;3)
>
> (The Muslim calls Saccha pir
> The Marathas call Sadguru
> But open your eyes and see
> These two are not different)

Syncretic ideas

During Medieval period, Islam entered in Maharashtra and the rule of different Muslim kingdoms like Bijapur and Ahmadnagar have started over it. Initially, the government of Muslim Sultans remained by and large foreign in nature, as most of the nobles in the court were Turk, Persian, Arab and Irani. But slowly the local Marathas also got place of authority in the administration. The southern part of India was far away from the main recruiting ground for the Muslim nobles and soldiers i.e. Iran and Persia. As a result the Muslim kingdoms of south India had to take the help of the local Marathas. This changing political scenario also contributed to the growth of composite culture. '*Yavana*' is a term used in Sanskrit for foreigners. Earlier it was used for the Greeks. Later it was also used for the Muslims. The word is having a negative connotation. The poet, though Muslim uses the word *Yavana* for the Muslims. He says,

"*Yavanacha Acharya Mulla Kazi*
Sakal Adharmas Dhyavi Bazi
Gotras Karave Bhaktis Razi
To Acharya Khara" (5;99)

(Mulla Kazi is an *Acharya* of Yavana
We should discard all *Adharmas*
One who makes the relatives inclined towards *Bhakti* is a real Acharya)

Syncretic thinking is obvious in *Yogsangram* at different places. The poet mentions the name of Narayana and Allaha in the same verse.

"*Om Namoji Narayana*
Ya Allaha Mahanati Yavan" (1;52)

(I pray to Narayana and the Muslims calls *Ya Allaha*)

While describing qualities of a good *Kazi* i.e. Muslim judge, the poet says good *Kazi* is someone whose mind is not disturbed, who do not take bribe and who is engaged in praise of God. He uses the Hindu terminology

"*Ishwarbhajani Apule Man Govi*" (5;80)

(Who is engaged in devotion to *Ishwara*)

Ishwara is a term used for Hindu Gods. While describing the feeling of devotion of *Kazi* to God, Sheikh Mohammad uses the term '*Ishwarbhajan*', i.e. praise of *Ishwara*. This is reflective of his belief that there is no difference between the God of Hindus and the God of Muslim. It was very radical. The poet further writes that *Maulana* (A Muslim learned in Muslim theology) is someone who feels that other's problems are his own problems.

"*Aple Dukh Taise Parache Mane*" (5;81)

Caring for others and especially downtrodden is one of the qualities desirable in the Saint. While describing the qualities of a Fakir, Sheikh Mahammad says,

"*Fakir To Jo Rag Vishaya Sandawala*
Swas Ucchwase Nitya Athvi Alla
Dekhoni Pale Bashkal Galbala, Ekanta Sukh Bhogi
Fakirpanacha Dawina Tora.
........*Jo Swye Sawastacha Karil Nash*
Tochi Sanyasi Akhand Udas" (5; 85)

(The real Fakir is someone who had discarded anger and desire Who remember *Allaha* with every in and out breath Who runs away from unnecessary talks and crowds, who enjoys the happiness while alone Who do not show off his asceticism ....who kills six enemies himself, He is a real detached *Sanayasi*)

The poet uses the words like Fakir and *Sanayasi* as synonym. The qualities described above are also the qualities expected of Hindu ascetics.

Sheikh Mahammad gives a different definition of the word Mussalman. He says that he is a Mussalman, because he stayed for nine months in *Mus*; i.e. womb. According to him as everybody is born of *Mus*, everybody is Musslaman. (6; 13). However everybody is trying to hide this truth and calls themselves as *Viashyas, Kshtriyas* or *Brahmins*. He criticizes Vedas for spreading these false beliefs. (6; 16).

Many Sufis have adopted *Yogic* practices from the Hindus. Sheikh Mahammad is also familiar with the *Yogic* practices as is obvious from his writings. In the third chapter he describes different *Chakras* in the human body like a practitioner of the Yoga believes.

Bhakti and *Mukti*

In the *Bhakti* literature sometimes the *Bhakti* saints give higher place to *Bhakti* than *Mukti*. Similar thinking has found its reflection in *Yogsangram*. In a reported dialogue between God and the poet (Ch.7), the God asks Sheikh Mohammad to discard *Bhakti* and in return the God will give him *Mukti* in the *Vaikuntha*. But Sheikh Mahammad rejects it and says that he have no desire of *Viakuntha*. His only desire is that God should give him love.

However his concept of *Mukti*; liberation from the cycle of birth and death is different. He says that the *Mukti* that God is offering is like a prostitute. As a prostitute comes near a man when a man is having money and goes away when a man loses his fortune. Similarly the *Mukti* will give him temporary abode in *Vaikuntha*, but he will be hurled back to this cycle of birth and death after his *Punyas*; the accumulated virtues deeds are over.

So his concept of *Mukti* is a temporary abode in *Vaikuntha*; the abode of Vishnu. But the generally accepted concept of *Mukti* in Hindu philosophy is permanent liberation from the cycle of birth and death. This concept of *Mukti* is different than the concept of *Swarga*; the haven. In the concept of *Swarga* people reach heaven as a result of the virtuous deeds. They enjoy all the privileges there as a reward of accumulated *Punyas*. But as they enjoy in the heaven, their accumulated virtues gets dissipated. As soon as their accumulated *Punyas* gets exhausted they fall back on the earth. So according to this *Swarga* is a distraction, which will distract a person from *Mukti*, the final aim.

Sheikh Mahammad's concept of *Mukti* seems to be similar to *Swarga*, but the difference is that in *Swarga* people are believed to have all kind of enjoyments and in *Vaikuntha* one enjoys the eternal bliss in the presence of God. Sheikh Mahammad's concept of *Mukti* is similar to Ramanuja's. In this also an individual soul reaches near God and enjoys eternal bliss. But according to Ramanuja *Mukti* achieved by an soul is permanent. The soul does not come back. That is not a case with Sheikh Mahammad, here the soul comes back after he had exhausted his good *Karma*.

It is not certain if Sheikh Mahammad had studied the work of Ramanuja or Shankaracharya. But like many *Bhakti* saints of medieval period, Sheikh Mahammad seems to have recorded his experience spontaneously. Generally we do not find *Bhakti* saint subscribing to one particular school of thought about the concept of God like *Advita, Vishisthaadvita* or *Dvita*. They record their spiritual experience as they experience it. It was a creative poetical outburst of the mystical experience. Same is the case with Sheikh Mahammad.

Different type of *Bhakti*

Bhakti movement had provided space for those who were neglected and stigmatized by the society. In the Bhakti movement of Maharashtra, Kanhopatra, daughter of a prostitute was also given space. Her devotional compositions are sung even today. Sheikh Mahammad also narrates a story of a prostitute (11;35 to 53). In the story, a prostitute named Pingla achieves liberation by following her profession sincerely without attachment.

The prostitute was well known for her equal treatment of all her patrons. After hearing this God Sankara came to her disguised as a wood cutting laborer. The laborer was wearing old, torn cloths. The laborer says to the prostitute that he had desired her for a long and earned some money with great efforts. The prostitute agrees to be his for a night in exchange of that money. The God in the disguise of a woodcutter goes out and comes in as a king. The king now demands that the prostitute now spend a night with him. But as the prostitute refuses and requests the king to come on some other day as she had promised her service to the laborer for that night. At this the king gets angry and says that he can give her much more wealth than the laborer. But the prostitute remains firm on her commitment.

The king goes back and the laborer comes in again. The prostitute gives him bath and food and the laborer lies on a couch. God Sankara then leaves the mortal body of the laborer and returns to his abode Kailasa to tell his consort Parvati about the prostitute. The prostitute sees the lifeless body of the laborer and starts crying that her husband is dead. As she had accepted the laborer as her husband for a night, she prepares to immolate herself as *Sati* along with him. Everybody including the king of the place tries to dissuade her but she burns herself with the laborer and goes to *Vaikuntha*.

Though there is obviously a dramatization, the story gives many messages. The patriarchal influence on the story is obvious. It demands unflinching loyalty even from a prostitute and expects that she should burn herself with her husband. A husband who was a husband for a night only! But the story is also indicative of a struggle of the poet in particular and humanity in general to find purity among the apparently impure. The message is clear 'a prostitute who does not discriminate, who does her duty without attachment can have a place in *Vaikuntha*'. The prostitute is a very loud example of *Karmayogi*. The spiritual accomplishment is not a monopoly of few, it can be found at any place. Evan unusual place like a house of a prostitute.

Sheikh Mahammad also mentions *'Virodhi'* Bhakti of Ravana and Kansa. (3;83). This is rather a strange kind of *Bhakti* mentioned in the *Bhakti* literature. According to this Ravana and Kansa achieved God, because they constantly hated the God. It is out of this hatred they constantly thought about the God and this had finally led to their liberation.

Mystic experience

According to a belief in Indian spiritual tradition, our true nature is soul and the physical body is just a temporary cover. According to this our parents and relatives are nothing but the parents and relatives of this body only. Sheikh Mahammad says,

"Mother and father take care of me. I found them like a people who had stayed with me for few days only" (3;40)

The mystic experience of that we are someone beyond this material existence is reflected in the poem. Sheikh Mahammad's Guru tells him that he, i.e. his Guru is his real father and mother and Sheikh Mahammad came to him as a river finally goes to sea and this is a result of his accumulated good deeds i.e. *Punyas.*(22;53)

While describing the qualities of a spiritually accomplished person, Sheikh Mahammad says,

> "*Pacha Tattvacha Na Kari Adhar*
> *Nirashene Pahe He Mayakar*
> *Avikalpa Dharuniya*" (5;97)

(A spiritually accomplished person does not remain dependent on the five elements, He remains detached with this illusory world and he do not have '*Vikalp*' i.e. doubt in his mind)

Like Kabir, Sheikh Mahammad is also not in favor of unnecessary mortification of human body. Self realization is the main motive of spirituality. He says that if one has realized his true self, he will not be bound by anything. The asceticism of different kinds are only means towards that end. This state self realization is understood by a person who had realized it, it cannot be explained. As a dumb person cannot explain the taste of sugar. (13;79)

Sheikh Mahammad describe that stage of the highest bliss as,

"*Mag Apla Anand Apan Pahi,*
Bodhtwe Niji Nivant Rahi" (3;4)

(He experience his own happiness, with self realization he remains stable within)

The experience of divine bliss cannot be explained in the words. Says the poet,

"The experience of self-realization
Everybody knows it himself, it cannot be explained" (13;81)

About pleasure and happiness

Scriptures generally takes stand that indulgence in sensual pleasure is harmful for the growth of soul. The poet gives different examples to explain that how attraction to sensual pleasure lead human beings towards destruction. Like moth is attracted by a burning lamp and is killed (4;36)

The poet advises that one should control his/her sensual desire and concentrate on God. If one indulges in sensual pleasure throughout the life and lastly at the time of death remembers God, then it is not going to help. It is like setting your house on fire and then start digging a well in a hurry. (9;93)

The poet makes use of different simile to make his philosophy simple. He gives example of a cultivated field. If a field does not have a caretaker, the birds will eat the grains and fly away. The peasant will cry by seeing this. Similarly, the birds of sensual pleasure will fly away during the young age and after that an individual will be caught in the trap of Yama; death of God and will be tortured in a different way. A fish is attracted by a bait, but he is caught and pulled out of water and then he is in pain (4;32 to 34)

Sheikh Mahammad says that sensual pleasure is like a sugar kept on a blade of sword. If someone goes to lick it, his tongue will be cut. Similar is the result of sensual pleasure on this body. (4;40)

While explaining that addiction to sensual pleasure is dangerous, the poet gives different examples,

> "*Hivache Hudhudine Kapu Lagla*
> *Phanguran Jalun Jari Tapo Lagla*
> *Pudhe Bahut Divas Hive Mela*
> *Taisi Vishyachi Godi*" (9;88)
>
> (A person was shivering due to cold
> He burnt his blanket and got some heat
> But after that he died due to cold.
> This is a nature of sensual pleasure.)

According to the poet Obsession of people with sensual pleasure is an important reason for their ruins. He says that the people constantly think about sensual pleasure, if they think with the same intensity about the God, they will immediately achieve liberation. (11; 103)

The poet also explains the futility and shifting nature of human attachments. He says a man gets attached to his wife and indulges in sensual pleasure. But if the same woman becomes seriously ill, same man will not look at her and wishes her dead. (11; 105)

Scriptures preach that real happiness does not depend on external factors, but it comes from within as a result of spiritual enlightenment. We find reflection of similar kind of thinking in the compositions of many Bhakti saints. Sheikh Mahammad also says that a spiritually accomplished person will not try to show off his spirituality,

> "*Te Janas Disti Vede Bawale*
> *Antari Bhogti Bramsukhache Sohale*" (2; 97)
>
> (The spiritually accomplished person may appear as foolish to the world, But he enjoys '*Brahmsukha*'; the supreme happiness within.)

Mind and Ego

Sheikh Mohammad says that mind is like a leader of all other organs of the body. He calls it *Mananayaka,* mind the leader.(4;47)

A person should treat his mind like a horse, ride over it and kill the desires. A person who can do that will surely reach a stage of self-realization. (4; 31)

Yogsangram says that mind is everything. By controlling mind one gets God and if mind is spoiled, it will make one to suffer in hail. The poet says,

> "*Are Are Mana Chatura*
> *Ekas Ghavila Chauranciicha Fera*
> *Ekas Nele Muktichiya Dwara*" (18;5)
>
> (O mind you are very clever
> You make someone to born and die repeatedly
> And take somebody on the threshold of liberation)

Greatness of mind is depicted in scriptures. Sheikh Mahammad says that mind had made someone a sage and someone a businessman. Controlling of mind is essential for spiritual accomplishment. The poet says,

> "*Skeikh Mahmamad Bolile Khun*
> *Adhi Man Karave jatan*
> *Labhel Parbrhma Nidan*" (18;19)
>
> (Sheikh Mahmmad gives an hint
> The mind should be controlled first
> After that one can get the God)

People who have little knowledge are prone to become proud says Sheikh Mohammad,

> "*Taisa Ha Garva Mipana Lavakari*
> *Dhaytiyala Badhi*" (14;4)
>
> (This pride and ego affects the knowledgeable person quickly)

The person who had acquired complete *Jnana* does not show off.

> "*Paha Samudra Purntve Bharla*
> *Pari to na Uallanghi Maryadela*

Taisa Jnana Pahije Vartala
Rankamadhe Rankpane" (14; 9)

(As sea is complete in itself
It does not cross its boundary
Similarly a *Dhayata*, learned person should behave
He should behave like a poor among the poor)

Dhayata is translated as learned. But in Indian tradition the word *Dhayata* or *Jnani* is applied to someone who is spiritually accomplished. It does not indicate theoretical knowledge, but a state of self-realization.

The poet emphasizes on humility.

"*Mi Ek Janata, Jan Murkh Vede*
He Jethe Umto Lage Vadekode
Tethuni Shigra Atmagyan Dhadpude
Paluniya Jaye" (14; 8)

(If a spiritually accomplished person thinks that he is wise and others are fools, the spiritual realization will go away immediately from him.)

In the 17th chapter, Sheikh Mohammad explains the struggle of a soul against ego. Ego stands as a barrier between individual soul and the God.

He metaphorically explains the struggle. In this metaphor, he treats mind like a horse, which a soul should subdue and ride. The desires are like reins, which the soul holds under control. The detachments are like arrows and with those arrows the ego is subdued. The soul cuts *Vikalp*, i.e. doubt. The other supporters of the ego is also killed by the soul

"*Kam Krodha mad Matsar*
He Shrestha Ahankarache Vajir
Dhamb Prapanch Moh Sardar
He Padav kele" (17; 129)

(Desire, Anger, conceit and jealousy are the minister of ego.
Pride, possession and illusion are his knights
All these are killed by the soul)

About Hypocrisy and Superstitious

During the medieval Maharashtra, there was a system of '*Murali*' which was similar to the system of *Devadasi*. A girl was declared as a consort of God and was called '*Murali*'. She will not marry anybody else. People indulged in illicit relation with *Murali* and this obviously contributed to the moral degradation of society. The poet wonders how people could have relation with a woman, who is declared as belonging to God and it is surprising that God also do not do anything to them. (14; 55)

The poet criticizes hypocrisy in the society. He says that when people get lot of wealth, to show off, they create idols of gold and silver. But if the famine comes, they break the same idols for want of money. The goldsmith beat these Gods with hammers, now why the God do not do anything to these people. (14; 75)

When the idols are created out of stone, the artists keep their feet on the idols. How these Gods become eligible for worship. It is all delusion. (14; 76)

Sheikh Mahammad reflects upon the hypocrisy among the people. Some people do little act of charity and then go around boasting about it. He writes,

> "*Eke Dahas Didhle Vastra Anna*
> *To Jagi Manhe Mya Posile Santjan*
> *Puslyawin Mirvi Bhushan*
> *Abhiman Dharuniya*" (7; 36)
>
> (Somebody had given cloth and food to ten people
> He proclaims to the world that he had supported the saints
> Without asking he praises himself and feels pride)

He further says that the God supports everyone, but do not boast about it to anybody. He cools the living being by rain.

Sheikh Mahammad is critical of superstitious in the society. Some people make sacrifice of a cock or goat when son is born. Same son, when grows up indulge in a sin and thus add to the sins of the family. Inflicting self torture to please God is a practice in vogue at many places. The poet makes reference to the practice of people putting sharp iron hook in their flesh and hanging from it in front of God. (12;76). He is critical of these kinds of practices. At many places the superstitious Hindus believe that the spirit of the dead people possess the human beings. Sheikh Mohammad says,

> "*Mele Jitache Dehi Sancharle*
> *Tar Jitache Jiv Konikade Gele*"
>
> (If a dead person's soul enters in the body of a living being
> Where the soul of living person goes)

The poet further says that if somebody can get liberation by staying in water, why not the aquatic creatures become pure. He also does not agree that one can get God by adopting a celibate life or discarding cloth and going to forest. He also criticizes mechanical engagements in rituals and going to pilgrimage. He says that what people search from place to place is in fact near us.

Earlier the spiritual knowledge was passed from Guru to disciple. Sheikh Mohammad is cautious about accepting someone as a disciple. He says that anybody can not be accepted as disciple. (4;51 to 93). A person who is addicted to sensual pleasure, who do not have liking for taking the name of Hari, who sacrifices animals in front of Gods, who is very proud, who betrays your trust, who is *Vivadi* (argumentative), who insults others, who talks about spiritual knowledge but keeps looking at other's wives, who drinks liquor, who abuses should not be accepted as disciple.

Bakti saints have tried to purge society of social evils like gambling and drinking and also tried to build character of the people as we find reflected in the *Yogsangrama*.

Sheikh Mahammd also narrates the desirable qualities in the disciple. He says the people who have faith and are steady in devotion to god, a person who is generous to all, who had discarded the pride, vanity and anger should be trusted as a disciple. (4;98)

In spiritual training, Guru is having a significant place. People who have dedicated their body, speech and mind to Guru, these people are suitable to be accepted as disciple. (4;98, 99)

Hinduism and Islam, two important religion of India had coexisted for centuries. As Islam is not only a religious doctrine, but is a well defined way of life. This had made it impossible for Hinduism to absorb

Islam as it had done with many other religious cults during ancient times. In fact Hinduism is an amalgamation of the different religious doctrines and practices that had emerged at different places in the Indian sub continent.

In spite of the distinct differences in Islam and Hinduism, there were few people like Sheikh Mahammad, Kabir, Rahim and Dara Shikoha in the medieval period who tried to build the bridges. Unfortunately, their influences have remained to limited people as is obvious from the tragic experience of the partition. But much water had flown down since 1947 and probably, there could be many like Sheikh Mahammad, waiting for discovery. Their syncretic ideas will contribute towards generating inter-faith dialogue which is sadly lacking in India.

Explanatory Notes

1. *Ovi* is a two line rhythmic verse. This poetic style is very popular in the Bhakti literature of Maharashtra. Most of the prominent Maharashtrian Bhakti saints have used this style for their devotional compositions. It is similar to what Hindi Bhkati poets like Kabir and Rahim had used in their *Dohas*.
2. *Jnaneshwari* is a Marathi commentary on *Bhagavad Gita* by Jnaneshwara(13th century). This is one of the most important scripture of *Bhakti* movement of Maharashtra. It has influenced the writings of later Marathi *Bhakti* Saints like Eknatha (16th-17th century).
3. *Saguna* and *Nirguna*- These are the two broad categories in which the Bhakti saints of medieval periods are categorized. *Saguna* worshipers believed that the God is having *Gunas*, i.e. attributes and *Nirguna* worshippers believed that the God is without attribute. Tulsidas, whose devotion was directed to Rama was a *Saguna* Bhakt and Kabir who conceptualized God as someone incomprehensible, indescribable was a *Nirguna* Bhakt. But this distinction is difficult to apply to the Bhakti saints of Maharashtra. In the writings of the Maharshtrian *Bhakti* saints there seems to be a realization that through *Saguna* one can reach *Nirguna*.
4. Chapter no; *Ovi* No/ Nos.
5. *Adwita* - A belief that there is only one soul. Sankaracharya, (7th -8th century) is considered as an important apostle of this belief system.
6. *Antyaj* - these communities were considered as beyond four Varnas and were rated lower than Shudras in the social ladder.
7. *Mlenchha* - The word is used as a derogatory term for the outsiders.
8. *Avindha* - Another derogatory term used for Muslims in Marathi.

References

1. Bahirat and Bhalerao, '*Warkari Sampradaya: Udaya ani Vikas*', Vinus Prkashan, Pune, 1998 (Marathi).
2. Deshmukh Bhagavant, '*Eknath Vangmaya Darshan*', Sahitya Academy, New Delhi, 2003 (Marathi).
3. Deshpande A.N. '*Prachin Marathi Vangmayacha Itihas*' (History of ancient Marathi literature), Part-II, Part-V, Vinus Prkashan, Pune (Marathi).
4. Gosawi R.R., '*Samarth ani Samarth Sampradya*', Vinus Publication, Pune, 1981 (Marathi).
5. Pangarkar L.R. '*Jay Jay Raguvir Samarath*' Keshav Dhavle, Mumbai, 2003 (Marathi).
6. Parlikar Sacchidanand, '*Loknayak Samarth Ramdas*', Lokbharati, Allahabad, 2002 (Hindi).
7. Pendse S.D. '*Gyandev ani Namdev*', Continental Publishers, Pune, 1998 (Marathi).
8. Pendse S.D. '*Rajguru Samarth Ramdas*', Continental Publishers, Pune, 2003 (Marathi).
9. Sakhre Nanamaharaj, '*Sarth sri Gyaneshwari*', Sarathi Prakashan, Pune, 2001.
10. Sheikh Mahammad, '*Yogsangram*' (edited by R.C. Dhere), Varda Books, Pune, 1981.
11. Yardi M.R., 'The Jnaneshwari', Bharatiya Vidya Bhavan, Pune.
12. Sharma Krishna, 'Bhakti and the Bhakti Movement; A New Perspective', Munshiram Manoharlal, New Delhi, 1987.

22

Passages on Music in Śivadharma Corpus

– *Anil Kumar Acharya*

Śivadharma corpus consists of nine texts, viz. Śivadharmaśāstra, Śivadharmottara, Śivadharmasaṅgraha, Śivopaniṣad, Umāmaheśvara-saṃvāda, Uttarottaramahāsaṃvāda, Vṛṣasārasaṅgraha, Dharmaputrikā and Lalitavistara. These are composed before 12th century CE and composition of most of these texts is believed to be started in the era of the supremacy of Śaivism, i.e. after sixth century CE, over its rival Buddhism. These texts preach Śaiva religion for lay Śaivites, thus in general these texts have been considered as texts of Paurāṇic or Āgamic corpus; though except the first text others have not been mentioned in the list of *Upapurāṇas*[3], and only the first two are mentioned in the list of *Upāgamas*.

Of these above mentioned texts, the *Umāmaheśvarasaṃvāda* (UMS), in its twenty-first chapter, and the *Uttarottaramahāsaṃvāda* (UttMS) which is otherwise titled as *Uttarottaram, Uttarottaratantram* and *Uttarottara-umāmaheśvarasaṃvāda*, in its seventh chapter, mentions various facts pertaining to the notes of the gamut (*svaras*) of Indian music. The styling of these two texts suggests that both are connected with each other, not only due to the similarity of main interlocutors, i.e. Umā and Maheśvara, but also because of the alikeness in their subject matter, i.e. preaching ethics for lay devotees. The text *Umāmaheśvarasaṃvāda* seems to be very much influenced by the great epic *Mahābhārata*. For, the great epic has been eulogized throughout the eighteenth chapter of this text and the epic has been mentioned as the fifth Veda (*paṃcamaveda*)[5]; therefore in colophon it has been titled: *Bhāratakīrtana* [6]. Besides, this text bears resemblance, not only in styling but also in subject matter, with the *Umāmaheśvarasaṃvāda* section of the *Anuśāsanaparva* of the great epic[7], though no parallel verses could be found therein. And the second text, irrespective of different titles, could be considered as the later part of the first text, as it has been prefixed with the term *Uttarottara*, which means subsidiary. The same styling could be seen in the first two texts of the *Śivadharma* corpus, i.e. *Śivadharma/Śivadharmaśāstra,* and *Śivadharmottara*, and this very idea could be seen endorsed by the statement of *Śaivakalpadruma*[8], authored by a seventeenth century Śaivite author of Odisha named Laxmidhara Mishra. Both texts have twenty-two and ten chapters respectively, and preach various mundane duties, good conducts, bad effects of the age of *Kali* etc.

The twenty-first chapter of the *Umāmaheśvarasaṃvāda* begins with the query regarding the nature and creation of *varṇas*, *Ṣabdas* etc. by Devī (i.e. Umā). She poses this interesting question after having approached to the blue-necked (*Ṣitikaṇṭha*) great God (*mahāprabhu*) who is worshiped by Brahmins (*vipras*) and sages (*brahmacāris*) and is seated comfortably on the seat covered with Vaidurya gems (*maṇis*) and decorated with many jewels. As an answer to the above mentioned main query and other subsidiary queries of Devī in due succession, the great god did mention various facts of *svaras* of Indian music which have been recorded in this chapter. The subject matters of this chapter could be divided into three main sections, viz. narration of seven *svaras*, merits of singing those, and demerits of committed faults during singing.

The first section mainly counts the names of seven *svaras*, viz. Ṣaḍja, Ṛṣabha, Gāndhāra, Madhyama, Paṃcama, Dhaivata and Niṣāda, and their corresponding colours, viz. complexion of lotus (*padmavarṇābha*), white (*Ṣuklavarṇaka*), golden (*hiraṇyābha*), complexion of *kuṅkuma* (*kuṅkumaprabha*), red (*rakta*), mixed coloured (*nānāvarṇa*) and colour of the cloud (*meghavarṇa*), respectively; corresponding animal sounds, viz. sound of peacock, sound of cock (*kukkuṭa*), sound of horse, sound of cow, sound of cuckoo, sound of frog and sound of elephant, respectively; their presiding deities, viz. Agni, Brāhmaṇa, Soma, Viṣṇu, Tryambaka, Varuṇa and Nārada, respectively; their places in human body, viz. throat (*kaṇṭha*), head (*Ṣiras*), nose (*nāsikā*), chest (*uras*), thai (*ūru*), forehead (*lalāṭa*) and in whole body (*sarvagātreṣu*), respectively; classes of beings please therewith, viz. gods (*deva*), great sages (*maharṣi*), ancestors (*pitṛ*), great serpents (*mahoraga*), all creatures (*sarvabhuta*), demi-gods (*yakṣa* & *gandharva*) and demons (*rākṣasa*), respectively; corresponding letters, viz. '*a*' & 'ā', 'ṛ'& 'ḷ', '*i*' & '*ī*', '*lṛ*' & '*lḹ*', '*e*' & '*ai*', '*u*'&'*ū*', and '*o*'&'*au*', respectively; corresponding corners, viz. north-west (*vāyavya*), north (*saumya*), north-east (*aiśāna*), east (*aindra*), south-east (*āgneya*), south (*yāmya*), south-west (*nairṛta*), respectively.

In addition to those, it mentions the numbers of *mūrchanā* and *tāna*, viz. twenty-one (*ekaviṃśati*) and forty-nine (*ekonapaṃcāśat*), respectively. And a small section therewith records names of different gods and goddess who will be pleased by sweet singing of *svaras* in the seventh part (*saptame bhāge*) of a day on various *tithis* of the both quarters (*pakṣas*) of a month, viz. Agni on the first day of the lunar fortnight (*pratipadā*); Narasiṃha on the second day (*dvitīyā*); Devarāja (Indra) on third day (*tṛtīyā*); Vināyaka on fourth day (*caturthī*); Sriyā (lakshmi) on fifth day (*paṃcamī*); Mahāgaurī on sixth day (*ṣasṭhī*); Āditya on seventh day (*saptamī*); Īśvara on eighth day (*aṣṭamī*); Durgāon ninth day (*navamī*); Pitāmaha (Brahmā) on tenth day (*daśamī*); Vasava on eleventh day (*ekādaśī*); Viṣṇu on twelfth day (*dvādaśī*); Brāhmaṇa on thirteenth day (*trayodaśī*); Śiva on fourteenth day (*caturdaśī*); and Soma on full-moon day (*pūrṇimā*).

The second section records different merits of uttering seven *svaras* in different months of a year and in various occasions. Those merits are: having been purified, wearing white dress and observing fast, if one sings on the eighth day of the light and dark half of the month of Āṣāḍha, he will obtain haven (*svarga*) and enjoy great pleasure; in the same way, singing in the month of Śrāvaṇa will earn the merit of [donating] thousand cows; in the month of Bhādrapada Śaṅkara will be pleased and will earn the merit of Rājasūya sacrifice; in the month of Āśvayuja (Āśvina) will earn the merit of a Naramedha sacrifice; in the month of Kārtika will earn the merit of dying at confluence of rivers (*prayāga*); in the month of Mārgaśīrṣa will earn the merit of thousand Aśvamedha sacrifices; in the month of Pauṣa will earn the merit of (donating) thousand cows and will be respectable being blessed with charming figure and good fortune; in the month of Māgha the singer will enjoy all mundane pleasures in this life and after death will obtain haven (*parāṃgati*) and again will back to the earth and take birth in a family of a rich after his acquired merits comes to an end; in the month of Phālguna will attain Rudraloka crossing Brahmaloka and at the end of acquired virtues he will reborn in a great family (*vipule kule*) on earth; in the month of Caitra the singer will became a master, brave and wealthy, un-doubtfully Lord Śaṅkara and Vāsudeva will be pleased, the singer will be adorned everywhere, will have good figure and enough wealth, no child will die in his family and there will be no misery, and moves in chariot carried by swan; in the month of Vaiśākha the singer undoubtedly and truthfully pleases the great god (*mahādeva*), moves to haven in Puṣpaka chariot, and stays there till sixty years and then will reborn as an elder son, and becomes a rich owner of cows, wealthy, parent of son and handsome; in the month of Jyeṣṭha the singer acquires merits of all kinds of sacrifices, charities and pilgrimages.

The last part of this section records various merits of singing pertaining to different occasions, viz. he who sings during the worship of God he will be freed form misery; singing on the occasion of obsequial oblation (*Ṣrāddha*) the singer will pleases ancestors and [oblation will be eternal]; singing inside the site of a house (*vāstu*) will destroy diseases related to children (*bālaroga*); singing inside paddy field will enrich yielding; singing amongst cowherd will enrich possession of cows; singing inside a royal palace (*rājavāsa*) will surely makes one victorious; singing amongst crowd will destroy discordance; he who hears *svara*s at the time of death he will not reborn in a bad source of birth (*viyoni*); sings during forenoon (*pūrvāhna*) destroys bad dreams.

The third section mainly narrates the episode of the rescue of the king of elephants (*ganjendramokṣa*) by lord Vishnu in the context of describing the demerits of the incomplete singing of seven *svaras*. Before commencement of the narration of this episode, there are few verses which prescribes time limit in a period of forty-eight minutes (*muhūrta*s) for singing of the seven *svara*s, and thus suggests that each *svara* in their due order should be sang for four *muhūrta*s.

Narrating the episode of *gajendramokṣa* it has been mentioned that seven *svara*s are presided by seven demi-gods (*gandharva*s), viz. Nārada, Tumbura, Hāhā, Huhu etc. One of them [i.e. Hāhā], who has prevailed in the universe due to his expertise in singing and playing musical instruments, once was cursed by the sage Devala and as a result of that Hāhā becomes a crocodile and resides in the beautiful lake situated in Trikuta mountain. In the mean while a herd of elephant reaches there and the king of elephant herd was caught by the invisible cruel crocodile while playing happily inside the assemblage of lotus being surrounded by other elephants, and the elephant king while crying loudly in pain was drawn deep inside the water. Being pained, the king of elephant moved towards the western direction and called Lord Vishnu to save him, holding a golden lotus like lotus up in the air as an offering. And hearing the call and prayer of the elephant Lord Vishṇu came to the rescue and separated the crocodile's head by his disc and save his devotee, the king of elephants, and the demi-god Hāhā. To our interest, the colophon of the above mentioned chapter reads: "*iti bhagavato gītapurāṇe dharmaguhye gajendramokṣaṇam umāmaheśvarasaṃvāde ekaviṃśatitamodhyāyaḥ*".

It is worthy to mention herewith that the above mentioned version of the episode of *gajendramokṣa* is in some point different from the popular version which is found in the eighth chapter (*skanda*) of the *Bhāgavatapurāṇa*. According to the *Bhāgavatapurāṇa* the crocodile in its previous life was a demi-god named Huhu; but the version of the *Umāmaheśvarasaṃvāda* names it as Hāhā, and the story is quite different from the version of *Bhāgavatapurāṇa*. In popular belief the sage Devala did curse the demi-god because of his mischief by pulling the leg of the sage while he was offering prayer to the Sun god after taking bath in the river; but from the context of the *Umāmaheśvarasaṃvāda*, though verses depicting the exact cause of Devala's curs is unclear (vide ṣ Appendix, underlined verses 64-66), it could be assumed that the demi-god was cursed due to incomplete singing of *svara*s. For, this episode has been presented on the background of narrating the demerits of incomplete singing of the *svara*s.

Though not in a complete chapter like in the *Umāmaheśvarasaṃvāda*, but a section of the seventh chapter of the *Uttarottaramahāsaṃvāda* narrates the seven *svara*s in the context of musical rendering of Vedic mantras (*vedapāṭha*). Therein in reply to the question of Umā regarding *svara*s pertaining to the singing of Vedic mantras along with few auxiliary questions related to Veda, Īśvara, i.e. Lord Śiva, did mention along with answers to all other questions that the seven *svara*s have been created by him for singing Vedic mantras and they are divided in to three major groups, viz. acute accents (*udātta*s), grave accents (*anudātta*s) and mixed accents (*svarita*s). Niṣadha and Gāndhāra are acute accents, Ṛiṣabha and Dhaivata are grave accents and rest are mixed accents. And in few succeeding verses, replying Umā's questions on nature, colours, etc. of the seven *svara*s, Īśvara narrates sounds, which are considered to be the origin of the seven *svaras*, of different animals, and colours of different *svaras* as has been narrated earlier in the passages of the *Umāmaheśvarasaṃvāda*; however, there are some disagreements between two texts on this topic (vide ṣthe table at the end). These *svaras* are being divided into three groups (*grāmas*) and those are presided by Brahmā, Viṣṇnu and Maheśvara, and there are Śādava etc. (*Ṣādavapramukhā*) which differentiates *svaras* from each other. Narrating the origin of seven svaras it has been mentioned that, five which are originated from Pitṛvahni are called Paṃcama; Ṛṣabha and Dhaivata are originated in the family of Ṛṣabhāga; Ṣaḍja, Gāndhāra and Madhyama are originated from family of Devajāti; and Niṣāda is originated from demons (*asuras*). Next few passages narrate different *svaras* which are to be sung in different segments of a day, viz. Śādava in noon, Madhyama in afternoon, Mālava-Kauśika in the evening, Niṣāda in the first part of the night, Dhaivata in the second part, different Paṃcamas in the third part, different Ṣaḍjas in the fourth part, Gāndhāra before sunrise, Rarka?-Kauśika in the first part of the day and Saurāṣṭra and Paṃcamas after breakfast (*bhuktentare*). Mūrchanās, which have been presented in three groups in accordance to their relation with three different groups, viz. *devatā, pitṛ* and *ṛṣi*, have been delineated in next few verses. Mūrchanās, viz. Nandī, Viśālā, Sumukhī, Citrā and Citravatī belongs to gods; Apyāyanī, Viśvadhṛtā, Candrahema, Kapardinī, Caitrī and Āvāhanī belong to Pitṛs; Uttarā, Mandā, Dvitīyā, Atiraṅgikā, Aśvakrāntā, Śuddha-ṣaḍja, Nārāyaṇī and Rajanī belongs to Ṛṣis.

References

1. According to R. C. Hazra – "…. it appears that the *Śivadharma* was written later than the *Yājṃavalkyasmṛiti*. So, this work is to be dated between 200 and 500 A.D.; and this early origin of the work explains why it is totally free from Tantric influence" & "Thus, the date of composition of the *Śivadharmottara* (in its present form) falls between 700 and 800 A.D." - *The Śivadharma & The Śivadharmottara*, (R. C. Hazra, 1952-53).

   And the eighth text of this corpus is believed to be "composed in 1069 AD. In the reign of Śankara Deva Nepal. . . . . Q. by Śivānanda Saraswatīin *Yogacintāmaṇi*, ..." (NCC, Vol. IX, p.253).

   Also some of the available manuscritps, viz. MSS. G4007 (1036 A.D.) & G3852 of Asiatic Society, Culcutta, MS. Add 1645 (1136 A.D.) of Cambridge University Library, MS. प-1075 (1170 A.D.) of National Archives,

Svaras	Texts	Colours	Sounds	Deities	Places	Beings	Letters	Corners
	UMS	Lotus	Peacock	Agni	throat	gods	a & ā	vāyavya
Ṣaḍja	UttMS	Red (like Pomegranate flowers)	-do-	--	--	--	--	--
Ṛṣabha	UMS	White	Cock	Brāhmaṇa	head	Great sages	ṛ&]	saumya
	UttMS	Yellow (like Kiṅkarāta)	Vipyakāka/ Vipyāhaka					
	UMS	Golden	horse	Soma	nose	ancestors	i & ī	aiśāna
Gāndhāra	UttMS	Pale (pāṇḍura)	goat					
Madhyama	UMS	Kunkuma	Cow (gavedaka)	Viṣṇu	chest	Great serpents	lṛ& l]	aindra
	UttMS	White	Curlew (krauṃca)					
Paṃcama	UMS	Red	cuckoo	Tyambaka	thai	All creatures	e & ai	āgneya
	UttMS	Green (like atasi flower)	-do-	--	--	--	--	--
Dhaivata	UMS	Mixed	frog	Varuṇa	forehead	Demi-gods	u & ū	yāmya
	UttMS	Not mentioned	-do-					
Niṣāda	UMS	Black(megha)	elephant	Nārada	Whole body	demons	o & au	nairṛta
	UttMS	Black (like the neck of cuckoo)	-do-					

Kathmandu, Nepal, of this corpus are dated in 11th-12th century CE. Thus it has been concluded that these texts must have been composed before 12th century CE.

2. "Yet Saivism exerted an influence on the religious life of the Indian world that far exceeds what might be expected of such a minority, especially from one outside the maninstream of Brahmanical observance. For there can be no doubt that for several centuries after the sixth it was the principal faith of the elites in large parts of Indian subcontinent and in bothe mainland and insular Southeast Asia. Only Mahayana Buddhism was able to rival it during this period; ....

   An unpublished corpus of texts comprising principally the *Śivadharma* and the *Śivadharmottara*, contains the observances recommended to this laity, revealing that following the example of the Buddhist the Śaivas had propagated a lesser religion of merit gathering that centred on the support and veneration of the persons and institutions of the religion proper, " *-Introduction of Religion and the State: Śaiva officiants in the territory of the king's Brahmanical chaplain*, (Sanderson 2004, p.231).

   In this connection it is worthy to quote two verses from *Śivadharmaśāstram* which apparently indicate the state of religious rivalry, which gave birth the Śaiva scriptures of laity: *buddhenāpyarcitaṁ liṅgaṁ jambūnadamayaṁ śubham| tena buddhatvamāpnoti sadāśāntamavasthitam|| ārhatastu sadākālaṁ puṣpaliṅgārcanātparam| tenārhatvamavāpnoti yogaṁ cāpi sudurlabham||* (*Paśupatimataṁ śivadharmaśāstraṁ paśupatināthadarśanam -Śivadharmaśāstraṁ tṛtīyo'dhyāyaḥ,* page-7)

   But it is to be noted her that these verses are missing in the transcript of IFP, no T0032, which is a copy of a South Indian MS of the *Śivadharmaśāstram*.

3. *caturthaṁ śivadharmākhyaṁ sākṣānnandikeśabhāṣitam* [*@nandieśabhāṣ itam*-emd.]| (Kūrmapurāṇa I. 1.18a); *caturthaṁ śivadharmākhyaṁ purāṇaṁ nandineritam*| (Skandapurāṇa-saurasamhitā)

4. *īśānaṁ śivadharmaṃca Ṣivadharmottaraṁ tathā||66|| divyaproktaṁ kuberākhyaṁ śārvoktasyaiha paṃcamam|67|* (Uttarakāraṇāgamaḥ, prathamapaṭalaḥ) / *īśānaṁ śivadharmaṃca Ṣivadharmottaraṁ tathā| divyaproktaṁ kuberākhyamiti bhedasya paṃcakam||* (Ajitāgamaḥ, kriyāpādaḥ, prathamapaṭalaḥ)

5. *bhāratampaṃcamo veda itihāseti nāmataḥ*|

6. The colophon reads: *iti Ṣivadharma-umāmaheśvarasaṃvāde bhāratakīrtanannāma aṣṭādaśo'dhyāyaḥ*|

7. Mahabharata, BORI Publication

8. Explaining the term *Ṣivadharmaparāḥ* and *Ṣvadharmaparipālavān* in the third *kāṇḍa* of the *Śaivakalpadruma* Laxmidhara Mishra has mentioned:

Ṣivadharme Ṣivadhrmaśāstre purvottaracaturviṃśatyadhyāye parāyaṇāniratāḥd and *svadharmaṃśivadharmaśāstramd pūrvottaracaturviṃ śatyadhyāyasahitaṃpālayanti ye tānd,* respectively. Ms. R3348, GOML, pp. 63-64.

Appendix

उमामहेश्वरसंवादे एकविंशतितमोऽध्यायः

उवाच देवी देवेशं शितिकण्ठं महाप्रभुम्।
पूज्यते भक्तिमद्देवो विप्रैस्तु ब्रह्मचारिभिः ।।1।।

सुखोपविष्टमासीनमासने गोवृषध्वजम्।
वैदूर्यमणिस छन्ने बहुरत्नविभूषिते ।।2।।

अभिगम्य तु तन्देवी प्रा जलिर्वाक्यमब्रवीत्।
सर्वो में धर्म आख्यातः सप्तस्वरपरिच्छदः ।।3।।

किं शब्दः कीदृशो वर्णः कथं देवेन कीर्तितः।
कथमक्षरसम्प्राप्तः कथमङ्गे प्रतिष्ठितः ।।4।।

कथं हि देवदेवेन प्रोक्त आगीयते नृणाम्।

भगवानुवाच
शृणु देवि रहस्यानि गूढः स्थाने प्रकाशिताः ।।5।।

षड्जर्षभौ सगान्धारौ मध्यमं प चमं तथा।
धैवतः सनिषादश्च स्वराः सप्त प्रकीर्तिताः ।।6।।

षड्जस्तु पद्मवर्णाभ ऋषभः शुक्लवर्णकः।
हिरण्याभस्तु गान्धारो मध्यमः कुङ्कुमप्रभः ।।7।।

प चमस्तु स्वरो रक्तो नानावर्णस्तु धैवतः।
निशादो मेघवर्णस्तु इत्येते स्वरवर्णकाः ।।8।।

मयूरः षड्जसन्नादी कुक्कुटस्तु ऋषभन्नदेत्।
अश्वो वदति गान्धारं मध्यमन्तु गवेदकः ।।9।।

उत्कृष्टं प चमं विद्यात् कोकिलाभीरुतं स्वरम्।
माण्डूको धैवतो ज्ञेयः कु जरस्तु निषादवान्।।10।।

अग्निना गीयते षड्ज ऋषभो ब्राह्मणेन तु।
सोमो गायति गान्धारं विष्णुना मध्यमः स्वरः ।।11।।

प चमस्तु स्वरो गीतस्त्र्यम्बकेन महात्मना।
धैवतो वरुणोद्गीतो निशादो नारदेन तु ।।12।।

कण्ठे उत्तिष्ठते षड्ज ऋषभश्च शिरस्तथा।
नासिकायान्तु गान्धार उरसि मध्यमस्तथा ।।13।।

प चमस्तु स्मृतश्चोरो ललाटे धैवतस्तथा।
निशादः सर्वगात्रेषु विज्ञेयः स्वरचिन्तकैः ।।14।।

सप्त स्वरास्तु ये प्रोक्ता एकविंशतिमूर्चनाः।
ताना एकोनप चाशत् स्थाने दैवतवर्णतः ।।15।।

षड्जेन प्रीयते देव ऋषभेन महर्षयः
गान्धारस्तु पितृन्नित्यं मध्यमस्तु महोरगान् ।।16।।

प चमेन स्वरेणाशु सर्वभूतसुखं भवेत्।
धैवतो यक्षगन्धर्वा निशादो राक्षसा हि वै ।।17।।

अ आ षड्जस्वराः प्रोक्ता इ ई गान्धार इष्यते।
उ ऊ तु धैवतो ज्ञेय ऋ ॠ तु ऋषभः श्रुतः ।।18।।

लृ ॡ मध्यम इष्यते ए ऐ तु प चमः स्वरः।
ओ औ इति निशादस्तु स्वराक्षरविनिर्णयः ।।19।।

वायव्यः सौम्य ऐशान्य ऐन्द्र आग्नेय एव च।
याम्य नैर्ऋत इत्येते स्वराः षड्जादयो बुधैः ।।20।।

ऊर्ध्वाधो वारुणीभागा मिश्रकस्तु यदृच्छया।

देव्युवाच
मासाना च कथं चाष्टौ दिवसानां कथं विभो ।।21।।

एतन्मे संशयो देव कथं पर्व च गीयते।

महेश्वर उवाच
षडर्तु द्वादशा मासाः दिवसास्त्रिंशदेव तु ।।22।।

अग्नेः प्रतिपदः प्रोक्ता द्वितीया नरसिंहः च।
तृतीया देवराजस्तु चतुर्थ्यस्तु विनायकः ।।23।।

प चम्यान्तु श्रिया देवी महागौर्यस्तु षष्ठके।
सप्तम्यान्तु तथादित्य अष्टम्यामीश्वरस्तथा ।।24।।

दुर्गादेवी नवम्यान्तु दशम्यान्तु पितामहः।
एकादश्यान्तु वसवो द्वादश्यां विष्णुरेव च ।।25।।

ब्रह्मणस्तु त्रयोदश्यां चतुर्दश्यान्तथा शिवः।।
पूर्णमास्यान्तथा सोम उभयोरपि पक्षयोः ।।26।।

दिवसे सप्तमे भागे गीयते मधुरः स्वरः।
यदैवऊ्गीयते पुंसा स्वरः सम्पूर्णलक्षणः ।।27।।

तदा देवगणाः सर्वे दिवि घोषवती तदा।
दिव्यं शब्दन्तदा श्रुत्वा तथा हि वरवर्णिनि ।।28।।

देव्युवाच
एवं गायन्ति ये पुंसः स्त्रियो वापि प्रयत्नतः।
किं स्वरन्दीयते देव श्रोतुमिच्चामि तत्वतः ।।29।।

देवदेव उवाच
आषाढमासे सम्प्राप्ते शुक्लकृष्णाष्टमी तथा।
गीयते सोपवासेन शुक्लवस्त्रः शुचिर्नर : ।।30।।

स्वर्गलोकमितो याति सुख च परमम्भवेत्।
तर्थव श्रावणे मासे शुक्लकृष्णाष्टमी तथा ।।31।।

गीयते सोपवासेन गोसहस्रफलं भवेत्।
शुभे भाद्रपदे मासे शुक्लकृष्णाष्टमी तथा ।।32।।

गीयन्ते सोपवासेन देवस्तुष्यति शङ्करः।
राजसूयस्य यज्ञस्य फलं प्राप्नोति मानवः ।।33।।

तर्थवाश्वयुजे मासे शुक्लकृष्णाष्टमीन्तथा।
गीयते उपवासेन नरमेधफलं लभेत् ।।34।।

गीयते कार्तिके मासे शुक्लकृष्णाष्टमीन्तथा।
प्रयागे म्रियते यश्च तस्य पुण्यफलं लभेत् ।।35।।

गीयते मार्गशीर्षे तु शुक्लकृष्णाष्टमीन्तथा।
अश्वमेधस्य साहस्रं फलं प्राप्नोति मानवः ।।36।।

तथैव पौषमासे तु शुक्लकृष्णाष्टमीन्तथा।
गीयते सोपवासेन गोसहस्रफलं लभेत् ।।37।।

रूपसौभाग्यसम्पन्नो जायते पूजितो नरः।
गीयते माघमासे तु शुक्लकृष्णाष्टमीन्तथा ।।38।।

इहलोकसुखं प्राप्य परत्र च परां गतिम्।
तस्य क्षयादिहागत्य जायते स महाधने ।।39।।

तर्थव फाल्गुने मासे शुक्लकृष्णाष्टमीन्तथा।
गीयते शुचिवस्त्रेण उपवासः समाहितः ।।40।।

ब्रह्मलोकमतिक्रम्य रुद्रलोके महीयते।
तस्यान्ते पुनरागत्य जायते विपुले कुलं ।।41।।

ईश्वरश्चैव शूरश्च धनाढ्यश्चैव जायते।
उत्तमश्चैत्रमासे तु गीयते सुव्रतो यतः ।।42।।

शङ्करो वासुदेवश्च परितुष्टो न संशयः।
सर्वत्र लभते पूजां रूपवान्धनवान् भवेत! ।।43।।

न बालो म्रियते तस्य न च व्यसनमाप्नुयात्।
हंससारसयुक्तेन विमानेन स गच्चति ।।44।।

वैशाखे गीयते यस्तु उपवासः समाहितः।
न मिथ्या न च सन्देहो महादेवश्च तुष्यति ।। 45।।

पुष्पकेन विमानेन स्वर्गलोके महीयते।
षष्टिवर्षसहस्राणि देवलोके स तिष्ठति ।।46।।

तस्यान्ते पुनरागत्य ज्येष्ठपुत्रश्च जायते।
गवाढ्यश्च धनाढ्यश्च पुत्रवान् रूपवान् भवेत् ।।47।।

ज्येष्ठे मासे तु सम्प्राप्ते उपवासेन गीयते।
सर्वयज्ञफलावाप्तिः सर्वदानफलं लभेत् ।।48।।

सर्वतीर्थफल चैव प्राप्यते नात्र संशयः।
एतत्ते कथितन्देवि गीयमानेषु सर्वदा ।।49।।

एतद् धर्म्यं यशस्य च इहलोके परत्र च।
यश्चेमां गायते नित्यं यश्चेमां शृणुयान्नरः ।।50।।

दुःखन्तु न तु सेवेत देवं पूज्येत गीयते।
श्राद्धकाले च सम्प्राप्ते यस्तु गायति मानवः ।।51।।

तुष्यन्ति पितरस्तस्य हव्यकव्यमिवाक्षयम्।
वास्तुमध्ये तु गीयेते बालरोगस्तु नश्यति ।।52।।

क्षेत्रमध्ये तु गीयते सर्वसस्याभिवर्धनम्।
गोष्ठमध्ये तु गीयेत वर्धन्ते सर्वधेनवः ।।53।।

राजवासे तु गीयेत ध्रुवश्च विजयी भवेत्।
जनमध्ये तु गीयेत तर्थव कलिनाशनम् ।।54।।

मृत्युकाले श्रुतिं प्राप्त वियोनिं न स गच्चति।
पूर्वाह्ने चापि गीयेत दुःस्वप्न च प्रणश्यति ।।55।।

एतेत्ते कथितन्देवि किम्भूयः श्रोतुमिच्चसि।

देव्युवाच
यदि तुष्टोऽसि भगवन् देव कौतूहलं हि मे ।।56।।

अतः परन्तु पृच्चामि व्युत्क्रमेण प्रगीयताम्।
को दोषो भवते तस्म किं च भवति लक्षणम् ।।57।।

देवदेव उवाच

षणमुहूर्तेषु वेलासु सृकृच्चैव प्रगीयते।
एवं सर्वानुपूर्वेण येन येन हि गीयते ।।58।।

स्वरसप्तक्रमेणापि षणमुहूर्ते तथैव च।
ऋषभः षड्जागान्धारौ चतुर्मुहर्तो गीयते ।।59।।

मध्यमः चतुर्मुहूर्ते प चमश्च तथैव च।
मध्यम चतुर्मुहूर्ते यथाक्रमेण गीयते ।।60।।

चतुर्मुहुर्तो धैवतो निषादश्च तर्थव च।
भक्तिभावात्प्रगीतेन नास्ति दोषो मया विदः ।।61।।

असम्पूर्णं यद गीतं विघ्नन्तस्य प्रटृश्यते।
पूर्वन्तावत् प्रवक्ष्यामि शृणु देवि यथाक्रमम् ।।62।।

नारदस्तुम्बुरादीनि गन्धर्वश्च हहा हुहू।
गन्धर्वाः सप्त इत्येते तेभ्यो व्याप्तमिदं स्वरैः ।।63।।

गन्धर्वगीतवाद्येषु जगदासनकारिताः ।
गीते चार्द्धं प्रमुक्तानां केषु मध्ये प्रगीयते ।।64।।

प्रभाते तत्र वेज्ञेयः सर्वभूतसमागमम्।
ऋषीणा चैव सर्वेषां देवाना च समागताम् ।।65।।

न प्रभातं प्रभातेन कोपेनाविष्टदेहके।
देवलस्य तु शापेन ग्राहोऽभूत्तत्क्षणादपि ।।66।।

तस्य शापप्रभावेन त्रिकूटो नाम पर्वतौ।
तस्मिन्दिव्यह्रदे नूनं गन्धर्वोऽभूत्पपात सः ।।67।।

एतस्मिन्नन्तरे काले जनयूथं समागमम्।
तस्मिन् सरसि दुष्टात्मा विरूपान्तर्जलेशयः ।।68।।

आसीद् ग्राहो गजेन्द्राणां निपुरा केकरेक्षणः।
दन्तोज्ज्वलमुखस्तस्मिन् कदाचिद्गजयूथपः ।।69।।

सलिले पङ्कजवने युथमध्यगतः सुखी।
खेलत्युत्पङकजवने युथेन महतावृतः ।।70।।

गृहीतस्तेन रौद्रेण ग्रहेणाटृश्यमूर्तिना।
पश्यन्तीनां करेणूनां क्रोशन्तीना च दारुणाम् ।।71।।

ह्रियते पङ्कजवने ग्राहेणाटृश्यमूर्तिना।
व्यवस्थितः स निरुद्वेगः पश्चिमामगमद् दिशाम् ।।72।।

जगाम मनसा देवं शरणं मधुसूदनम्।
प्रगृह्य पुष्पगग्रेण का चनं कमलोत्तमम् ।।73।।

आपद्विमोक्षमन्विच्छन् गजः स्तोत्रमनुस्सरन्।
भक्तिन्तस्यानुसंचिन्त्य नागस्यामेघसम्भवाम् ।।74।।

उज्जहाराप्रमेयात्मा तरसश्चरिसूदनः।
सरस्थं दारयामास ग्राहं चक्रेण माधवः ।।75।।

मोक्षयामास स गजं पापेभ्यः शरणागतम्।
स हि देवलशापेन हाहा गन्धर्वसत्तमः ।।76।।

ग्राहत्वमगमत्कृष्णाद्वधं प्राप्य दिवङ्गतः।
आपद्विमुक्तो युगपद् गजो गन्धर्व एव च ।।77।।

एवं हि कथयामास तुष्टोऽस्मि वरवर्णिनि।
देवस्य वचनं श्रुत्वा धर्मं कथितसंस्मरन् ।।78।।
हृष्टतुष्टा मया देव शिरसा वन्दितः प्रभुः ।।78।।

इति भगवतो गीतपुराणे धर्मगुह्ये गजेन्द्रमोक्षणम्
उमामहेश्वरसंवादे एकविंशतितमोऽध्यायः।

उत्तरोत्तरमहासंवादे सप्तमोऽध्यायः

उमोवाच

एते वेदस्वराः सप्त कथिता वेदकारणाः।
कीदशास्ते तु विज्ञेयाः कंवर्णं वि चलक्षणम् ।।45।।

अष्टौ भावास्ततो देव मूर्छना एकविंशतिः।
एकैकस्य तु किन्नाम वद शम्भो प्रसीद मे ।।46।।

ईश्वर उवाच

स्वरा चैव प्रवक्ष्यामि यैरिदं वर्तते जगत्।
स्वरहीना निवर्तन्ते वायवः स्वरलक्षणाः ।।47।।

स्वरं नन्दन्ति श्रोत्राणि वातश्चङ्गिरते स्वरम्।
स्वरप्रणीतं त्रैलोक्य स्वरे शब्दाः प्रतिष्ठिताः ।।48।।

मयूरो वदले षड्जं निषादं वदते गः।
काले प्रावृषि वै देवि दर्दुरो धैवतं वदेत् ।।49।।

विप्यकाको (विप्यहाको) वेदेद्देवि स्वरमृषभमेव च।
एते चैव स्वराः प्रोक्ताः वर्णं वै कथयाम्यहम् ।।50।।

षड्ज आरक्तवर्णाभो दाडिमीकुसुमप्रभः।
ऋषिभस्तु भवेत्पीतः किंकरातसमप्रभः ।।51।।

गान्धारः पाण्डराभश्च शुक्ल चैव तु मध्यमः।
प चमः श्यामवर्णस्तु अतसीकुसुमप्रभः ।।52।।

कृष्णवर्ण निषादस्तु ोकिलग्रीवसन्निभः।
एते देवि त्रयो ग्रामे ब्रह्मविष्णुमहेश्वराः ।।53।।

शादवप्रमुखाः ज्ञैयाः स्वरान्योऽन्यप्रभेदकाः।
सजातीषु विजातिषु सहस्रगुणविस्तराः ।।54।।

पितृवह्निसमत्पन्नाः प च ये प चमाः स्मृताः।
ऋषभागकुले देवि उत्पन्ना ऋषभधैवताः ।।55।।

जितान्योऽन्यभेदेन प्राकृतं संस्कृतेन च।
देवजातीकुलोत्पन्नाः षड्जगान्धारमध्यमाः ।।56।।

असुराणां समुत्पन्ना निषादस्तु यशस्विनि।
मध्याह्ने शादवं कुर्यादपराह्ने च मध्यमम् ।।57।।

सन्ध्याकाले तु सम्प्राप्ते कुर्यान्मालवकौशिकम्।
रात्रौ तु प्रथमे यामे निषादं कारयेद्बुधः ।।58।।

द्वितीये प्रहरे चैव धैवतन्तु विचक्षणः।
यामे तृतीयके चैव यानि भिन्नानि प चमम् ।।59।।

तानि सर्वाणि मेधाविर्गायते भवितात्मवान्।
यामके तु चतुर्थेऽस्मिन् भिन्नषड्जं समाश्रयेत् ।।60।।

गान्धारं पूर्वमादित्यैर्देविकायां प्रयु जते।
दिवसे प्रथमे यामे कुर्याद्वैरर्ककैशिकम् ।।61।।

भुक्तेऽन्तरे तु कर्तव्यः सौराष्ट्रं प चमानि तु।
एवं वेलाविशेषेण गान्धार्वं सुविचारितम् ।।62।।

मूर्छनां कथयिष्यामि यथा नामानि सुन्दरि।
नन्दी विशाला सुमुखी चित्रा चित्रवती तथा ।।63।।

शुभा वेला तु विज्ञेया देवानां सप्त मूर्छना।
आप्यायनी विश्वधृता चन्द्रहेमकपर्दिनी ।।64।।

चैत्री चावाहनी चैव पितृणां सप्त मूर्छना।
उत्तरा च तथा मन्दा द्वितीय चातिरङ्गिका ।।65।।

अश्वक्रान्ता च भौम्येषु शुद्धषड्जस्तथैव च।
नारायणीतिरजनी ऋषीणां सप्त मूर्छना ।।66।।

....

इति उत्तरोत्तरमहासंवादे सप्तमोऽध्यायः

23

Manuscripts and Miniature Paintings of Assam

– *Swadhinata Das*

The art of miniature painting was known in Assam from early period. The manuscript is commonly known as *chitralekha*. The art of this type of painting in Assam was developed around manuscript illumination. The manuscripts of Assam were written during the Bhakti Movement under the supervision of Srimanta Sankardeva in 15th-16th Century CE. The movement gave birth to a vigorous culture of literature accompanied by artistic resurgence with multiple ramifications. The sole aim of the Assamese manuscript painting is to tell the story swiftly and vividly by throwing the medium of line and colour.[1] Manuscripts with illuminated margins is known as *latā-katāputhī*. *Latā-katāputhī* illustration is often used in Madhabdeva's *Namagoshā* manuscripts.

In Assam the Bhakti movement was started by Srimanta Sankardeva. In this movement *sattra* institution of Assam played a great role as religio-cultural centre. The *sattra* institution patronized and supported the literary and artistic renaissance, taking beneath its facade, a vast repertoire of arts and crafts. Sankardeva and his followers gave importance in the field of art and craft. As result of this, the number and title of manuscripts were increased and *sattras* emerged as one of the great repositories. The other repository was the archives of the Āhom and Koch kings.

The manuscripts of Assam can be broadly divided into two major styles i.e. (a) Tai style or Tai *Ahom* style, affiliated to the Buddhist style of Burma, and (b) The Assamese Style, which bears local traditional features.

Tai style: The Tai manuscripts represent the earliest school of the manuscript painting in Assam. There are two kinds of paintings found in Tai Ahom style- *Phung Chin* manuscript dated 1473 CE and *Suktantakyempong*. The *Phung-Chin* deals with 16 heavens and 16 hells. The second manuscript deals with *Lokadharma*. The style and theme of these religious paintings preserved in some Buddha *Viharas* of Assam have their origin in South-East Asia and not in Assam. Of late, few more such illustrated Tai manuscripts have come to light in Assam.

The Assamese style: The Assamese style manuscript is divided into two kinds- (a) The *Sattriya* style, which was developed in the *sattras* proper and(b) The Royal court style or *rajaghariya* style which travelled from *sattras* to the royal Ahom court.[2] The development of *sattriya* style was older than the *rajaghariya* style. Again, the royal school developed intotwo styles, viz (a) the Garhgaon, under the patronage of Ahom rulers and (b) the Darrang under the patronage of Koch rulers.

The Assamese script developed three distinct modes namely-*Gadgāya, Bāmuniya* and *Kāthali* or *Kahkari*.[3] The *Gadgāya* style was mainly related to the Ahom capital, Gadgão. Though it was centered and connected around the Ahom administration, but it became the most widely used scripts even in *Sattra* circles. In general the Sanskrit *Pandits* used the *Bamuniya* style. They used it to copy the Sanskrit lore. The *Kāithāli* script probably originated with the *kaiths* and *kāyasthas*. This script was used by them in official documents and books of accounts. Speaking generally about illustrated manuscripts in Assam, Dr. S.K. Bhuyans writes, "The skill of a painter was generally requisitioned to decorate the labours of the transcriber by sketching appropriate pictures on spaces left blank for the purpose."[4]

The documented manuscripts were done in 17th and 18th centuries in Assam, but they represent an older tradition, which is closer to the western Indian tradition. Some scholars though that manuscript painting style was derivate of Pala School. It may be pointed out here that many scholars believe that north Indian style of painting have originated from the western Indian tradition. Samiran Baruah establishing by citing some peculiarities of the Assamese school that it had originated before the Persian influence was in vague in North Indian.

Sattriya School: The great Srimanta Sankardeva introduced the *Sattriya* School of painting in Assam. It is the earliest indigenous school of painting in Assam. The *Citra Bhāgawat (Bhāgawat* book X, dated 1539, CE 1461) from *Bali Satra* of Nagaon is the earliest example of *Sattriya* style. Regarding this book R Dasgupta mentions, "The earliest extant example of an illustrated manuscript of this school is the Bhāgawat book X dated 1539 from Bāli Statra". The style initiated in the early 16th century has marked similarity with the various North Indian schools of miniatures of these Mahāpurāna manuscripts dated Ad. 1540 from Palam near Delhi and Mrigavati belonging to mid century are stylistically closest to the above manuscript.[5]

This school continued till the last days of the Tungkhugiyas though in the meantime a superior style developed in royal patronage in Upper Assam. The association of *Sattriya School* with the religious atmosphere of the*sattra* was perhaps responsible for its popularity as a medium especially when religion texts had to be illustrated. This is seen in preference of royal patrons for this style when they commissioned the artists to illustrate religious text like *Gitā Govīnda*, the *Ananda Lahari* or the *Rama Yana* in the same style. The important manuscripts of this school are as follows:

Vanamali Devar Carita of Ramakanta Dwija, *Sri Bhagavata Matsya Carita* of Nityananda Kaystha, (1644-50 AD) *Lava-Kusa-Yuddha* of Harivar Vipra (1714-44 CE) *Ananda Lahari* of Ananta Acarya Dwija (1714-44 CE) *Ramayana, Sundara Kanda* (1715 CE) *Sankara Carita* (Date not known) *Ramayana, Lanka Kanda* (1791-1806 CE) etc.

In general, the text and picture follows each other and narration continued in several strips. The nature of the strips is horizontal. In *Sattrya* style of painting the picture penal is divided into two registers constituting active and negative spaces for pictorial narration. Pictorial figures are set in the active space in such a manner that they move horizontally in frame through time. Like the script the pictorial figures can read one after another.

Most of the panels depict more than one event happening in many moments of the correlation between the events is achieved either through placing a couple of figures on either side of an imaginary dividing line showing their backs to each other or by placing them aface.

Royal School: As per the name suggests, the school was grown under the patronage of royal courts of Koch and Ahom. The birth place of Royal school is Darrang Raj of Mangaldoi. The royal school style is close to the *Sattriya* School. It grew up at royal patronage of the Koch royal family of Mangoldoi. The line of *Sattriya* School soon developed its own characteristics. Maheswar Neog has rightly said, "It is, thus, seen that Assam Vaisnavism developed a school of painting of its own and this art was later patronized by the Ahom monarchs and Koch chief in the 17th and 18th centuries."[6] Slowly the art of royal school was influenced by the Ahoms culture, because the sources of the Rajas of Darrang were not enough. The Ahom royal style is found in several manuscripts. This style is known as Garhgaon School. The school named after the capital Garhgaon as under the patronage of Ahom Kings a good number of manuscripts were written in there. It was a real court art with its own secular character. This style is a good combination of Mughal in technique and Assamese in spirit. It was under the patronage of Ahom kings that the beautiful paintings were executed in some manuscripts such as the *Hastī-vidyārnava, Śankhacūda Badha, Gīta-Govinda, Lava-kuśar Yudha, Dharma Purana, Bhagavata* (Book VI) etc. Ahom kings like Rudra Singha and Siva Singha and their queens were responsible for the development of this new and secular branch of art and painting in Eastern Assam.

The basis of the royal school of art was of course the traditional religious painting with new infiltration of Mughal influence. But it is interesting to notice thateven during the Mughal rule the independent Ahom never lost ties with the mainland. The native Muslims of Assam mixed up with local population. During the days of Ahom artists were invited from the other parts of the community. Ahom king Rudra Singha invited and gave well settlement to Mughal artists near his capital. In the paintings of Assam the three quarter profile is noticed which was an inheritance from Persian paintings for the Mughal artist. Though these Assamese paintings bear the essential features of the Mughal, yet they all breathe the atmosphere of an aristocrat Hindu household of Northern India.

The Ahom court art was not influenced by the European style even in later period. Another noteworthy feature of the painting is that it depicts the portrait of the royal family members and other important persons connected. This is why portraits of Sukumar Barkath, the author of

Hastividarvana, the painters Dilwar and Dosai and the patrons of Siva Singha and Ambika Devi are found.

Artisian:

The painter belongs to a class of people known as *Khanikars*. In the Ahom period there was whole *khel* or guild of *Khanikars*. In such of *khel* Muslims people were also including. The scribes were called *likhaks* or *lekhaks*. A*khanikar* might be an illiterate person; but he could copy all the paintings as well as writings. The *khanikars* also made idols and masks for the theatrical performances, and the word *pratimā* came to be applied indiscriminately to both idols and paintings. The *Khanikars* made *simhasanas* (holy pedestals), *puthi-thagās* (book-rests), *gachās* (lamp-stands), etc. from wood and painted them generally with vermilion and yellow arsenic.

The artists or *Khanikars* were initially associated with copying of transcripts and make-up the actors of dramatic performance produced in*sattras*. Later on they extended their work field and started to drown the pictures in manuscripts. They used their practical knowledge of brush and colour in context of traditional dramatic presentation now became very useful in defining pictorial forms for transforming verbal imageries in the pages of a manuscript. The artist of work must have been a master in his subject. They had the sense of proportion and vision.

The *Khanikars* were patronized and supported to work with their penmanship by the *Sattras* and Ahom kings. Moreover many bibliographies came forward to support the *Khanikars* for their penmanship. The Ahom kings patronized and supported an army of clerks and copyists under the supervision of an officer named *Likhakar* Barua (meaning superintendent of scribes). The royal members attached a set of compartments called *Gāndhiya-bharāl* for preservation of royal manuscripts, records and letters to the royal palace.[7]

The traditional paintings of Assam were the illustrations of the texts. As such artists were basically concerned on the context of the texts. They deal with the context which already existing meanings of the texts, instead of creating new meaning with form and colour. The artist generally copy one manuscript to another, so it is hard to understand how much they understand inspired by the text.

The Assamese paintings are primarily a product of the village culture. Generally the manuscripts were prepared by the traditional scribes and painters who lived in the village.In Assam, the painters *(Khanikars)* had to depend on farming for their livelihood and so it was not possible for them no settle in urban centre near his clients to do the paintings exclusively. Moreover the *Vaisnava* monasteries which were also the production of manuscript were also situated away from the urban centre.

Writing Materials and their making process:

Sāci-Pāt: The *Sāci-pāt* is made from the inner bark of the *Sāci* tree (*Aquilariaagallocha*). It is mentioned in *Harsacharita* that *Sāci* tree were presented to king Harsha of North India by the messenger of Bhāskarbarman of Kāmarupa (*aguru-valka-kalpita-saücayāni. Subhāsita-bhāüji-pustakani-parinata-pātala-patolatvimsi*)[8] A tree is selected of about 15 or 16 years growth and 30 to 35 inches in girth, measured about 4 feet from the ground. From this the bark is removed in strips, from 6 to 18 feet long, and from 3 to 27 inches in breadth. These strips are rolled up separately with the inner or white part of the back outwards, and the outer or green part inside, and are dried in the sun for several days. They are then rubbed by hand on a board, or some other hard substance, so as to facilitate the removal of the outer or scaly portion of bark. After this, they are exposed to the dew for one night. Next morning the outer layer of the bark *(nikari)* is carefully removed, and the bark proper is cut into pieces of a convenient size, 9 to 27 inches longs long and 3 to 18 inches broad. These are put into cold water for about an hour, and the alkali is extracted, after which the surface is scraped smooth with a knife. They are then dried in the sun for half an hour, and, when perfectly dry, are rubbed with a piece of burnt brick. A paste prepared from *mātimāh* (*Phaseolusraduantus*) is next rubbed in, and the bark is dyed yellow by means of yellow arsenic. This is followed again sun-dying, after which the strips are rubbed as smooth as marble. The process is now complete, and the strips are ready for use.[9] The universal custom of applying harital or yellow arsenic was not only for colouring the folios but protecting these from the attack of insects and micro-organism. The fumes of *gandhaka* (surplus) were used in the finished manuscript. The *gandhaka* acted as an insecticide also.

Describing *sācipātiyaputhi* in his "Note on Assamese manuscript", Dr. Bhuyan says, "The leaves were numbered, the figures being inserted at the second page of a folio. The centre of each leaf was perforated for the fasting string to pass through. Leaves thicker than those used in the body of the manuscript were used for covers; and occasionally wooden pieces were also used. These were always some spare leaves or pages to record change of ownership, on the other important events in the life of the owner or his family. These additional leaves were known as Beti pat or attendant leaves." [10]

Tulā-Pāt: Another writing material was *tulā-pāt* (cotton leaf). The *tulā-pāt*was not used as much as *sāci-pāt.* In *Kotha Guru Carita* it is mentioned especially in connection with painting. *Tulā-pāt* looks like fine lint. It was made by ginning, felting and processing cotton *(tulā)* into sheets. The Ahom people has followed a well process to make strong and tough writing sheets from a pulp obtained by the beating of the barks of a few varieties of trees.

The process of making *tulā-pāt* as described by Chaikhang Gohain, an Ahom scholar of Namphakial village, is as follows- "*Tulā-pāt* is essentially a paper made from wood pulp. Three kinds of trees were usually selected for making *tulā-pāt*, while *tulā-pāt* was made from *maihai* tree. The dark brown variety of *tulā-pāt* was made from *yaman*tree. There was also a red variety of *tulā-pāt* but the tree from which this was made is not known. The *yaman* tree has been identified with the hsa tree of the Shan people and the *nuni* of the Assamese or the paper-mulbary. The barks of above mentions trees were cut into convenient sizes and then boiled till they disintegrated and formed a fine pulp and became clear of the impurities. The pulp was next poured water and kept in rectangular ditches of required size where it floated on the water surface and left to cool. When cold, the film of pulp lying on a surface of watergave a sheet of strong tough paper. Usually, a *tulā-pāt* folio was made by stitching two single sheets together or by folding a longer sheet into two and the stitching them. This was done to give strength to the folios." [11]

***Tāl-Pāt, Bānh-Pāt* etc:** Some other writing materials of that period were made of bamboo strips, silk treated with *mātimah* paste, palm-leaves (*tālpāt*) treated with lac resin smoothened animal hides and even bamboo sticks considered to be a magical value.[12] Leaves of the *nahar* tree (*Mesueferre*) and a kind of leaf known as alpal were also used for same purpose.

***Muga* Fabric:** The manuscripts of *muga* and silk were also common in Assam. Sometimes folios made of *muga* stitched along the top to form a pad. These materials were not as popular *sacipat*. The Purani Samaguri Satra of Sibsagar district has the important *Padaputhi* manuscript done on *Muga* silk cloth.[13]

Lamination

With the help of lac lamination process of paintings and folios were done. A piece of finished lac was selected for lacquering. A quantity of good shellac is boiled in water to make it soft and clean. Then blobs of clean red shellac are dropped on several places of the surface and leave it to cool down. After that a piece of red hot iron is held above each blob and makes it sticky. Next with a blade of *keteki* leaf the sticky blob is spread on the surface as extensively as possible, so that the resulting film became thin and to allow the painting to be visible under it. Then a second blob is tried until the whole surface is coated with a transparent golden yellow film of shellac of uniform thickness. All excess shellac is scrapped off the surface.[14]

Colour and Ink

The most common ink that used for writing in early was very deep as Chinese black, which was also very fast colour. The characteristic of the ink is that it was water proof and long lasting. The ink is not fade even after long exposure. Another characteristic of Assamese ink is its tenacity of adherence to glossy and slippery surfaces. Some other colours of inks were also available in early Assam. The golden ink or '*sonar pani'*, white ink and invisible ink were also used, but not common as black. On green folios of *tulā-pāt* the colour ink had been used to write. Gold paint was also used. But this paint was used occasionally, mainly in royal letters and manuscripts. The Buddhists of Assam used gold paint to illustrate the...

The preparation of ink for writing manuscripts was a very interesting process. The ink making formula and process was commonly known to the printers and writers. The ink was made of using by various kinds of natural ingredients. To make this ink *śilikha* (*Terminalia citrine*) is mainly used. A few fruits of this variety are kept steeped in water in an earthen bowl for a few days. After this the bowl is exposed to dew for several nights with a non-porous basin below it. The water turns black in few days and by this time percolates it through the earthen bowl and drops into the non-porous basin as a very fine and deep black ink.Sometime peopleadd iron and iron sulphas to make it blacker. Some people put the blood of a variety of fish known as *kuciyā* to make it dark and thick.[15] Cow's urine was also added to the *śilikha* extract.

Kotha Guru Charita has given the list of colours that used in manuscripts of Assam. The *hengul*and *haital* was used as colour in painting and writings. In *Chinha Yatra* and manuscripts, Sankardeva used these colours for painting. Besides, king Naranaraya supplied twelve varieties of colours in powered state to Sankaradev,for priming the *pirali* of *Chandan Chora*.[16] The commonly used colours in Assamese manuscripts are-Indigo for the blue colour *(Nila*), yellow arsenic for yellow (*Haital),* vermillion (*Hengul*) and Lamp black (*Kajol Mahi*).

Some other different inks used in early Assam were :

a. *Kajal Mahi* (lamp Black)
b. *Narikal Mahi*- It was mad from soot collected on the inner side of a coconut shell by placing above the flame of an oil lamp.
c. *Tel Mahi*-This kind of ink was probably prepared with oil instead of water.
d. *Kare Mahi*-This was made from roasted rice. The rice is roasted to black powdered finally and mixed water.
e. *Sanchi Mahi*-This was another commonly used ink of early Assam. But the preparation process of this type of ink was not known. May be this ink prepared with black on extract of *sanchi* wood as it name indicates.
f. Other ink- The Buddhists of Lakhimpur and Sibsagar used a kind of ink made from gold dust. Many manuscripts in Tai scripts were written with this ink.[17]

Brush, Pen and Pencil

In Bana's *Harshacharita*, references of writing and painting materials are found. From *Harshacharita,* written in the 7th century CE, it is known that Bhaskarvarma, the king of Kamrupa, or ancient Assam, gifted

Harshavardhana, king of northern India, 'volumes of fine writing with leaves made from aloe bark and the hue of ripe cucumber.' Bana has mentioned that the gifts from Bhaskarvarma also included a pair of wooden panels, to one side of which were attached coloured pots of small gourds and brushes.

The pen used was a goose quill or reed. Pens were also made of bamboo shoots and known as *jeng*. In native language of Assam pen known as *kap*. In ancient Assam, pencils were also used, which were made from a kind of earth known as *hamsila*. The *hamsila* was probably imported from Bhutan, which might have had a golden or yellow colour.[18] Pencil made of terracotta was used. This was used for writing as well as for drawing the outlines of painting. The bamboo tubes were filled with finely kneaded earth. This is the backed till the earth hardened and was thoroughly burnt. Then the tubes spilt of and the pencil was ready for use.[19]

Features

The miniature paintings of Assam have its own characteristics. The study of these paintings can give us a picture of contemporary society of Assam along with its economic and religious situation. The paintings show human figures, divine and semi divine characters, demons, natural sceneries, animals, birds, architectural design, etc. Both men and women figures of manuscripts are depicted with thin waist and broad chest. The facial appearances of the characters conventionally or flatly drown which appear all alive. Facial features are uniformly drawn in profile. The eyes are drawn in almond shape.

Rāksasas have been painted in black with monstrous appear, while *Asurās* and *Danavās* are generally shown either in black or red in colour. Maximum *Devās* are painted in red or yellow. Mahadevā, Balabhadra and Brāhmanas are drowning in white colour. Lord Vishnu or Krśna always depicts in black, blue or green colour. The different colour identifies the different characters. All the divine characters are depicted with their particular *ayudhās* or weapon and *vāhanās*. Therefore it is easy to recognize the particular characters.

Men are usually depicted in wearing three pieces of cloth viz., dhoti, waist-band (*kamarbandh*), and scarfcloth *(dopātta)* and the women were also wear three pieces of cloths viz., *ghāgra* or *sāri*, waist band and gaily colour scarf or *chaddar* with both end hanging loosely over the two sides of the body. The female used to make coil or bun. Sometime male characters are depicted with pure medieval Muslim noble dresses e.g. long frock type garment (*angaraksa*) and *ornās* wrapped round the upper part of body along with the *mughlaipāg*. On the other hand in some case female were wearing long skirt which is similar to Rajasthani pattern.The *Danavas* and *Asurās* generally wore the *muglāipāg*, long flowing garment (*chāpkan*), short skirts type garments and *pyjamas* and containing beard like those of Muslims.

It is noticed that both men and women were decorated with various kinds of ornaments from top to bottom. The women were depicted with more ornaments like *haśtalaṇkāra, karṇabharāna, pādābharna, grīvabharana* etc. Sometimes *mukutās* are noticed, which wore by the royal figures.

In defining hills and hillocks, rivers and oceans, the artists' treatment is always stylish. The birds and animals are drawn like realistic. Birds of different colour and species have been depicted in both static and moving position. Many kinds of animals are drawn in manuscripts such as horse, monkey, elephant, tortoise, crocodile etc. Trees are beautifully depicted having each leaf clearly differentiated. Trees are generally painted like sprays. Mountains are depicted as sites of multi coloured convex bodies. Sometimes hill is defined by some wave like blocks each super-imposed one above the other. Water is generally indicated by broad wavy parallel lines of green colour interspersed with thin white lines.

From the view of time period the manuscripts of Assam can be divided into two divisions—17th Century's manuscripts and 18th Century's manuscripts. Both of them have some specific features. Commenting on the medieval landscape painting as seen in manuscripts of Assam, Dr. S.K Chatterjee remarks: "The earlier style is simpler, more vigorous and more sincere and have a stately epic character about them' and about the new style he says, 'the 18th century shows a happy blending of the basic Eastern Indian style of religious miniatures found in Orissa, Bengal and Assam, which more sophisticated Mogul and Rajasthani as possibly also Kangara art of the West."[20]

Most of the paintings of 17th century can be grouped together for their common features. The manuscripts of 17th century share some of the characteristics with the early Western Indian tradition. A comparison with some of the published 18th Century Nepali and Bengali paintings show that the Assamese paintings are closer to the 15th and 18th century Northern Indian tradition rather than the paintings of Nepali and Bengali of 18th Century:

a. The pictorial figures are set in the active space in such a way that they move horizontally in the frame through time. Like the script, the pictorial figures can be read only one after another.

b. Most of the panels depict more than one event that happened many movements of time. Correlation between the events is established by using various way of presentation.

c. The text and picture follow each other and the narration continues in several strips. The strips are horizontal in nature.

d. The lavish decoration, mastery of execution and expansion of the palette with mixed colours are some characteristic of the later day paintings which show the influence of Tungkhungia in court.

e. Basket pattern, the use of *mudras* and stylized poses of the human figures etc continued even in the Sattra School.

f. In manuscripts lying and sleeping position is indicated by drawing the figures horizontally.

g. Some of the pure Assamese instruments and objects are noticed in manuscript, suc as-drums *(khol)*, cymbals *(tāl),* hope pipe *(pepā),* Bihu drum *(dhol)*, assamese trays *(śarāi),* sitting stools *(tāmulipirā),* bed steads *(chālpirā)* and country made sun shades *(jāpi)* etc.

h. Generally the manuscript of Assam is consisted of a large central area, where the subjects are depicted. This area generally painted in red, though sometime yellow and pink are also noticed, whereas the subjects are painted with many colours. The surrounding broader and top broader are seen in blue and green colour. The top broader forming a series of canopies over the central area.

i. Except the portrayal of Brahma, all the male and female figures are always in convention ways which are depicted in profile.

j. In general a male costume consists of a dhoti and scarf. The scarf is hanging from the neck with its two ends freely falling over the shoulders on either side. The female dress is consisted of *mekhela* (lower garment) and a *riha* (upper garment).

k. The treatment of the land is always conventional. The natural elements are depicted as the same way.

l. The architecture is very simple, consisting of a cross section view of the Assam type house with roofs and supporting pillars. In many cases only the door is drown instead of the complete house. Sometime only the pillar is depicted independently to present the whole house. The umbrella is depicted as hanging from a hook like handle.

m. Pictorial abstraction is one of the significant features of the Assamese school.

n. Miniature paintings of the Assamese school have invariably remained in horizontal format while in other parts of India they changed to the vertical format.

18th Century Manuscript

The manuscripts of 18th century bear all the elements of 17th Century's manuscripts. The Rajput-Mughal elements have been found to converge a unique manner. The combination of Rajput-Mughal idiom and local idiom form a new and unique style. When the flavor of Rajput-Mughal idioms translated from its vertical format to the horizontal formed of Assamese manuscripts, naturally they formed a unique style.

a. In the manuscripts of 18th century the background green colour was replaced by the red colour. Many new shades of colours were noticed in the manuscripts of 18th Century. At that time the painters were introduced with new colours.

b. The convention of dividing the composition into the composition border of the 17th century's manuscripts has almost abandoned in the 18th century group of painting.

c. The general composition division of the central and surround border of the 17th century manuscript has been completely given up by his group of painting. But in this type of manuscript an attempt to differentiate the planes is clearly noticed. But the effort of defining perspective failed to maintain the depth of the Rajput-Mughal idioms.

d. The depictions of the male and female figures are nice and solid. The male and female faces are drowning in different ways. Generally faces are shown in profile, three-quarter and frontal views.

e. The female costumes became very elaborate. In many cases the dresses became identical with the costume of late *Rajasthani* paintings.

f. In 18th Century's manuscripts the plants and animals are depicted in more naturalistic and conventional way.

g. In some manuscripts some flowering plants are noticed which are used for ornamented decorative purpose and because of this reason they are not look like natural. The depiction of hills and mountains are different from the 17th century's manuscripts.

h. The architectural depiction is quite complex. Some elements of the Rajput mughal art is noticed in these paintings. But sometime in some particular cases the style of depicting single door instead of whole building is noticed which a common element of 17th century paintings is.

i. The chariots are depicted in many ways. In some cases chariots are like platform mounted on four wheels and some mounted on two wheels. Some chariots are elaborately decorated. Some of chariots have canopies overhead. The style of umbrella is different from the hanging style umbrella of 17th Century.

It could be known from the above discussion, that the manuscripts play a great role in early cultural History of Assam. The uniqueness and the provincial flavor of simplicity are the basic reason of beauty of Assamese manuscript. The manuscripts of Assam have its own characteristics which is helpful to create a new and unique field in cultural history. When we study the common features of manuscripts it is shown that the Assamese paintingwhether cultivated in *sattras* or in court is basically bear the same category and technique. They are different in degrees of perfection only.

Dr. Kapila Vastsyayan for the first time in her editorial note on *Gita Govinda* declared that "the Assamese miniature paintings can safely be placed as an independent school in the tradition of Indian manuscript painting."[21] Art has to borrow from others and gives to others. Thus, Assamese miniature painting though have borrowed many elements from Rajasthani, Mughal and other style, it retained its indigenous character and personality and house it forms a separate school. Certain special features e.g. gestures household objects, utensils and *sarai* (decorates dish on stand with and without lid) architectural style of house or buildings, costumes, flora fauna abstractness in depiction, the unusual themes taken for illustration and the size of manuscript distinguish Assamese paintings in the panorama of Indian manuscript painting tradition as a separate school.

References

1. Sarma, S.N. (1966): *The Neo-Vaisnavite Movement and the Satra Institution of Assam*, Department of Publication, Guwahati University, Guwahati, p. 246.
2. Choudhury, R.D and Kalita, N (1998): *Manuscripts painting from Kamarupa Anusandhan Samiti, Directorate of Museums: Assam*, p. XI.
3. Neog, M. (1965): *Sankardeva and His Time: Early History of Vaisnava Faith and Movement in Assam*, Lawyers' Publication, Guwahati, p. 308.
4. Sarma, S. (1999): *Descriptive Catalogue of Assamese Manuscripts*, Publication of Guwahati University, Assam, p. XVII.
5. Dasgupta. R. (1972): *Eastern India Manuscript Painting*, Db Publication, Bombay, p. 57.
6. Neog, M. (1965): *Sankardeva and His Time: Early History of Vaisnava Faith and Movement in Assam*, Lawyers' Publication, Guwahati, p. 257.
7. Bhuyan. Dr. S.K. (1930): *Descriptive Catalogue of Assamese Manuscripts*, Publication of the University of Calcutta, p. XIX.
8. Cowell, E.B and Thomas, F W. tr (1897): Bana, *Harsa Carita*, London, p. 214.
9. Gait. E. A. (1905): *History of Assam*, Bina Library, Guwahati, p. 428.
10. Sarma, S. (1999): *Descriptive Catalogue of Assamese Manuscripts*, Publication of Guwahati University, Assam, p. XV.
11. Baishya, D. (2009): *Traditional Science and Material Culture of Early Assam*, EBH Publication, Guwahati, p. 254.
12. Gogoi, L. (1981): *Ahom Jātiāru Asmiyā Samskriti*, Sibsagar, pp. 126-29.

13. Baishya, D. (2009): *Traditional Science and Material Culture of Early Assam*, EBH Publication, Guwahati, p. 254.
14. Neog, M. (1948): *Sri Sri Sankardeva*, Bina Library, Guwahati, p. 303.
15. Medhi, K (1963): *Likhār Sājuli*, writing material, Asām Bandhava Publication, Jorhat, p. 40.
16. Baishya, D. (2009): *Traditional Science and Material Culture of Early Assam*, EBH Publication, Guwahati, p. 256.
17. Baishya, D. (2009): ibid, p. 256.
18. Baishya, D. (2009): ibid, p. 257.
19. Handique, K.K, and Dutta Baruah, H.R (1999): *ChitraBhagawat*, Publication Board Assam, Guwahati, p. 87.
20. Chatterjee, S.K. (1970): *Place of Assam in the History and Civilization of India*. Guwahati University Publication, Assam, p. 38.
21. Vastyana, K and Neog, M. (1986): *Gita-Govinda* in the Assam School of Painting, Publication Board Assam, Guwahati, p. 85.